America's Healthcare Transformation

Strategies and Innovations

America's Healthcare Transformation

Strategies and Innovations

Edited by **Robert A. Phillips**

Rutgers University Press Medicine
New Brunswick, New Jersey, and London

Library of Congress Cataloging-in-Publication Data

Names: Phillips, Robert A., 1951–, editor.
Title: America's healthcare transformation : strategies and innovations /
    edited by Robert A. Phillips.
Description: New Brunswick, New Jersey : Rutgers University Press,
    [2016] | Includes bibliographical references and index.
Identifiers: LCCN 2015042932 | ISBN 9780813572222 (hardcover : alk.
    paper) | ISBN 9780813572239 (e-book (ePub)) | ISBN 9780813572246
    (e-book (Web PDF))
Subjects: | MESH: Delivery of Health Care—United States. | Efficiency,
    Organizational—United States. | Health Care Reform—United States. |
    Patient Safety—United States. | Quality of Health Care—United States.
Classification: LCC RA445 | NLM W 84 AA1 | DDC 326.10973—dc23
LC record available at http://lccn.loc.gov/2015042932

A British Cataloging-in-Publication record for this book is available from
the British Library.

This publication was supported in part by the Eleanor J. and
Jason F. Dreibelbis Fund.

Visit our website: http://rutgerspress.rutgers.edu

Manufactured in the United States of America

CONTENTS

v

PREFACE AND ACKNOWLEDGMENTS

In the United States, we are in the midst of a fundamental transformation of the practice of medicine and of the $3 trillion per year healthcare industry. Landmark events in the 1990s that stimulated these dramatic shifts include the conceptualization and widespread adoption of evidence-based medicine, the introduction of computerized physician order entry, and elevation of patient safety and quality as a healthcare priority following the 1999 report by the Institute of Medicine (IOM) titled *To Err Is Human: Building a Safer Health System.* In the first two decades of the 21st century, events that have spurred the transformation of healthcare include the completion of the Human Genome Project in 2003, the passage of the Affordable Care Act in 2010, emergence of precision medicine, advanced analytics to enable population health management, the widespread use of smartphones and associated apps that enable remote monitoring, and the shift toward patient-centered care with emphasis on the patient experience. It is not an exaggeration to state that we are in the middle of the largest change in healthcare practice and delivery in history.

The mission of this book is to provide a comprehensive roadmap for navigating these historic and sometimes confusing times by focusing on the five major domains that are influencing and experiencing the greatest paradigm shifts. These domains are "Patient Safety and Quality," "Healthcare Delivery Redesign," "Emerging Paradigms in the Practice of Medicine," "Healthcare Reform and New Payment Methods," and "Patient Experience, Engagement, and Services." In doing so, this book touches on virtually every facet of the ongoing transformational changes in healthcare and the practice of medicine.

To achieve this aim, we assembled a group of experts who are at the leading edge of thought and implementation of these transformational changes. Authors were invited with a request to compose their expert opinion in the style of a keynote address—academic but understandable to the general educated public, physicians, and policy makers. It is our goal to provide these groups, as well as healthcare administrators, clinical leaders, and all practitioners, the tools required to understand the healthcare's trajectory and be successful leaders of change.

Part I, "Patient Safety and Quality," features several comprehensive reviews of methodologies. The topics are developing a highly reliable organization, fundamental approaches to measuring the safety of care, illustrations and learnings from organizations that have focused on eliminating unintended variation and waste, the role of health information technology in creating safer healthcare, the development of a culture of safety, the imperative and emerging methodologies for training providers in patient safety and quality, and the use of registries and public reporting to drive quality improvement.

Part II, "Healthcare Delivery Redesign," explores many emerging models. Included are evaluations of innovative high-quality and low-cost care delivery solutions from around the United States and from abroad, a primer on population health management, an analysis of team-based care, a review of the rise of convenience retail clinics, an exploration of high-tech solutions such as telemedicine and mobile health, and a description of the novel coordination of care program "Grand-Aides."

Part III, "Emerging Paradigms in the Practice of Medicine," views the use of guidelines through the lens of the rationale for their development and the impact they are having on improving quality of care and outcomes. This part goes on to explore how evidence-based medicine can be implemented in a model of shared decision making, and it ends with a review of the basic concepts, implementation, and challenges of precision medicine.

Part IV, "Healthcare Reform and New Payment Methods," begins with a strong case that insurance reform will fundamentally and irreversibly drive healthcare delivery reform. This is followed by a primer on the path and skills required to create value in the U.S. healthcare system, which is moving along the spectrum from fee for service to bundled payments and accountable care.

Part V, "Patient Experience, Engagement, and Services," introduces the concept that a fundamental goal of healthcare delivery is to reduce patient suffering by addressing needs that arise from the patient's disease as well as by removing dysfunction in healthcare delivery that cause emotional and physical distress. This is followed by reports from two major medical centers—Stanford Health Care and Houston Methodist—on how behaviorally based strategies, both of which are anchored in values, can successfully energize and empower employees to deliver a superior patient experience.

I am indebted to many people who helped make this book possible. Dana Dreibelbis, Executive Editor of Rutgers University Press, was highly receptive to the concept proposal for this book and quickly championed it through the press's review and approval process. Throughout the book's development and progress, Dana offered invaluable editorial and technical advice. I want to thank all of the authors who generously agreed to give their time and expertise to this first edition. I hope they will be pleased with the outcome and will be encouraged to contribute to future editions. Finally, this book would not have been completed without the organizational and creative skills of my assistant, Susie Lee. I owe her a debt of gratitude.

This book was conceived as an opportunity to engage the wisdom and vision of today's leading healthcare thought leaders and innovators to create a textbook that would provide a roadmap for success in this unique time in U.S. healthcare. It is my hope and that readers will find this book to be a valuable resource as they endeavor to improve the practice of medicine and the delivery of healthcare in our communities and nation.

Robert A. Phillips, MD, PhD, FACC
Executive Vice President and Chief Medical Officer, Houston Methodist
President and CEO, Houston Methodist Physician Organization
Professor of Cardiology, Houston Methodist Institute for Academic Medicine
Professor of Medicine, Weill Cornell Medical College

CONTRIBUTING AUTHORS

Susan A. Abookire, BSEE, MD, MPH, FACP
Assistant Professor in Medicine
Harvard Medical School

Julia D. Andrieni, MD, FACP
Vice President, Population Health and Primary Care
Houston Methodist
President and CEO
Houston Methodist Physicians' Alliance for Quality

David W. Bates, MD, MSc
Senior Vice President for Quality and Safety
Chief Quality Officer
Brigham and Women's Hospital
Brigham and Women's Physicians Organization

Kasey R. Boehmer, MPH
Knowledge and Evaluation Research Unit
Mayo Clinic

Marc L. Boom, MD, MBA
President and CEO
Houston Methodist

Mark R. Chassin, MD, FACP, MPP, MPH
President and Chief Executive Officer
The Joint Commission and Joint Commission Center for Transforming Healthcare

Nana E. Coleman, MD, EdM
Assistant Dean for Graduate Medical Education, Healthcare
*   Quality, and Patient Safety*
Assistant Professor of Pediatrics
Baylor College of Medicine
Section of Critical Care Medicine
Texas Children's Hospital

Erin S. DuPree, MD, FACOG
Chief Medical Officer and Vice President
Joint Commission Center for Transforming Healthcare

Thomas W. Feeley, MD
Helen Shafer Fly Distinguished Professor of Anesthesiology
Head, Institute for Cancer Care Innovation
Senior Fellow, Institute for Strategy and Competitiveness
The University of Texas MD Anderson Cancer Center
Harvard Business School

Mauro Ferrari, PhD
Ernest Cockrell Jr. Presidential Distinguished Chair
President and Chief Executive Officer, Houston Methodist Research Institute
Director, Institute for Academic Medicine at Houston Methodist Hospital
Executive Vice President, Houston Methodist
Senior Associate Dean and Professor of Medicine, Weill Cornell Medical College

James L. Field, MBA, DBA
President of Research and Insights Division
The Advisory Board Company

Arthur Garson, Jr., MD, MPH
Chairman, Grand-Aides USA and International
Director, Health Policy Institute
Texas Medical Center

Jason Gorevic
Chief Executive Officer
Teladoc

Philip Greenland, MD
Harry W. Dingman Professor of Cardiology
Departments of Preventive Medicine and Medicine
Director, Institute for Public Health and Medicine
*   Center for Population Health Sciences*
Feinberg School of Medicine
Northwestern University

Tine Hansen-Turton, MGA, JD, FCPP, FAAN
Chief Executive Officer, National Nursing Centers Consortium
Chief Operating Officer, Public Health Management Corporation
Executive Director, Convenient Care Association

Hanh H. Hoang, PhD
Research Operations Manager
Office of Strategic Research Initiatives
Houston Methodist Research Institute
Institute for Academic Medicine
Houston Methodist Hospital

Gary S. Kaplan, MD, FACP, FACMPE, FACPE
Chairman and CEO
Virginia Mason Health System

Kunal N. Karmali, MD, MS
Departments of Preventive Medicine and Medicine
Feinberg School of Medicine
Northwestern University

Ju Young Kim MD, PhD
Scripps Translational Science Institute
Clinical Associate Professor
Seoul National University Bundang Hospital

Thomas H. Lee, MD
Chief Medical Officer
Press Ganey Associates

Kasaiah Makam, MD
Center for Heart and Vascular Health
Christiana Care Health System

Elizabeth Malcolm, MD, MSHS
Director of Implementation and Evaluation, Clinical Excellence Research Center
Instructor in Medicine
Stanford University School of Medicine

Arnold Milstein, MD, MPH
Professor of Medicine
Director of the Clinical Excellence Research Center
Stanford University School of Medicine

Alicia D. H. Monroe, MD
Provost and Senior Vice President for Academic and Faculty Affairs
Professor, Family and Community Medicine
Baylor College of Medicine

Victor M. Montori, MD, MSc
Professor of Medicine
Knowledge and Evaluation Research Unit
Mayo Clinic

Deirdre Mylod, PhD
Executive Director, Institute for Innovation
Senior Vice President, Decision Analytics & Research
Press Ganey Associates

Kenneth W. Patric, MD, DABFM
Chief Medical Officer
The Little Clinic

Alberta T. Pedroja, PhD, CPHQ, HACP
President
ATP Healthcare Services, LLC

Amir Dan Rubin, MBA, MHSA
Executive Vice President
Optum / UnitedHealth Group
Former President and CEO
Stanford Health Care

Sarah P. Slight, MPharm, PhD, PGDip
Associate Professor in Pharmacy Practice
School of Medicine, Pharmacy, and Health
Wolfson Research Institute
Durham University, UK

Steven R. Steinhubl, MD
Director of Digital Medicine
Scripps Translational Science Institute

Janet J. Teske, DNP
Director of Retail and Employer Clinics
Aurora Health Care QuickCare Clinics

Nikhil G. Thaker, MD
Division of Radiation Oncology
The University of Texas MD Anderson Cancer Center

Henry H. Ting, MD, MBA
Senior Vice President
Chief Quality Officer
NewYork-Presbyterian
Professor of Medicine at Columbia University Medical Center
Columbia University College of Physicians and Surgeons

William S. Weintraub, MD, MACC, FAHA, FESC
John H. Ammon Chair of Cardiology
Center for Heart and Vascular Health
Christiana Care Health System

Sandra A. Weiss, MD
Center for Heart and Vascular Health
Christiana Care Health System

Sharyl Wojciechowski, MA
Patient Experience Knowledge Manager
Press Ganey Associates

America's Healthcare Transformation

Strategies and Innovations

PATIENT SAFETY
AND QUALITY

Organizing Performance Management to Support High-Reliability Healthcare

Erin S. DuPree
Mark R. Chassin

Abstract

Quality and safety problems abound in healthcare despite intensive efforts across the industry to eradicate them. To rectify these problems, healthcare organizations are beginning to adopt lessons from organizations in so-called high-reliability industries. These high-reliability organizations (HROs) routinely produce stellar safety records despite operating under extremely hazardous conditions. This chapter discusses the concept of high reliability and its goal of zero harm, briefly describes a pathway that healthcare organizations might follow to pursue this goal, and focuses on how performance management can best be structured to support a high-reliability journey in healthcare.

Healthcare is complex, depends heavily on human behaviors, and is subject to unexpected occurrences at every level from the individual patient to the organizational and system levels, making it inherently unsafe. Problems such as wrong site surgeries and healthcare–associated infections persist in healthcare despite widespread attention to improvement[1] in the years following reports from the Institute of Medicine (IOM), especially *To Err Is Human*[2] and *Crossing the Quality Chasm*.[3] One study updated the estimated number of deaths from error–related injuries published by the IOM in 1999 from 98,000 per year to 210,000–400,000 per year, with serious harm events ranging from 10 to 20 times the number of deaths.[4]

This level of harm is foreign to high-reliability organizations (HROs), which include nuclear power plants, commercial air carriers, military aircraft carriers, and even zoos and theme parks. Weick and Sutcliffe describe these organizations as managing unexpected events through five processes: (1) preoccupation with failure, (2) sensitivity to operations, and (3) reluctance to simplify; and when errors occur (4) commitment to resilience and (5) deference to expertise. These processes enable organizations to contain errors and prevent harm.[5] Together these processes create a state of collective mindfulness in which workers look for and report unsafe conditions before harm occurs and when these problems can be more easily fixed. These industries thus learn continuously and strive for zero harm. For example, from 1990 through 2001, U.S. commercial aviation had a death rate of 13.9 deaths per million flights. From 2002 to 2013, however, that death rate plummeted by a remarkable 90% to 1.4 deaths per million flights, even though the average annual number of flights increased by 12%.[6] This may demonstrate how HROs are never satisfied with their current level of safety.

Interest has been growing in the methods used in other industries and how they might be applied to clinical safety and quality issues[7] within healthcare to ensure reliability for every patient, every time. Reliability in healthcare is failure-free operation from the patient's viewpoint. First and foremost, it is safe care, and it is effective, timely, accessible, efficient, and patient centered. Healthcare is far from highly reliable even with routine safety practices such as hand hygiene, which does not occur 60% of the time.[8] Yet there is no guidance in the high-reliability literature about how to get from low to high reliability. A roadmap has been developed at the Joint Commission, taking what has been learned from high-reliability organizations, the accreditation surveys of thousands of organizations, and some hospitals that have started to adapt high-reliability principles. The first step toward high reliability in healthcare is a leadership commitment to zero harm. The second major change for healthcare is the incorporation of safety culture principles and practices throughout the organization. A leadership commitment to zero harm and a culture of safety are essential components of HROs. Healthcare, though, requires a third component: the adoption of highly robust performance improvement methodologies. This is absent from the high-reliability literature because these industries do not have key safety processes that fail most of the time. Performance improvement methodologies originated in manufacturing industries and have evolved over time. Individual companies and healthcare organizations have seen dramatic improvements with business processes and billions of dollars saved using performance improvement methodologies.[9–11] Again, healthcare must take lessons from other industries to address the magnitude of errors and harm currently present today.

LEADERSHIP COMMITMENT

Moving toward high reliability requires a healthcare organization to adopt the long-term aim of zero harm starting with the board of trustees or directors of the healthcare organization and its chief executive officer (CEO). This commitment leads to a change in investment strategies and leadership behaviors. The board is responsible for financial performance and the quality of care delivered to the community: clinical outcomes, accessibility, patient experience, and productivity. Because board members are typically community leaders who are more comfortable with finances than clinical information, the CEO must ensure the board has ongoing education regarding the organization's clinical performance. Adopting the goal of zero harm is critical, because a main principle of healthcare is "First, do no harm"; this clearly and succinctly establishes the long-term vision necessary for leadership alignment. Leadership includes the board and CEO, senior management, and nursing and physician leaders. The vision of zero harm creates a burning platform, a place around which everyone can rally, leading to profound inspiration and respect for the work in which front line workers are engaged every day. The leaders' attitudes, beliefs, and behaviors, especially the CEO's, are central to the changes in organizational culture.

SAFETY CULTURE

A culture of safety has three central attributes: trust, reporting, and improvement.[12] Front line workers trust their peers and management to routinely recognize and report errors and unsafe conditions. Trust is established through the elimination of intimidating behaviors, fixing problems that have been reported, implementing improvements, and communicating the improvements consistently and broadly. Visible, meaningful improvements strengthen trust and reporting and create a positive reinforcing cycle (Figure 1.1). Holding everyone accountable for consistent adherence to safe practices is another critical ingredient for trust. Healthcare organizations often punish staff for blameless acts while failing to implement equitable disciplinary procedures across disciplines and departments, a failure that leads to confusion around accountability and diminished trust. Workers fail to report because they are afraid that the errors will end up in their personnel files.[13] Many physicians continue to work largely as independent craftsmen, claiming their own approach to patient care

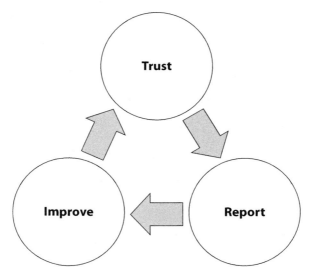

FIGURE 1.1 Safety Culture. Adapted from Reason J, Hobbs A.[12]

without accountability to the care team or system that supports the diagnosis and treatment plan.[14] If physicians who bring in high revenues are allowed to misbehave, then workers see the priority of leadership as production over safety. Nurses still "eat their young," also contributing to the pervasive issues with behavior and accountability in healthcare.[15]

High-reliability organizations recognize that errors and harm are always possible and seek to continuously learn and improve. Humility on the part of healthcare leaders is required so they can understand that the vast majority of adverse events are the result of "system" or management failures, not individual failures. Even with the elimination of harm and system failures, organizations do not "arrive" at high reliability. Organizations continuously learn and strive to deliver better care. Creating an infrastructure for performance improvement provides an organization with the cultural underpinnings—the foundation—to be a high-reliability organization.

IMPROVEMENT: SIX SIGMA, LEAN, AND THE IMPORTANCE OF CHANGE MANAGEMENT

Modern quality improvement methods were developed initially in manufacturing industries in the decades after World War II by W. Edwards Deming and others. Deming combined statistical process control with transformational change for superior performance, or what has become known as *operational excellence*.[16] Dramatic results in performance are evident in diverse companies such as General Electric, Motorola, and Toyota,[9] which have embraced process improvement methods. These effective process improvement approaches based on Deming's management principles have not been incorporated effectively into healthcare delivery. Healthcare organizations too often look to external agencies to create their quality agenda and strategy, instead of leading from within and determining strategic objectives from their own analysis of the needs of the patients and communities they serve. Quality "strategies" are typically produced in reaction to the ever-growing list of federal and state requirements and public demands, leading to "project fatigue" throughout the industry.

The performance improvement infrastructure is a critical component to the creation of a high-reliability organization in healthcare. In the 1970s, Motorola, a company at the leading edge of industrial America, recognized it had a quality problem and adopted Deming's postulate that a focus on quality decreases cost while increasing customer satisfaction; this ran counter to the prevailing focus on cost, which can lead to decreased quality and eventually increased costs and decreased customer satisfaction. Variation was linked to defects and waste: eliminate the variation and quality will increase, costs will decrease, and customer satisfaction will increase. Motorola assembled the problem-solving methodology of DMAIC—that is, define, measure, analyze, improve, and control (Figure 1.2). This alignment with the scientific method addressed variation and became known as *Six Sigma*, or *zero defects*. Sigma is the symbol for standard deviation in statistics, and standard deviation levels help us understand how much the process deviates from perfection. The higher the sigma level, the less variation there is and the better the process is. Today, Six Sigma emphasizes a structured organizational approach to competency-based deployment so that the entire workforce is trained and the methodology becomes the way the organization does its work. Six Sigma has become a philosophy of management that emphasizes the importance of understanding factors critical to quality and customer expectations through the measurement and analysis of data, the implementation of solutions designed to improve processes to affect the most statistically significant sources of variation, and sustaining these solutions. With billions of dollars of documented savings in individual companies, Six Sigma has proven to be the most effective process-improvement method in history.[17]

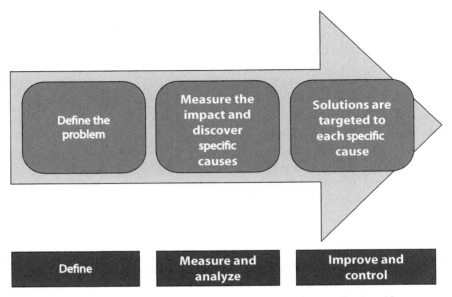

FIGURE 1.2 DMAIC (Define, Measure, Analyze, Improve, and Control), A problem-solving methodology

The lean concept also evolved in the Japanese automotive industry as an integrated system of principles, practices, tools and techniques focused on increasing customer value, improving work flows throughout the value stream, and reducing waste.[18] Rather than organizing work processes to accommodate physicians and nurses, lean in the healthcare industry stresses the need to make the patient—the customer—the starting point for all process design, with all subsequent decisions guided by the notion of narrowing all actions to only those the patient deems valuable. Occurrences that patients do not perceive as valuable include waiting to be seen and getting hospital-associated infections. This not only includes lost lives and resources but also lost human potential, which could be applied more usefully to providing better care if waste and defects were eliminated.[19] Lean emphasizes operational change driven by the front line staff who best understand the processes, recurrent errors, and unsafe conditions that need to be improved, which results in profound respect for the front line staff. However, lean is weak on organizational infrastructure, deployment plans, analytical tools, and control.[20]

Combining lean approaches with Six Sigma leads to an expanded breadth of application and enables an organization to benefit from both types of improvement, depending on the nature of the problem. Six Sigma is the best method for chronic, complex problems when solutions are not known; lean tends to work best with problems that have known solutions that are not being implemented, enabling rapid improvements with minimal data collection.

Many quality improvement initiatives fail or are not sustained because of a lack of acceptance and accountability. Change management is a set of actions supported by a tool set that is used to address these aspects of improvement by providing guidance at every stage of performance to everyone at every level. The tools increase the exposure and participation of staff and leadership in shaping new solutions and interventions; this increases the speed in which a proposed change is adapted and accepted, reinforces its effectiveness, and strengthens sustainability. The tools facilitate employees' ability to improve processes by engaging them in managing and directing the constant change that is inherent in any dynamic business environment, especially healthcare.

A blend of Six Sigma, lean, and change management emphasize data-driven problem solving to understand the root causes for performance failure, removing waste from processes, and recognizing and harnessing the needs and strengths of the people who will implement and sustain the required changes. Collectively called Robust Process Improvement® (RPI®), these methods build on the strengths of prior methodologies and offer a systematic approach to dissecting complex safety problems; this can help guide an organization to deploy focused, highly effective solutions.[21] The tools from one or two methods and toolboxes are not adequate to address the layers of complex issues in healthcare today: Countless deep problems in healthcare require RPI.

RPI strategies, methods, and training programs have been used effectively to improve business processes as well as patient-centered processes and outcomes (Figure 1.3).[1,11,21] These results emphasize the importance of developing a measurement system that will lead to targeted solution development and reliably assess whether the solution actually leads to improvement. The link to overall organizational strategy, patient-centered definition of problems, inclusion of change management, and data-driven approach to analysis leads to changing processes critical to system performance. To date, although there is a growing awareness of lean and Six Sigma, much of the diffusion in healthcare has been inconsistent and thus limited in effectiveness: isolated consulting engagements, a brief leadership introduction to the concepts, or dependency on a specific organization leader who has brought enthusiasm to the topic. Increasing improvement capacity is the basis for transforming individual healthcare organizations and the delivery system at large.

THE MILBANK QUARTERLY
A MULTIDISCIPLINARY JOURNAL OF POPULATION HEALTH AND HEALTH POLICY

PMC full text: Milbank Q. 2013 Sep; 91(3): 459–490.

Published online 2013 Sep 13. doi: 10.1111/1468-0009. 12023

Copyright/License ▶   Request Permission to reuse

TABLE 1

Improvements Seen in Four Projects Using Robust Process Improvement

Problem Addressed	Number and Type of Health Care Organizations	Measure	Before (%)	After (%)	Relative Improvement (%)
Hand hygiene	8 hospitals	Hand hygiene compliance [a]	47.5	81	71
					p = 0.000
Handoff communication	10 hospitals	Ineffective handoffs at care transitions [b]	41	18	56
					p = 0.007
Wrong-site surgery risks	5 hospitals, 3 ambulatory surgery centers	Risk of wrong-site surgery [c]			
Scheduling			39	21	46
					p = 0.000
Preoperative area			52	19	63
					p = 0.000
Operating room			59	29	51
					p = 0.000
Colorectal surgical-site infections (SSI)	7 hospitals	Cases with an SSI [d]	15.8	10.7	32
					p = 0.000

Notes: Robust Process Improvement is a combination of three complementary process improvement methods: lean, six sigma, and change management.

[a] Percentage of times that caregivers cleaned their hands before walking into or out of a patient's room.

[b] Percentage of handoffs that failed to provide complete information necessary to patient care.

[c] Percentage of cases with any risk of wrong-site surgery.

[d] Percentage of colorectal surgery cases with any surgical-site infection.

Source: http://www.centerfortransforminghealthcare.org/projects/projects.aspx.

FIGURE 1.3 RPI improves patient–centered processes and outcomes. Reproduced from Chassin MR, Loeb JM.[1]

HOW TO BUILD AN RPI PROGRAM THAT LASTS

A consistent approach to improvement across an entire organization is needed in order to effectively move toward an organization's vision, mission, and strategic imperatives. If a consistent approach is not part of the organizational culture, then transformation and sustainability will remain elusive. A commitment to performance improvement is aligned with patient interests, organizational reputation, employee engagement, and a favorable return on investment. For example, the Mayo Clinic has documented a 5:1 return on its investment in effective performance improvement methods.[22] Patients, providers, insurers, and employers all benefit. Companies such as General Electric, BD, Cardinal, and Eli Lilly have shown how to embed a program into an organization, yet these successes cannot be imported directly from Fortune 500 companies.[11] Implementation of performance improvement methodology can fail for many reasons, including a lack of financial or human resources, poor training, project selection that is not tied to strategic imperatives, and a lack of leadership.[23] To ensure that the methodology becomes the way the organization does its work and becomes part of its culture, leadership commitment and support to the ongoing investment of financial and human capital are critical.

A board-level commitment to implementation of a performance improvement methodology ensures that it will be more than a "flavor of the month" type of initiative. It enables performance improvement to not be dependent on one person or department. Ongoing education of the board in quality principles, RPI tools, and its role in providing that oversight is a necessary component to ensure that the commitment is sustained. Keeping the board abreast of the progress and results of strategic projects and organizational change is critical to successful integration. A financial commitment enables the senior management team to invest in effective training and develop the internal capacity over time to train management and staff across the organization in the tenets of improvement and to avoid costly consultants who helicopter in and out of an organization.

The CEO's role is to create and foster an environment that sets the stage for success. He or she must signal by committing time and energy that implementing RPI is a principal organizational priority. The CEO must educate the board and also align senior managers around an understanding of RPI: what it is, why the organization will benefit from it, and how the organization will operationalize the training, methods, and spread of the methodology. Management alignment on the importance of training is necessary because training can take up to 25% of a staff member's time over many months. If management does not see the training as important, then staff members will not have the time or support from their supervisors to do the work necessary to complete the training.

Getting the buy in of the chief financial officer (CFO) is critical because he or she will want to see a return on the investment. The CFO should lead efforts to track the costs of training and validate the financial results of any improvement initiative. The head of human resources is also important to sustaining improvement in the organization because completion of RPI training and the use of improvement methods and tools are incorporated over time into staff development and performance expectations. Performance expectations of leaders and managers should include goals for spreading RPI in their areas of responsibility.

The clinical leadership (e.g., chief medical officer, chief quality officer, vice president of medical affairs, and chief nursing officer) have the responsibility of promoting the program, working with leaders to identify trainees, and operationalizing training time and support for large groups of workers across the organization. Their alignment with the program is essential. They often take the brunt of dealing with influential resisters and need the explicit support of the board, CEO, and CFO to do their jobs.

Project selection, or the right work, is critical to the success of RPI in an organization. Initiatives should be tied to issues of strategic importance. For example, the Red Cross Hospital in Beverwijk, Netherlands, realized that the projects they worked on were not necessarily always strategic or did not have significant drivers aligned with the organization's business. The hospital lacked a systematic process for project management and tracking, and projects were often not completed. Management adopted Six Sigma to overcome these challenges to improvement.[23]

Measuring the results of the RPI program allows for adjustments and midcourse corrections when necessary. The return on investment, progress spreading across the entire organization, staff knowledge, and the use of RPI are all indicators that can be tracked over time to measure how well RPI is being implemented. RPI integration in an organization is a strategic goal in and of itself, the progress of which is reported to the board.

To embed the management philosophy and methodology throughout the organization, the training must go beyond a few select individuals or just the quality department: Limited expertise leads to limited results in improvement. To transform to a learning and improvement culture, everyone must be trained at a level appropriate to their positions so that RPI becomes the way work is done in the organization. This internal capacity allows management and staff to speak the same language and work across silos to achieve organizational objectives. The knowledge and skills gained empower front line staff to identify and act on opportunities to improve.

The creation of multiple levels of training allows opportunities for all staff to participate. RPI training includes courses for leadership, RPI experts, change leaders, full-time trainers and mentors, and foundational tools and concepts. Training starts with leadership. Leaders learn how to be role models for behavior, providing motivation and support, and accepting specific program and project responsibilities. Leaders are taught how to select staff and projects for training. Leaders also learn the critically important task of embedding the program in their organization. An early objective is to create a group of internal experts and trainers.

The most talented formal and informal leaders across the organization are selected to become the organization's RPI experts (e.g., green belts, black belts). The training for green belts can take up to 25% of their time over 6 to 12 months. Typically, several teams of green belt trainees are trained at once, with each team drawn from different parts of the organization. The teams work on projects as they learn the tools; this allows each team of 3 to 5 trainees to see how RPI works for a variety of initiatives. This approach also fosters cross-departmental communication and breaks down internal silos. Once they have been trained, the green belts remain embedded throughout the organization to facilitate and lead ongoing improvement initiatives.

A few select green belts undergo additional training to become black belts. Once trained and certified as black belts, these individuals spend 100% of their time on organization-wide strategic initiatives. A few black belts and change leaders undergo even more advanced training to become full-time RPI trainers and mentors for the organization: master black belts and master change leaders. This group will become the critical mass of trainers who can facilitate spread of the methodology and capacity across the organization.

The importance of change management cannot be underestimated. Accepting solutions and being accountable for change are usually the most difficult aspects of implementing, sustaining, and spreading improvement. Staff throughout the organization are trained as "change leaders." These individuals are trained only in change management tools and techniques, ensuring that change is thoughtful and managed to support continuous improvement. In addition to the change leaders, everyone in the organization incorporates change management tools as part of daily work. The tools are used to ensure that meetings are purposeful and run efficiently with clear accountability for decisions made and work to be done. When discussions lead to differing opinions and ideas even when decisions must be made, change management tools can help achieve consensus. When conflicts arise across the organization, change agents facilitate meetings to work through the issues and move forward.

The rest of the workforce is trained in the principles and basic tools of RPI (yellow belts) so workers understand the language, execute small-scale process improvements in their work area, and participate in larger organizational initiatives. This is the introductory, or foundational, level of training. All three toolkits (lean, Six Sigma, and change management) are introduced and a project is completed using some of the tools. Participants do not need to learn in-depth statistical analysis for this level of training but do learn meaningful ways to present data and the practicality of statistical process control in the early detection and prevention of problems rather than inspecting problems.

To be sustainable, the integration of performance improvement management and methodology requires substantial change and ongoing employee engagement. Programs and infrastructure need to be developed to ensure trainee skills are used and maintained after the initial training. RPI training and projects should be a consistent presence in the employee newsletter. Celebrations at the close of projects and annual fairs can keep implementation fun and rewarding. The CEO must visibly champion and recognize those individuals who undergo training and use improvement methodology in their work. The CEO can include the progress of the RPI program and project results in town halls, daily meetings, and board reports, as well as when speaking with external stakeholders.

A fundamental shift in healthcare quality from a top-down, externally driven process that tells providers what to do to a blend of top-down and bottoms-up approaches is critical for the transformation to high reliability in healthcare. Front line caregivers are in a unique position to address the fundamental barriers to improving clinical care: Only they fully understand how complex the work is and the strengths and weaknesses of the electronic health record; they are also the ones involved in high-risk communication processes. Leadership commitment and clear strategic direction allows and empowers front line providers who are trained in robust improvement methods to identify variations in care and develop interventions that ensure safe, excellent care. Without improved knowledge and skills, clinical teams have only limited abilities to innovate and effectively improve local processes. RPI is an approach to performance and organizational culture change that enables transformation. Much of healthcare improvement today rests in the hands of leaders to take the initiative to learn about performance methodologies and increase improvement capacity within their own organizations. Leadership commitment to performance improvement management and methodology is essential to high reliability in healthcare.

REFERENCES

1. Chassin MR, Loeb JM. High-reliability health care: getting there from here. *Millbank Q,* 2013;91(3):459–490.

2. Kohn LT, Corrigan J, Donaldson MS, eds. *To Err Is Human: Building a Safer Health System.* Washington, DC: National Academy Press; 1999.

3. Institute of Medicine. 2001. *Crossing the Quality Chasm: A New Health System for the 21st Century.* Washington, DC: National Academy Press; 2001.

4. James JT. A new, evidence-based estimate of patient harms associated with hospital care. *J Patient Safety.* 2013;9(3):122–128.

5. Weick K, Sutcliffe K. *Managing the Unexpected: Resilient Performance in an Age of Uncertainty.* 2nd ed. San Francisco, CA: John Wiley & Sons, Inc.; 2007.

6. U.S. Department of Transportation. U.S. air carrier safety data. Washington, DC: Research and Innovation Technology Administration, Bureau of Transportation Statistics; 2013. Retrieved from http://www.rita.dot.gov/bts/sites/rita.dot.gov.bts/files/publications/national_transportation_statistics/html/table_02_09.html.

7. Chassin MR, Loeb JM. The ongoing quality improvement journey: next stop high-reliability. *Health Affair.* 2011;30(4):559–568.

8. ErasmusV, et al. Systematic review of studies on compliance with hand hygiene guidelines in hospital care. *Infect Cont Hosp Ep.* 2010;31(3):283–294.

9. Bartlett CA, Wozny M. GE's two-decade transformation: Jack Welch's leadership. Harvard Business School Case Study 9-399-150; 2005. Retrieved July 7, 2015, from http://www.hbs.edu/faculty/Pages/item.aspx?num=67.

10. Rao J. 2011. Best Buy: merging lean sigma with innovation. Harvard Business School Case Study BAB697; 2011. Retrieved July 7, 2015, from https://hbr.org/product/best-buy-merging-lean-sigma-with-innovation/an/BAB697-PDF-ENG.

11. Chassin R. The Six Sigma initiative at Mount Sinai Medical Center. *Mt Sinai J Med.* 2008;75(1):45–52.

12. Reason J, Hobbs A. *Managing Maintenance Error: A Practical Guide.* Burlington, VT: Ashgate; 2003.

13. Agency for Healthcare Research and Quality. Hospital survey on patient safety culture: 2014 user comparative database report: executive summary; 2014. Available at http://www.ahrq.gov/professionals/quality-patient-safety/patientsafetyculture/hospital/2014/hosp14summ.html.

14. Swensen SJ, et al. Cottage industry to post-industrial care: the revolution in health care delivery. *New Engl J Med.* 2010;362(5):e12.

15. Rowe M, Sherlock H. Stress and verbal abuse in nursing: do burned out nurses eat their young? *J Nurs Manag.* 2005;13(3):242–248.

16. Deming, WE. *Out of the Crisis.* Cambridge: MIT Center for Advanced Educational Services; 1986.

17. Hoerl RW, Gardner MM. Lean Six Sigma, creativity, and innovation. *Int J Lean Six Sigma*. 2010;1(1):30–38.

18. Womack JP, Jones DT. *Lean Thinking: Banish Waste and Create Wealth in Your Corporation*. New York, NY: Free Press/Simon & Schuster; 2003.

19. Hines S, et al. *Becoming a High Reliability Organization: Operational Advice for Hospital Leaders*. Rockville, MD: Agency for Healthcare Research and Quality; 2008: 45–46.

20. deKoning H, et al. Lean Six Sigma in healthcare. *J Healthc Qual*. 2006;28(2):4–11.

21. DuPree E, et al. Improving patient satisfaction with pain management using Six Sigma tools. *Jt Comm J Qual Patient Safety*. 2009;35(7):343–350.

22. Swensen, SJ. The business case for health-care quality improvement. *J Patient Safety*. 2013;9(1):44–52.

23. Ahmed S, Noor NA, Rafikul I. Effects of lean Six Sigma application in healthcare: a literature review. *Rev Environ Health*. 2013;28(4):189–194.

CHAPTER 2

Elimination of Unintended Variation in Patient Care

Gary S. Kaplan

Abstract

This chapter explores challenges presented by unnecessary variation and centers on the work Virginia Mason teams have done in the areas of prescribing antibiotics, operating room time-outs, sepsis treatment, and patient rooming, using a foundational element of the Virginia Mason Production System, which was developed from practices of the Toyota Production System. These systems were created with the goal of eliminating unintended variation in patient care.

Eliminating unnecessary variations in healthcare is an essential step toward improving both the quality and affordability of care in the United States. A foundational element of the Virginia Mason Production System, which was adapted from the principles and methods of the Toyota Production System, is designed to honor variation in care when it is in the best interest of a particular patient. The system is further designed to eliminate variation in care that is not evidence-based and not in the interest of a patient and consequently generates overuse and waste. This chapter focuses on several ways that teams at Virginia Mason in Seattle have reduced unnecessary variation in care and explores challenges presented by unnecessary variation in:

- prescribing antibiotics
- time-outs in the operating room
- treatment of patients with sepsis
- rooming patients in ambulatory care.

FOUNDATIONAL ELEMENTS TO ELIMINATE UNNECESSARY VARIATION

At Virginia Mason, two particularly important foundational elements have enabled us to adapt the Toyota Production System to healthcare and make significant reductions in unnecessary variation. Our strategic plan creates alignment throughout our organization on our single most important idea—that the patient always comes first. The idea of the patient at the top of our pyramid is deeply embedded within our culture. We have developed compacts with our physicians, leaders, and board members. The strategic plan is one of our foundational documents. The others are compacts that are the product of deep conversations and define the responsibilities that physicians, leaders, and board members have to the organization as well as the reciprocal obligations the organization has toward them. These documents serve to bolster the effectiveness of our management method, the Virginia Mason Production System, which is the foundation of our strategic plan (Figure 2.1).

RAMPANT UNNECESSARY VARIATION IN HEALTHCARE

Donald Berwick, MD, former administrator of the Center for Medicare and Medicaid Services, has addressed the issue of unnecessary variation:

> As industrial quality management techniques find their place in healthcare, professionals may feel threatened by the effort to reduce variation. Understanding may reduce this fear. Variation of the types addressed in quality control efforts erodes quality and reliability, and adds unnecessarily to costs. Such undesirable variation derives, for example, from misinterpretation of random noise in clinical data, from unreliability in the performance of clinical and support systems intended to support care, from habitual differences in practice style that are not grounded in knowledge or reason, and from the failure to integrate care across the boundaries of components of the healthcare system. Quality management efforts can successfully reduce each of these forms of variation without insult to the professional autonomy, dignity, or purpose of healthcare professionals. Professionals need to embrace the scientific control of variation in the service of their patients and themselves.[1]

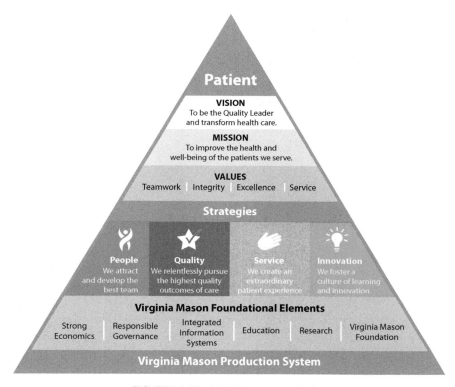

FIGURE 2.1 Virginia Mason strategic plan

Niranjan Kissoon, MD, has observed that "unnecessary variation in the use of diagnostic tests and therapies . . . is anathema to quality and safety in medicine. . . . Variation can most likely be ascribed to physician practice preferences, opinion of guidelines, knowledge translation gaps, training, and local culture. . . ."[2]

Provost and Murray observe that "One of the key strategies in improvement is to control variation":

> Often, when first presented, this concept sounds threatening to healthcare professionals whose job is to make judgments and treat the conditions of unique patients. So first we must differentiate intended versus unintended variation (Berwick 1991). Intended variation (often called purposeful, planned, guided, or considered) is an important part of effective, patient-centered healthcare. A physician, for example, purposely prescribes different doses of a drug to a child and an adult. Certainly, in a patient centered healthcare system, it is desirable

to have variation to best match preferences for communication style, interaction with family, and so forth.

Unintended variation is due to changes introduced into healthcare process that are not purposeful, planned, or guided. The changes can come from decisions made, but usually show up through equipment, supplies, environment, measurement, and management practices.[3]

CLINICAL VALUE STREAMS

Unnecessary variation is waste. The Toyota Production System was designed to eliminate waste, and the system's application in healthcare in the form of the Virginia Mason Production System also targets waste. Virtually all improvement work at Virginia Mason in some way targets unnecessary variation. Thousands of *kaizen* (Japanese for "continuous improvement") events through the years have identified and reduced or eliminated unnecessary variation in every area of the organization. At Virginia Mason, our work demonstrates the cure for unnecessary variation is thoughtfully crafted standard work that is defined by teams doing the work. Once standards are created, all team members are trained on those standards and rigorous measurement guides the ensuing improvement work. There is no improving without measurement; no measurement without standards.

Ever since adapting the Toyota method to healthcare in 2001, Virginia Mason teams have eliminated significant unnecessary variation by constructing clinical value streams that identify best practices. Teams then embed decision rules within the electronic health record so that it is a simple matter—rather than a burden—for team members to adhere to the standard work. A critically important element is that the team members doing the work are the ones who have created and defined the standard work.

In addition to thousands of kaizen events targeting variation, Virginia Mason has also stabled the Center for Health Care Solutions (founded in 2007) to reduce unnecessary healthcare costs. Unwarranted variation is a major barrier to quality, efficiency, and affordability. Much of this follows wide variations in physician education in medical schools and training programs. Young doctors in one medical center might be taught to treat low back pain or migraines in ways that are significantly different. The question in attempting to eliminate unnecessary variation is not whose training is superior, but what does the evidence say? In seeking to answer that question, teams at Virginia Mason have assessed the evidence on what works best for a number of different common conditions and used that evidence to set an evidence-based pathway for each condition. Among the common costly conditions for which teams have established standard evidence-based treatments are:

- abdominal pain
- asthma
- chest pain
- depression and anxiety
- diabetes
- headache
- hyperlipidemia
- hypertension
- acute respiratory infection
- uncomplicated low back pain
- urinary tract infections

Literature Review

Creating a clinical value stream begins with rigorous research in the existing literature. A highly skilled medical librarian works in partnership with a physician and a resident to identify articles in the literature that have direct bearing on treating a particular condition. They seek to identify a standard approach that will provide the safest and highest quality care at the most affordable cost. The standard pathways identified seek to eliminate all defects.

The process also includes input from those front line physicians who have the greatest experience and expertise with the particular condition being discussed. The literature search and physician input are buttressed by reliance on the Strength of Recommendation Taxonomy (SORT) method, which is considered a reliable arbiter of best practices. This process identifies standard work to implement the best practices for a given condition.[4] But if the process were to end at this point, it would not prove particularly effective.

Decision Rules

The clinical value stream process results in a product. That product comes in the form of decision rules that are embedded within the electronic health record. Figure 2.2 shows the screen where physicians are required to select the evidence-based reason to order a lumbar MRI, for example. With this decision tool in place, MRI use for uncomplicated low back pain was reduced by approximately 25%.[5,6]

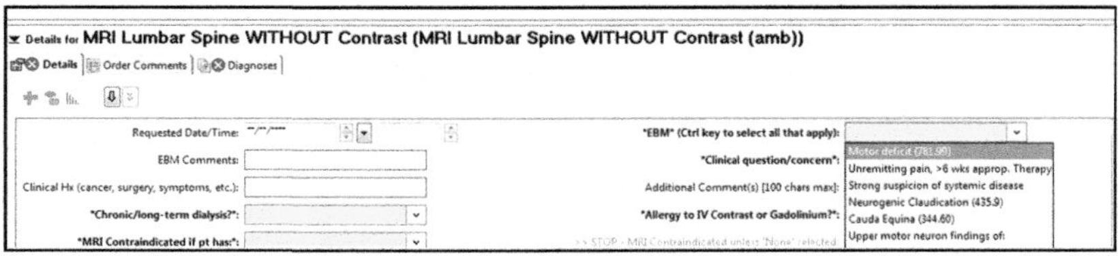

FIGURE 2.2 Evidence-based order for lumbar MRI

VARIATION IN OPERATING ROOM TIME-OUT

Surgeons perform precisely the type of surgery that is appropriate for each patient. This type of variation in care is value added and patient centered.

Unnecessary variation in the OR—in a wide variety of forms—can be highly dangerous and wasteful. Variation in how surgeons deal with other OR team members, for example, can put patients at risk. At Virginia Mason, we have found that different surgeons, depending on how and where they were trained and their personal preferences, required varying support from staff. Research has indicated that a time-out at the start of surgery can improve outcomes and patient safety.[7]

At Virginia Mason, there was significant variation in how (and even whether) surgeons were conducting presurgical time-outs. The goal was to create a standard time-out to be followed by every surgical team every time—without exception. We owe this to our patients. After a series of kaizen events—including videotaping presurgical time-outs to help instruct teams—we identified a standard process for precisely how a time-out would be done, including who would call it and how people would participate. The standard work includes a simple checklist (Figure 2.3) that is posted on the wall of every OR at Virginia Mason. Although the checklist is extremely important, so is the atmosphere that we sought to create within each OR. The time-out process has been important in attaining that atmosphere in which all team members feel comfortable speaking up and indicating whether they might have any concerns about the procedure. The idea is to level the power gradient within the surgical team.

The surgeon starts by calling for the time-out. Everyone in the room stops what they are doing. Each person speaks, attesting only to things he or she has personally confirmed (e.g., the correct implant is in the room, there are four units of blood on hand, etc.). At the end of the time-out, the surgeon asks anyone with a safety concern to speak up.

<u>**Attending Surgeon or Primary Surgery Resident**</u>

1. Circulating RN

☐ Identify self / guest (PRN) – full name & role
☐ Attest that patient matches checked name band
☐ Consent signed (state site & procedure)
☐ Devices: ☐ Foley ☐ VTE prophylaxis ☐ Warmer
☐ Room Status Board Updated
☐ Counts Done

2. Surgical Scrub Tech

☐ Identify self / guest / vendor (PRN) – full name & role
☐ Instrumentation ready
☐ Implants present?
☐ Drugs AND Solutions Labeled
☐ Prepped field appropriate and "YES" is visible, if applicable
☐ Call for Time out

3. Anesthesiology

☐ Identify self / guest (PRN) – full name & role
☐ State significant Drug Allergies
☐ Preop meds ☐ Antibiotics ☐ Heparin SQ ☐ Insulin
☐ ASA class ___ due to ___ (comorbidities) ___
☐ Blood Loss Plan ☐ Products ☐ Cell Saver Plan

4. Surgeon

☐ Identify self / guest – full name & role
☐ State Procedure / Site / s, Time Needed, Indication
☐ ABO compatibility verified and documented electronically
☐ Verify Imaging Matches – Patient / Site / Sidedness
☐ State Anticipated Difficulties
☐ State Anticipated Blood loss
☐ Post-op Plan – Disposition / Special bed?
☐ Encourage Team Input or Safety Concerns

FIGURE 2.3 Surgical time-out checklist

REDUCING VARIATION IN TREATING PATIENTS WITH SEPSIS

The leading cause of death in our hospital is not cancer or heart disease. It is sepsis. Throughout the country, there is significant variation in how sepsis is treated.[8] We also found unnecessary variation within our hospital, and when our teams worked on this challenge, they made an important discovery: One-quarter of patients who died met the technical definition of septic shock. In a review of the work, our sepsis team observed, "To our team, this meant that focusing efforts on recognition and treatment of early sepsis in the acute care setting could have a significant impact on mortality. . . ." Thus, we sought an approach that would enable clinical staff members to both identify less severe sepsis early on and treat it quickly.[9]

To reduce variation in the treatment of sepsis, we started by defining it and educating our clinicians on that definition. It is not that our clinicians were unfamiliar with sepsis. They surely were. But for many years in medicine, the focus has been on septic shock—with good reason—and much less so on early identification of sepsis. At Virginia Mason, we define sepsis as the "suspicion of infection and two positive SIRS (systemic inflammatory response syndrome) criteria." Since an educational campaign among caregivers began in 2011 and 2012, the incidence of sepsis diagnosis at Virginia Mason has increased by an estimated 30%, largely because of our improved ability to recognize the condition.

Before the significant changes we made to treating sepsis, treatment variation was widespread. Best practice evidence for treating sepsis is well established. The Surviving Sepsis guidelines[10] call for a treatment bundle that includes antibiotics, intravenous fluids, blood cultures, and a lactic acid. The recommendation is that this bundle should be completed within three hours. During our internal study, our clinicians found that these steps were sometimes completed in three hours but other times not. Doctors and nurses would get busy and sometimes forget to complete the bundle in the appropriate time. Some physicians had their own preferred way of treating the condition that, in some cases, were not consistent with agreed-on best practices. Our teams found that a significant barrier to rapid treatment was time: Nurses suspecting a sepsis diagnosis in a patient were required to wait to begin treatment until they received the go-ahead from a physician. This additional time often further endangered patients.

Our senior leadership was aggressive in prescribing a goal of completing the sepsis bundle not in three hours but within one hour. This was a major challenge to our clinical teams, yet they came up with an approach that has paid significant dividends for our patients. The clinical teams prescribed standard work for what we call the sepsis "power hour." It begins by recognizing the essential nature of the nurse's role because it is the nurse in most cases who sees the patient's symptoms often long before a physician does. Therefore, the standard approach at Virginia Mason empowers a nurse who suspects sepsis in a patient to start an IV with 500 mL of fluid and order a white blood cell count, blood cultures, and a lactic acid. This rapid intervention establishes a baseline treatment that can be continued and enhanced—with additional fluids and antibiotics—when a physician confirms the sepsis diagnosis. (The physician may determine that the patient does not have sepsis, but the early treatments will have caused no harm to the patient). This work has resulted in significant improvements.[11]

STANDARD ROOMING PROCESS IMPROVES CONSISTENCY OF CARE

In 2007, our clinical teams conducted careful analysis and found widespread variation in our primary care practices. Some clinics performed at a high level, making sure all patients had age- and gender-appropriate tests and screenings.

Other clinics performed unevenly. One particular clinic had several dozen exam rooms, all configured differently. Many physicians had personal preferences for everything, ranging from how the patient was roomed to the kind of instructions patients received at the conclusion of a visit.

This variation meant some patients were up-to-date on mammograms and colonoscopies, for example, and others were not. It meant that medical assistants working with physicians were less productive than their potential because of confusion about the widely varying demands of doctors. The flaw in this system—or lack of a system—was the virtual absence of standardization. A series of Rapid Process Improvement Workshops (RPIWs) focused on eliminating variation in the visit, starting with rooming. The rooming process may initially appear pro forma, but it is a pivotal aspect of caring for our patients, not only because it sets up the physician and patient for a productive visit, but also because elements crucial to the patient's health are essential elements of the rooming process. The result of this work was a standard rooming process spread throughout all of Virginia Mason's clinics.

An important component of standard work in the primary care rooming process involves "external setup." This lean management concept calls for a medical assistant preparing everything needed for a patient's visit *before* the visit. This frees the physician to focus on the work that doctors do best: diagnosing and treating patients, particularly those with complex medical conditions.

Under the revised rooming protocol, all medical assistants throughout Virginia Mason follow the same procedures when rooming patients. This systematic approach—which takes nine minutes—follows well-defined standard work intended to eliminate variation in the rooming process. It eliminates the unnecessary variation that previously meant some patients received all preventive tests and screenings and others did not. This standardized approach has also spread to specialty care areas because many patients—particularly those with multiple chronic conditions—have appointments with specialists far more often than they might see their primary care doctors.

The standard process includes a detailed checklist and sequence, which ensures that each patient is current on important tests and procedures (Figure 2.4 shows a portion of the checklist). This checklist is in the electronic health record and clearly visible to all caregivers. Its purpose is stated at the top of the form: "To ensure that all safety and quality rooming steps are accomplished completely in the correct sequence for every primary care patient visit."

Quality Check	Safety Precaution	Standard WIP
◇	✚	◯

Purpose:
To ensure that all safety and quality rooming steps are accomplished completely in the correct sequence for every primary care patient visit

Related Policies or Evidence: Visit Set-up by Concern Adult & Pediatric

Roles/Work Units Who Must Adopt This Process:
Flow Managers (FM) & RNs in all Primary Care Practices

STEP	TASK DESCRIPTION	TOOLS/ SUPPLIES REQUIRED	CYCLE TIME
1.	Patient arrival validation: if it appears patient has not arrived by scheduled appointment time, FM calls patient's name in all waiting areas at appt time, and again 5 minutes later.		
2.	a.) Retrieve patient's labels b.) Gather Paperwork: • Charge Slip, attach label • Patient Visit Worksheet (PVW); attach label • Cerner Problem Summary List (PSL)	a.) Arrival label b.) Charge Slip c.) Patient Visit Worksheet	
3. ◇	a.) 💜 Greet patient at reception with a smile, introducing yourself. Walk at same pace as patient to scale. b.) Perform "It Takes 3" (Name, DOB, PCP) c.) Measure patient weight in pounds (without shoes) d.) Measure or ask for height in inches (without shoes) e.) Seat patient in location for blood pressure Note: If patient is early & room available, perform visit set-up as usual, but advise patient that PCP may not able to see before appointment	a.) "Ms. Pat Smith? Hello, I'm Mary, a Medical Assistant" b.) "Please verify your date of birth"	
4. ✚ ◇	a.) Review and update Health Maintenance Module (HMM). b.) Address items in HMM in order in which they appear, with goal of addressing each **DUE** or **OVERDUE** item at every visit. c.) For scripting, click on Clinical Decision support tools as needed. d.) Complete HMM communication tool on PVW as HMM reviewed with patient. e.) Tests that automatically update HMM if performed at VMMC include: mammogram, DEXA, Chlamydia, pap, LDL, GLUCOSE, PSA, BMR/BMF, TSH, A1c, urine microalbumin. f.) For tests performed outside VMMC, request outside record by assisting patient to fill out Release of Information form to obtain report (or fax Cerner message using autotext osrreq SW), then communicate records request to PCP on PVW. When record arrives, satisfy by selecting "Performed Else-where" tab, selecting date performed and enter in Comments: • Results • Clinic/Provider Name		

FIGURE 2.4 Ambulatory care rooming protocol

STEP	TASK DESCRIPTION	TOOLS/ SUPPLIES REQUIRED	CYCLE TIME

	g.) CANCEL: because of the potential seriousness of missing a diagnosis, "CANCEL" may only be selected by Provider. POSTPONE: selected by Provider, RN or FM, for one month duration only, while outside record of element is requested, with comment indicating location from which record is being requested. Provider may postpone items based on clinical indication (e.g. severity of osteopenia, previous pap history) h.) Specific elements:
	• **Mammogram:**
	   ◦ If **DUE**, order on PVW. If patient asks to arrange herself, offer patient self-schedule information
	   ◦ If "**DUE**" but actually completed outside VM, request outside records as above
	• **Colonoscopy**
	   ◦ Completed, report available, f/u year recommendation available: satisfy element in HMM by selecting f/u year recommendation. Enter into comments the gastroenterologist plan verbatim, with his/her name.
	   ◦ Completed, report available, f/u year NOT available: do not satisfy element. Print colonoscopy report and pathology report and bundle with visit paperwork for PCP to satisfy. Indicate "see attached" on PVW near "Colonoscopy."
	   ◦ If "**DUE**" but actually completed outside VM, request outside records as above
	   ◦ If **DUE,** inform provider by circling on PVW.
	• **Pap:**
	   ◦ If **DUE** and patient visit is for Preventive Case Review, set up specimen collection as per Standard Process and inform provider by circling on PVW.
	   ◦ If **DUE** and visit is for unrelated concern, schedule appointment.
	   ◦ If "**DUE**" but actually completed outside VM, request outside records as above
	   ◦ If **DUE** but done outside VM, request outside records as above
	• **Chlamydia:** if **DUE,** set up Micro Lab form for urine specimen collection, unless pap/pelvic exam anticipated today, then set up for cervical screen as per Standard Process.
	• **DEXA**: if **DUE**, order on PVW.
	• **Labs:**
	   ◦ If **DUE** for LDL, GLUCOSE, PSA, BMR/BMF, TSH, A1c, urine microalbumin, chlamydia screen, order labs in Cerner through VM Pages Pre-Visit-Testing
	   ◦ If "**DUE**" but actually completed outside VM, request outside records as above
	   ◦ If this is not a care management visit and patient is due for LDL or A1c, schedule DM CM visit
	• **Tobacco Use**: update this yearly query. If patient uses tobacco, circle "Tobacco," which is prompt for PCP to counsel, then to open this element in HMM to document counseling.
	• **Immunizations:**		

(continued)

REDUCING UNNECESSARY VARIATION
IN PRESCRIBING ANTIBIOTICS

Unnecessary variation in prescribing antibiotics is rampant throughout the United States.[12] Providers routinely supply patients with antibiotics despite the fact there is little if any evidence these medications are effective in certain cases. An unintended consequence of this wasteful practice has been the development of drug-resistant infections that are fatal for thousands of Americans each year.[13] A report from one of our teams found the following:

> In 2011, within the Virginia Mason Department of Primary Care, antibiotics were being prescribed inappropriately for cases of acute bronchitis 82% of the time, and visits for upper respiratory infection syndromes led to prescription of antibiotics 56% of the time.

Our clinicians sought "to develop an intervention to reduce inappropriate antibiotic use by primary care providers at Virginia Mason." Implementing the project in 2011, the intervention included a multipronged approach:

1. Academic detailing and standard workflow
   A team of experts at Virginia Mason reviewed best evidence for management of upper respiratory tract infections and developed a standardized clinic workflow for upper respiratory infections, including an electronic medical record template that is completed by both a medical assistant and primary care provider.
2. Measurement and transparent reporting
   Using billing and prescribing data collected via the electronic medical record, the analytics team created a year-to-year antibiotic prescribing report that identified inappropriate antibiotic-prescribing patterns for each primary care provider that is internally shared every year. The data was used to identify both positive and negative outliers and to collectively develop strategies to reduce inappropriate antibiotic prescribing behavior.
3. Symptom support and virtual care
   Starting in April 2012, the team developed an RN phone call protocol in which patients calling in to request a visit for symptoms suggestive of upper respiratory infection are offered a phone call by a registered nurse to help manage symptoms without visiting the primary care provider. After only six months of offering this extra care service, about half the patients chose the nurse phone call.

The result of this work was a decline in the prescription of antibiotics from 41.8% (January 2011) to 18.6% (July 2014).

A NOTE ON APPROPRIATENESS

An important element in reducing unnecessary variation is applying a rigorous appropriateness standard. An orthopedic operation, for example, may meet quality outcomes criteria, but if it was not needed in the first place it is not only wasteful but also dangerous. At Virginia Mason, a foundational element in our surgical treatments is an appropriateness test: Does the patient need the surgery or is there another treatment that could prove beneficial? In addition, there is an important shared decision-making element to appropriateness: Does a fully and well-informed patient—aware of all options—want the procedure?

CONCLUSION

This chapter covers a small sample of the rigorous work being conducted at Virginia Mason that seeks to eliminate unnecessary variation in care delivery. The Virginia Mason Production System is designed to enable teams to identify waste inherent in unneeded variation and then find improved practices that eliminate that waste and variation. This management method enables improvements in quality, safety, access, affordability, and other metrics that are meaningful to patients. Eliminating variation is essential to improving these metrics and many more. It is an essential aspect of the work we do every day.

REFERENCES

1. Berwick DM. Controlling variation in health care: a consultation from Walter Shewhart. *Med Care.* 1991;29:1212–1225.

2. Kissoon N. Unnecessary variation cloaked as discretion in medical decisions. *Can J Emerg Med* 2013;15(1):1–2.

3. Provost LP, Murray S. *The Health Care Data Guide: Learning from Data for Improvement.* San Francisco, CA: Jossey-Bass; 2011:107.

4. Ebell, MH, et al. Strength of Recommendation Taxonomy (SORT): A patient-centered approach to grading evidence in the medical literature. *Am Fam Physician.* 2004; 69(3):548–556.

5. Blackmore CC, Mecklenburg RS, Kaplan GS. At Virginia Mason, collaboration among providers, employers and health plans to transform care, cut costs, and improve quality. *Health Affair.* 2011;30:1680–1687.

6. For doctors who wish to override the system, there is an "escape route" within the electronic health record. Still, the test cannot be ordered without the provider providing the evidence-based indication.

7. World Alliance for Patient Safety. *Implementation Manual: Surgical Safety Checklist.* Geneva, Switzerland: World Health Organization; 2008. Available at http://www.who .int/patientsafety/safesurgery/tools_resources/SSSL_Manual_finalJun08.pdf.

8. Wang H E, Devereaux RS, and Yealy DM. National variation in United States sepsis mortality: a descriptive study. *Int J Health Geogr.* 2010;9:9.

9. Coates E, Villarreal A, Gordanier C, Pomernacki L. Sepsis power hour: a nursing driven protocol improves timeliness of sepsis care. Paper presented at Society of Hospital Medicine Annual Meeting; March 29 to April 1, 2015. National Harbor, MD. http:// www.shmabstracts.com/abstract/sepsis-power-hour-a-nursing-driven-protocol-improves -timeliness-of-sepsis-care/.

10. Society of Critical Care Medicine and the European Society of Intensive Care Medicine. Surviving Sepsis Campaign. April/May 2013. Available at http://www .survivingsepsis.org/About-SSC/Pages/default.aspx.

11. Qualis Health Award submission: "Results suggest that the use of the Sepsis Power Hour process improves the timeliness of sepsis care at Virginia Mason Medical Center. Among patients who receive a sepsis Power Hour 90% received a fluid bolus within one hour, as compared to only 36% prior to the intervention. Similar improvements were seen across all four bundle elements."

12. Steinman MA, Yang KY, Byron SC, Maselli JH, Gonzales R. Variation in outpatient antibiotic prescribing in the United States. *Am J Manag Care.* 2009;15(12):861–868.

13. Washington Health Alliance. Virginia Mason: Reducing inappropriate antibiotic prescribing in primary care; 2015, January. Available at http://wahealthalliance.org/wp -content/uploads.php?link-year=2015&link-month=01&link=spotlight-on-improvement -virginia-mason.pdf. According to the American Academy of Family Physicians and the American Academy of Allergy, Asthma, and Immunology, antibiotics are prescribed for more than 80% of outpatient visits for acute sinusitis, despite the fact that viral infections cause the majority of acute rhinosinusitis and only 0.5% to 2% of these infections progress to bacterial infections.

Fundamental Approaches to Measuring and Improving Patient Safety

Sarah P. Slight
David W. Bates

Abstract

Healthcare should be safe, patient centered, effective, and timely. Measuring and improving the safety and quality of care is critically important. This chapter outlines several fundamental approaches to measuring and improving safety and quality, including patient safety indicators, retrospective medical chart reviews, voluntary anonymous incident-reporting systems, patient safety culture tools, information technology, quality standards, the plan-do-study-act (PDSA) cycle, lean thinking and Six Sigma. Patients can also reveal important insights into the delivery of care in a particular setting and the kinds of changes needed to bring improvements. The importance of the patients' voice is discussed in further detail in this chapter.

Patient safety represents the foundation of high-quality healthcare. The Institute of Medicine (IOM) defined patient safety as "the prevention of harm to patients."[1] Potential injuries may occur because of errors of commission and omission; in recent years, the latter has been perceived to pose an even greater threat to health.[2] Medical errors are costly, not only in terms of human suffering, patients' loss of trust, and diminished satisfaction in their healthcare system but also in terms of opportunity costs. According to the IOM's first report on patient safety, *To Err Is Human: Building a Safer Health System*, errors are commonly caused by "faulty systems, processes, and conditions that lead people to make mistakes or fail to prevent them."[3] Correction of these systems and processes is regarded as key to improving patient safety, making it harder for healthcare providers to do the wrong thing and easier for them to do the right thing.[3]

Quality of healthcare relates to striving for excellence and value. The idea that varying degrees of excellence exist in healthcare was highlighted at least as far back as 1976.[4] The IOM defined quality then as the "the degree to which health services for individuals and populations increase the likelihood of desired health outcomes and are consistent with current professional knowledge."[5] The notion is that patients should be able to feel safe in the knowledge that a particular medical procedure or course of treatment will help them achieve the intended outcome. This landmark report attempted to raise public awareness about quality-of-care concerns, the opportunities for improvement, and the need to set standards and expectations around the delivery of healthcare. A more specific agenda for quality improvement was outlined in the IOM's second report in the quality series—*Crossing the Quality Chasm*—with the committee proposing that care should not only be *safe* but also *effective* (providing services based on scientific knowledge), *patient centered* (providing care that is respectful of and responsive to patients), *timely* (reducing wait times and sometimes harmful delays), *efficient* (avoiding waste), and *equitable* (providing consistent care that does not vary because of personal characteristics).[6]

Patient safety is integral to quality improvement. According to the IOM first report, "it would not be desirable to have one agency focused on quality issues and a separate agency focused on patient safety."[3] Organizations can develop safer processes and improve quality at the same time by identifying, evaluating, and reducing the risks and hazards associated with patient care. In this chapter, we will describe the frequency and types of patient safety incidents, outline the different approaches used to measure and improve patient safety and quality, the importance of establishing a safety culture, and the critical role of information technology as a tool for improvement.

FREQUENCY AND TYPES OF PATIENT SAFETY INCIDENTS

A medical error may or may not result in an adverse event (an injury that results from a medical intervention such as the use of a drug). In other words, medical errors have the potential to cause harm, whereas adverse events relate to the actual harm caused.[7] Adverse drug events that are associated with medication errors are considered preventable.[8] There has been considerable debate around whether efforts should focus on measuring error-prone aspects of the medication use process (e.g., errors in prescribing or administration) or concentrate on adverse drug events.[7] A recent systematic review commissioned by the World Health Organization estimated that 1.4% (95% CI 0.5–2.2) of patient encounters result in a patient safety incident, with major harm caused from 12.8% (95% CI 9.8–15.8) of these incidents globally.[9] The most common patient safety incidents involve errors with communication, diagnostic investigations, prescribing, and administration. In the U.S. outpatient setting alone, some 1 in 13 prescriptions was found to contain a prescribing error; half of these had the potential to cause harm.[10] This rate was substantially higher than those reported in the inpatient setting (0.4 to 5 per 100 orders) using similar methods.[11] The frequency of outpatient diagnostic errors—which includes missed, delayed, and incorrect diagnoses—was estimated to be 5.08% in the United States or approximately 12 million adults every year.[12] A delayed cancer diagnosis can be one of the most harmful and costly types of errors in the outpatient setting.[13] The rates of chemotherapy and home medication errors in cancer outpatients were also reported to range from between 0.3 to 5.8 per 100 visits and 0 to 14.5 per 100 visits, respectively, at different sites.[14] Administration errors were found to be the most common (56%) and often resulted from confusion over two sets of orders, one written at the time of diagnosis and another written at a later date if doses needed to be changed (initial dose was administered).[14]

MEASURING AND IMPROVING SAFETY

A variety of approaches have been used to measure safety, including chart reviews, direct observation, and sorting through claims for signals that an adverse event may have occurred. Patient safety indicators use claims data to identify measurable items that can *indicate* problems or unacceptable variations in patient care. More specifically, they can identify potentially preventable complications or adverse events related to a patient's exposure to the healthcare system.[15] The Agency for Healthcare Research and Quality's Patient Safety Indicators (AHRQ PSIs) have been used to mine administrative data to measure the rate of adverse events. Although these datasets are often readily available and at low cost, concerns have been raised over the reliability of their information in relation to the completeness and timing of entries and the accuracy of coding; they are thus likely to be more suitable for research purposes than for operational purposes such as identifying institutions or providers who deliver less safe care.[16] Quality indicators are easier to define and can more broadly be used to measure three conceptually distinct aspects of care—structure, process, and outcome—as first proposed by Avedis Donabedian in 1966.[17] *Structural indicators* can provide information on the healthcare setting, such as qualifications of care providers and adequate facilities and equipment. *Process indicators* describe how healthcare has been provided in terms of appropriate diagnosis and treatment, completeness of information, illness prevention (e.g., cancer screening), and the acceptability and continuity of care. *Outcome indicators* measure the end result of healthcare such as mortality, morbidity, readmission rates, and patients' experience—for example, patient-reported outcome measures (PROMs). Nationally, the focus has often been on improving patient outcomes and experiences; for example, the U.K. government announced in 2011 that the National Health Service (NHS) would be held to account for delivering measurable results from treatment activities.[18] To maximize the effectiveness of safety and quality indicators in improvement strategies, measures should be as feasible as possible (to collect and report), reliable (comparing like with like or determining the mix of risk and cases), and sensitive to change (capable of detecting changes).[19]

Other approaches used to measure the incidence of adverse events include retrospective medical chart reviews and voluntary anonymous incident-reporting systems. The Harvard Medical Practice Study used retrospective chart review as part of a two-stage process to detect adverse events in the inpatient setting.[20] Although reviews can be costly and resource intensive, the use of "triggers" or "clues" can help guide chart reviewers to specific cases at high risk of adverse events. The use of trigger tools such as the Institute for Healthcare Improvement's Global Trigger Tool,[21] have become popular techniques for more efficiently identifying adverse events and measuring their rates over time, though mainly in the inpatient setting.[22,23] A limitation of chart review is that the quality of charts is often highly variable and adverse events are not always recorded. Anonymous incident-reporting systems also play an important role in capturing patient safety information, relying on those involved in a safety event (e.g., nurse or physician) to provide detailed information voluntarily, especially for near misses, which are rarely recorded in records.[24] Although incident reporting has the advantage of involving front line staff in identifying these potential hazards, reports are subject to selection and recall bias, and they only capture a small fraction of the adverse events that can occur in a particular setting.[25,26] The usefulness of an incident-reporting system may also be limited by underreporting partly because of providers' misperceptions about what constitutes harm and concerns that a reported error may lead to punitive action.[27,28]

Within a culture of safety, however, providers need to be able to report errors without fear of retribution, and they must recognize that most preventable adverse events result from system failures, not individual failures.[29] The importance of establishing this positive safety culture in healthcare organizations is widely recognized. The culture should promote openness, teamwork, collaboration, and communication across all hierarchical levels as well as reporting mistakes and learning from them.[6] High-risk industries—including organizations that have worked extensively on safety (also known as *high reliability organizations*)—have shown a strong commitment to establishing cultures of continuous learning and willingness to change.[30] However, achieving sustained improvements in healthcare organizations can be difficult. The culture instilled during medical training has contributed to a belief that mistakes should not happen.[3] Rather than simply singling out particular individuals as being at fault, organizations should make concerted efforts to identify the ways a system allowed errors to occur. In the United States, the AHRQ-sponsored *Hospital Survey on Patient Safety Culture* is a measurement tool designed to help hospitals access the culture of patient safety in their organizations.[31,32] The Safety Attitudes Questionnaire was also developed to compare attitudes in diverse healthcare settings, including inpatient and outpatient settings.[33,34] This tool measures providers' attitudes about job satisfaction, perceptions of management, teamwork, safety climate, working conditions, and stress recognition. A third tool, which was developed in the United Kingdom and used extensively around the world, is the Manchester Patient Safety Framework (MaPSaf),[35,36] which helps healthcare teams in different settings assess their progress in developing a safety culture.

Information technology (IT) can play a major role in improving safety for many patients. The introduction of computerized physician order entry (CPOE) with decision support can increase the likelihood of catching and preventing medication-related errors.[24] Computerized tools can also improve communication between clinicians, provide access to online reference sources, assist with calculations and monitoring, and improve compliance with preventive service protocols.[37–39] IT can also help reduce the frequency of different types of errors, including errors of omission (through corollary orders)[40] and transcription (through bar-code technology),[41] and associated adverse events.[42,43] Computer databases that contain laboratory test results and current medication orders for the same patient increase the opportunities for real-time screening and analysis.[7]

MEASURING AND IMPROVING QUALITY

Measuring and improving quality is critically important in the healthcare environment. The development and availability of quality and safety standards in healthcare organizations can serve many purposes. As noted in *To Err is Human*,[3] they can define a minimum level of acceptable performance and establish consistency and uniformity across healthcare organizations. Standards also help set expectations and values, not only for healthcare providers but also for patients. Although the implementation of quality standards has been an effective approach in the Western world, for resource-restricted settings international standards can be difficult if not impossible to achieve. Launched in March 2011, the SafeCare Initiative was designed to address this issue. The SafeCare approach is based on internationally acknowledged quality standards, and it dissects the improvement process of healthcare providers in surveyable and measurable steps. Thus, an improvement trajectory is created that provides positive incentives for healthcare providers to move upward in quality, ultimately to the level that qualifies them for full accreditation. That objective might be out of reach for most providers starting out, but this guided way can help them work toward that objective and boost client, investor, and regulator confidence in the motivation and capacity of healthcare providers to steadily enhance their performance.[44,45]

Quality improvement is a continuous process that draws on a wide variety of approaches, many of which were developed in the manufacturing sector and transferred to healthcare. The plan-do-study-act cycle, also known as the *Deming* or *Shewhart cycle*, supports quality-improvement efforts by testing change in rapid, informative cycles. The *plan* step involves deciding on what change or in what way a process could be improved and then implementing the change as part of the subsequent *do* step on a small scale and over a relatively short period of time. The *study* step involves analyzing the results obtained before finally deciding what actions should be taken to effect the desired change as part of the *act* step. This PDSA cycle is one of the key elements incorporated into the Institute for Healthcare Improvement's *Breakthrough Collaborative Model*,[46] which accelerates the pace of change by promoting performance improvement across a network of clinics or hospitals rather than trying to improve the facilities of a system one at a time. Two other approaches, lean and Six Sigma, build on the basic PDSA cycle. Lean thinking aims to improve quality by eliminating all activities that do not add value and serve the patient's needs. Two crucial components of this process are (1) determining what patients consider of value and (2) involving all staff in redesigning the process to reduce waste.[47]

The Six Sigma philosophy seeks to identify and reduce variation in a process, which is synonymous with eliminating errors. Six Sigma applies elements in the acronym DMAIC: define, measure, analyze, improve, and control. The *measure* step involves gathering data to show how much variation is present, with the additional *control* step emphasizes continuously measuring and monitoring the process after the change has been made. By achieving Six Sigma (a statistical unit of measure), the failure rate is minimized to 3.4 defects (errors) per million opportunities.[48]

Many of these quality-improvement approaches share common underlying principles.[49] These include (1) understanding the problem by studying the data collected and concentrating on the areas in greatest need of improvement; (2) understanding the processes and systems within the organization, focusing in particular on the patient pathway; (3) improving the reliability of the system and clinical processes to help reduce errors and deliver high-quality consistent care; (4) measuring and analyzing the demand (the number of patients requiring access to the service), flow (when the service is needed), and capacity (sufficient staff and equipment) to help reduce waste; (5) enthusing, involving, and engaging front line staff (particularly clinicians) to help bring about change; and (6) involving patients, caregivers, and the wider public in designing improvements and monitoring the impact of a change.[49] Patients can reveal important insights into the quality of care delivered in a particular setting and the kinds of changes that are needed to bring about improvements.

In the United Kingdom, the events at Mid Staffordshire NHS Foundation Trust came to national attention when apparently high mortality rates were reported in patients admitted with emergencies.[50] The National Advisory Group on the Safety of Patients in England studied the various accounts of Mid Staffordshire and the recommendations of Robert Francis to specify changes that were needed in moving forward.[51] The most important single change called for in the advisory group's report was for the NHS to embrace an ethic of learning and involve patients and their carers at all levels of healthcare organizations from wards to the boards of hospitals. Thus, the patients' voice was considered an essential asset in monitoring the safety and quality of care.

To conclude, there have been numerous calls for healthcare organizations and professionals to make patient safety and quality improvement a top priority.[3,6] This chapter has outlined several different approaches for measuring and improving safety and quality. These include the use of (1) patient safety indicators, (2) retrospective medical chart reviews, (3) voluntary anonymous incident-reporting systems, (4) patient safety culture tools, (5) information technology, (6) quality standards, (7) use of the PDSA cycle, (8) lean thinking, and (9) Six Sigma. The current safety and quality of healthcare varies among hospitals, cities, and countries. Clearly, more needs to be done to ensure that patients get the best care possible.

REFERENCES

1. Aspden P, Corrigan JM, Wolcott J, Erickson SM. 2004. *Patient Safety: Achieving a New Standard for Care.* Washington, DC: National Academy Press.

2. McGlynn EA, Asch SM, Adams J, Keesey J, Hicks J, DeCristofaro A, et al. The quality of health care delivered to adults in the United States. *N Engl J Med.* 2003;348(26): 2635–2645.

3. Kohn L, Corrigan JM, Donaldson MS, eds. *To Err Is Human: Building a Safer Health System;* 1999. Consensus Report of Institute of Medicine. Accessed March 15, 2015, from http://www.iom.edu.

4. M. A. Wandelt. 1976. Definitions of words germane to evaluation of health care. *NLN Publ.* 1976;15–1611):57–58.

5. Institute of Medicine. *Medicare: A Strategy for Quality Assurance,* vol. 2; 1990. Washington, DC: National Academy Press.

6. Committee on the Quality of Health Care in America. *Crossing the Quality Chasm: A New Health System for the 21st Century;* 2001. Washington, DC: National Academy Press.

7. Classen DC, Metzger J. Improving medication safety: the measurement conundrum and where to start. *Int J Qual Health Care.* 2003;15(suppl 1)i41–i7.

8. Kaushal R, Bates DW. Computerized Physician Order Entry (CPOE) with Clinical Decision Support Systems (CDSSs). U.S. Department of Health & Human Services, Agency for Healthcare Research and Quality. Accessed March 15, 2015, from http://archive.ahrq.gov/clinic/ptsafety/chap6.htm.

9. Panesar SS, deSilva D, Carson-Stevens A, Cresswell K, Salvilla SA, Slight SP, et al. How safe is primary care? a systematic review. *BMJ Qual & Safety.* 2015;1–10.

10. Gandhi TK, Weingart SN, Seger AC, Borus J, Burdick E, Poon EG, et al. Outpatient prescribing errors and the impact of computerized prescribing. *J Gen Intern Med.* 2005;20(9):837–841.

11. Bates DW, Boyle DL, Vander Vliet MB, Schneider J, Leape L. Relationship between medication errors and adverse drug events. *J Gen Intern Med.* 1995;10(4): 199–205.

12. Singh H, Meyer AN, Thomas EJ. The frequency of diagnostic errors in outpatient care: estimations from three large observational studies involving U.S. adult populations. *BMJ Qual & Safety.* 2014;23(9):727–731.

13. Singh H., Hirani K, Kadiyala H, Rudomiotov O, Davis T, Khan MM, et al. Characteristics and predictors of missed opportunities in lung cancer diagnosis: an electronic health record-based study. *J Clin Oncol.* 2010;28(20):3307–3315.

14. Walsh KE, Dodd KS, Seetharaman K, Roblin DW, Herrinton LJ, Von Worley A, et al. Medication errors among adults and children with cancer in the outpatient setting. *J Clin Oncol.* 2009;27(6):891–896.

15. Farquhar M. AHRQ quality indicators. In: Hughes RG, *Patient Safety and Quality: An Evidence-Based Handbook for Nurses*; 2008. Rockville, MD: Agency for Healthcare Research and Quality.

16. Rosen AK, Rivard P, Zhao S, Loveland S, Tsilimingras D, Christiansen, CL, et al. Evaluating the patient safety indicators: how well do they perform on Veterans Health Administration data? *Med Care*. 2005;43(9):873–884.

17. Donabedian A. Evaluating the quality of medical care. *Milbank Q*. 1966;44(3)(suppl):166–206.

18. National Health Service. NHS Outcomes Framework 2012–13; 2011. London: Author. Available at http://www.dh.gov.uk/en/Publicationsandstatistics/Publications/PublicationsPolicyAndGuidance/DH_131700. Accessed March 15, 2015.

19. Campbell SM, Braspenning J, Hutchinson A, Marshall M. Research methods used in developing and applying quality indicators in primary care. *Qual & Safety in Health Care J*. 2002;11(4):358–364.

20. Leape LL, Brennan TA, Laird N, Lawthers AG, Localio AR, Barnes, BA, et al. The nature of adverse events in hospitalized patients: results of the Harvard Medical Practice Study II. *N Engl J Med*. 1991;324(6):377–384.

21. Griffin F, Resa RK. *IHI Global Trigger Tool for Measuring Adverse Events*, 2nd ed. Cambridge, MA: Institute for Healthcare Improvement; 2009. Available at http://www.IHI.org. Accessed 15 March 2015.

22. Classen DC, Resar R, Griffin F, Federico F, Frankel T, Kimmel N, et al. "Global trigger tool" shows that adverse events in hospitals may be ten times greater than previously measured. *Health Affair*. 2011;30(4):581–589.

23. Landrigan CP, Parry GJ, Bones CB, Hackbarth AD, Goldmann DA, Sharek PJ. Temporal trends in rates of patient harm resulting from medical care. *N Engl J Med*. 2010;363(22):2124–2134.

24. Jha AK, Kuperman GJ, Teich JM, Leape L, Shea B, Rittenberg E, et al. Identifying adverse drug events: development of a computer-based monitor and comparison with chart review and stimulated voluntary report. *J Am Med Info Assoc*. 1998;5(3):305–314.

25. Cullen DJ, Bates DW, Small SD, Cooper JB, Nemeskal AR, Leape LL. The incident reporting system does not detect adverse drug events: a problem for quality improvement. *Jt Comm J Qual Improve*. 1995;21(10):541–548.

26. Nuckols TK, Bell DS, Liu H, Paddock SM, Hilborne LH. Rates and types of events reported to established incident reporting systems in two U.S. hospitals. *Qual & Safety Health Care J*. 2007;16(3):164–168.

27. Leape LL. Why should we report adverse incidents? *J Eval Clin Pract*. 1999; 5(1):1–4.

28. Resar, RK, Rozich JD, Classen D. Methodology and rationale for the measurement of harm with trigger tools. *Qual & Safety Health Care J*. 2003;12(suppl 2):ii39–ii45.

29. Leape LL, Bates DW, Cullen DJ, Cooper J, Demonaco HJ, Gallivan T, et al. Systems analysis of adverse drug events. *JAMA*. 1995;274(1):35–43.

30. Sagan SD. *The Limits of Safety: Organizations, Accidents, and Nuclear Weapons*. Princeton, NJ: Princeton University Press; 1993:xvi.

31. Blegen MA, Gearhart S, O'Brien R, Sehgal NL, Alldredge, BK. AHRQ's hospital survey on patient safety culture: psychometric analyses. *J Patient Safety.* 2009;5(3): 139–144.

32. Colla JB, Bracken AC, Kinney LM, Weeks WB. Measuring patient safety climate: a review of surveys. *Qual & Safety Health Care.* 2005;14(5):364–366.

33. Sexton JB, Helmreich RL, Neilands TB, Rowan K, Vella K, Boyden J, et al. The Safety Attitudes Questionnaire: psychometric properties, benchmarking data, and emerging research. *BMC Health Serv Res.* 2006;6:44.

34. Modak I, Sexton JB, Lux TR, Helmreich RL, Thomas EJ. Measuring safety culture in the ambulatory setting: the Safety Attitudes Questionnaire—ambulatory version. *J Gen Intern Med.* 2007;22(1):1–5.

35. Law MP, Zimmerman R, Baker GR, Smith T. Assessment of safety culture maturity in a hospital setting. *Healthcare Q.* 2010;13(special no.):110–115.

36. Wallis K, Dovey S. Assessing patient safety culture in New Zealand primary care: a pilot study using a modified Manchester Patient Safety Framework in Dunedin general practices. *J Primary Health Care.* 2011;3(1):35–40.

37. Bates DW, Gawande AA. Improving safety with information technology. *N Engl J Med.* 2003;348(25):2526–2534.

38. Balas EA, Weingarten S, Garb CT, Blumenthal D, Boren SA, Brown GD. Improving preventive care by prompting physicians. *Archiv Intern Med.* 2000;160(3): 301–308.

39. Bates DW, Leape LL, Cullen DJ, Laird N, Petersen LA, Teich JM, et al. Effect of computerized physician order entry and a team intervention on prevention of serious medication errors. *JAMA.* 1998;280(15):1311–1316.

40. Overhage JM, Tierney WM, Zhou XH, McDonald CJ. A randomized trial of "corollary orders" to prevent errors of omission. *J Am Med Info Assoc.* 1997;4(5):364–375.

41. Poon EG, Keohane CA, Yoon CS, Ditmore M, Bane A, Levtzion-Korach O, et al. Effect of bar-code technology on the safety of medication administration. *N Engl J Med.* 2010;362(18):1698–1707.

42. Bates DW. Using information technology to reduce rates of medication errors in hospitals. *BMJ.* 2000;320(7237):788–791.

43. Bates DW, Miller EB, Cullen DJ, Burdick L, Williams L, Laird N, et al. Patient risk factors for adverse drug events in hospitalized patients. *Archiv Intern Med.* 1999; 159(21):2553–2560.

44. SafeCare. Introducing standards to improve health care delivery in resource-restricted countries. Retrieved from http://www.jointcommissioninternational.org/; n.d. Accessed March 15, 2015.

45. SafeCare. Basic health care standards. Retrieved from http://www.safe-care.org/;nd. Accessed March 15, 2015.

46. The Breakthrough Series. *IHI's Collaborative Model for Achieving Breakthrough Improvement.* Boston: Institute for Healthcare Improvement; 2003.

47. Institute for Healthcare Improvement. *Going Lean in Health Care.* Cambridge, MA: Institute for Healthcare Improvement; 2005.

48. Lanham B, Maxson-Cooper P. Is Six Sigma the answer for nursing to reduce medical errors and enhance patient safety? *Nurs Econ.* 2003;21(1):38–41.

49. The Health Foundation. *Quality Improvement Made Simple: What Every Board Should Know about Quality Improvement.* United Kingdom: The Health Foundation; 2011.

50. Commission for Health Care Audit and Inspection. *Investigation into Mid-Staffordshire NHS Foundation Trust.* United Kingdom: Commission for Health Care Audit and Inspection; 2009.

51. National Advisory Group on Safety of Patients in England. *A Promise to Learn: A Commitment to Act. Improving the Safety of Patients in England.* London, UK: Crown Press; 2013.

The Organizational Culture that Supports Patient Safety

Alberta T. Pedroja

Abstract

The culture of safety is a function of the values, attitudes, perceptions, competencies, and patterns of behavior that influence the context in which care is delivered. The culture of an organization is believed to have as much an impact on patient safety as the use of best clinical practices.

This chapter offers the characteristics of the culture of safety and the strategies employed to promote them. Characteristics include patient safety as an organizing principle, leadership engagement, teamwork, transparency, flexibility, and a learning environment. Strategies for preventing patient harm include designing safe and reliable systems and team building among others. Examples of strategies to mitigate risk are alerts and reminders built into the electronic medical record and team huddles. Finally, recovery after an incident includes storytelling and the use of root cause analysis.

Despite the many barriers to the culture of safety's development, leadership engagement, voluntary initiatives, and regulation have had positive influences to help overcome such traditional values as steep authority gradients and hierarchical structures with physicians as unquestioned leaders. These must now give way to a flat configuration. Acknowledging human fallibility and at the same time expecting accountability is a dilemma that all healthcare leaders must face in the effort to create and sustain the culture of safety.

THE CULTURE OF SAFETY

The landmark report from the Institute of Medicine, *To Err is Human*,[1] states that evidence-based practices are critical, but the contextual framework in which care is delivered also contributes to patient safety. By 2004, articles describing the culture of safety[2–4] concluded that preventing adverse incidents depends as much on cultural changes as on structural changes in healthcare organizations. Thus, the culture of safety is defined as "the product of individual and group values, attitudes, perceptions, competencies, and patterns of behavior that determine the commitment to, and the style and proficiency of, an organization's health and safety management."[5]

Evidence-based medicine provides the rules, which are often in the form of policies and procedures. The culture determines how we behave when the rulebook is gone or no one in authority is watching, a situation that occurs regularly given the exigencies of patient care.

TYPES OF WORK

According to James Reason,[6] much of the work performed in healthcare can be categorized into three types: skill based, rule based, and knowledge based. Skill-based work is performed automatically and takes little conscious thought. Taking vital signs is skill-based work. Activities performed infrequently are rule based, as are complicated processes that need a series of reminders to be sure that every step is performed as expected. On a regular basis, staff follows the rules enumerated via guidelines, protocols, and hospital policies. Knowledge-based work is required in circumstances where the situation is unique and rules do not apply. Professionals draw on previous experience, similar situations, other team members, or the literature in the field to devise a course of action.

The following example is illustrative of how knowledge-based work can devolve from rules-based work. The patient was a 92-year-old male with a previous history of peptic ulcer disease requiring multiple surgeries for internal bleeding; he was undergoing a procedure to insert a Jackson Pratt drain to remove excess fluids from the body. As per protocol, the staff performed the first of three sponge and instrument counts at the start of the surgery. The second count performed before the closure was short by one sponge. The staff looked in the OR but did not find the sponge. The surgeon explored the field but was unable to feel the sponge, so he called for an x-ray. The radiologist saw a foreign object, and since the procedure called for a drain, he erroneously concluded that he was looking at a Penrose drain when he was actually looking at the missing sponge. He wrote a brief note on the film stating, "No foreign object other than the drain." Based on this report, the surgeon closed the patient because patient safety would recommend that additional time under general anesthesia was more dangerous than closing the patient and conducting a CT scan the next day. A CT scan did, in fact, identify the location of the missing sponge, and the patient was taken back to the OR to have the sponge removed.

The policy for sponge and instrument count did not anticipate a situation in which the sponge count was off and the staff could not account for it in the OR or in the patient via the radiologic image. The policy could have dictated a response (rules-based work), but it was assumed that if the sponge was not in the OR—it was in the patient—and that the radiologic image would be conclusive. An organization committed to patient safety offers skills training to support skills-based work, ready access to the steps in the process to support rules-based work, and a culture of safety to encourage staff members to make good decisions when the rules no longer apply and they are required to use critical thinking skills to perform knowledge-based work.

Performance-improvement activities can help identify weak links in the hospital's processes and turn knowledge-based work into rules-based work. When problems are identified, tools to support rules-based work may be developed after which time the processes are implemented via the electronic medical record. In this way, the electronic medical record offers the opportunity to refine the delivery of patient care by ensuring that clinicians use best practices and evidence-based care. The example below is a case in point.

The organization was alarmed to discover an increase in the number of patients who had hospital-acquired *Clostridium difficile*. According to the Centers for Disease Control and Prevention (CDC), 250,000 people require hospital care for *C. difficile* infections every year, and it is thought that many of these infections could have been prevented with proper hand hygiene. Although *C. difficile* is commonly found in the digestive tract, it becomes harmful when the balance of intestinal flora is upset by toxins released by the bacteria that attack the lining of the intestine. It is recommended that testing for *C. difficile* occur after the patient is observed to have three unformed stools.[7]

With no change in the patient population, the incidence of *C. difficile* jumped to 20 cases per quarter when the previous 18 months saw just 6 to 9 cases per quarter. The hospital had already switched to the appropriate dilution of bleach, the use of UV lights after the patient is discharged and major initiatives for hand hygiene commonly associated with the prevention of *C. difficile* infections. The team came together to determine whether a nursing home was admitting patients with *C. difficile*, whether the clustering of cases suggested that staff education might be needed, or there was a correlation with length of stay (LOS). A review of the literature uncovered a study in which positive outcomes of *C. difficile* were associated with turnaround times, and that possibility was added to the list of hypotheses investigated.

The investigation found no correlation with LOS, nursing home admissions, or unit clusters, but it was found that the onset of diarrhea could be found in the medical record for only 57% of the *C. difficile* cases. Because we know that we manage what we measure, it was clear that we were not measuring or managing *C. difficile*. The lab director clarified the definition of the specimen to be collected, and the nursing directors instructed the informaticists to add a check for diarrhea to the initial nursing assessment and every shift assessment. In addition, a *C. difficile* tab in the electronic medical record was created for any patient with suspected *C. difficile*. The number of cases fell to five in the following quarter and remained at that level ongoing. The process for patients with suspected *C. difficile* became rules-based work with the help of the electronic medical record.

CHARACTERISTICS OF THE CULTURE OF SAFETY

The aviation industry has contributed important ideas to the culture of safety in healthcare because flying a plane is also considered a high-risk, complex endeavor, dependent on human factors and reliable systems. Their investigations established the significance of leadership, teamwork, situational awareness, and safety by design.[8,9] In healthcare, as in aviation, the understanding that human error is inevitable is integral to systems designed for safety; the risk of human error reaching the patient and causing harm will only be reduced through systems that support safe practices. The most notable of these systems in the automation of documentation so that we no longer leave important aspects of patient care to rote learning (skills-based work) or professional judgment (knowledge-based work).

Teamwork is the lynchpin of the culture of safety. Effective team performance requires team members to cooperate in a shared vision—that is, patient safety demands that there is good communication free of the authority gradient.[10] An example of a teamwork technique borrowed from aviation is the so-called time-out process before operative and invasive procedures where all members of the team must acknowledge a common understanding of the procedure about to be performed. In the preceding knowledge-based error example, the surgical team, deeply affected by the failure of their system to protect the patient from a retained foreign body, instituted a "count pause." Now surgery is halted while the surgical technician performs the instrument count to minimize the risk of error. More importantly, direct physician-to-physician communication is the key. The attending surgeon must directly communicate with the radiologist to make sure they share an understanding of the indication and interpretation of the radiological image findings.

The approach to teamwork in aviation has been crew resource management (CRM). The Agency for Healthcare Research and Quality (AHRQ) used the CRM principles to develop a program called TeamSTEPPs[©] that focuses on the knowledge, skills, and attitudes needed for teamwork in healthcare. The AHRQ website (http://teamstepps.ahrq.gov/) offers a review of the literature, a patient safety culture survey, and a variety of other resources to adapt the principles of teamwork into the challenges of clinical practice.

Other characteristics of the culture of safety have been identified by studying high reliability organizations (HROs) such as nuclear power generation plants, firefighters, and hostage negotiating teams. Weick and Sutcliffe[11] found that HROs track small failures, resist oversimplification, remain sensitive to operations, maintain capabilities for resilience, and take advantage of shifting locations of expertise. Small failures are treated as symptomatic of larger and potentially more serious problems in the system; timely resolution of small failures are seen as necessary to avert adverse safety events.

In the following example, the patient sustained no permanent harm. However, staff treated each incident as a sentinel event because it was clear that the systems were not fail safe. A 50-year-old patient arrived in the emergency department (ED) via ambulance with a diagnosis of pulmonary embolism. The ED physician ordered intravenous unfractionated heparin, which requires weight-based dosing. The patient was not ambulatory and unable to step on the scale, so the ED nurse estimated the weight to be 80 kg and ordered the heparin dose accordingly. She initiated the heparin per protocol based on the estimated weight of the patient, and the patient was transferred to the intensive care unit (ICU). The patient's actual weight taken in the ICU was 60 kg, but no one made a correction in the heparin dose being administered to the patient. The lab reported the partial thromboplastin time (PTT) result, taken six hours after the loading dose, to be 113.3, well above the normal therapeutic range. The ICU staff recognized the error and adjusted the dose based on the actual weight of the patient. The error was classified as a class E medication error—that is, the error reached the patient and required treatment but did not cause permanent harm. As a result, the process was changed. Any patient transferred from the ED to the ICU automatically has his or her weight checked and heparin dose adjusted if necessary to ensure patient safety. This example also illustrates rules-based work (heparin dosing) and the potentially serious consequences that can ensue if the rules are not followed.

Resilience speaks to the ability to change focus and adapt to changing realities. Aggressive use of the electronic health record (EHR) as in the preceding examples have wrought significant changes in healthcare delivery and in the way we develop and ensure high reliability organizations. Given the number of specialties involved and the frequently unexpected turns in patients' conditions, the locus of expertise also often changes from one situation to the next. With its members working together to provide the range of services when they are needed, the team has the best hope of achieving optimal patient outcomes.

James Reason[12] attributes additional characteristics to the culture of safety, including a "reporting culture" that fosters a nonpunitive environment encouraging incident reporting, a "just culture" that assures staff that mistakes will be handled fairly, a "learning culture" that encourages everyone to learn from their mistakes and adverse events, and a "flexible culture" in which staff quickly adapt to changing circumstances.

In the just culture model proposed by David Marx,[13] individuals have three fundamental duties: avoid causing unjustified risk or harm, produce an outcome, and follow procedural rules. Against this background, a mistake can be classified into three categories. The first is the human error—inadvertently doing what should not have been done, also referred to as *slips* and *lapses*. The second is the at-risk behavior where risk is not recognized or is mistakenly believed to be justified. The third is reckless behavior—the choice to consciously disregard a substantial and justifiable risk. The model proposes the following actions: console for human error, coach for at-risk behavior, and punish for recklessness.

SAFEGUARDS: PREVENTION, MITIGATION, AND RECOVERY

Strategies to promote the culture of safety can be categorized into three phases: prevention, mitigation, and recovery. The prevention phase focuses on proactively anticipating potential risks in the system and correcting them. Mitigation occurs when there are known risks. Finally, when patient harm does occur, recovery includes a series of steps that often result in strategies that prevent or mitigate these risks in the future. Taken together, these strategies support the culture of safety.

Prevention

Reliability is the "probability of a product performing a specified function without failure under given conditions for a specified period of time."[14] Reliability is usually reported as a defect rate—for example, 10^{-1}, 10^{-2}, 10^{-3}, and so forth. One error in 10 tries is 10^{-1}; one error in 100 tries is 10^{-2}; one error in 1,000 tries is 10^{-3}, and so on. Table 4.1 provides examples of what would occur if society were content with a 10^{-3} defect rate—that is, 99.9% accuracy. With so much at stake, healthcare professionals hold themselves to an even higher standard; consequently, Six Sigma, or 10^{-6}, is the goal of many healthcare organizations.

Unconstrained human performance guided by discretion only is generally estimated to be at a reliability level between 10^{-1} and 10^{-2}. Constrained human performance with limits on discretion such as alerts built into the system or forcing functions can reach levels between 10^{-2} and 10^{-3}. Strategies likely to bring clinical practice to a level of 10^{-1} reliability include training and awareness, checklists, information and feedback mechanisms on compliance, and standardization of equipment and supplies. More sophisticated failure preventions to reach a reliability of 10^{-2} necessitate decision aids and reminders built into the system, defaults to desired actions, multiple layers of redundancy, habituated patterns, standardization of processes, opt-out versus opt-in choices, and forcing functions.[15]

Every time another check or another signature is required, we are reducing the probability of human error using forced redundancy.[16–18] The count pause implemented in the OR demonstrates the team's recognition of the importance of forced redundancy. The use of automation improves those odds further. For

TABLE 4.1 If 99.9% Were Good Enough*

IRS lost documents	2 million per year
Major plane crashes	3 per day
Lost items in the mail	16,000 per hour
ATM errors	37,000 per hour
Pacemakers incorrectly installed	291 per year
Babies given to the wrong parents	12 per day
Erroneous medical procedures	107 per day

*With permission from the Massachusetts QIO

example, computer-based physician ordering systems (CPOE) have built-in forcing functions to freeze the order-entry screen until medication-allergy information is entered. Furthermore, it may provide warning alerts and reminders in the case of drug–drug interactions. Forcing functions essentially stop the process from moving forward, preventing a step from occurring; this improves the likelihood that evidence-based practices known to improve outcomes and reduce patient harm will be implemented. The requirements and incentives of the Affordable Care Act (ACA) have necessitated the use of 10^{-2} strategies in which forcing functions, standardization of processes, and defaults are common in the electronic health record.

Mitigation

In the mitigation phase, the culture of safety is characterized by teamwork and communication using patient safety as the organizing principle. Well-functioning teams demonstrate a common purpose of safe patient care. The roles of various team members are clear but not overly rigid, allowing members to easily adapt when needed. Power is decentralized and autonomy eschewed to prevent error. The importance of teamwork is particularly acute when circumstances deviate from the norm, when the rules are absent, and when the team must rely on an educated guess. This is also known as "critical thinking." Each member of the team must be free to act or contribute because sometimes the hierarchy is unwieldy or, worse, an impediment.

A word of caution is necessary during the initial implementation of the electronic health record. The clinician's task list in the EHR overwhelms nursing care, and higher-level nursing skills associated with critical thinking and knowledge-based work can take a back seat. It is here that leadership must help the clinician work through these early growing pains to enable clinical practice and the culture of safety to remain intact. So long as the team is committed to safe and effective care first and the necessary documentation to achieve it, this will be a passing phase.

Good teamwork relies on good communication to achieve desired outcomes. Regulatory and accreditation agencies such as the Joint Commission require standardization of communication between providers to ensure that communication is comprehensive and complete. The process known as *situation, background, assessment, and recommendation* (SBAR), which is commonly used to standardize communication in healthcare, is an example of a risk-mitigation strategy.[19] In the example of the missing sponge, the communication between the radiologist and the OR staff was wholly responsible for the problem associated with the missing sponge. The solution was a more structured form of face-to-face communication or telephonic communication during off-hours to guard against errors or unnecessary time under general anesthesia.

Another initiative to mitigate risk is the team huddle in which staff members regularly convene, typically at the start of the shift, to review risks associated with patient care such as wound care, surgical procedures, and restraints, among others. This alerts the staff to watch for problems that may arise over the course of the shift and increases situational awareness. A time-out is required by regulation before the start of a procedure to achieve the same effect.

Recovery

In a culture of safety, the recovery phase after a near miss or actual adverse event is focused on learning from the event. A full investigation that includes individual interviews with staff members and a rigorous analysis of the processes associated with the failure is required for all sentinel events, but if the organization is a "fanatic for failure,"[11] process analysis is also used more widely for near misses. The root cause analysis (RCA) is employed for sentinel events, and an intensive analysis, a streamlined process investigation, is used for any case that did not go as planned even though there was no harm to patients. An RCA is a systematic review of every structure and process associated with patient care, including staffing, communication, leadership, training, information, and the environment to name a few. An intensive analysis will review some, though not all, of the issues specified in an RCA. Intensive analyses vary, but one such process relies on staff preparation of the case, including a timeline and a description of the incident that details the time, date, and patient condition. Staff then reviews selected processes that need a drill down such as the equipment, staffing, education, communication, information, environment of care, or leadership. This information is taken to a weekly risk meeting where the cases are discussed and recommendations made. These may go out to the entire organization if it is seen as a weak spot. The RCA or intensive analysis process during the recovery phase provides an opportunity to learn from the potential system vulnerabilities and develop policy and protocols to effectively transition knowledge-based work into rule-based work.

During the root cause analysis in which the team explored the medication error that occurred when the ED patient transferred to the ICU, one manager recommended counseling action against the employees who ordered and administered the heparin without getting a weight on the patient. Hearing that there are no gurneys in the ED with built-in scales, another team member recommended the purchase of new equipment. On further consideration, this solution also was rejected as impractical. There is no guarantee that this gurney would be available when a patient who needed to be weighed arrived in the ED, which may be why this is not the community standard at this time. The solution devised by the team, therefore, was that heparin dosed in the ED with an estimated weight will include an alert in the system for the unit staff that indicates heparin was dosed with estimated weights. The patient then needs to be weighed immediately on arrival in the unit and the heparin dose will be adjusted as needed. The policy now includes a procedure in which the pharmacist will adjust the dosing if the estimated weight is more than 10 pounds off in either direction. With the help of an alert in the system, we can be assured that this high-risk medication will be delivered safely to every patient every time, thus supporting the culture of safety.

Thus, the recovery phase often leads to additional steps for prevention and mitigation of risks, completing the cycle. None of this would be possible without a staff willing to report the error in an environment that promotes transparency. To foster transparency, institutional leadership must ensure that those who report adverse events are safe from unfair retribution, that the process for reporting is easy and well understood, and that the process analysis is just. In addition, staff must be confident that the purpose of the discussion is to learn from the experience and not to unjustifiably prosecute those who were involved.[12]

Storytelling is also becoming an important part of patient safety armamentarium in the recovery phase. Dennis Quaid,[20] Sorrel King,[21] Linda Kenney,[22] and others have had a national impact telling their stories to large audiences of healthcare workers. At the local level, hospitals across the country are using stories to facilitate the implementation of new patient safety policies and procedures; sometimes patients are also included in the discussions so that they can provide staff with firsthand accounts. The quality reports to the board that include such features as "Lessons Learned" or "Stories from the Field" provide board members with a deeper understanding of the complexities associated with delivering safe patient care. One of the six recommendations from the IHI on engaging boards in improving quality and safety includes storytelling.[23] Specifically, the IHI recommends the following: "Select and review progress toward safer care as the first agenda item at every board meeting, grounded in transparency, and putting a 'human face' on harm data."

MEASURING THE CULTURE OF SAFETY

The truism, "you manage what you measure," prompted AHRQ to sponsor the development of a Culture of Safety Survey. The Joint Commission and other accrediting bodies require that organizations administer such a survey on a regular basis. The dimensions on the AHRQ survey that can be found on its website[24] include leadership, the learning environment, willingness to report, teamwork, and communication to enumerate a few critical ones. The purpose of the survey is to raise staff awareness, assess the current situation of the organization, and support the improvement efforts.

The ACA has implemented financial penalties for errors, which has led to reporting of these measures to the medical staff and the board. The Joint Commission requires that sentinel events be reported along with lessons learned or other process improvements that are designed to prevent these errors from happening again. DNV GL NIAHO® methodology requires that the organization's Patient Safety System process be documented and available for review during the annual survey.

Barriers to the Culture of Safety

Competing priorities, fragmentation of work among different disciplines, and hierarchical structures are a few of the long-standing challenges for organizations that are striving to create a culture of safety. Steep authority gradient is still common in hospital operations that must give way to the shared responsibility needed for patient safety. Cost pressures may lead to greater efficiency, but they can also create obstacles to the checks and double checks on high-risk operations by an increasingly busier staff. Finally, redesigning processes is a costly endeavor and often undertaken after an adverse event rather than proactively to design safe systems.

In a culture of safety, autonomy and trust in an individual professional is not enough; it must be supplemented by fail-safe processes designed to prevent errors. Double checks when transfusing blood products or administering high-risk medications are not inefficiencies but precautions that serve to protect patients from harmful healthcare errors.

Other traditional viewpoints have had to change as we have become more sensitized to patient safety. When guidelines and protocols were introduced, they were disparaged as "cookbook medicine" and seen as threats to the autonomy of clinicians. Now we understand them as important tools to facilitate the implementation of best practices. The acknowledgement of human fallibility still remains problematic in healthcare. Transparency has had an uphill battle for acceptance. Physicians and staff are well aware of the threat of litigation, and it may seem that to admit wrongdoing is to put themselves and the hospital in financial jeopardy if a patient sues. In addition, courts typically search for someone to blame. It seems counterintuitive to many physicians and hospitals that disclosure may actually reduce the overall risk of patient dissatisfaction and litigious behavior.

The greatest dilemma facing the culture of safety has been the need to balance accountability while promoting a nonpunitive environment that encourages reporting and transparency.[25] Hospital administrators have sought to strike a balance using James Reason's types of work (skills, rules, and knowledge based) in conjunction with just culture algorithms to determine the appropriateness and type of staff counseling and disciplinary action. Figure 4.1 displays one method to determine accountability for human error is by first determining the type of work performed and asking relevant questions. If all questions can be answered in the positive, then the staff is believed to have acted in a responsible manner. If any are answered in the negative, then it is reasonable to hold the staff accountable and offer solutions such as counseling, coaching or other disciplinary actions.

Building and Improving the Culture of Safety

Despite these challenges, changes have occurred, some voluntarily and others under duress. The Leapfrog Group,[26] the IHI's "100,000 Lives Campaign,"[27] and the "5 million Lives Campaign"[28] are voluntary initiatives that have affected sweeping changes. For example, the Leapfrog Group was among the first to recommend the implementation of CPOE to reduce medication errors. Federal funding is now available for CPOE implementation through incentive payments for the use of certified electronic health records. Rapid response teams (RRTs), a voluntary initiative in the 100,000 Lives Campaign, was considered so valuable that it is now incorporated in the Joint Commission's regulations requiring that hospitals recognize and respond to a patient's change in condition using RRTs (Hospital Accreditation Standards, PC.02.01.19).

Regulation has played an important part in promoting a culture of safety. The Joint Commission requires a staff climate survey that includes questions on willingness to report errors and other dimensions associated with the culture of safety; the leadership standards for accreditation require hospital administration to provide the resources needed for a patient safety program. The DNV GL NIAHO® Patient Safety System process requirement specifies that the organization's process address detection; that preventative and corrective actions be taken; that processes to reduce risk are defined; that action plans are implemented; that measurement be ongoing to ensure action effectiveness; and that management review of response and resource allocation uses the results of patient adverse events and other data analysis.[29]

To determine whether staff should be counseled, review the criteria for each type of work. If all can be answered in the affirmative, staff cannot be held responsible. If any of the questions is negative, staff is accountable.

Type of work: Skill-based

Questions for Skill-Based Work
1. Did staff assigned to the task have the appropriate skill?
2. Was the skill something that could be expected for this job category?
3. Did the hospital adequately train staff to ensure competencies are present?
4. Was the activity known to carry risk?
5. Were safeguards performed properly?

Example: Staff held accountable

The case: A nurse was dosing insulin for a diabetic patient. Hospital policy requires a second signature because insulin is considered a high-risk medication. However, the unit was very busy and the nurse was a seasoned professional so she handed the chart to the second nurse who co-signed without checking.

Analysis
1. Did staff assigned to the task have the appropriate skill? Yes.
2. Was the skill something that could be expected for this job category? Yes.
3. Did the hospital adequately train staff to ensure competencies are present? Yes.
4. Was the activity known to carry risk? Yes.
5. Were safeguards performed properly? No.

Result: Both nurses were counseled.

Discussion: "Busy" cannot be an excuse for unsafe care.

Example: Staff not held accountable

The case: A patient with blood type AB needed fresh frozen plasma (FFP) at 2 a.m, but the blood bank did not have the AB type. The blood bank technician (BBT) removed the informational chart from the wall and erroneously noted that Type A FFP was a clinically appropriate substitution. After a discussion with his supervisor, he released the FFP to the clinical area where an astute nurse caught the error and prevented patient harm. The analysis revealed that the BBT had mistakenly read the informational chart for packed cells where type A is an appropriate substitution.

Analysis: BBT
1. Did staff assigned to the task have the appropriate skill? Yes.
2. Was the skill something that could be expected for this job category? Yes.
3. Did the hospital adequately train staff to ensure competencies are present? Yes.
4. Was the activity known to carry risk? Yes.

FIGURE 4.1 Determining accountability for medical error

5. Were safeguards performed properly? Yes.

Result: The technical was apprised of the mistake but was not counseled. However, the supervisor was counseled as he failed to double-check the work of the technician.

Discussion: The technician committed a slip, but slips are a part of the human condition. Hospital processes include double, triple and quadruple checks to accommodate this reality.

Questions for rules-based work
1. Did staff know the rules?
2. Should staff have known them?
3. Were the rules available for review if needed?
4. Was it reasonable to make an exception in this circumstance?

Example: Staff held accountable
The Case: The surgical checklist includes verifying the presence of a valid history and physical (H&P) performed within 30 days. The nurses were responsible for assuring the completeness of the surgical checklist. The H & P on the chart was 31 days old and the physician had little tolerance for rules he thought were foolish; so, the nurse let the patient go through.

Analysis

1. Did staff know the rules? Yes.
2. Should staff have known them? Yes.
3. Were the rules available for review if needed? Yes.
4. Was it reasonable to make an exception in this circumstance? No.

Result: The nurse was counseled and this was included in the physician's OPPE profile.

Discussion: Staff knew the rules and the extenuating circumstances were not sufficient for ignoring them. A current H & P is a patient safety concern. If the nurse was uncomfortable, she should have spoken to her supervisor.

Example: Staff not held accountable
Case: Nurses were asked to provide gentle reminders to physicians to sign their telephone orders within 48 hours. One physician did not take kindly to these and let the nurses know it, but the Joint Commission had recently cited the hospital for this offense. When the physician came on the floor, the staff nurse looked for her supervisor but she was not available.

Analysis

1. Did staff know the rules? Yes.
2. Should staff have known them? Yes.
3. Were the rules available for review if needed? Yes.

(continued)

FIGURE 4.1 *(continued)*

Type of work: Skill-based

4. Was it reasonable to make an exception in this circumstance? Yes.

Result: The nurse was not counseled.

Discussion: The hospital took the position that it has a responsibility to protect its staff from disruptive physicians. She discussed the situation with the nurse and the supervisor approached the physician in an alternative venue.

Type of work: Knowledge-based

Questions for knowledge-based work

Given the choices this person made, did s/he show good judgment?

Example: Staff held accountable

The Case: An ICU Nurse floating to the ED had an order for Solu-Medrol. Solu-Medrol was in the ICU smart pump library, but not in the ED library. Hence, she delivered the medication free-flow. The error was discovered when the patient received an overdose.

Analysis: Given the choices this person made, did s/he show good judgment? No.

Result: The nurse was counseled.

Discussion: Given the risks of the medication, the nurse did not show good judgment protecting the patient from harm because no attempt was made to contact a physician or the supervisor. She was floating from another unit and could be expected to encounter slightly different circumstances which she had the responsibility to check.

Example: Staff not held accountable

The Case: The operating room staff performed the sponge and instrument count per policy. When the count was off, staff called in the radiology technologist who performed an X-Ray. The radiologist indicated that sponge was not inside the patient. Staff could not account for the missing sponge but they closed anyway.

Analysis Given the choices this person made, did s/he show good judgment? Yes.

Result: Staff was not counseled.

Discussion: Staff followed the policy and acted in the best interest of the patient under the circumstances. The risk of prolonged anesthesia was greater than the risk of the sponge inside. A CT performed the next day provided the location of the sponge.

Many states have laws that require hospitals to report their serious adverse events and publish their findings on the Internet. In 2005, the federal government authorized the creation of patient safety organizations (PSOs) to encourage reporting of adverse events by hospitals without the fear of reprisals. The goal of the PSOs is to improve quality and safety through the collection and analysis of data on adverse events.[30]

Leadership engagement has taken many forms. One example includes the implementation of executive walkabouts where members of the executive team walk around the units to directly hear patient safety concerns from the staff.[31] Many have embraced transparency and a balanced view of the responsibility of the organization and the individual.

Conclusion and Lessons Learned

The following are key considerations in building and sustaining an organizational culture that promotes safety:

Patient safety as an organizing principle: Given the inherent risks in patient care, are the processes designed to keep patients free from harm caused by medical mistakes? Does staff hold patient safety as an inviolable principle?

Leadership: Does the organization commit the resources needed to address safety concerns? Do the leaders encourage transparency?

Teamwork and communication: When faced with a problem, does everyone within and between departments step forward to help regardless of the roles and hierarchy? Is everyone free to alert the team to threats to patient safety?

Transparency: Is a team willing to report errors without fear of reprisals?

A learning environment: When an error occurs, does the team come together to understand what happened and how this can be prevented in the future? Can the organization adapt to the changes needed when a risk to patient safety is uncovered?

If your organization has a culture of safety, you are likely to find a team willing to work together, to see communication within and between departments, and to have a robust process for analyzing process. In short, you will have patient safety as an organizing principle pervasive throughout the organization.

REFERENCES

1. Kohn LT, Corrigan JM, Donaldson MS. *To Err Is Human: Building a Safer Health System.* Committee on Quality and Healthcare in America. Washington, DC: National Academy Press; 2000.

2. Sammer C, Lykens K, Singh K, et al. What is a patient safety culture? A review of the literature. *J Nurs Scholarsh.* 2010;42(2):156–165.

3. McCarthy D, Blumenthal D. Stories from the sharp end: case studies in safety improvement. *Milbank Q.* 2006;84(1):165–200.

4. Walshe K, Shortell SM. When things go wrong: how health care organizations deal with major failures. *Health Affair.* 2004;23(3):103–111.

5. Sorra, JS, Nieva, VF. Hospital survey on patient safety culture. Rockville (MD): Agency for Healthcare Research and Quality (Publication No. 04-0041); 2004.

6. Reason J. *Human Error.* Cambridge, MA: University Press; 1992.

7. Centers for Disease Control and Prevention. Healthcare-associated infections: *Clostridium difficile.* Available at http://www.cdc.gov/HAI/organisms/cdiff/Cdiff_clinicians .html.

8. Denham CR, Sullenberger CB, Quaid DW, et al. An NTSB for healthcare— learning from innovation: debate and innovate or capitulate. *J Patient Safety.* 2012;8(1): 3–14.

9. Lewis GH, Vaithianathan R, Hockey PM, et al. Counterheroism, common knowledge, and ergonomics: concepts from aviation that could improve patient safety. *Milbank Q.* 2011;89(1):4–38.

10. Baker DP, Gustafson S, Beaubien J, et al. Medical teamwork and patient safety: the evidence-based relation. AHRQ Publication No. 05-0053. Rockville, MD: Agency for Healthcare Research and Quality; 2005. Accessed October 28, 2012, from http://www .ahrq.gov/qual/medteam/.

11. Weick KE, Sutcliffe KM. *Managing the Unexpected: Resilient Performance in an Age of Uncertainty.* San Francisco, CA: John Wiley & Sons; 2007.

12. Reason J. *Managing the Risk of Organizational Accidents.* Burlington, VT: Ashgate; 1997.

13. Marx D. *Patient Safety and the "Just Culture:" A Primer for Health Care Executives.* New York, NY: Columbia University; 2001.

14. Advisory Group on Reliability of Electronic Equipment (AGREE). *Reliability of Military Electronic Equipment.* Report. Washington, D.C.: US Government Printing Office; 1957.

15. Amalberti R, Hourlier S. Human error reduction strategies in health care. In: Carayon P, ed. *Handbook of Human Factors and Ergonomics in Health Care and Patient Safety.* Boca Raton FL: CRC Press; 2011.

16. Pinsky HM, Taichman RS, Sarment DP. Adaptation of airline crew resource management principles to dentistry. *J Am Dent Assoc.* 2010;141(8):1010–1018.

17. Weiser TG, Haynes AB, Lashoher A, et al. Perspectives in quality: Designing the WHO surgical safety checklist. *J Qual Health Care.* 2010; 22(5):365–370.

18. Gawande AA. *The Checklist Manifesto: How to Get Things Done Right.* New York, NY: Picador; 2009.

19. Heinrichs WM, Bauman E, Dev P. SBAR "flattens the hierarchy" among caregivers. *Stud Health Technol Inform.* 2012;173:175–182.

20. Quaid D, Thao J, Denham CR. Story power: The secret weapon. *J Patient Safety.* 2010;6(1):5–14.

21. King S. *Josie's Story: A Mother's Inspiring Crusade to Make Medical Care Safe.* New York, NY: Grove Press; 2010. See also http://www.josieking.org.

22. Kenney LK, van Pelk RA. To err is human; the need for trauma support is, too. A story of the power of patient/physician partnership after a sentinel event. Marietta, GA: Patient Safety and Quality Healthcare; 2005. October 28, 2012, from http://www.psqh.com/janfeb05/consumers.html.

23. Conway J. Getting boards on board: Engaging governing boards on quality and safety. *Jt Comm J Qual Patient Safety.* 2008;34(4):214–220.

24. Information on the Patient Safety Survey can be found at http://www.ahrq.gov/professionals/quality-patient-safety/patientsafetyculture/index.html.

25. Wachter RM, Pronovost PJ. Balancing "no blame" with accountability in patient safety. *N Engl J Med.* 2009;361(14):1401–1406.

26. The Leapfrog Group. Washington, DC: 2012. October 28, 2012, from http://www.leapfroggroup.org.

27. Berwick DM, Calkins DR, McCannon CJ, et al. The 100,000 lives campaign: Setting a goal and a deadline for improving health care quality. *JAMA.* 2006;295(3):324–327.

28. Protecting 5 million lives from harm. Cambridge, MA: Institute for Healthcare Improvement; 2012. Retrieved October 28, 2012, from http://www.ihi.org/offerings/Initiatives/PastStrategicInitiatives/5MillionLivesCampaign/Pages/default.aspx..

29. NIAHO Accreditation Requirements. Interpretive Guidelines & Surveyor Guidance—Version 11. Rev.2014-06-17, QM.8, Patient Safety System, SR.2.

30. Patient Safety Organization information. Rockville, MD: Agency for Healthcare Research and Quality. Retrieved October 28, 2012, from http://www.pso.ahrq.gov/psos/overview.htm.

31. Thomas EJ, Sexton JB, Neilands TB, Frankel A, et al. The effect of executive walk rounds on nurse safety climate attitudes: a randomized trial of clinical units. *BMC Health Serv Res.* 2005;5(1):4.

The Role of Health Information Technology in Patient Safety

CHAPTER 5

Sarah P. Slight
David W. Bates

Abstract

The Institute of Medicine (IOM) estimates that between 44,000 and 98,000 people die each year in U.S. hospitals as a result of healthcare injuries. The cost of these injuries can be substantial. Health information technology (HIT) can play a vital part in intercepting errors and improving patient safety in many different clinical settings. HIT can also improve communication between healthcare professionals, make knowledge more readily accessible, assist with dose calculations, perform clinical checks in real time, assist with monitoring, and provide clinical decision support. This chapter discusses specific HIT prevention strategies that target the ordering stage (e.g., computerized provider order entry and clinical decision support), and transcribing and administration stages (e.g., bar-coded electronic medication administration record technology and smart infusion pumps) of the drug-delivery process. It also considers HIT applications that assist with the delivery of care, such as the follow-up of abnormal test results and patient monitoring, and the broader implications of HIT for medical care and policy.

Patient safety is receiving growing attention worldwide. The U.S. Joint Commission, the U.K. Care Quality Commission, and the Canadian Patient Safety Institute have all published guidance and standards to help improve patient safety in healthcare settings.[1–3] Many different healthcare professionals and procedures may be involved in a patient's treatment, thus making it increasingly difficult to ensure safe care. The Institute of Medicine (IOM) estimates that between 44,000 and 98,000 people die each year in U.S. hospitals as a result of healthcare injuries.[4] An adverse event is an injury due to a medical treatment[5]; it is caused by poor medical management and substandard care rather than the patient's underlying disease process. Some adverse events are unavoidable, such as an unanticipated allergic reaction to an antibiotic, while others are often preventable.[6]

One important indicator of patient safety is the rate of adverse events among hospitalized patients. In the United States, the overall rates of adverse drug events (ADEs) and potential ADEs were found to be 6.5 and 5.5 respectively per 100 admissions in two large Harvard-affiliated teaching hospitals.[7] Of the 12% life-threatening ADEs and 30% serious ADEs reported in this study, 42% were judged preventable. Patient safety is an important issue for other countries, too. The overall rate of adverse events among patients in 20 Canadian acute care hospitals was found to be 7.5 per 100 hospital admissions.[8] Almost 37% of these adverse events were considered preventable, with more than 20% found to be associated with permanent injury and even death. In England and New Zealand, the respective rates were a little higher with 11.7% and 11.2% reported.[9,10] Half of these adverse events found in the English study were judged to be preventable with ordinary standards of care.[9] Furthermore, the use of more intensive approaches and broader definitions of adverse events have found even high rates of adverse events. Notably, Classen recently found an adverse event rate of 49 events per 100 admissions in three hospital settings using a trigger tool.[11]

The cost of these injuries can be substantial. The United Kingdom's National Health Service pays out around £400 million to simply settle clinical negligence claims every year.[12] Jha et al estimated that the elimination of readily preventable adverse events in U.S. hospitals could have saved more than $16.6 billion (5.5% of total inpatient costs) in 2004 alone.[13] Many countries have accepted the significant economic and human costs associated with adverse events and understand the need for healthcare systems to have built-in defenses and safeguards to decrease the level of harm.

Health information technology (HIT) can play a vital part in intercepting errors and improving patient safety in many different clinical settings. Medication safety is one domain that is amenable to improvement with HIT. Errors resulting in preventable ADEs have been found to occur at the stages of medication ordering (56%), transcription (6%), dispensing (4%), and administration (34%).[7] HIT can also improve communication between healthcare professionals (e.g., serious laboratory abnormalities), make knowledge more readily accessible (e.g., access to reference information), assist with dose calculations, perform clinical checks in real time, assist with monitoring, and provide clinical decision support.[14] The U.S. government recognizes the huge potential of HIT and, through the Health Information Technology for Economic and Clinical Health (HITECH) Act, agreed to provide incentive payments to clinicians and hospitals for the adoption and meaningful use of HIT. In this chapter, we discuss specific HIT prevention strategies that target the ordering, transcribing, and administration stages of the drug-delivery process, as well as consider the broader implications of HIT for medical care and policy.

At the medication ordering stage, the prescriber must select the appropriate medication and its dose and frequency. Mistakes can happen for a variety of reasons such as illegible handwriting, ambiguous abbreviations, or a lack of knowledge on the part of the prescriber. CPOE can help overcome some of these problems and has been defined as "a provider's use of computer assistance to directly enter medical orders (for example, medications, consultations with other providers, laboratory services, imaging studies, and other auxiliary services) from a computer or mobile device."[15] CPOE replaces the more traditional order methods of paper, fax, telephone, and oral communications. Although CPOE orders are more legible than those written by hand, it is the addition of clinical decision support (CDS) systems that makes it such a powerful application for improving patient safety, efficiency, and healthcare quality. CDS can provide physicians with real-time, relevant, treatment-related information and guidance at various stages in the healthcare process.[16] This can include basic CDS (e.g., drug-allergy checking and drug–drug interaction checking) and more advanced CDS (e.g., dosing support for renal insufficiency and geriatric patients).

A recent systematic review was undertaken to quantitatively assess the effectiveness of CPOE at reducing preventable ADEs in acute care settings.[17] The 16 studies included in the analysis had varying intervention and implementation designs: CPOE developer (homegrown versus commercial), presence or absence of CDS, CDS sophistication (basic, moderate, or advanced), and extent of implementation (limited number of units versus hospital-wide). The analysis showed that CPOE was associated with a significant reduction in preventable ADEs, with medication errors approximately halved. These findings are generally consistent with those of earlier systematic reviews and meta-analyses.[18–20] However, two studies of commercial CPOE systems in hospital-wide implementations reported increases in medication errors but statistically significant decreases in preventable adverse drug events.[21,22] Potential explanations may be that CPOE systems can make errors easier to detect but also cause new medication errors.

Another noteworthy study came from Han et al, who observed an unexpected increase in the mortality rate from 2.58% to 6.57% with the introduction of a commercial CPOE application at the Children's Hospital of Pittsburgh.[23] During the 18-month study period, 1,942 children were admitted to this hospital via interhospital transfer, of whom 1,102 (56.7%) were specifically admitted to the intensive care unit (ICU). According to the authors, the usual "chain of events" that occurred after admission changed after CPOE implementation. These included an inability to "preregister" patients into the system (until they had physically arrived in the hospital) and the need for additional time to enter the orders through CPOE as compared with written form. This in turn led to potential delays in treatment and diagnostic testing. However, while the rise in mortality coincided with the CPOE implementation, it is unclear whether the CPOE system itself actually caused the increase.[24] The hospital chose to make other system changes at the time as the CPOE implementation, such as the complete centralization of medications in the pharmacy department, which meant that nurses were no longer able to obtain time-sensitive medications from a satellite medication dispenser located in the ICU. This was a separate decision made by the hospital that generated further delays in the administration of these medicines; yet the authors attributed its effect to CPOE.[24] Hospitals need to carefully plan for the implementation of key technologies such as CPOE because the process can be difficult and marked by challenges. There also needs to be engagement and collaboration from all involved, appropriate training and support offered to staff (especially when the system becomes operational), and clear leadership and commitment to patient safety from the very top of the organization.

No statistically significant differences in effect were found between systems with or without CDS in the systematic review previously mentioned.[17] Realizing the promise and full potential of CDS is not straightforward. Most healthcare organizations will only realize a moderate proportion of the potential benefits, unless the complexities of the application are addressed. The implementation of CDS must be done thoughtfully. Each organization needs to understand the CDS-related technical capabilities of their CPOE applications and find the best way of using CDS to achieve their medication safety goals. Organizations also need to decide whether they will purchase vendor CDS or develop their own. Until now, most of the CDS that has been shown to be useful has been custom developed by large academic medical institutions such as Partners Healthcare in Boston, Massachusetts. Smaller organizations do not have the resources and expertise to do this. However, these organizations do need to be able to review and customize the vendor knowledge base (which should survive version upgrades) and have control over the specific alerting rules they want to implement. The knowledge presented to clinicians should be evidence based (with links for clinicians to review if possible), and the wording of alert messages needs to be clear and concise to allow clinicians to directly act on the information received. The effectiveness of the CDS implemented locally should be monitored, including how alerts are transmitted and whether clinicians choose to accept or override these alerts.

CPOE with CDS should be implemented in such a way as to improve medication safety. The Leapfrog Group, an association of some of the largest U.S. employers, developed a tool to specifically measure the ability of implemented CPOE systems with CDS to detect and avert prescribing errors in hospital settings.[25] This tool used fictitious patients created solely for the purposes of assessments and test orders judged likely to cause serious harm to adult patients. To achieve high scores in the test, hospitals needed to have implemented advanced CDS (e.g., alerts that take into account a patient's renal function or age when calculating the dose) as well as basic tools that are more straightforward to implement (e.g., drug–drug interaction checking and drug-allergy interaction checking). A sample of 62 hospitals that voluntarily used the tool were found to be far outside safe limits; 47% of the test orders, which were judged to result in patient fatality, were not detected by the CDS in use in these hospitals. This may relate to the fact that the hospitals as a group used basic decision support far more than the advanced tools. Significant variability was observed in the use of CDS between hospitals, with the six top-performing hospitals using six different software products. Several factors were believed to have contributed to this variability, including the ease of applying the tool, relevant knowledge and expertise of staff, the availability and commitment of dedicated CDS resources, and the length of time CDS had been used in the hospital.

At the transcription stage of the drug-delivery process, information needs to be entered or transferred accurately between systems or settings. This helps ensure that the right drug is given to the right patient at the right dose and at the right time. Bar-code technology can address medication administration and transcription errors at the point of care before administration. However, the adoption of bar-code technology by hospitals has been slow. Bar-code verification technology is usually implemented with an electronic medication administration system (eMAR) in hospitals, which enables medication orders to be electronically imported directly from either the CPOE or the hospital pharmacy system. The nurse administering the medication at the patient's bedside is required to scan the bar-codes on the patient's wristband and on the medication; a warning will sound if the application identifies either a discrepancy (e.g., the scanned dose does not correspond to the medication order) or the patient is not due or is overdue for the dose. One study assessed the effects of bar-code eMAR technology on administration and transcription errors, as well as on the associated potential ADEs.[26] Using a prospective, before-and-after, quasi-experimental study design, data were collected on transcription and medication administration in 35 adult medical, surgical, and intensive care units in a 735-bed tertiary academic medical center. The implementation of bar-code medication-verification technology was associated with a 41% reduction in non-timing administration errors and a 51% reduction in associated potential ADEs.[26] Errors in the timing of medication administration (e.g., administered either early or late by more than one hour) fell by 27%, with no significant change in associated potential ADEs. Transcription errors and associated potential ADEs were essentially eliminated on the units with bar-code eMAR; this was an important finding because each erroneous transcription can lead to repeated erroneous administrations. Although this study showed how bar-code eMAR could substantially improve medication safety, the results reflect the experiences of only one hospital that already had fully implemented CPOE and bar-code verification for pharmacy staff. The application was designed in close collaboration with clinical users and leaders.

At the administration stage, computerized patient infusion devices (*smart pumps* or *smart infusion pumps*) can also greatly decrease the rate of medication errors in hospitals.[27] Intravenous (IV) medications are more likely to be associated with significant patient harm because of their narrow therapeutic ranges and the nature of their potential adverse events (e.g., bleeding).[28,29] Smart pumps are different from older pumps in that they can be programmed to include dose error-reduction systems and drug libraries and thus address the clinical risks associated with the use of these high-risk medications.[30] The smart pump can prompt the user to choose a drug from the library and input a volume and infusion rate (which can automatically calculate the dose).[31] The drug library contains a list of standard concentrations and volumes for IV drug infusions and dosing limits for specific drugs, and it is usually customized for each hospital's specific needs.

Many literature reviews have assessed the potential for smart pumps to improve patient safety in the hospital setting.[30,32] One systematic review described the impact of smart pumps on error reduction and found the types of errors most commonly intercepted were wrong dose, wrong rate, and pump-setting errors.[30] They can alert the clinician to an error (e.g., wrong concentration), and the clinician can then choose to correct the error, cancel the infusion, or simply ignore these "soft" alerts by overriding them (usually with confirmation). Hard limits are restrictive and cannot be overridden; the clinician would either have to reprogram the infusion rate within the acceptable range or cancel the infusion.

Several studies have reported on the number of errors potentially avoided with the use of smart pump technology.[27,33,34] In one study, for example, the administration of unfractionated heparin generated 501 hard alerts in 246 patients, which included 250 overdose alerts (29.0%) and 178 underdose alerts (20.6%).[31] The authors also quantified the magnitude of overdose errors, with the infusion-device software preventing 10-fold potential overdoses in 31 patients (15%), 100-fold potential overdoses in 40 patients (19%), and greater than 100-fold potential overdoses in 8 patients (4%). This study also demonstrated how programming errors were frequently duplicated, with clinicians attempting to reprogram the device with the same incorrect information. It is important to identify the reasons for this behavior as it may be that the parameters of soft and hard limits are set too high or too low and need to be adjusted to avoid alert fatigue. Clinicians should also have flexibility when administering medications, depending on the patients' specific situation, so that IV pumps will not cause delays in treatment.

The impact of smart pump technology on ADEs is less clear. One study assessed the impact of smart pumps with integrated decision support software on the incidence and nature of ADEs and found no difference in the ADE rate.[35] However, users frequently bypassed the drug library and overrode the smart pump alerts in this study; after correcting for these two practices in the analysis, the rates of preventable ADEs during the intervention would have decreased from 0.28 to 0.18 ($p = .27$) and nonintercepted potential ADEs from 2.12 to 0.36 ($p < .0001$) per 100 patient pump days.[35] Smart pumps also have the advantage of being able to record objective data about the infusion process and intercepted potential errors.[31] Another study used the number of potential serious errors averted to estimate a total savings of more than $29 million per year for Carolinas Medical Center, the largest facility in the Carolinas HealthCare System.[36] Although it is unclear whether all of these errors would have resulted in harm, it does show the potential cost savings that may accrue with the implementation of such a system.

HIT applications can also assist with the delivery of care more broadly, such as the follow-up of abnormal test results and patient monitoring. The failure to follow up abnormal test results is an important patient safety concern.[37,38] Ambulatory patients may be particularly vulnerable to these failures, given the many different individuals and settings involved. A recent systematic review was undertaken to quantify the extent to which laboratory and radiology tests were not followed up[39]; it reported wide variation of 6.8% to 62% for laboratory tests and 1% to 35.7% for radiology tests. The authors also reported how the impact on patient outcomes included missed cancer diagnoses. HIT can play an important role in supporting and managing the reporting and follow-up of test results.[40] Partners Healthcare developed a comprehensive results-management application called Results Manager, which classified the degree of abnormality for each test result, presented guidelines to clinicians to help them manage abnormal results, and allowed clinicians to generate result letters to patients.[40] The U.S. Veterans Administration system adopted the use of a "view alert" system to notify clinicians of abnormal test results. This system allowed a radiologist, for example, to alert the provider electronically to the presence of an abnormal imaging test result. The referring provider could click on this alert to view the patient's report, an action that also indicated receipt of the result. However, one study conducted by Singh et al showed how providers in an ambulatory multispecialty clinic failed to acknowledge receipt of 36% ($n = 368$) of these transmitted alerts, with 4% ($n = 45$) of these abnormal tests completely lost to follow-up.[41] Even if physicians opened the electronic alert message, a second study showed how this does not necessarily guarantee that they will act on the abnormal result.[42]

HIT is a key component of any solution. However, similar to the bar-code eMAR technology and CPOE previously mentioned, this technology is only effective if users acts on the information received. It is important to also understand the varying demands, workload and time pressures on healthcare professionals, all of which can influence their actions. HIT devices can also be used to monitor a patient's vital signs and provide an alert to the clinician when there are signs of deterioration, thus allowing them to intervene early. The Early Sense System is an example of one such contactless device; placed under the bed mattress, it can continuously monitor a patient's heart rate, respiratory rate, and movement level.[43,44] The effects of this motion-sensing monitor were assessed in a medical-surgical unit in a community hospital and found to significantly reduce total length of patient stay in the hospital and in intensive care unit for those transferred.[43]

As a consequence of HIT adoption, the amount of electronic data we now hold about National Health Service patients has dramatically increased. Data about their mental health, clinical problems, outcomes, and socioeconomic status can be held in multiple locations, including GP practices, acute hospitals, and mental health services. Techniques have been developed to aggregate these disparate data sources and uncover patterns or trends and thus help predict patient outcomes.[45] For example, these data can be used to identify potentially high-cost patients or patients at risk of ADEs and allow interventions to be precisely tailored to their specific problems, thus ensuring they are managed more effectively. With limited resources in healthcare, data analytics presents an exciting and significant opportunity for improving care delivery and reducing costs.[45] It is likely to play a key role in future patient care and almost certainly be useful across the healthcare divide between primary and secondary care.

To conclude, HIT is an important tool for improving patient safety in different healthcare settings. It can help in a multitude of ways such as structuring actions, providing evidence-based knowledge at the point of prescribing, preventing medication errors, reducing transcription and administration errors, and ADEs. Better use of HIT can help reshape healthcare systems in response to increasing demand and constrained resources. It can improve information flows, identify patients at particular risk of adverse events, and help healthcare professionals provide highly personalized care. That said, HIT is simply a tool, and it is only effective if used as intended. All HIT can give rise to unintended consequences, and although some may be caused by technical flaws, many can be the result of sociotechnical issues. Policies that provide incentives for the adoption of HIT should ensure that investment in infrastructure supports new care paradigms.

REFERENCES

1. The Joint Commission. Available at http://www.jointcommission.org/standards_information/prepublication_standards.aspx. Accessed March 15, 2015.

2. Care Quality Commission. Available at http://www.cqc.org.uk. Accessed March 15, 2015.

3. Canadian Patient Safety Institute. Available at http://www.patientsafetyinstitute.ca/English/Pages/default.aspx. Accessed March 15, 2015.

4. Kohn L, Corrigan, JM, Donaldson, MS. *To Err Is Human: Building a Safer Health System*; 1999. Available at http://www.qu.edu.qa/pharmacy/development/documents/14ay/To_Err_is_Human_1999__report_brief.pdf. Accessed March 15, 2015.

5. Brennan TA, Leape LL, Laird NM, et al. Incidence of adverse events and negligence in hospitalized patients. Results of the Harvard Medical Practice Study I. *N Engl J Med*. 1991;324(6):370–376.

6. Leape LL, Lawthers AG, Brennan TA, Johnson WG. Preventing medical injury. *Qual Rev Bull*. 1993;19(5):144–149.

7. Bates DW, Cullen DJ, Laird N, et al. Incidence of adverse drug events and potential adverse drug events. Implications for prevention. ADE Prevention Study Group. *JAMA*. 1995;274(1):29–34.

8. Baker GR, Norton PG, Flintoft V, et al. The Canadian Adverse Events Study: the incidence of adverse events among hospital patients in Canada. *Can Med Assoc J*. 2004; 170(11):1678–1686.

9. Vincent C, Neale G, Woloshynowych M. Adverse events in British hospitals: preliminary retrospective record review. *BMJ*. 2001;322(7285):517–519.

10. Davis P, Lay-Yee R, Briant R, Ali W, Scott A, Schug S. Adverse events in New Zealand public hospitals I: occurrence and impact. *NZ Med J*. 2002;115(1167): U271.

11. Classen DC, Resar R, Griffin F, et al. "Global trigger tool" shows that adverse events in hospitals may be ten times greater than previously measured. *Health Aff*. 2011; 30(4):581–589.

12. Department of Health. *An Organisation with a Memory. Report of an Expert Group on Learning from Adverse Events in the NHS Chaired by the Chief Medical Officer*. London: The Stationery Office; 2000.

13. Jha AK, Chan DC, Ridgway AB, Franz C, Bates DW. Improving safety and eliminating redundant tests: cutting costs in U.S. hospitals. *Health Aff*. 2009;28(5): 1475–1484.

14. Bates DW, Gawande AA. Improving safety with information technology. *N Engl J Med*. 2003;348(25):2526–2534.

15. The Centers for Medicare and Medicaid Services. Eligible hospital and critical access hospital meaningful use core measures measure 1 of 16. Stage 2; 2014. Available at https://www.cms.gov/Regulations-and-Guidance/Legislation/EHRIncentivePrograms /downloads/Stage2_HospitalCore_1_CPOE_MedicationOrders.pdf.

16. Kuperman GJ, Bobb A, Payne TH, et al. Medication-related clinical decision support in computerized provider order entry systems: a review. *J Am Med Info Assoc*. 2007;14(1):29–40.

17. Nuckols TK, Smith-Spangler C, Morton SC, et al. The effectiveness of computerized order entry at reducing preventable adverse drug events and medication errors in hospital settings: a systematic review and meta-analysis. *Syst Rev*. 2014;3:56.

18. Radley DC, Wasserman MR, Olsho LE, Shoemaker SJ, Spranca MD, Bradshaw B. Reduction in medication errors in hospitals due to adoption of computerized provider order entry systems. *J Am Med Info Assoc*. 2013;20(3):470–476.

19. Shamliyan TA, Duval S, Du J, Kane RL. Just what the doctor ordered. Review of the evidence of the impact of computerized physician order entry system on medication errors. *Health Serv Res*. 2008;43(1)(pt 1):32–53.

20. van Rosse F, Maat B, Rademaker CM, van Vught AJ, Egberts AC, Bollen CW. The effect of computerized physician order entry on medication prescription errors and clinical outcome in pediatric and intensive care: a systematic review. *Pediatrics*. 2009; 123(4):1184–1190.

21. Leung AA, Keohane C, Amato M, et al. Impact of vendor computerized physician order entry in community hospitals. *J Gen Intern Med*. 2012;27(7):801–807.

22. Menendez MD, Alonso J, Rancano I, Corte JJ, Herranz V, Vazquez F. Impact of computerized physician order entry on medication errors. *Revista de calidad asistencial: organo de la Sociedad Española de Calidad Asistencial.* 2012;27(6):334–340.

23. Han YY, Carcillo JA, Venkataraman ST, et al. Unexpected increased mortality after implementation of a commercially sold computerized physician order entry system. *Pediatrics.* 2005;116(6):1506–1512.

24. Phibbs C, Milstein, A, Delbanco, SD, Bates, DW. No Proven Link Between CPOE and Mortality. Pediatrics Post-Publication Peer Review Forum; December 19, 2005.

25. Metzger J, Welebob E, Bates DW, Lipsitz S, Classen DC. Mixed results in the safety performance of computerized physician order entry. *Health Aff.* 2010;29(4):655–663.

26. Poon EG, Keohane CA, Yoon CS, et al. Effect of bar-code technology on the safety of medication administration. *N Engl J Med.* 2010;362(18):1698–1707.

27. Fields M, Peterman J. Intravenous medication safety system averts high-risk medication errors and provides actionable data. *Nurs Admin Q.* 2005;29(1):78–87.

28. The Institute of Safe Medical Practices. ISMP's list of high alert medications; 2014. Available at http://www.ismp.org/tools/highalertmedications.pdf. Accessed March 15, 2015.

29. Institute for Healthcare Improvement. High-alert medication safety; 2011. Available at http://www.ihi.org/topics/highalertmedicationsafety/pages/default.aspx. Accessed January 16, 2016.

30. Ohashi K, Dalleur O, Dykes PC, Bates DW. Benefits and risks of using smart pumps to reduce medication error rates: a systematic review. *Drug Saf.* 2014;37(12): 1011–1020.

31. Fanikos J, Fiumara K, Baroletti S, et al. Impact of smart infusion technology on administration of anticoagulants (unfractionated heparin, Argatroban, lepirudin, and bivalirudin). *Am J Cardiol.* 2007;99(7):1002–1005.

32. Murdoch LJ, Cameron VL. Smart infusion technology: a minimum safety standard for intensive care? *Br J Nurs.* 2008;17(10):630–636.

33. Manrique-Rodriguez S, Sanchez-Galindo AC, Lopez-Herce J, et al. Impact of implementing smart infusion pumps in a pediatric intensive care unit. *Am J Health Syst Pharm* 2013;70(21):1897–1906.

34. Tran M, Ciarkowski S, Wagner D, Stevenson JG. A case study on the safety impact of implementing smart patient-controlled analgesic pumps at a tertiary care academic medical center. *Jt Comm J Qual & Patient Safety.* 2012;38(3):112–119.

35. Rothschild JM, Keohane CA, Cook EF, et al. A controlled trial of smart infusion pumps to improve medication safety in critically ill patients. *Crit Care Med.* 2005;33(3):533–540.

36. Mansfield J, Jarrett S. Using smart pumps to understand and evaluate clinician practice patterns to ensure patient safety. *Hosp Pharm.* 2013;48(11):942–950.

37. Bates DW, Leape LL. Doing better with critical test results. *Jt Comm J Qual & Patient Safety.* 2005;31(2):61, 66–67.

38. World Alliance for Patient Safety. Jha A, Ed. *Summary of the Evidence on Patient Safety: Implications for Research.* Geneva, Switzerland: World Health Organization; 2008.

39. Callen JL, Westbrook JI, Georgiou A, Li J. Failure to follow-up test results for ambulatory patients: a systematic review. *J Gen Intern Med.* 2012;27(10):1334–1348.

40. Poon EG, Wang SJ, Gandhi TK, Bates DW, Kuperman GJ. Design and implementation of a comprehensive outpatient results manager. *J Biomed Inform.* 2003; 36(1–2):80–91.

41. Singh H, Arora HS, Vij MS, Rao R, Khan MM, Petersen LA. Communication outcomes of critical imaging results in a computerized notification system. *J Am Med Inform Assoc.* 2007;14(4):459–466.

42. Singh H, Thomas EJ, Sittig DF, et al. Notification of abnormal lab test results in an electronic medical record: do any safety concerns remain? *Am J Med.* 2010;123(3): 238–244.

43. Brown H, Terrence J, Vasquez P, Bates DW, Zimlichman E. Continuous monitoring in an inpatient medical-surgical unit: a controlled clinical trial. *Am J Med.* 2014; 127(3):226–232.

44. Slight SP, Franz C, Olugbile M, Brown HV, Bates DW, Zimlichman E. The return on investment of implementing a continuous monitoring system in general medical-surgical units. *Crit Care Med.* 2014;42(8):1862–1868.

45. Bates DW, Saria S, Ohno-Machado L, Shah A, Escobar G. Big data in health care: using analytics to identify and manage high-risk and high-cost patients. *Health Aff.* 2014;33(7):1123–1131.

CHAPTER 6

Training Physician Leaders in Patient Safety and Quality

PROGRESS AND CHALLENGES

Susan A. Abookire

Abstract

The practice of medicine has seen dramatic changes. Quality improvement was introduced by W. Edwards Deming, and studies established the need for patient safety. Payment models evolved through diagnosis-related group (DRG) payments, managed care, and the Affordable Care Act. It is imperative that physician training move beyond models established years ago that focus solely on disease evaluation and treatment; physicians must be prepared to participate in the ongoing transformation of healthcare. Physicians need skills to work in teams, to provide care that is patient centered, participate in improvement, and use evidence and informatics. The American College of Graduate Medical Education established the *Clinical Learning Environment Review* to set standards for residency training that include these elements. Specialized training programs in quality improvement and patient safety have emerged across the country, but competencies in the broader context of healthcare must be embedded in all physician training so that future healthcare providers are empowered to lead clinical transformation.

THE NEED FOR TRAINING THE NEXT GENERATION

The practice of medicine has changed remarkably since the 1960s. Several advances have contributed to this dramatic change. Technology has developed markedly and now plays a key role in the delivery of healthcare. Appreciation for the social determinants of health, the impact of poverty, the need for access, and the merits of equity have become central in ways that were barely discussed a half-century ago. Also dating back to the 1960s, the role of quality improvement in healthcare has grown from a set of skills adapted from other industries such as auto manufacturing to the emerging foundation of market value and payment models. Along with this rapid and persistent change, the paradigm of medical training founded on *The Flexner Report*, established in the early 20th century, must undergo radical updates to prepare physicians and nurses for the new century of medicine.

Two legendary professors of medicine, Sir William Osler and Francis W. Peabody, were responsible for establishing much of the foundation of professional standards and medical education. During the late 19th century at Johns Hopkins, Sir William Osler founded what is essentially the precursor to medical residency programs at Johns Hopkins Hospital, requiring young physicians to reside in the hospital without pay to learn how to care for patients under the close and supportive relationship of senior physician mentors. Although contrary to current pressures for work hours and duty limits, residents thrived under these mentoring relationships, and the notion of the residency program spread throughout the country.

In the early 20th century, as the profession of medicine grew in stature as a body of rigorous scientific inquiry combined with compassion and art, hospitals assumed an increasing role in scientific research and medical education.[1] A prevailing belief was that scientific research improved the rigor of outcomes in medicine and medical education provided an ongoing intellectual stimulus and accountability for ensuring excellence in the medical profession.[1] As teaching hospitals emerged and accepted this view, Francis W. Peabody, a Harvard Medical School professor, advanced the teaching mission of academic hospitals. In addition, he advocated the balance of medical knowledge with compassion as in his famous essay "The Care of the Patient," in which he memorably stated "The secret of the care of the patient is in caring for the patient."[2] For the majority of the 20th century, medical education thrived on the ideals of scientific knowledge and apprenticeship, with student physicians learning from senior physicians at the bedside. From World War II until the late 20th century, an abundance of scientific advancement and federal funding set the tone and pace of medical training for professionals.

The national priority of reducing healthcare costs emerged sharply in the 1980s. The advent of prospective payments and the diagnosis-related group (DRG) system had a dramatic shift on how hospitals payments were made.

Although physicians were practicing in an environment that placed increasing demands for competence on cost constraints and judicious use of resources, neither the medical education system nor the majority of physician incentives shifted rapidly to embrace these changes, resulting in a discrepancy between healthcare payment imperatives and physician training. While physician training continued to focus on clinical diagnosis and management, the healthcare industry was waging a nationwide debate about reform and payment.[3,4]

Although quality improvement had become part of other industries such as automobile manufacturing in both Japan and the United States, healthcare only began to embrace it when W. Edwards Deming pioneered adapting improvement methods from industry to healthcare. Trained in engineering and management, Deming championed the statistical process work of Dr Walter Shewart[5] and established what become known as the plan-do-study-act (PDSA) method of quality improvement. Deming's contributions to improving production began during the 1950s in postwar industrial Japan and led ultimately to the foundation of his "14 Points" of quality-improvement efforts worldwide.[6] Gradually, in the late 1990s and early 2000s, healthcare organizations such as Virginia Mason in Seattle[7]; ThedaCare in Appleton, Wisconsin[8]; and Seattle Children's Hospital[9] began to adapt the principles learned in Japanese manufacturing, which was termed the *Toyota production system* and eventually became known as *lean*. When Dr Donald Berwick published "Continuous Quality Improvement in Healthcare" in the *New England Journal of Medicine* in 1989,[10] he sounded the call to adapt improvement principles to American healthcare and subsequently went on to found the Institute for Healthcare Improvement (IHI) in 1991.

In 1999, the Institute of Medicine (IOM) published its landmark report in 1999, titled *To Err is Human: Building a Safer Health Care System*,[11] which stated that 44,000 to 98,000 otherwise preventable deaths occur annually from medical errors in hospitals, with 7,000 preventable deaths related to medication errors alone. The science of patient safety—focusing on systems to reduce harm from medical error—became a centerpiece of healthcare improvement. In 2004, the IHI launched its "100,000 Lives Campaign."

Despite profound changes in healthcare design and delivery, interns, residents, and fellows receive little to no training on how to improve outcomes and reduce medical errors on a systems level. The 2001 Institute of Medicine report *Crossing the Quality Chasm: A New Health System for the 21st Century*[12]called for the reform of health professions education to address the needs in American healthcare for improved quality and patient safety. *Health Professions Education: A Bridge to Quality*[13] in 2003 identified major changes needed in health professional education and established a set of competencies. A roundtable convened by the Lucian Leape Institute in 2010 published its findings, *Unmet Needs*, which identified the need to include quality and patient safety in professional education as one of the foremost challenges facing healthcare.[14]

What Does the Next Generation Need?

Evaluating and treating patients to prevent, cure, or palliate illness has been a cornerstone of physician expertise, and it must remain as such for society to achieve the best healthcare outcomes possible. While necessary, however, this is no longer sufficient. Physicians not only must navigate a transforming healthcare landscape of changing payment models but also provide critical perspective and leadership to balance this transformation and cost focus with the long-held ideals of the medical profession.[3]

Numerous drivers are shaping the transformation of healthcare, and each driver encompasses a set of values. Led by the Center for Medicaid and Medicare Services (CMS), payers constantly apply pressure for better outcomes and lower costs through numerous mechanisms, including the CMS inpatient and outpatient quality-reporting systems, value-based purchasing, penalties for healthcare acquired conditions, and meaningful use incentives and penalties. Patient advocacy groups demand transparency, data, and comparative information to drive the choices of healthcare systems. Widespread medical information—of varying quality and accuracy—is available to patients who want a more active role in their healthcare. If healthcare professionals remain focused solely on the pathophysiology of disease, healthcare transformation and resource reallocation will continue to occur at a spellbinding pace without the critical input of the devoted professionals who provide it.

For the past few decades, the question has been, What do healthcare professionals need to know beyond scientific medical knowledge?

THE QUALITY CHASM

The IOM's quality chasm report identified 10 important "rules" to guide the transformation of healthcare (12); see Table 6.1.

In response, the Committee on the Health Professions Education Summit established a set of priorities needed to meaningfully engage professionals in healthcare design and improvement. The group outlined overall needs for systems improvement, such as better accommodating patient needs—including chronic diseases; better, safer, and more effective technology adoption; and

TABLE 6.1 Ten Simple Rules of Performance in a Redesigned Healthcare System for the 21st Century

Current Approach	New Rule
Care is based primarily on visits.	Care is based on continuous healing relationships.
Professional autonomy drives variability.	Care is customized according to patient needs and values.
Professionals control care.	The patient is the source of control.
Information is a record.	Knowledge is shared, and information flows freely.
Decision making is based on training and experience.	Decision making is evidence based.
Do no harm is an individual responsibility.	Safety is a system property.
Secrecy is necessary.	Transparency is necessary.
The system reacts to needs.	Needs are anticipated.
Cost reduction is sought.	Waste is continuously decreased.
Preference is given to professional roles over the system.	Cooperation among clinicians is a priority.

shared decision making with patients—and the compelling role of team work on patient outcomes, workforce satisfaction, and access. Based on the 10 rules and identified weaknesses, the committee established a set of five core competencies for all healthcare professionals: (1) provide patient-centered care, (2) work in interdisciplinary teams, (3) employ evidence-based care, (4) apply quality improvement, and (5) utilize informatics.

These competencies identify observable abilities of healthcare professions rather than testable specific medical knowledge and aim to establish an array of abilities across domains that will foster our collective power to achieve safe and high-quality systems.

These competencies and their proposed interrelationships are shown in Figure 6.1.

THE ROLE OF ACCREDITATION IN PROPELLING NEW COMPETENCIES

In what has been described as the *Flexnerian revolution* of the 21st century,[15] in 1999 the Accreditation Council for Graduate Medical Education (ACGME) initiated a profound change in training standards for all physicians. Many forces were at play. There had been increasing public demand for physician competency standards. Rising national healthcare costs heightened the need for accountability in public funding of physician training programs, and national

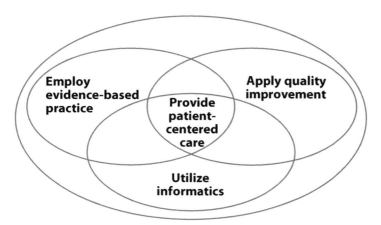

FIGURE 6.1 Team-based collaboration

policy making took on a major role in ensuring patient safety. Consumers, providers, and payers have all driven healthcare quality standards toward outcomes of care. The healthcare quality movement is fundamentally a public health response to improving care for all patients; public health leaders also called for competency-based training and sought a workforce capable of managing the needs of populations by deepening a focus of the contexts of care in our training programs[16] and producing a workforce that is cost conscious while remaining patient centered.

Responding to these many forces, the ACGME launched a competency-based curriculum with evaluation of outcomes for physicians. This replaced the structure- and process-based curriculum previously in place, which only required established time frames for various clinical rotations (e.g., one month of gastroenterology) without evaluating the goals and outcomes of those clinical rotations.

This has been a sea change in medical education, partly because the drive toward an outcomes-based notion of physician competency mirrors the parallel drive toward improving measurable outcomes in healthcare, which is the foundation of the healthcare quality-improvement movement. Another reason for the profound effect of the ACGME milestone-based outcomes project is that, from its beginning, it sought to establish competencies for physicians that accounted for broader, system-oriented, population-based physician competencies, moving from a standard of knowing medical facts to full functionality in a modern healthcare system in ways that foster high quality and coordinated and effective care for patients, populations, and communities.

In 1999, the ACGME endorsed six general competencies as the foundation of graduate medical education:

1. Patient care
2. Medical knowledge
3. Practice-based learning and improvement
4. Interpersonal and communication skills
5. Professionalism
6. Systems-based practice

The first two competencies incorporate traditional notions of clinical competence, but the last four embrace many of the essential needs for our healthcare system to achieve goals of the highest quality and patient safety. In 2002, the ACGME phased in these competencies as the new requirements for medical residency accreditation.[17]

To advance the process, the ACGME proposed that medical education further articulate milestones for these competencies in each clinical discipline. In 2009, requirements for accreditation for internal medicine residencies changed and became based on these new milestones.[18] Residencies for surgery, pediatrics, and other disciplines also were developed and articulated milestones for these six core competencies, as well as methods to define and evaluate their outcomes.

Although these competencies do not explicitly include all of the fundamentals of quality and patient safety, they do provide a solid foundation. Insofar as these competencies are becoming established standards for all physicians, implementation and achievement of these competencies will significantly advance the ability of the physician workforce to participate in the healthcare transformation around population-based outcomes and effectiveness that underlie the goals of the quality and patient safety movement.

Professionalism has been shown in multiple settings to be an essential component of patient safety. The domain of competence in professionalism includes an understanding of and commitment to professional conduct, and it encompasses values of honesty, integrity, and compassion.

Identifying communication as an explicit domain is pivotal to advancing quality and patient safety in the medical profession. Communication lapses are elements of more than 80% of all adverse events, and communication skills have been demonstrated to be teachable and effectively learned. These skills include how to lead teams and how to provide effective and clear communication to patients, peers, and other members of the healthcare team. These skills also include setting a zone of "psychological safety" so that all members of the healthcare team can express concerns and observations.

The domain of practice-based learning and improvement refers to a physician's individual internal motivation for ongoing reflection, learning, and improvement. The skills acquired in this domain include being able to evaluate one's own practice patterns, apply evidence-based medicine to clinical decisions, compare one's own performance to standards and best practices, and achieve improvement goals for one's own practice outcomes.

Whereas the domain of practice-based learning is more individual, the domain of systems-based practice confers the need for physicians to understand how healthcare functions as a system, at both their organizational level and the local, state, and national levels. At the organizational level, an example of this competence is learning the skills to coordinate care across the continuum. At the national level, knowledge of healthcare reform, payment models, and external quality measurement engenders participation and engagement by the physician competent in this domain.

ACGME NEXT ACCREDITATION SYSTEM AND CLINICAL LEARNING ENVIRONMENT REVIEW

The ACGME's Next Accreditation System (NAS) phased in implementation of these milestones in 2012; by 2014, program accreditations were governed by these standards. To promote successful implementation of these standards, site visits to establish the Clinical Learning Environment Review (CLER) began to explore how well these objectives were being met in medical residencies across the country.[19] CLER site visits focused on resident engagement in hospital programs in quality improvement, patient safety, supervision, transitions, mitigation of fatigue, and professionalism. For many organizational leaders in quality and patient safety, this alignment of residency requirements with quality and patient safety goals served as a motivating and strengthening driver of alignment between the residencies and the organizational requirements of the quality and patient safety programs. This was particularly true with physicians in ongoing work to improve safety reporting and recognizing the importance of care coordination (19).

CLER evaluations have highlighted multiple obstacles in the current environment that limit the successful implementation of fundamental principles of patient safety and quality. Chief among these is an insufficient appreciation and working knowledge of a culture of safety by attending physician and faculty. You can't teach what you don't know. Hence, all too often, residents are still told to "be more careful" after making a medical error, rather than becoming involved in leading the systems changes to improve patient safety and prevent harm.[20] This perpetuates the pipeline of future physician leaders who are chastised for human error and deprived of the opportunity to learn compassion, professionalism, and systems skills in the practice of medicine.

Development of Quality and Patient Safety Training Programs

While the ACGME has tackled the core competencies for all physicians, several programs have been developed to train physicians in quality and patient safety nationally and internationally.

These programs have emerged to serve the rapidly increasing demand for training of the rich, emerging, and rapidly evolving underpinnings of quality and patient safety. These programs are generally for physicians who desire a specific leadership role in quality and patient safety rather than for all physicians. The growth in this area is in response to increasing demands among physicians for training programs that will prepare them to become organizational leaders in system transformation. A review of these many programs shows how common the core dimensions are in this rapidly evolving field.

WORLD HEALTH ORGANIZATION

The *Multi-professional Patient Safety Curriculum Guide* released by the World Health Organization (WHO) in October 2011, promotes the need for patient safety education.[21] This comprehensive guide assists universities and schools in the fields of dentistry, medicine, midwifery, nursing, and pharmacy in teaching patient safety. It also supports the training of all healthcare professionals on priority patient safety concepts. The list of topics is shown in Table 6.2.

Recognizing the developmental nature of medical education and the importance of patient safety, the American Medical Student Association (AMSA) created the Patient Safety Scholars Program, with a curriculum based on the WHO's patient safety curriculum framework.[22] The program provides participants with a comprehensive introduction to current challenges to patient safety, teaches students how to work toward patient safety solutions, and establishes future leaders in the patient safety movement. The following is a summary of the AMSA curriculum:

TABLE 6.2 World Health Organization Patient Safety Curriculum Topics

Topic	Page
1: What is patient safety?	92
2: Why applying human factors is important for patient safety	111
3: Understanding systems and the effect of complexity on patient care	121
4: Being an effective team player	133
5: Learning from errors to prevent harm	151
6: Understanding and managing clinical risk	162
7: Using quality-improvement methods to improve care	176
8: Engaging with patients and careers	192
9: Infection prevention and control	210
10: Patient safety and invasive procedures	227
11: Improving medication safety	241

- What is patient safety?
- What is human factors engineering, and why is it important to patient safety?
- Understanding systems and the impact of complexity on patient care
- Being an effective team player
- Understanding and learning from errors
- Understanding and managing clinical risk
- Introduction to quality-improvement methods
- Engaging with patients and their caretakers
- Minimizing infection through improved infection control
- Patient safety and invasive procedures
- Improving medication safety
- Patient perspectives on medical errors

DEGREE PROGRAMS

Several degree programs, primarily Masters degrees, have been developed across the country in quality and patient safety. For example, there are currently Masters degrees offered by:

Northwestern University Feinberg School of Medicine Institute for Healthcare Studies
 Degree: Master of Science in Healthcare Quality and Safety
 Website: http://www.feinberg.northwestern.edu/ihs/education/certificate

Jefferson School of Population Health
Degree: Master of Science in Healthcare Quality and Safety
Website: http://www.jefferson.edu/population_heath/quality_safety

George Washington University Health Sciences Programs
Degree(s): Master of Science in Nursing, Healthcare Quality
University of Illinois College of Medicine at Chicago
Degree: Master of Science in Patient Safety Leadership
Website: http://uic.edu/orgs/online/programs/master-of-science-in-patient
-safety-leadership/index.shtml

These programs are not aimed at training all physicians, but rather focus on the emerging interest among physicians in leading healthcare change through quality and patient safety.

In 2008, the Jefferson School of Population Health established a master's program in healthcare quality and patient safety that is primarily designed for working professionals seeking part-time educational opportunities.[21] Courses are offered asynchronously online using best practices, interactive learning, and practitioner faculty with years of experience and recognized expertise. The degree is finalized with a capstone project to apply lessons to real-time organizational healthcare quality and patient safety issues. The core domains covered in this master's program are as follows:

U.S. Healthcare Organization and Delivery or Comparative Models of Healthcare for the International Track Health Informatics
Healthcare quality and safety measurement and outcomes analysis
Tools and methods
Organization development and change in healthcare
Advanced HQS tools and methods in clinical settings
Population health management
Health law and regulatory issues
Health research methods health economics
Healthcare financing and reimbursement

IHI OPEN SCHOOL

The Institute for Healthcare Improvement launched another program in 2008: an "open school" with a mission "to advance healthcare improvement and patient safety competencies in the next generation of health professionals worldwide."[22]

This training program offers students of medicine, nursing, public health, pharmacy, health administration, dentistry, and other allied health professions the opportunity to learn about quality improvement and patient safety at no charge. The major domains covered within the IHI open school, listed below, span the foundation of quality and patient safety.

Improvement capability
Patient safety
Leadership
Person- and family-centered care
Quality cost and value
Triple aim for populations
Graduate medical education

ASSOCIATION OF AMERICAN MEDICAL COLLEGES

The Association of American Medical Colleges (AAMC) also recognized the dramatic shifts in healthcare delivery and the evolution of accreditation requirements and established "Integrating Quality," a five-year joint initiative by the AAMC and the University Healthsystem Consortium. The AAMC has played a leadership role not only in contributing to the body of knowledge of core competencies for this emerging and dynamically evolving field but also by recognizing the need for faculty development in this area. The AAMC established a Delphi-based methods approach to identifying the competencies needed for all physicians to meaningfully participate in transforming healthcare quality and patient safety.[23]

There are few established leaders in this field who are also medical educators, and few medical educators have the expertise in this broad specialty. Therefore, the AAMC also developed a strategy to support curriculum design and learning scenarios to foster the much needed faculty development. In this work, the critical core requirements for proficiency and mastery of teaching quality and patient safety were established.[23]

The following competencies are critical to QI and PS. In all cases, the ability to role model and teach the competency is requisite to attaining proficient status.

- Practicing EBM
- Analyzing one's practice and making improvements
- Incorporating feedback into practice
- Using information technology to improve practice and reduce errors

- Working effectively in an interprofessional team
- Adapting to a variety of systems and settings
- Understanding and improving systems
- Incorporating considerations of cost awareness and risk–benefit analysis in patient or population-based care
- Knowing one's limitations

HARVARD MEDICAL SCHOOL

Recognizing the needs for future physician leaders in quality and patient safety and the overlap between population health, public health, and healthcare quality, the Harvard Medical School launched a two-year postgraduate fellowship in 2010.[24] The six core domains of this fellowship are show in Table 6.3. Those who complete the fellowship receive training and a master's in public health.[25]

TABLE 6.3 Six Core Domains Covered in Harvard Medical School's Quality and Patient Safety Fellowship

Competency Domain	Examples
Clinical effectiveness	Biostatistics, population management
Patient safety theory	Error, root cause analysis, teams
Quality improvement	Quality improvement, lean
System design	Principles system design
Leadership, self, and change management	Leadership, self-Awareness
Healthcare operations and policy	Contracts, revenues

TRAINING THE NEXT GENERATION: CONCLUSIONS

The era of medical education has shifted, and medical professionals now recognize that all future healthcare providers need to be proficient in the broader context of healthcare practices. There is ongoing debate about what degrees of expertise are needed in these areas for an individual physician to effectively practice clinical medicine in the dynamic environment. Some awareness of payment models, costs versus benefits, systems, and healthcare improvement methods are essential for meaningful participation in this organizational transformation. For leaders in this field, the domains of expertise are more robust, encompassing skills in quality improvement, the science of patient safety, epidemiology, population management, change management, leadership, and payment model reform.

REFERENCES

1. Ludmerer KM. *Time to Heal: American Medical Education from the Turn of the Century to the Era of Managed Care.* New York, NY: Oxford University Press; 1999.

2. Peabody FW. The care of the patient. *JAMA.* 1927;88:877–882.

3. Iglehart JK. The role of physicians. *New Engl J Med.* 1994;330:728–731.

4. Iglehart JK. Physicians and the growth of managed care. *New Engl J Med.* 1994; 331:1167–1171.

5. Deming WE. *The New Economics for Industry, Government, and Education.* 2nd ed. Cambridge, MA: MIT Press; 2000:266.

6. Deming WE. *Out of the Crisis.* Cambridge, MA: MIT Press; 2000:507.

7. Kenney C. *Transforming Health Care: Virginia Mason Medical Center's Pursuit of the Perfect Patient Experience.* New York, NY: Productivity Press; 2011.

8. Toussaint J, Womack J. *Management on the Mend: The Healthcare Executive Guide to System Transformation.* Appleton, WI: ThedaCare Center for Healthcare Value; 2015.

9. Wellman J, Jeffries H, Hagan P. *Leading the Lean Healthcare Journey: Driving Culture Change to Increase Value.* London, UK: Productivity Press; 2010.

10. Berwick DM. Continuous improvement as an ideal in health care. *New Engl J Med.* 1989;320:53–56.

11. Kohn LT, Corrigan JM, Donaldson MS. *To Err Is Human: Building a Safer Health System.* Washington, DC: National Academy Press; 1999.

12. Institute of Medicine, Committee on Quality of Health Care in America. *Crossing the Quality Chasm: A New Health System for the 21st Century.* Washington, DC: National Academy Press; 2001:337.

13. Committee on Health Professions Education Summit, Board on Healthcare Services, Institute of Medicine, *Health Professions Education: A Bridge to Quality.* Greiner, AC, Knebel E, eds. Quality Chasm Series. Washington, DC: National Academy Press; 2003:192.

14. Education, Lucian Leape Institute Roundtable on Reforming Medical Education. *Unmet Needs: Teaching Physicians to Provide Safe Patient Care.* Boston, MA: National Patient Safety Foundation; 2010.

15. Carraccio C, Wolfsthal S, Englander R, et al. Shifting paradigms: from Flexner to competencies. *Acad Med.* 2002;77(5).

16. McGaghie WC, Miller GE., Sajid AW, Telder TV. Competency-based curriculum development in medical education: an introduction. *Public Health Pap.* 1978;68:11–91.

17. Accreditation Council for Graduate Medical Education. The ACGME outcome project: retrospective and prospective; 2007.Available at https://www.acgme.org /acgmeweb/Portals/0/PDFs/ACGMEMilestones-CCC-AssesmentWebinar.pdf.

18. Green, ML, Aagaard EM., Caverzagie KJ, et al. Charting the road to competence: developmental milestones for internal medicine residency training. *J Grad Med Ed.* 2009; 1(1):5–20.

19. Accreditation Council for Graduate Medical Education. Clinical Learning Environment Review (CLER): Expectations for an optimal clinical learning environment to achieve safe and high quality patient care; 2014. Accessed March 12, 2015. Available at http://www.acgme.org/acgmeweb/Portals/0/PDFs/CLER/CLER_Brochure.pdf.

20. Nasca TJ, Weiss KB, Bagian JP. Improving clinical learning environments for tomorrow's physicians. *New Eng J Med*. 2014;370(11):991–993.

21. World Health Organization. The multi-professional patient safety curriculum guide; 2011. Available at http://www.who.int/patientsafety/education/curriculum/tools-download/en/.

22. American Medical Student Association. Member center; 2015. Available at http://www.amsa.org/members/.

23. Association of American Medical Colleges. Teaching for quality: Integrating quality improvement and patient safety across the continuum of medical education; 2013. Available at https://www.aamc.org/initiatives/cei/te4q/366184/te4qreportarticle.html.

24. Gandhi TK, Abookire SA, Kachalia A, et al. Design and implementation of the Harvard fellowship in patient safety and quality. *Am J Med Qual*. 2016;31(1):22–26.

25. Abookire SA, Gandhi TK, Kachalia A, et al. Creating a fellowship curriculum in patient safety and quality. *Am J Med Qual*. 2016;31(1):27–30.

CHAPTER 7

Use of Registries and Public Reporting to Improve Healthcare

Kasaiah Makam
Sandra A. Weiss
William S. Weintraub

Abstract

This chapter discusses the use of registries and public reporting to improve healthcare outcomes. Use of registry data is evolving rapidly in healthcare and public reporting of healthcare outcomes. Quality improvement has largely been made possible with use of these registries. This chapter will cover a variety of information: defining and finding source of registries along with validated tools for proper risk adjustment for public reporting in healthcare, both at the physician and institutional levels. Also, the impact of public reporting of registry data on healthcare outcomes is discussed here, including advantages and limitations, as it may pose a potential challenge to healthcare professionals' traditional concept of autonomy. In conclusion, we will explore why public reporting of healthcare quality performance is considered to be an important step in improving accountability among healthcare professions.

PATIENT REGISTRIES

Patient registries are very helpful if they are properly designed and executed as these can provide detailed information such as a real-world view of clinical practice, patient outcomes, safety and comparative effectiveness.[1] Patient registries focus on health information from various record sets and E.M. Brooke delineated registries in health information systems as "a file of documents containing uniform information about individual persons, collected in a systematic and comprehensive way, in order to serve a predetermined purpose."[2] The National Committee on Vital and Health Statistics describes registries used for a broad range of purposes in public health and medicine as "an organized system for the collection, storage, retrieval, analysis, and dissemination of information on individual persons who have either a particular disease, a condition that predisposes them to the occurrence of a health-related event, or prior exposure to substances (or circumstances) known or suspected to cause adverse health effects."[3]

The Patient-Centered Outcomes Research Institute (PCORI) recognizes registries as an important potential source of data to support patient-centered outcomes research (PCOR). PCOR "assesses the benefits and harms of preventive, diagnostic, therapeutic, palliative, or health delivery system interventions to inform decision making, highlighting comparisons and outcomes that matter to people."[4] It is with these registries that public reporting, an important component of quality improvement, is made possible.

PUBLIC REPORTING

Public reporting started after the 1986 publication of unadjusted mortality rates by the Health Care Financing Administration (HCFA), the predecessor of the Centers for Medicare and Medicaid Services. Mortality statistics were then released annually between 1986 and 1992. However, the execution of public reporting by HCFA was based on administrative claims data (billing data) rather than clinical data, which resulted in inadequate risk adjustment and ultimately led to termination of the program in 1993.[5,6] New York state's Cardiac Surgery Reporting System (CSRS) was the first statewide program to produce public data on outcomes for cardiac surgery and is the nation's longest-running program of this kind.

This form of healthcare performance data reporting has grown for more than a decade in the United States; the production and dissemination of report cards is currently a multimillion-dollar industry.[7] However, there has been only minimal agreement among the various stakeholders about potential benefits, such as promoting quality improvement or choosing a highest-quality provider by the consumers from the release of comparative performance data. Therefore, it is difficult to assess whether the benefits of public disclosure of performance data outweigh disadvantages such as risk aversion, which means providers avoiding high-risk patients out of fear of public reporting without appropriate risk adjustment because these high-risk patients are most likely to suffer complications or death.[8] Policy makers have emphasized the public release of hospital performance data with the goal of improving quality of care.[9,10] On the one hand, report cards on hospital performance are believed to stimulate hospitals and clinicians to initiate and engage in quality-improvement activities and increase the accountability and transparency of the healthcare system.[11,12] However, the downside in publicly releasing the report cards is that it may contain data that are misleading or inaccurate and may unfairly harm the reputations of hospitals and clinicians.[13,14]

REPORT CARDS

Werner et al[14] described two general types of healthcare report cards; one measures outcomes, and the other measures the process leading to certain outcomes. Examples of outcomes-based reports include those from cardiac surgeons and hospitals' risk-adjusted mortality rates following coronary artery bypass graft (CABG) surgery.[15–18] Process-based report cards, which are also called *quality indicators*, are reports on the rates of medical interventions such as screening tests and medications use that are assumed to be related to but separate from outcomes.[14] In other words, these report cards evaluate the *process* by which a certain outcome is achieved or mitigated.

Outcomes are the most important healthcare quality metrics and are of greatest relevance to patients.[19] Outcomes combine the net effects of measured and unmeasured structures and processes of care. CABG mortality remains the paradigm for public reporting, and we will discuss the public reporting pattern of CABG mortality.[20] Many states with public report cards publish results at both surgeon and program levels.

DATA SOURCE FOR PUBLIC REPORTING

For reporting publicly at either the individual provider or program level, data need to be obtained. The source of these data can be administrative from claims or from clinical registries. Administrative data usually consist of demographic, diagnosis, and procedural codes and are derived primarily from insurance claims. Administrative data can be flawed for public reporting because they lack critical clinical variables for appropriate risk adjustment, and outcomes results may be misleading.[5,6] From using the administrative data, cases may be missed or misclassified, and sometimes nonreimbursable diagnoses may be excluded.[21] Clinical registries contain the clinical variables that are of paramount importance for appropriate risk adjustment for public reporting, and clinical data registries are still considered the gold standard for public reporting, either alone or in combination with administrative registries, which can provide information regarding the long-term survival, readmission, and re-intervention data.[22,23]

To identify the extent of the problem using the administrative data for profiling, Hannan et al compared New York CABG results determined from their dedicated clinical database (CSRS) with those derived from the New York administrative database and the federal Medicare administrative database.[24,25] From these comparisons, models derived from clinical database provided superior discrimination and accuracy in explaining variations in patient mortality. To improve the value of administrative data, sometimes it can be mixed with limited number of clinical variables, laboratory data and other indicators like "present on admission."[26,27] However, there are some reported models for certain conditions based on administrative data which showed to have excellence performance compared with models derived from clinical data.[28]

While reporting outcomes measures, risk adjustment should always be performed based on clinical variables. Absence of appropriate risk adjustment resulted in considerable criticism of the hospital mortality rates released by HFCA between 1986 and 1993 and also termination of public reporting program in 1993.[5,6] For the past two decades, risk adjustment has been an integral feature of credible outcomes report cards.[21,29,30]

RISK ADJUSTMENT FOR OUTCOMES REPORTING

Statistical methods without proper risk adjustment based on administrative data (claims data) were used for public reporting by the HCFA, which was the first public reporting on CABG mortality that included observed and expected mortality data for all acute-care nongovernmental hospitals. Hospitals with higher than expected mortality rates were classified as underperforming institutions. There are various methodological flaws that were criticized in early HCFA for public reporting. These included variable sample sizes among providers, failing to estimate the inter- and intrahospital variance components, ignoring the statistical dependence among outcomes within a hospital and use of a classification system that labels a predetermined number of hospitals as having quality problems when excess mortality could be to the product of random error.[31]

Hierarchical models can be used to describe hospital mortality to overcome the statistical limitations of the HCFA approach.[31] The use of hierarchical models helps to mitigate concerns of small sample sizes and unreliable risk-adjusted mortality rates. The hierarchical model simulates the hypothesis that underlying quality leads to systematic differences among true hospital outcomes. When these hierarchical models are used, provider results are shrunken toward the population mean by an amount that is inversely related to sample size. Independent of sample volume, the final shrunken estimate is a combination of the provider's observed rate and the average rate among all providers. The hierarchical model assumes that hospital mortality is independent of the number of patients treated at the hospital. It has also been reported that the relation between institutional volume and mortality is relatively weak in the case of CABG surgery.[32]

Even after risk adjustment, results from various hospitals cannot always be directly compared with one another because there many variables can affect the outcome for direct standardization. Rather, indirect standardization can be used based on multiple regression modeling, which can permit simultaneous assessment of the effect of many risk factors on any given patient.[33] With indirect standardization, any particular provider's results may be compared with those of the benchmark population. This provides the basis for star rating provided by the Society of Thoracic Surgeons (STS), which compares an individual program's performance with national benchmarks for similar mixes of patients.[34]

Based on the calculated performance scores such as risk-adjusted mortality rates, providers are often classified into rating categories. Because short-term results of a provider are only a limited sample of a provider's true long-term performance, classification into rating categories should address random sampling variation by applying principles from inferential statistics.[34] Criterion-referenced methods and norm-referenced methods have been used to classify rating categories.[34]

Criterion-referenced method is the simplest method that does not rely on the distribution of observed data but rather on a predetermined threshold of performance established by regulators. The main advantage of this method is its simplicity. The disadvantages include that the bar could be set so low that quality differences among providers could not be discriminated because all of the providers could pass that bar; another disadvantage is that it does not account for random statistical fluctuation between and within reporting cycles.

Norm-referenced methods are the most commonly used methods for classifying provider performance. This method takes the distribution of observed results among all the providers in the population. The choice of a benchmark population could be national, which is preferable for its generalizability, but it also could be regional or state benchmark data. Investigators reported using a statistical quality-control approach, with outlier warnings indicated by results outside the 95% or two standard deviation control limits, and confirmed outlier status designated when they lie outside the 99.7% or three standard deviation control limits.[35] Bayesian methods for determining outliers have been used as in the STS CABG composite score.[36] The 99% Bayesian certainty criterion used by the STS CABG composite score for public reporting has high specificity and high sensitivity. All methods used to classify providers into multiple performance categories should be based on pilot testing to achieve the optimal balance of sensitivity and specificity.

The robust information for public reporting on outcomes measures has been achieved in some areas such as mortality rates from CABG among providers. However, there is no one common platform where the outcomes measures are reported publicly. There is not enough literature on the topic where and how one can find the places where public reporting is done. This is especially difficult for consumers who have no common platform to consult.

WHAT IS REPORTED

Various report cards of CABG surgery provide different information; for example, a report card of CABG surgery the from Pennsylvania Health Care Cost Containment Council includes information on the number of surgeries performed, in-hospital and 30-day mortality rates, readmission rates within 7 and 30 days, and postsurgical lengths of stay for both hospitals and surgeons as well as average hospital charges and average Medicare payments for hospitals only.[37] Another example includes report cards from the New York state department of health, which reports data for percutaneous coronary intervention, CABG, and valve procedures at both the hospital and surgeon levels, which includes acute-care and 30-day observed, expected, and risk-adjusted mortality rates. The New York state reports data every 3 years to have enough volume for statistically significant results. The New York state also started reporting the 30-day readmission rates following percutaneous coronary intervention (PCI), CABG, and valve procedures.[38]

As reported by Hannan and colleagues,[39] public reporting at the individual surgeon level may benefit consumers by discouraging less capable surgeons from practice. After public reporting was initiated, there was a report of an exodus of lower volume, lower performance surgeons from New York, which may partly explain the improved state outcomes. But, as described by Shahian et al,[34] there are several problems in reporting at the individual surgeon level because cardiac surgical outcomes are highly dependent on effective, coordinated team functioning, including surgeons, nursing, anesthesia, perfusion, intensive care units, and cardiology. Reporting at the surgeon level does not reflect this complex team effect, and sample size is also a major issue because the frequency of CABG is declining, with many surgeons performing fewer than 100 isolated procedures in a year. A potential solution to mitigate the low annual sample size at the individual surgeon level is to collect the surgeon level data over several years, thereby increasing the sample size. The biggest limitation of reporting at the surgeon level includes the fear that high–risk cases may have a much greater negative effect on their individual report card ratings, despite evidence that risk models adequately protect them.[40] Risk aversion was first described by Omoigui and colleagues.[8]

The other unit of public reporting is at the program level. The Society of Thoracic Surgeons is the leading society in public reporting for CABG and valve surgeries. The STS adult cardiac surgery data base was introduced in 1989, and it enrolls patients from the majority of cardiac surgery programs in the United States. The STS provides a CABG composite score that consists of 11 individual measures of cardiothoracic surgery performance endorsed by the National Quality Forum and grouped within four outcomes (Table 7.1) and process of care domains of quality.[41]

The STS CABG composite score has been widely accepted by providers, patients, and other stakeholders. The STS does the public reporting of cardiac surgery outcomes at the program level as it believes that cardiac surgery involves the teamwork and overall outcomes of cardiac surgery do not depend solely on surgeons unless there are specific concerns regarding individual surgeon performance. In addition to numerical scores for individual domains,

TABLE 7.1   The Society of Thoracic Surgeons Coronary Artery Bypass Grafting Composite Score

Domains	Component Measures
Risk-adjusted operative mortality	Risk-adjusted operative mortality
Risk-adjusted morbidity ("any or none")	Renal failure
	Stroke
	Sternal infection, mediastinitis
	Reoperation for cardiac causes
	Prolonged ventilation
Use of the internal mammary artery	Use of the internal mammary artery
Use of recommended perioperative medications ("all or none")	Preoperative β-blockers
	Discharge antiplatelet agents
	Discharge antilipid agents
	Discharge β-blockers

Quality Domain	Participant Score (98% CI)	STS Mean Participant Score	Participant Rating[1]	Distribution of Participant Scores ● = STS Mean					
2006 Overall	95.3% (94.1 , 96.3)	94.5%	★ ★	Min 83.8		10th 92.7	50th 94.7	90th 96.3	Max 97.8
2006 Avoidance of Mortality	98.2% (97.1 , 98.9)	97.8%	★ ★	Min 93.4		10th 96.9	50th 97.9	90th 98.6	Max 99.2
2006 Avoidance of Mortality[2]	86.6% (81.8 , 90.7)	86.2%	★ ★	Min 48.1		10th 79.8	50th 86.9	90th 91.9	Max 96.2
2006 Use of IMA[3]	85.6% (80.0 , 91.1)	92.9%	★	Min 57.8		10th 86.6	50th 94.4	90th 97.8	Max 99.4
2006 Medications[4]	70.6% (64.3 , 76.7)	57.6%	★ ★ ★	Min 9.9	10th 38.3	50th 58.4		90th 76.0	Max 90.3

FIGURE 7.1 The Society of Thoracic Surgeons coronary artery bypass grafting composite star rating system. This typical participant report shows star ratings and numerical scores with confidence intervals (CIs); IMA = internal mammary artery.

the STS also assigns a star summary rating based on the statistical probability that a provider's performance is above or below the STS average. The STS started reporting the numerical scores and star ratings in September 2010 (Figure 7.1).

BENEFITS OF PUBLIC REPORTING FOR CONSUMERS

Regardless of type, the purpose of medical report cards is to provide healthcare consumers with some objective evidence of quality care provided by a health practitioner, allowing them to select the best clinical providers. In turn, this assessment could improve the quality of healthcare provided by all. But for this to happen, patients must be able to find the report cards and understand and trust the ratings to find the best quality provider. Public report cards evaluated as part of ongoing quality-improvement research initiatives over the last couple of decades were not shown to be encouraging because most patients did not know that this comparative performance information was publicly available.[15–18,42,43] However, the uptake of this quality information increased from 27% in 2000 to 35% in 2004.[44–46] In addition, even among patients who were aware of and used these report cards, many were unable to understand or trust this information.[47,48] The common misunderstandings include the language and terms used in report cards, what an indicator is supposed to reveal about the quality of care, and whether high or low rates of an indicator reflect good performance.[49] This problem of misunderstanding is more common among patients of lower socioeconomic status.[49]

In fact, evidence suggests that the report cards are too complex for most patients and rarely influence their decisions in choosing physicians and where to be admitted for procedures. Data from Pennsylvania indicate that less than 1% of patients who were to undergo cardiac surgery knew the quality ratings for their physicians and hospitals.[44] In light of this available information, helping patients through report cards has not yet been realized, even though there is significant potential in improving patients' choice of providers.

Even though public report cards may not have helped patients in choosing high-quality providers, they fill another important need for the patients. By publicly reporting the quality performance, report cards help the public hold healthcare providers accountable for the quality of care they deliver.[50] Surveys show that public accountability in quality is important to the public because reporting is considered an effective way of reducing errors.[51] In one study, 92% of Americans answered that reporting of serious medical errors should be required.[45]

Although the ability of report cards to assist the public in choosing high-quality providers has been limited, physicians might use the public report cards in their choice of referrals.[52,53] Even though most physicians report being aware of the public report cards, many do not trust the information. In one study, only 13% responded that the report card had a moderate or substantial influence on their referral recommendations.[52] Despite providers' mistrust of such data, there is growing evidence that physicians and hospitals respond to public rankings, and the resulting efforts to improve ratings can lead to improvements in healthcare outcomes for patients.[49]

THE RELATIONSHIP OF PUBLIC REPORTING AND OUTCOMES

The most important and fundamental question about public reporting is the extent to which it influences the outcomes of care. Hannan et al reported that in-hospital mortality for CABG patients decreased from 3.52% in 1989 to 2.78% in 1992.[39] After risk adjustment to reflect differences across the years in severity of patient illnesses, the decrease in relative risk-adjusted mortality was 41% in this time period—from 4.17% in 1989 to 2.45% in 1992. The improvement has been attributed to several factors, including quality-improvement programs at high-mortality hospitals; restriction of privileges of low-volume, high-mortality surgeons; practice improvements in low-volume surgeons; and better training and performance among surgeons new to the system.[11,20]

Furthermore, the public reporting of risk-adjusted cardiac outcome information from cardiac registries in New York has resulted in several hospital-specific quality-improvement initiatives. Hannan et al described the following three initiatives that resulted in a decrease of the risk-adjusted mortality. St. Peter's Hospital in Albany, New York, was identified as having a significantly higher mortality in the early years of the program (1991 and 1992).[54] The excess mortality was identified to be secondary to emergency cases, for which St. Peter's experienced a 26% mortality rate compared to a 7% mortality rate for the state. After a review of the management of the emergency cases, St. Peter's concluded that the patients were not stabilized adequately before surgery. This then led to a major change in the management of these patients. In 1993, there were no deaths among the 54 emergency patients who underwent CABG surgery.[55] Similar improvement in risk-adjusted mortality was noted at Winthrop Hospital, New York, with rates falling from 9.2% to 4.6% to 2.3% between 1989 and 1991,[56] and at Erie County Medical Center, Buffalo, New York, where the hospital's risk-adjusted mortality fell from 7.31% (1989 to 1991) to 2.51% (1993 to 1995), just below the statewide average of 2.57%. The very low annual volume at this facility of slightly more than 100 cases rose to 219 cases per year in the 1996 to 1998 time period, during which the mortality rate was 1.77%.[56]

As the outcomes for CABG surgery have improved across the country and around the world as a result of newer techniques and advances in care, it stands to reason that the improvement in mortality could be entirely unrelated to public reporting. In light of this, the accurate manner of assessing the risk-adjusted outcome changes in New York was compared to other regions over the same period. Peterson et al used national Medicare data between 1987 and 1992 to examine the CABG mortality rate and changes in rate.[57] The researchers confirmed a 33% reduction in New York's 30-day unadjusted mortality rate in New York, well above the national average of 19% during the period studied. The only other area with similar figures was northern New England, where provider profile reports were provided for internal use only rather than for publication.[58]

In an evaluation of Cleveland Health Quality Choice project, Rosenthal and colleagues reported improved outcomes associated with the publication of mortality data for six common medical conditions and two surgical operations.[59] The authors reviewed 101,060 discharges from 30 northeastern Ohio hospitals and found significant and sustained reduction in risk-adjusted mortality for most conditions following the publication of the mortality data.

Other public report cards have also been hailed for improving healthcare quality. The National Committee on Quality Assurance publishes its Health Plan Employer Data and Information Set (HEDIS) measures of health plan performance annually, and over the past five years has reported that performance on key measures of clinical quality improved over the preceding year.[60] The *Boston Globe* recently reported that fewer nursing home residents experience untreated pain or are placed in restraints since the first report card was published in 2002. However, there has been no significant change in other areas of nursing home quality such as the occurrence of pressure sores among residents or the ability of residents to walk or feed themselves.[61]

However, the improvement in risk-adjusted mortality rate after CABG surgery has been challenged by simultaneous reports of cardiac surgeons turning away the sickest and most severely ill patients in states with CABG report cards apparently in an effort to avoid poor outcomes and lower publicly reported ratings. Omoigui et al noted that the number of patients transferred to the Cleveland Clinic from New York hospitals increased by 31% after the release of CABG report cards in New York, and that these transfer patients generally had higher risk profiles than patients transferred to the Cleveland Clinic from other states.[8] In contrast, Peterson et al found that the percentage of New York residents receiving out-of-state CABG surgery decreased between 1987 and 1992, and the likelihood of bypass surgery following myocardial infarctions increased.[57] Surveys of surgeons and cardiologists in New York state indicated that they believe that avoidance of high-risk patients is a problem. Burack et al reported that 67% of New York surgeons claimed they had refused to treat at least one patient in the previous year and 18% refused to treat more at least five patients.[62] In another study, Narins et al found that 83% of interventional cardiologists in New York "agreed" or "strongly agreed" that the publication of statewide report cards decreased the chance that patients needing PCI actually received it.[63]

Moscucci et al reported marked differences in unadjusted mortality rates in people undergoing PCI in Michigan and New York, with significantly lower unadjusted in-hospital mortality in New York than in Michigan (0.83% versus 1.54%).[64] It has been reported that a propensity in New York toward not intervening with higher-risk patients out of fear of public reporting of high mortality rates is a possible explanation for these differences. However, after adjusting for comorbidities, there was no significant difference in mortality between the two groups.

CONCLUSION

The first major problem we identified in this topic is an absence of a common platform to search for public reporting on healthcare outcomes. At the consumer level, it might be even more difficult to do this search. One way to improve consumer access to public reporting is, for example, the way the Society of Thoracic Surgeons joined with *Consumer Reports* to showcase the results of the cardiac surgery mortality rates.

The second problem is the interpretation of these results. For example, as reported by Donelan et al, comprehension of surgeon performance data by consumers is limited and variable, based on the display format.[67] To properly interpret these published results, consumers should be educated on how to analyze the results properly.

In conclusion, public reporting of healthcare quality performance might be an important step in improving accountability among healthcare professions. But whether public reporting results in improving healthcare quality is uncertain. Public disclosure of performance data is a major health policy initiative that also poses a potential challenge to healthcare professionals' traditional concept of autonomy.[65] Therefore, it is most important to ensure data completeness and accuracy because these reports can affect the quality of patient care as well as the success and profitability of healthcare providers. It is also important to improve the acceptance of these reports to the public and providers. Leaders in healthcare have suggested that the principal obstacle to broader action on quality improvement is a lack of consensus on publicly reporting quality measures. The public, however, is unambiguously positive about the accountability public reporting provides.[51,64]

REFERENCES

1. Gliklich RE, Dreyer NA, Leavy MB, eds. *Registries for Evaluating Patient Outcomes. A User's Guide*. 3rd ed. Rockville, MD: Agency for Healthcare Research and Quality; 2014.

2. Brooke EM. *The Current and Future Use of Registries in Health Information Systems*. Geneva, Switzerland: World Health Organization; Publication No. 8; 1974.

3. National Committee on Vital and Health Statistics. *Frequently Asked Questions About Medical and Public Health Registries*. Rockville, MD: Agency for Healthcare Research and Quality; 2012.

4. Patient-Centered Outcomes Research Institute. Patient-centered outcomes research. Retrieved August 28, 2012, from http://www.pcori.org/research-results/patient-centered-outcomes-research.

5. Rosen HM, Green BA. The HCFA excess mortality lists: a methodological critique. *Hosp Health Serv Adm.* 1987;32:119–127.

6. Blumberg MS. Risk adjusting health care outcomes: a methodological review. *Med Care Rev.* 1986;43:351–393.

7. Epstein A. Rolling down the runway: the challenges ahead for quality report cards. *JAMA.*1998; 279:1691–1696.

8. Omoigui NA, Miller DP, Brown KJ, et al. Out migration for coronary bypass surgery in an era of public dissemination of clinical outcomes. *Circ.* 1996;93:27–33.

9. Steinbrook R. Public report cards—cardiac surgery and beyond. *New Engl J Med.* 2006;355(18):1847–1849.

10. Lee TH, Meyer GS, Brennan TA. A middle ground on public accountability. *New Engl J Med.* 2004;350 (23):2409–2412.

11. Chassin MR, Hannan EL, DeBuono BA. Benefits and hazards of reporting medical outcomes publicly. *New Engl J Med.* 1996;334(6):394–398.

12. Hibbard JH, Stockard J, Tusler M. Does publicizing hospital performance stimulate quality improvement efforts? *Health Aff.* (Millwood) 2003;22 (2):84–94.

13. Jollis JG, Romano PS. Pennsylvania's focus on heart attack—grading the scorecard. *New Engl J Med.* 1998;338(14):983–987.

14. Werner RM, Asch DA. The unintended consequences of publicly reporting quality information. *JAMA.*2005;293(10):1239–1244.

15. Pennsylvania Health Care Cost Containment Council. *A Consumer Guide to Coronary Artery Bypass Graft Surgery.* Harrisburg, PA: Pennsylvania Health Care Cost Containment Council;1992.

16. New York State Department of Health. *Coronary Artery Bypass Surgery in New York State, 1990–1992.* Albany, NY: New York State Department of Health;1993.

17. New Jersey Department of Health and Senior Services. Cardiac surgery in New Jersey: consumer report; 2003. Accessed February 4, 2005, from http://www.nj.gov/health/healthcarequality/cardiacsurgery.shtml.

18. Office of Statewide Health Planning and Development. Website. http://www.oshpd.ca.gov/serp.html?q=cabg+mortality&cx=001779225245372747843%3Amdsmtl_vila&cof=FORID%3A10&ie=UTF-8&nojs=1. Accessed February 4, 2005.

19. Porter ME. What is the value in health care? *New Engl J Med.* 2010;363:2477–2481.

20. Hannan EL, Siu AL, Kumar D, et al. The decline in coronary artery bypass graft surgery mortality in New York State. The role of surgeon volume. *JAMA.*1995;273:209–213.

21. Krumholz HM et al. Standards for statistical models used for public reporting of health outcomes: an American Heart Association scientific statement from the Quality of Care and Outcomes Research Interdisciplinary Writing Group. *Circ.* 2006;113:456–462.

22. Jacobs JP, et al. Successful linking of the Society of Thoracic Surgeons adult cardiac surgery database to Centers for Medicare and Medicaid Services Medicare data. *Ann Thorac Surg.* 2010;90:1150–1156.

23. Klein LW, Edwards FH, DeLong ER, Ritzenthaler L, Dangas GD, Weintraub WS. ASCERT: the American College of Cardiology Foundation–the Society of Thoracic Surgeons Collaboration on the comparative effectiveness of revascularization strategies. *JACC Cardiovasc Interv.* 2010;3:124–126.

24. Hannan EL, et al. Clinical versus administrative data bases for CABG surgery: does it matter? *Med Care.* 1992;30 892–907.

25. Hannan EL, et al. Using Medicare claims data to assess provider quality for CABG surgery: does it work well enough? *Health Serv Res.* 1997;31 659–678.

26. Pine M, et al. Enhancement of claims data to improve risk adjustment of hospital mortality. *JAMA.* 2007;297:71–76

27. Geraci JM, et al. Mortality after cardiac bypass surgery: prediction from administrative versus clinical data. *Med Care.* 2005;43:149–158.

28. Krumholz HM, et al. An administrative claims model suitable for profiling hospital performance based on 30-day mortality rates among patients with an acute myocardial infarction. *Circ.* 2006;113:1683–1692.

29. Selker HP. Systems of comparing actual and predicted mortality rates: characteristics to promote cooperation in improving hospital care. *Ann Intern Med.* 2993; 118:820–822.

30. Kassirer JP. The use and abuse of practice profiles. *New Engl J Med.* 1994;330: 634–636.

31. Normand S.-L. T, Shahian DM. Statistical and clinical aspects of hospital outcomes profiling. *Stat Sci.* 2007;22:206–226.

32. Peterson ED. Procedural volume as a marker of quality for CABG surgery. *JAMA.* 2004;291 195–201.

33. Harrell FE Jr. *Regression Modeling Strategies with Applications to Linear Models, Logistic Regression, and Survival Analysis.* New York, NY: Springer-Verlag; 2001.

34. Shahian DM, et al. Public reporting of cardiac surgery performance: part 2–implementation. *Ann Thoracic Surg.* 2011;92:S12–S23.

35. Shahian DM, et al. Applications of statistical quality control to cardiac surgery. *Ann Thorac Surg.* 1996;62:1351–1358.

36. Austin PC. A comparison of Bayesian methods for profiling hospital performance. *Med Decis Making.* 2002;22:163–172.

37. Pennsylvania Health Care Cost Containment Council. Cardiac surgery in Pennsylvania, 2005–2006: information about hospitals and cardiothoracic surgeons. September 2008. Retrieved from http://www.phc4.org/reports/cabg/06/docs/cabg2006 report.pdf.

38. New York State Department of Health. Cardiovascular disease data and statistics. Retrieved from http://www.health.ny.gov/statistics/diseases/cardiovascular/.

39. Hannan EL, Kilburn H Jr., Racz M, Shields E, Chassin MR. Improving the outcomes of coronary artery bypass surgery in New York state. *JAMA.* 1994;271: 761–766.

40. Hannan EL, Siu AL, Kumar D, Racz M, Pryor DB, Chassin MR. Assessment of coronary artery bypass graft surgery performance in New York: is there a bias against taking high-risk patients? *Med Care.* 1997;35:49–56.

41. Shahian DM, Edwards FH, Ferraris VA, et al. Quality measurement in adult cardiac surgery: part 1–conceptual framework and measure selection. *Ann Thoracic Surg.* 2007;83(4) (suppl):S3–12.

42. Centers for Medicare and Medicaid Services. Nursing home compare databases; 2003. Retrieved from http://www.medicare.gov/Nhcompare/Home.asp.

43. Agency for Health Care Research and Quality. National health care quality report; 2003. Retrieved from http://archive.ahrq.gov/qual/nhqr03/fullreport/index .htm.

44. Schneider EC, Epstein AM. Use of public performance reports: a survey of patients undergoing cardiac surgery. *JAMA.* 1998;279:1638–1642.

45. Kaiser Family Foundation and Agency for Health Care Research and Quality. *National Survey on Consumers' Experiences with Patient Safety and Quality Information.* Washington, DC: Kaiser Family Foundation; 2004.

46. Kaiser Family Foundation and Agency for Health Care Research and Quality. *Americans as Healthcare Consumers: An Update on the Role of Quality Information.* Washington, DC: Kaiser Family Foundation; 2000.

47. Jewett JJ, Hibbard JH. Comprehension of quality of care indicators. *Health Care Finance Rev.* 1996;18:75–94.

48. Robinson S, Brodie M. Understanding the quality challenge for health consumers: the Kaiser/AHCPR survey. *J Qual Improv.* 1997;23:239–244.

49. Marshall MN, Shekelle PG, Leatherman S, Brook RH. The public release of performance data: what do we expect to gain? a review of the evidence. *JAMA.* 2000; 283:1866–1874.

50. Lansky D. Improving quality through public disclosure of performance information. *Health Aff.* (Millwood). 2002;21:52–62.

51. Blendon RJ, Des Roches CM, Brodie M, et al. Views of practicing physicians and the public on medical errors. *New Engl J Med.* 2002;347:1933–1940.

52. Schneider EC, Epstein AM. Influence of cardiac surgery performance reports on referral practices and access to care: a survey of cardiovascular specialists. *New Engl J Med.* 1996;335:251–256.

53. Hannan EL, Stone CC, Biddle TL, DeBuono BA. Public release of cardiac surgery outcomes data in New York: what do New York State cardiologists think of it? *Am Heart J.* 1997;134:55–61.

54. Hannan EL, Cozzens K, King SB III, Walford G, Shah NR. History contributions, limitations and lessons for future efforts to assess and publicly report healthcare outcomes. *J Am Coll Cardiol.* 2012;59(25):2309–2316.

55. Dziuban SW Jr., McIlduff JB, Miller SJ, Dal Col RH. How a New York cardiac surgery program uses outcomes data. *Ann Thorac Surg.* 1994;58:1871–1876.

56. Chassin MR. Achieving and sustaining improved quality: Lessons from New York state and cardiac surgery. *Health Aff.* 2002;21:40–51.

57. Peterson ED, Delong ER, Jollis JG, Muhlbaier LH, Mark DB. The effects of New York's bypass surgery provider profiling on access to care and patient outcomes in the elderly. *J Am Coll Cardiol.* 1998;32:993–999.

58. O'Connor GT, Plume SK, Olmstead EM, Morton JR, Maloney CT. A regional intervention to improve the hospital mortality associated with coronary artery bypass graft surgery. *JAMA*. 1996;275:841–846.

59. Rosenthal GE, Harper DL. Cleveland health quality choice: a model for collaborative community based outcomes assessment. *Jt Comm J Qual Improv*. 1994;20:425–442.

60. National Committee for Quality Assurance. *The State of Health Care Quality: 2004*. Retrieved from http://www.ncqa.org/portals/0/Publications/Resource%20Library/SOHC /SOHC_2004.pdf.

61. Dembner A, Dedman B. Nursing homes show uneven gains: national effort at grading has mixed results. *Boston Globe*. December 13, 2004: A1.

62. Burack JH, Impellizzeri P, Homel P, Cunningham JN Jr. Public reporting of surgical mortality: a survey of New York State cardiothoracic surgeons. *Ann Thorac Surg*. 1999;68:1195–1202.

63. Nairns CR, Dozier AM, Ling FS, Zareba W. The influence of public reporting of outcome data on medical decision making by physicians. *Arch Intern Med*. 2005; 165:83–87.

64. Mouscucci M, et al. Public reporting and case selection for percutaneous coronary interventions. An analysis from two large multicenter percutaneous coronary intervention databases. *J Am Coll Cardiol*. 2005;45:1759–1765.

65. Marshall MN, Shekelle PG, Leatherman S, Brook RH. *The Publication of Performance Data in Health Care*. London, UK: Nuffield Trust. In press.

66. Altman DE, Clancy C, Blendon RJ. Improving patient safety—five years after the IOM report. *New Engl J Med*. 2004;351:2041–2043.

67. Donelan K, et al. Consumer comprehension of surgeon performance data for coronary bypass procedures. *Ann Thorac Surg*. 2011;91:1400–1406.

HEALTHCARE
DELIVERY
REDESIGN

Achieving Higher Quality and Lower Costs via Innovations in Healthcare Delivery Design

Elizabeth Malcolm
Arnold Milstein

Abstract

Performance-improvement strategies such as lean and Six Sigma can enhance operational efficiency but will not be adequate to shrink the portion of the economy devoted to healthcare spending while raising quality. This chapter describes three ways to approach improving healthcare value: (1) find and adapt care delivery methods where the lowest cost, highest quality care is being delivered today; (2) address patients' and providers' most deeply felt unmet needs; and (3) adopt emerging technology that replaces costly labor or enables the replication of new care delivery methods. Mobilizing these strategies to redesign healthcare delivery can bend the cost curve and accelerate the achievement of the five other aims of healthcare delineated by the Institute of Medicine.

Over the last 10 years, policy makers and clinical teams have increasingly focused on improving "value."[1] The United States spends the largest proportion of its income on healthcare relative to its international peers, yet many indicators of health system performance are not proportionally better. A 2014 survey of older adults in 11 industrialized countries found that U.S. respondents were the sickest, had the most difficulty accessing care, were most likely to use the emergency room for health issues that could have been cared for by a primary care provider, and were more likely to have problems paying their medical bills.[2] Although the rate of growth of spending in the healthcare sector recently slowed, it is still outgrowing the gross domestic product (GDP). Meanwhile, several factors, including the aging of the U.S. population and biomedical innovations, will continue to apply upward pressure on healthcare spending.[3]

Policy makers are using patient and provider incentives to improve care and lower health spending. For example, the so-called Cadillac tax, a provision in the Affordable Care Act set to go into effect in 2018, will levy a 40% excise tax on insurers and self-insured employers who spend more per insured than a specified ceiling amount.[4] Insurers have begun to prune lower-value providers from their networks and incentivize consumers to be more value conscious. In addition, the federal Department of Health and Human Services has set aggressive goals for the proportion of Medicare payments that will be tied to the quality and efficiency of care.[5] Inefficiencies in care delivery in the United States are not easy to eliminate. For example, nearly one-third of organizations in the Medicare Pioneer accountable care organization (ACO) demonstration dropped out after the first year, and only a minority were able to achieve the level of spending reduction needed to align per capita health spending growth with GDP growth.[6]

Lowering the cost of better care can be accomplished via industrial quality-management methods or heightened professionalism. This chapter describes three recently developed approaches to fundamentally rethink care delivery methods that may also be used.

1. Searching today's global value frontier for care delivery models that consistently produce good quality at a lower cost.
2. Addressing the most deeply felt unmet needs of patients and clinicians to improve the likelihood that a novel high-value method of care delivery will be adopted.
3. Applying technology to replace more costly labor or make high-value methods of care delivery easier to use.

SEARCHING THE GLOBAL FRONTIER

Scalable, high-value care innovations can be revealed by searching today's global value frontier for care delivery methods that consistently produce good quality at a lower cost.

Clinical teams that consistently deliver exceptional value in an area of interest are an important source of solutions for two reasons.[7] First, many have found solutions that are viable in financial and regulatory environments that have traditionally ignored or financially penalized higher value. Second, providers may be more likely to adopt innovations that have been demonstrated by those they regard as their peers.[8]

High-value clinical teams can be identified by publicly reported information on clinical performance or analysis of health insurance claims-paid databases containing health spending and clinical information. Once identified, care and context at positive outlier sites can be compared with sites not performing as well to learn what distinguishes the care being delivered by these higher value clinical teams. Finally, the distinguishing features can be tested in other settings to determine when and whether replication leads to higher value care.

It is relatively difficult to get access to annual total per capita spending for a patient population served by an identifiable clinical team. However, access has begun to improve via private-sector companies, all-payer claims databases, and qualified entities established under section 13014 of the Affordable Care Act. More painstaking methods of comparing providers on value can also be applied such as time-driven activity-based costing and patient-reported outcome measures.

Our examination of positive value outliers has revealed several types of replicable innovations, which are discussed as follows.

When "rules-based medicine" is feasible, higher-cost healthcare workers can be replaced by lower-cost clinical team members, including patients. Rules-based medicine is "the provision of care for diseases that can be precisely diagnosed, whose causes are understood, and which consequently can be treated with rules based therapies that are consistently effective."[9] An example of this is the retail store–based clinic, in which care is provided for minor acute conditions (e.g., urinary tract infections) and vaccinations are offered in a pharmacy or other retail setting by a nurse practitioner following diagnostic and treatment rules.[10] Care episodes in retail clinics cost substantially less[10] and provide equal or greater quality compared to physician offices, emergency rooms, and urgent care visits for the same conditions.[11]

Care can be moved from higher-cost to lower-cost settings via one of two methods.

- *Moving delivery of care from acute care settings to outpatient settings*: This is a cost-lowering solution in instances where the timeliness and intensity of outpatient care can be increased so that it safely and more economically meets what used to require acute hospitals stays. For example, a transient ischemic attack (TIA)—a "ministroke" in which all symptoms resolve—can safely be treated in the outpatient setting after imaging and initial evaluation in the emergency department.[12] Such outpatient treatment of TIA occurs routinely in the United Kingdom but rarely in the United States despite similar safety and quality outcomes at a far lower cost in the United Kingdom.[13]

- *Decentralization of healthcare to home settings:* Where patients previously went to care, now the care can come to patients.[9] For example, dialysis provided in the home is not only less costly than center-based dialysis but also has far better outcomes on average, including lower mortality, fewer hospitalizations, and fewer adverse events.[14–16] Evolving technology is opening up many possibilities for delivering more care in low-cost settings such as referral pharmacies and patients' homes.

Care intensity can be better matched with patients' needs. Some practices on the value frontier use this technique to lower the cost of care while improving quality. One key example is intensified management of patients with complex chronic illness. The ambulatory intensive caring unit (A-ICU) model, originally implemented for Boeing employees, is a care model in which patients at high risk of hospital admission for ambulatory care–sensitive conditions are treated in a primary care site that features team-based care, more frequent patient contact, and coordination of medical and nonmedical services.[17] Although the enrollment in the Boeing pilot test was not powered to determine statistical significance of the change, the initial evaluation showed improvements in health-related quality of life and a large trend toward reduction in total per capita healthcare spending because of fewer emergency room and hospital admissions.[18]

Procedures can be better matched to patient preferences. When there is more than one clinically appropriate treatment option for a condition, it becomes even more important to base decisions on the personal values and preferences of a well-informed patient—especially when the chosen option may irreversibly affect a patient's quality of life. A shared decision-making process with decision aids helps patients select treatment options that are more aligned with their preferences. Patients choose more costly options less often when given full information about risks and benefits.[19] Group Health was able to show that implementation of decision aids for hip and knee joint replacement—surgical care that is highly preference-sensitive—reduced health spending by 12% to 21% through reduction in surgeries over six months.[20]

A final example of a practice from today's value frontier is the preferential referral of patients from primary care to low-spending specialists who have favorable quality rankings.[21] For example, physicians at the Geisinger Health System maintain a value-based referral network of specialists for use by primary care physicians. The network includes specialists, imaging facilities, non-Geisinger, and other ancillary providers who deliver lower-cost and higher-quality care compared to their peers.[22]

MEETING UNMET NEEDS

If the most deeply felt unmet needs of patients and clinicians are met to their satisfaction, then it is more likely that a novel high-value method of care delivery will be adopted.

Because patients, caregivers, and providers of healthcare will decide whether to adopt new methods of care, eliciting and addressing their most deeply felt unmet needs is instrumental to improving value. The human-centered design technique allows innovators to gain a "thorough understanding of what people want and need, and what they like or dislike" about current care.[23] Human centered design has a particular focus on identifying areas of unmet need to use as "grip holds" for the development of novel solutions. Initial solutions are iteratively prototyped and fed back to end users for further refinement. When done well, the end result is an innovation that attracts the end user by eliminating pain points and creating delight.

One component of human-centered design is called *empathic research*. Empathic research consists of exploratory observation and interviews with the end users of an innovation using methods derived from anthropology adapted for the early stages of a design process (called *applied ethnography*). Through empathic research, innovators can begin to understand the real problems that patients and providers face when managing a health condition or situation.[24] Human motivation research suggests that incorporating solutions to problems that elicit strong negative emotions (called *disgusters*) are more likely to have value to the adopters, in theory leading to a stronger desire for uptake.

An excellent example of such design thinking in healthcare is the development of the bedside shift report. This innovation grew out of a desire at Kaiser Permanente in Northern California to reduce the inefficiency and error associated with the nursing handoff at shift change. A team of designers and stakeholders from four Kaiser hospitals worked with front line nurses and patients to identify unmet needs in shift changes. They found that nurses spent up to 45 minutes either in face-to-face debriefings or listening to recorded messages from the previous shift. Despite this significant investment of time, nurses often failed to transfer information that mattered most to patients. Nurses often started their shifts already behind because they had to spend long periods transferring information; the result was more stress during their shifts and the inability to end work on time. For patients, each shift change felt like a hole in their care. By focusing on these deeply felt unmet needs for nurses and patients, the Kaiser team designed a new care delivery method for handoff. Nurses would round together at the patient bedside and deliver the report in front of the patient and family. This revolutionary change in how information was transferred between nurses led to better patient safety, lower information transfer times, and enhanced nurse and patient satisfaction.[23,25]

MAKING HIGH-VALUE CARE METHODS EASIER TO USE

When applied correctly, technology can replace more costly labor and methods of care delivery with higher-value methods that are actually easier to use.

Healthcare providers are expected to follow increasingly specified protocols in a workplace that is the epitome of a complex system with many intersecting layers of interacting components. A busy intensive care unit exemplifies a complex system in which the layers range from the complicated physiology of a critically ill patient to the web of social interactions with patients, family members, and clinical team members.

Cognitive psychologists understand cognition as a "dual process."[26,27] One part of the process is intuitive and reflexive. The role of this intuitive process is to continuously scan the environment for patterns. When the intuitive process detects an unfamiliar pattern, a second process can engage that is analytical, effortful, and deliberate. When an individual or a team is handling multiple complex tasks and information streams, the analytical cognitive process can become overwhelmed, causing wasteful and dangerous errors in judgment or fumbles in intended activities.

Technology based in artificial intelligence (AI) can augment this dual process. It can scan for pattern recognition and alert human operators when consequential unfamiliar patterns arise. AI can lower costs by reducing the amount of human surveillance needed to detect sentinel events that require further investigation. As artificial intelligence technology becomes more robust, it may become more adept than humans at identifying important abnormal patterns. AI-based technology can also perform continuous surveillance in places where it is cost prohibitive to use healthcare workers—for example, in the homes of frail older persons.[28]

CONCLUSION

To meet the demand for lower cost and better health, we can learn what high-value clinical teams are doing today, rely on empathic service design, and apply artificial intelligence and communications technologies. Their combination offers near-term potential to lower population-wide health spending and improve health beyond what may be accomplished through use of traditional performance-improvement tools.

REFERENCES

1. Porter ME. What is value in health care? *New Engl J Med.* 2010;363:2477–2481.

2. Davis K, Stremikis K, Squires D, Schoen C. Mirror, mirror on the wall: how the performance of the U.S. Health care system compares internationally. 2014;1–32. Available at http://www.commonwealthfund.org/publications/fund-reports/2014/jun/mirror -mirror.

3. McClellan M, Rivlin A. *Improving Health While Reducing Cost Growth: What Is Possible?* Washington, DC: Brookings Institution; 2014.

4. Piotrowski J. Health policy brief: Excise tax on "Cadillac" plans. *Health Affair.* 2013. Available at http://www.healthaffairs.org/healthpolicybriefs/brief.php?brief _id=99.

5. Burwell SM. Setting value-based payment goals—HHS efforts to improve U.S. health care. *New Engl J Med.* 2015;363:1–3.

6. Kocot SL, White R, Katikaneni P, McClellan M. *A More Complete Picture of Pioneer ACO Results.* Washington, DC: Brookings Institution; 2014.

7. Bradley EH, Curry LA, Ramanadhan S, Rowe L, Nembhard IM, Krumholz HM. Research in action: using positive deviance to improve quality of health care. *Implement Sci.* 2009;4:25.

8. Greenhalgh T, Robert G, Macfarlane F, Bate P, Kyriakidou O. Diffusion of innovations in service organizations: systematic review and recommendations. *Milbank Q.* 2004;82:581–629.

9. Christensen CM, Grossman JH, Hwang J. *The Innovator's Prescription: A Disruptive Solution for Health Care.* New York: McGraw-Hill; 2009.

10. Mehrotra A. Comparing costs and quality of care at retail clinics with that of other medical settings for 3 common illnesses. *Ann Intern Med.* 2009;151:321–328.

11. Shrank WH, Krumme AA, Tong AY, et al. Quality of care at retail clinics for 3 common conditions. *Am J Manag Care.* 2014;20:794–801.

12. Martinez-Martinez MM, Martinez-Sanchez P, Fuentes B, et al. Transient ischaemic attacks clinics provide equivalent and more efficient care than early in-hospital assessment. *Eur J Neurol.* 2013;20:338–343.

13. Paul NL, Koton S, Simoni M, Geraghty OC, Luengo-Fernandez R, Rothwell PM. Feasibility, safety and cost of outpatient management of acute minor ischaemic stroke: a population-based study. *J Neurol Neurosurg Psychiatr.* 2013;84:356–361.

14. Liu FX, Treharne C, Culleton B, Crowe L, Arici M. The financial impact of increasing home-based high dose haemodialysis and peritoneal dialysis. *BMC Nephrol.* 2014;15:161.

15. Weinhandl ED, Liu J, Gilbertson DT, Arneson TJ, Collins AJ. Survival in daily home hemodialysis and matched thrice-weekly in-center hemodialysis patients. *J Am Soc Nephrol.* 2012;23(5):895–904.

16. National Institute for Health and Care Excellence. Guidance on home compared to hospital dialysis in patients with end-stage renal failure. In: Nice Technology Appraisal Guidance T48. United Kingdom; 2002. Accessed January 31, 2015, at http://www.nice.org.uk/guidance/ta48/chapter/1-guidance.

17. Milstein A. How ambulatory intensive caring units can reduce costs and improve outcomes. California Health Care Foundation; 2011. Accessed February 5, 2015, at http://www.chcf.org/publications/2011/05/ambulatory-intensive-caring-units.

18. Milstein A, Kothari P, Fernandopulle R, Helle T. Are higher-value care models replicable? Health Affairs Blog; 2009. Available at http://healthaffairs.org/blog/2009/10/20/are-higher-value-care-models-replicable/.

19. Stacey D, Legare F, Col NF, et al. Decision aids for people facing health treatment or screening decisions. *Cochrane Database Syst Rev.* 2014;1:Cd001431.

20. Arterburn D, Wellman R, Westbrook E, et al. Introducing decision aids at Group Health was linked to sharply lower hip and knee surgery rates and costs. *Health Affair.* 2012;31:2094–2104.

21. Milstein A, Gilbertson E. American medical home runs. *Health Affair.* 2009;28:1317–1326.

22. Paulus RA, Davis K, Steele GD. Continuous innovation in health care: implications of the Geisinger experience. *Health Affair* (Millwood). 2008;27:1235–1245.

23. Brown T. Design thinking. *Harvard Bus Rev.* 2008;86:84–92.

24. Savage J. Ethnography and health care. *BMJ.* 2000;321:1400–1402.

25. Evans D, Grunawalt J, McClish D, Wood W, Friese CR. Bedside shift-to-shift nursing report: implementation and outcomes. *Medsurg Nursing.* 2012;21:281–284,292.

26. Croskerry P. Clinical cognition and diagnostic error: applications of a dual process model of reasoning. *Adv Health Sci Educ.* 2009;14(suppl 1):27–35.

27. Evans JS. Dual-processing accounts of reasoning, judgment, and social cognition. *Ann Rev Psych.* 2008;59:255–278.

28. Asch DA, Muller RW, Volpp KG. Automated hovering in health care—watching over the 5000 hours. *N Engl J Med.* 2012;367:1–3.

CHAPTER 9

Population Health Management

THE LYNCHPIN OF EMERGING HEALTHCARE
DELIVERY MODELS

Julia D. Andrieni

Abstract

Population health management (PHM) is a data-driven integrated healthcare delivery model that provides individualized care plans to populations based on health risks and conditions. PHM uses data aggregation, risk stratification, and analytics to design and monitor the effectiveness of treatments and interventions tailored to individual health profiles. The PHM model requires functional integration to deliver coordinated care, clinical integration of providers, and advanced health information capabilities to risk stratify and manage the population for quality outcomes. Investments are needed in core components to include information technology, care management programs, a primary care network of providers with same-day access, and patient-engagement tools such as health apps or home health monitoring devices. Population health management programs have captured the interest of the healthcare community with a focus on lowering health risks and improving clinical outcomes at a lower cost.

In a rapidly changing healthcare landscape that is moving from fee for service to fee for value, several different risk-based health delivery models have emerged to address this paradigm shift, including accountable care organizations (ACOs), clinically integrated networks (CINs), and patient–centered medical homes (PCMHs). In each of these models, PHM is the lynchpin for the implementation and success of the best strategy to navigate the required measureable clinical and financial outcomes associated with value-based medicine. Private insurance exchanges, self-insured employers, and the Medicare Shared Savings Program (MSSP) are payment models that support PHM's development.

As providers face the challenge of providing high-quality care at lower costs, a strategy is needed to segment populations into various health risk groups in order to direct appropriate clinical and other resources. For example, a high-risk uncontrolled diabetic population would require a more aggressive care-management approach than a well controlled diabetic population. Furthermore, in the value-based model, it is important to identify the less complex patients who can be cared for in the outpatient setting or monitored at home with healthcare devices that interface with their electronic health records (EHRs). Higher-cost tertiary or quaternary acute healthcare settings would be reserved for more complex patients who need intensive management or hospitalization for procedures in the in-patient setting. In value-based medicine, there is impetus to allocate resources and design care plans so that the high-risk and rising-risk segments of a population can be shifted to a lower-risk group. All of these interventions and paradigm shifts require a patient-centric approach with shared decision making and the use of patient EHR portals, patient apps, and patient advisory councils as strategies to engage patients. This patient-centric approach continues to shape this new landscape of healthcare with patient-friendly tools for self management.

To manage segmented populations, the foundational components for a PHM program include patient data aggregation and advanced analytics (prognostic and predictive), stratification of patients into defined risk groups, development of individualized care plans matched to risk groups, patient outreach to address gaps in care, and specific tools to support patient engagement. In a more advanced PHM program, community resource partnerships are developed to address non-clinical patient needs (i.e., social and educational needs) for ancillary services that affect health risks and resource use.[1]

To test the foundational components of PHM, in October 2012, the Center for Medicare and Medicaid (CMS) collaborated with commercial and state health insurance plans in seven U.S. regions in the comprehensive primary care (CPC) initiative that offered population-based care management fees and shared shavings opportunities to participating primary care practices. The CMS defined five comprehensive primary care functions to support population health management: (1) risk-stratified care management, (2) access and conti-

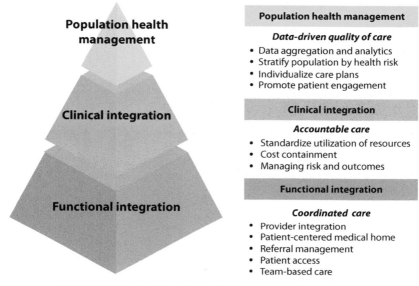

FIGURE 9.1 The building blocks of population health management

nuity, (3) planned care for chronic conditions and preventive care, (4) patient and caregiver engagement, and (5) coordination of care across the medical neighborhood.

These foundational components are reviewed and discussed in more detail in the following sections and include (1) data aggregation and analytics, (2) patient stratification by health risks into defined subgroups, (3) coordination of individualized healthcare plans, and (4) patient engagement.

DATA AGGREGATION AND ANALYTICS

Patient data aggregation can include clinical data sources from electronic health records, laboratory results, radiology results, other ancillary test reports, biometric screening results, and claims data (Figure 9.2). Other factors may influence and affect health outcomes to include demographics, social determinants, and behavioral health risk factors. Claims data are needed for a broader view of patients' use of health resources both within and outside their designated healthcare system. Self-insured employers are also including biometric screening parameters to track employee or beneficiary health trends. The use

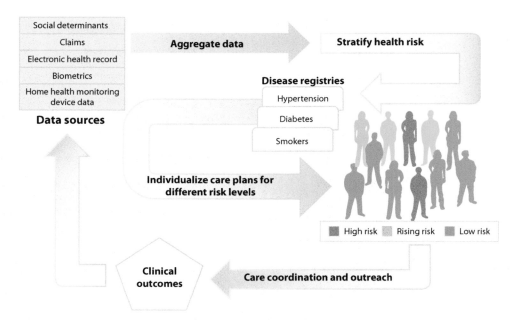

FIGURE 9.2 The mechanics of a population health management program

of biometric screening data to define the health risks for a population strategically informs the development of wellness programs and the matching of employees and beneficiaries to a primary care network.

After the data are aggregated, they can be stratified by health risk and segmented into chronic disease registries (diagnosis specific) or transitions in care registries (posthospitalization or post–skilled nursing facility). In this manner, data are utilized to identify patients who are at different risk levels for hospital readmissions or declines in health. Data analytics also defines the patients who are outliers in the use of healthcare resources, identifying patients who over- and underutilize health resources (gaps in care). Both are important in developing personalized care plans for each group. For overutilizers, a more intensive care-management approach with a 1:1 relationship with a nursing care manager may prevent readmissions. The typical ratio is one high-risk nursing care manager for 200 high-risk patients. A targeted outreach approach for patients who have increased health risks but are not engaged in their health may be appropriate for those who underutilize health resources. For example, the underutilizers may include a population that has not had evidence-based cancer screenings such as mammograms for breast cancer and colonoscopies for colon cancer. With outreach efforts and patient education to address patient concerns, prevention and early detection of cancer may be possible for the underutilizers. In population health management, there is an intentional focus on prevention and wellness to maintain the healthy segment of the population in a low-risk group.

A robust aggregation of patient data from multiple sources can also be used for predictive analytic models that predict which subset of patients are most likely to be readmitted in the future or which patients have the highest risk of developing poorly controlled disease. Predictive analytics can help target patient outreach efforts and personalized care plans to prevent poor health outcomes. Prescriptive analytic models are also being constructed to determine which patients are more likely to be nonadherent based on socioeconomic determinants and behavioral risk factors. The effective care plan for patients with the same chronic disease may vary based on the information from predictive and prescriptive analytics. For example, if social isolation and nonclinical factors such as food and housing challenges are not addressed, these factors could independently influence the health outcomes in chronic disease management. In addition, patients may be at different stages of readiness for change that may require a different approach with different goals of care.

PATIENT STRATIFICATION BY HEALTH RISKS INTO DEFINED SUBGROUPS

The population health pyramid is a stratification system of patients that places those at high risk at the top followed by the rising-risk and at-risk subgroups; the base of the pyramid comprises the largest group, those deemed low risk (Figure 9.3). High-risk patients at the top of the pyramid (usually high cost with complex comorbidities) account for approximately 5% of the total population. The rising-risk patient group—approximately 20% of a population— may have a behavioral risk or social determinant such as depression or poor health literacy that affects their chronic disease. The at-risk patient group is typically 40% of the population representing the predisease or borderline disease patients. The base of the population health pyramid is approximately the remaining 35%—healthy patients with no chronic disease or with controlled chronic disease.

The purpose of segmenting patients in these risk groups is to formulate individualized care plans for each subgroup with the most intensive interventions and the most use of resources reserved for the high-risk group. Population health managers who focus only on high-risk groups will not be able to lower

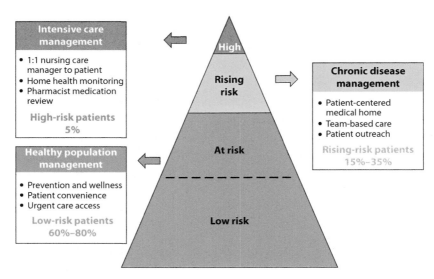

FIGURE 9.3 Populations health risks pyramid

those risks because approximately 20% of the rising-risk patients will become high-risk over the course of one year if these patients are not managed appropriately. The key to population health management is focusing on the coordination of individualized patient care plans for each risk group. When this type of integrated coordination of care is successful, it engages the patient and coordinates care plans with the primary care provider and other health team members.

We must go beyond the stratification of patient risk groups to understand why individual patients within a risk group are at a higher risk for failure of a care plan. Even within the high-risk patient subset, the number of reasons that could potentially place a patent at a higher health risk include the lack of a primary care provider, social determinants (health literacy level, lack of social support, unemployment, or other socioeconomic factors), behavioral risk factors (depression, anxiety, bereavement, etc.), and the lack of understanding of their health conditions with subsequent lack of engagement in their own health. Even within a population, it is important to dissect the barriers to healthcare within a subset to address and understand the drivers of outcomes. This type of comprehensive approach requires combining clinical data with nonclinical information in order to predict risk and to customize care plans with targeted resources directed to specific population subsets.

COORDINATION OF INDIVIDUALIZED HEALTHCARE PLANS

After defining patient health risk subsets, we can develop patient care plans matched to each risk level with more intensive management of high-risk groups and the appropriate delineation of resources for each subset. In many population health management programs, nursing care managers contact high-risk patients by the patient's preferred method of contact (i.e., telephone, text, e-mail) to help develop trusting relationships so they can understand the "why" for an individual in a high-risk group. The usual outreach ratio of high-risk nursing care managers to patients is 1 nurse to 200 high-risk patients. For rising-risk patients, the nursing care manager point of contact may be less frequent with the use of patient EHR portals or patient healthcare apps to engage patients with a less intensive approach. Rising-risk and at-risk patients are also managed within a patient-centered medical home model for a team-based approach to chronic disease management. A section of this chapter will be dedicated to PCMH because population health management is a core element of the PCMH model. The low-risk patients need a plan of care to accommodate wellness plans, prevention of disease, and convenient healthcare access when urgent unforeseeable medical issues arise. For the low-risk group, healthcare access is the key to decreasing the use of emergency departments and urgent care centers. The low-risk group needs to be linked to a primary care network to drive appropriate cancer and chronic disease screening and to provide access for urgent healthcare issues.

At Houston Methodist, our population health management strategy started with our own self-insured employees and beneficiaries in an effort to risk stratify and develop individualized care programs for diabetes, hypertension, and nicotine-dependent high-risk and rising-risk participants (Figure 9.4). One of the first lessons learned was that 47% of our employees and their beneficiaries did not have a designated primary care physician (PCP). This provided us with the opportunity to partner with the human resources (HR) department to assist in matching employees and their beneficiaries to our primary care network based on personal preferences. In addition, we partnered with our wellness department to develop programs specific to these populations at multiple hospital locations. Our physician population health partners were also asked

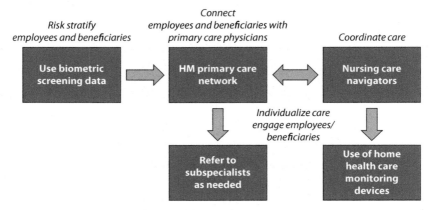

FIGURE 9.4 Houston methodist population health management program targets chronic disease management

to provide same-day access to our employees and their beneficiaries and were linked to our nursing care managers.

The Houston Methodist population health program contained three core elements for Houston Methodists' employees and beneficiaries that connected participants to our primary care network, wellness programs, and nursing care manager program for high-risk and rising-risk employees with diabetes, hypertension, or nicotine dependency. Participation was voluntary but supported by HR employee incentives. In addition, primary care physicians become physician population health partners to manage these participants if they agreed to quality initiatives providing same-day patient access, chronic disease management with the nursing care manager program, and home health monitoring devices. Communication was established between the participants, the nursing care managers, and the PCPs to support data-defined clinical goals and outcomes. Dashboards were created to exchange clinical data between patients' home health monitoring devices and the care management team to include the nursing care managers and primary care physicians.

PATIENT ENGAGEMENT

To increase the success of clinical outcomes, patient-engagement strategies are foundational to population health management. In the relationship between healthcare providers and patients, a shared decision making approach is not only

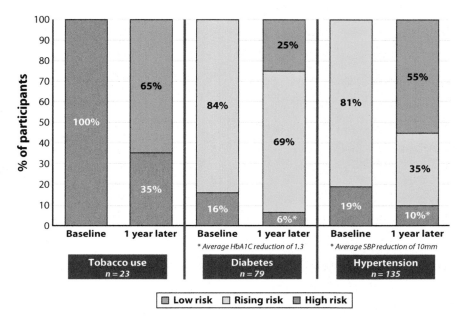

FIGURE 9.5 Comparison of 2014 and 2015 biometric data for participants who completed the population health pilot. Source 2014 and 2015 biometric data Houston Methodist San Jacinto population health pilot

patient centric but also care specific with an individualized plan. In population health management, patient-engagement tools have been developed with the use of game theory and interactive visuals to involve patients in their own health by tracking personal outcomes, peer groups, and rewards. Patient apps can interface with individuals and nursing care managers with the ability to send bulk messages to a population on a particular health issue. For established patients, the patient portal within the electronic health record can be used to target health reminders in bulk to a specific population. Patient apps and patient portals provide an asynchronous bidirectional form of communication that provides convenience to the growing population with smartphones. Even though technology plays an increasing role in patient engagement, the trusting relationship between high-risk patients and nursing care managers cannot be undervalued. Even when high-risk patients move to a lower-risk group, they usually want to continue the supportive relationship and coaching provided by a nursing care manager program. To manage resources in a population risk management program, a nursing care manager program should have clearly defined goals for the frequencies and types of patient interactions. In addition, there needs to be a method for graduating low-risk patients to a wellness program for health maintenance.

Home health monitoring devices can also engage patients in their health outcomes as well as export data to dashboards for management of these outcomes by nursing care managers in collaboration with primary care providers. A high-risk or rising-risk population can be managed between primary care visits by monitoring and intervening to influence health outcomes in real time based on exported patient data (e.g., blood pressure, blood sugar levels, and weight). Patients who may have experienced high blood pressures in their physicians' offices and thought they had "white coat hypertension" may realize for the first time that their blood pressure is equally high when they are at home sitting on the couch. This type of patient feedback can be eye-opening and can directionally change the course of health of an engaged patient. In our Houston Methodist population health management program, 74% of our high-risk and rising-risk employees and beneficiaries with home health blood pressure monitoring devices demonstrated normalization of blood pressures (Figure 9.6). With feedback from these devices, this group followed up with nursing care managers and their PCPs to achieve these outcomes. In addition, this group became engaged with their own health and wanted to keep these devices to maintain these outcomes.

Other patient-engagement strategies include web-based chat rooms where patients with the same diagnosis chat anonymously in patient groups to share and exchange information about their health. Some patients may be more comfortable with the traditional group meeting format with face-to-face discussions in their patient-centered medical home practices. Patient-engagement tools are customized to patient preference.

Clinical outcomes are more sustainable for chronic disease management if patients are engaged in their own health outcomes. Engaged patients also better understand their health issues and actively manage diet, physical activity, medications, and provider appointments. In addition, engaged patients are more aware of symptoms that can be communicated to a provider and often preempt a potential hospitalization or emergency department visit.

PATIENT-CENTERED MEDICAL HOME STANDARD: POPULATION HEALTH MANAGEMENT

The National Council for Quality Assurance (NCQA) recognizes and awards primary care practices who have met well-defined standards through an application process as patient-centered medical homes. The 2014 NCQA PCMH

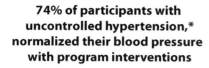

74% of participants with uncontrolled hypertension,* normalized their blood pressure with program interventions

55% of smokers who participated in the program stopped smoking

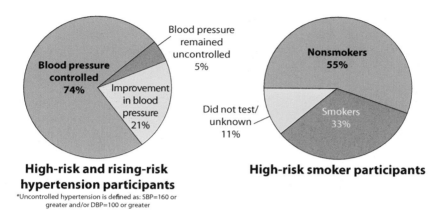

High-risk and rising-risk hypertension participants

*Uncontrolled hypertension is defined as: SBP=160 or greater and/or DBP=100 or greater

High-risk smoker participants

FIGURE 9.6 Houston Methodist population health program outcomes for hypertension and smoking cessation

guidelines have six standards; the third standard is defined as population health management. This NCQA standard sets the expectation that a primary care practice would use a comprehensive health assessment and evidence-based decision support based on complete patient information and clinical data to manage the health of its entire patient population.[2]

This population health management NCQA standard for PCMH recognition includes four healthcare domains: (1) prevention and screening, (2) chronic disease management, (3) immunizations, and (4) medication management. The NCQA population health management elements require the use of patient data to guide patient outreach efforts for at least two preventive care services. For example, the EHR can be queried to identify the appropriate population of women who have not had mammograms in order to target patient outreach efforts. This requirement also includes the use of patient data to identify the appropriate patient population for at least two immunization outreach efforts such as the zoster and pneumococcal vaccines. In addition, the NCQA also requires patient data to identify patients with chronic diseases who have been lost to follow-up in order to address any barriers to care and to schedule follow-up appointments. Patient data are also used to identify prescription refill gaps to address barriers to prescription refills (e.g., costs, side effects, health literacy). The population health management requirement for NCQA PCMH recognition advocates that primary care practices use patient registries and proactive patient reminders to address a variety of health needs in these four domains.

The other four elements outlined by the NCQA for the population health management standard are discussed as follows. The first element requires that a practice use an electronic system to record patient demographics, preferred language, dates of previous visits, legal guardian or health proxy, advance directives, primary caregiver, and other healthcare professionals involved in a patient's care. The second element requires the use of an electronic system to capture an up-to-date problem list, allergies, height, weight, body mass index, blood pressure, tobacco use history, family history, and a current list of prescription medications. Many of these requirements also meet stage 2's core meaningful use requirements. The third element requires that the practice updates a comprehensive health assessment so it can better understand the health risks and information needs of patients and families. Within this element, depression screening, health literacy, substance use history, communication needs, and cultural characteristics are captured to enrich the clinical data. The last element in the NCQA population health management standard emphasizes the importance of evidence-based decision support. This element requires that primary care practices implement evidence-based guidelines with clinical decision support such as point-of-care reminders for chronic and acute medical conditions, mental health issues (e.g., depression, anxiety, ADHD, dementia), or substance abuse issues (e.g., illegal drug use, prescription drug addiction, alcoholism). The practice is also required to use clinical decision support related to unhealthy behaviors such as obesity and smoking.

MEDICARE ADVANTAGE: A POPULATION HEALTH MANAGEMENT OPPORTUNITY

Medicare beneficiaries continue to grow and comprise an increasing proportion of a provider's population. CMS is already holding providers accountable for cost and quality of care with readmission penalties, value-based purchasing, and meaningful use. A strategy is needed to manage the cost and clinical outcomes of this growing population. Medicare Shared Savings Programs (MSSPs) for accountable care organization (ACO) performance yielded mixed financial results with only a quarter of ACOs earning a shared savings payment in the first performance year.[3] Medicare Advantage (MA) is a private health insurance option for Medicare beneficiaries. Most MA enrollees choose plans from health maintenance organizations or preferred provider organizations. These plans receive a capitated payment from CMS and can negotiate risk-based contracts with providers. Unlike MSSP, Medicare Advantage offers enhanced rewards with greater control over network providers. To succeed in this type of risk contracting, the infrastructure of population health management needs to be in place to include a comprehensive accessible primary care network, a strong management program to coordinate care, and the data infrastructure to guide outreach and clinical outcomes (Figure 9.1).

FUTURE SUSTAINABILITY AND SUPPORT FOR POPULATION HEALTH MANAGEMENT

In a relatively short span of time, population health management has captured the attention of accountable care organizations, clinically integrated networks, academic medical centers, public health agencies, primary care practices, corporate human resources departments, and healthcare systems. Population health management is flexible and can be adapted to all of the above structures based on how population health is defined. In addition, different payment models support population health management with an emphasis on the use of data to drive clinical outcomes and outreach. One challenge in this paradigm shift will be to accomplish improved clinical outcomes at a lower cost, which may require an extended period to realize.

Population health management requires the infrastructure of primary care network with sustainable access to primary care, the use of technology to aggregate, risk stratify data to affect clinical quality, and a coordinated patient care management program. These necessary components can each prove to be a challenge. With the current shortage of primary care providers, will PCPs be able to manage larger patient panel sizes in a team-based approach? How is patient engagement affected when a PCPs availability is reduced by an increasing patient panel size? Should collaborative partnerships with retail clinics be developed to enhance 24/7 patient access in this model of care? What is the role of virtual visits or telehealth in population health management? Does this strategy increase scalability? Duke University is creating a primary care leadership track to train physicians in leadership, community engagement, and population health so they have the skills to address population health needs.[4] This cultural shift from a traditional primary care model requires a new curriculum and infrastructure to support population health management.

Information technology (IT) tools and consulting services that support population health management are rapidly increasing. Currently, however, no single tool is satisfactory because one platform is needed for registry development, another tool is needed for risk stratification, and another tool is needed for care management documentation. Some IT tools accomplish predictive analytics, and some integrate behavioral risk factors and social determinants to enhance risk scoring. In this new science, we are still learning what the necessary components to maximize clinical outcomes are. New tools are still being developed to integrate and stratify the necessary elements necessary for population health.

One cornerstone of population health management is the individualized coordinated care plan for each risk segment of a population. Should care management services be outsourced or in-house to be scalable and effective? In this new territory, we have to define the most effective ratios of nursing care managers to patients for specific risk segments, the frequency of communication, and the preferred method of communication to drive outcomes. As the population increases, will it be financially sustainable to have large nursing care management programs for the continuum of health facilities for high-risk and rising-risk patients?

The business model for a population health management program may need to equate the savings from early chronic disease diagnosis, early cancer detection, and chronic disease prevention to realize gains. With increased outreach efforts and a focus on patient engagement, we expect to see an increase in outpatient visits and medication costs with a decrease in emergency department utilization and hospitalizations. In the short term, expenditures for the necessary infrastructure of a population health management program may exceed cost savings, which may not be realized until years later. Population health management also drives care to the most appropriate healthcare setting to save costs, which could be in conflict with maintenance of hospital volume in a fee-for-service payment model.

The shift to PMH may be especially challenging for academic health centers (AHCs). AHCs account for 6% of hospitals, 47% of organ transplants, 60% of level-one trauma centers, and 66% of burn unit.[5] These high-end AHC medical services have high fixed costs and incentivize patient volume in a fee-for-service payment model. The PHM disruption challenges AHCs in many ways, including shifting patient care to lower-cost outpatient settings, which can further affect the revenue of tertiary AHCs in the fee-for-service payment model. The disruptive forces of PHM could be mitigated by a new conceptual framework that includes new stratifications of health risks, innovation, community resources, and policy to demonstrate the added value of AHCs.[6] With this strategy, AHCs would be able to develop new metrics that could inform population health policy decisions and accountability for health outcomes.

Population health management has captured the interest of the healthcare community with a focus on lowering health risks and improving clinical outcomes at a lower cost. This team-based approach engages patients as core members of their healthcare teams. This paradigm for healthcare delivery has the potential to drive clinical outcomes with data, care coordination, and patient engagement. The Centers for Medicare and Medicaid Services may be a catalyst in supporting the development of population health with the CMS quality strategy, which aims to deliver higher-quality care and address social, behavioral, and environmental determinants of health.[7] Population health management could be a new frontier for managing risks, costs, and health outcomes but will require a shift in our current healthcare culture and our current payment models.

REFERENCES

1. Kassler JW, Tomoyasu N, Conway PH. Beyond a traditional payer—CMS's role in improving population health. *N Engl J Med.* 2015;372:109–111.

2. National Center for Quality and Assurance (NCQA). *Patient-Centered Medical Home 2014 Guidelines.*Washington, DC: National Center for Quality and Assurance; 47–60.

3. Gabriel S, Hasan H. *Why a Successful Population Health Strategy Must Include Medicare Advantage.* Health Care Advisory Board White Paper. 2014;3–11.

4. Sheline B, Tran AN, Jackson J, Peyser B, Rogers S, Engle D. The primary care leadership track at the Duke University School of Medicine: creating change agents to improve population health. *Acad Med.* 2014;89:1370–1374.

5. Stein D, Chen C, Ackerly, DC. Disruptive innovation in academic medical centers: balancing accountable and academic care. *Acad Med.* 2015;90:594–598.

6. Borden WB, Mushin AI, Gordon, JE, Leiman, JM, Pardes, H. A new conceptual framework for academic health centers. *Acad Med.* 2015;90:569–573.

7. Kassler WJ, Tomoyasu N, Conway PH. Beyond a traditional player—CMS's role in improving population health. *N Engl J Med.* 2015;372:109–111.

Healthcare Delivery Redesign

TEAM-BASED CARE

Nana E. Coleman
Alicia D. H. Monroe

Abstract

The presence of collaborative, high-reliability teams is the underlying component found in most favorable patient interactions, thriving medical systems, and healthy communities.

In this chapter, we propose a redesigned framework for team-based care that strengthens interactions between patients and providers, enhances acute care delivery and chronic illness management, supports the general health of populations, and results in reduced overall healthcare costs. We will further discuss the necessity of ongoing interprofessional training in patient-centered communication, values integration, and the teamwork that is essential for successfully actualizing this new model of team-based care.

Despite innovations in clinical practice and healthcare delivery, patients continue to suffer preventable adverse medical outcomes, feel disengaged from their providers and the medical process, and struggle with accessing quality healthcare.[1] We believe building a culture of teamwork and promoting team-based care is the greatest opportunity to enhance healthcare quality and safety, improve patients' care experiences, and foster communication and collaboration. We cannot expect to improve health outcomes, even in the face of scientific advancement, without a true commitment to improving the structure and function of healthcare teams. Through years of seminal work in quality improvement, we realize that the foundational element of most satisfying patient encounters,

128

successful medical systems, and healthy communities is the presence of collaborative, high-reliability teams.[2]

In the current era of transformative healthcare delivery, we propose a redesigned framework for team-based care that optimizes interactions between patients and providers, improves acute care delivery and chronic illness management, supports the general health of populations, and results in reduced overall healthcare costs—within the context of shared values and mutual respect between patients and their care providers.[3] Ongoing training in patient-centered communication[4] and teamwork using a variety of strategies—for example, simulation,[5–7] quality improvement and process redesign projects,[8] scheduled huddles and handoffs,[9] and debriefing with good judgment[10]—will be essential for implementing and sustaining this new model of team-based care.

HISTORICAL PERSPECTIVE: THE TRIPLE AIM

The origin of this proposed framework for healthcare delivery redesign lies within the Triple Aim, a paradigm defined by the Institute for Healthcare Improvement in 2008.[11] The Triple Aim outlines a strategic model for healthcare improvement that seeks to improve individual patient experience and population health at decreased per capita cost. We will first consider how improvements in clinical team performance have the potential to affect patient care, population health, and healthcare costs in the context of the Triple Aim.

Berwick et al further define five key components to the success of the Triple Aim: (1) macrosystem integration, (2) financial management, (3) population health management, (4) primary care redesign, and—perhaps the most important—(5) partnership with individuals and families. Although each domain is necessary for sustainable improvements in health outcomes, we believe that putting patients and families at the center of healthcare delivery facilitates safe, cohesive, and meaningful medical care experiences and shared decision making.[12] Hence, we direct our discussion toward an enhanced framework for team-based care aimed at integrating best evidence, enhancing patient care processes, and respecting patient values.[13]

Finally, as we consider models of best practice in team-based care, we acknowledge that gaps exist between the current trends in health professional education that primarily emphasize evidence-based practice as the catalyst for optimal care delivery and the proposed shift toward values-based practice as the principal paradigm on which clinical teams practice.

In the final section, we will consider interprofessional strategies for training the next generation of clinical teams and leaders to be guided not only by the science of medicine but also by the values that matter most to each and every patient they serve.

OPTIMIZING TEAM PERFORMANCE TO ENHANCE PATIENT EXPERIENCE, POPULATIONS, AND SYSTEMS

Enhancing the Patient Care Experience

Various disciplines have long recognized that patient-centered collaborative care models consider the patient to be at the core of the medical team; this results in enhanced patient satisfaction and may bring improved health outcomes.[14,15] When seeking to define what constitutes an "exceptional patient encounter," it is important to consider the following key elements of best practice in a model of patient-centered care:[16]

- Respect for patients' preferences, values, and needs
- Coordination and integration of care
- Clear communication, information, and education
- Attention to physical comfort
- Emotional support and management of fear and anxiety
- Appropriate involvement of family, friends, and caregivers
- Effective transitions of care and continuity
- Access to care

Cultivating these skills within clinical teams requires practice because although some of these behaviors are seemingly innate, if not used, they will not develop further.

Although patient satisfaction is increasingly cited as a catalyst for improving clinical team performance and as a central component of assessing healthcare quality across many clinical environments, the proactive engagement of patients and their families in the care process has other far-reaching benefits.[17,18] Countless medical errors are averted each year by family members who, as active team members, ask for and receive information about medications and treatments being administered to their loved ones. Similarly, historical clinical information from families is invaluable, particularly when a patient is unknown to the medical facility and care team. Family members and other caregivers thus must be considered along with the patient at the center of the medical team. Without this shared conceptual understanding, it becomes challenging for teams to form lasting and trustful relationships with their patients. True partnerships between patients, families, and the medical team are mutually rewarding. Patients and families who are actively engaged with the medical team are typically more satisfied with and less distrusting of the medical experience.

Patients wish to be respected, enabled, and engaged in the process of care delivery.[19] Among the primary goals of every healthcare encounter is to optimize the functional status and quality of life for every patient. By collaboratively engaging with patients and families, teams are better able to anticipate and overcome the barriers to attaining these goals. Similarly, when team-based care is focused on the patient, family and other caregivers, the transitions across zones of care are smoother and more cohesive. Given that active family engagement brings a consistent focus on the patient, it facilities a common mental model and shared goals even as patients traverse through the various aspects of the healthcare system. Likewise, patients throughout the continuum of care thrive in medical environments where their needs are both anticipated and met with the support of their families.

Well-functioning medical teams perform at their best when they seek to elicit a patient's values and align these beliefs with the goals of care. Although generally accepted standards of medical practice may guide much of their clinical decision making, it is equally important to integrate the preferences, expectations, beliefs, and concerns that each patient and family member brings to the medical encounter. Each patient's values are a product of his or her life experience, culture, education, and social circumstance; they cannot be separated from the individual. The ability to actively integrate patient values and expectations with scientific best practice represents a defining element of successful team-based care.

Improving Population Health

Beyond the clear value that consistently well-performing teams bring to the individual patient care experience, they also have tremendous benefit to communities at large. Although medical care is typically sought at the level of the individual, we recognize that the experience of illness and disease cannot be considered in a vacuum. Health promotion, public health, and disease prevention are deeply integrated with the individual health experience. The ability of clinical teams to leverage the science derived from public health and other social sciences to advocate for health promotion and disease prevention for each individual patient underlies our general health status as a society. Ultimately, it is this collective system that in many ways drives how, when, and to what standard individual patients are able to receive care.

Clinical teams also play a central role in facilitating both public and private partnerships that are designed to enhance community awareness, knowledge, and education. Through collaborative relationships with regulatory agencies, educational institutions, and governmental organizations, healthcare teams are often able to provide enhanced resources to individual patients and their families. The success of many public health campaigns such as "back to sleep" for the prevention of sudden infant death syndrome, breast cancer awareness and screening, and even influenza vaccination programs implicitly rely on clinical teams to guide patients toward the appropriate healthcare choices at every possible opportunity. To achieve the goal of better overall health for the community, clinical teams must be committed to strong interprofessional collaboration, remain adaptable in the face of evolving disease burdens and risks, and be willing to move away from the "silo" mentality that historically has driven much of medical care.[20]

In the current era of new and emerging threats to global health and life sustainability, perhaps in no previous time has the push to move from "cowboys to pit crews" been more fervent.[21] Teams that are aligned in their commitment to the benefits of preventive care, collective health risk reduction, and health security will ultimately have the greatest effect on reducing disease burden and minimizing public health risks.

Reducing Overall Healthcare Costs

Besides the value that high-performing clinical teams bring to patients, families, and populations, their value to healthcare systems is indisputable. Without organized and efficient teams, health systems become disorganized and unproductive; their performance, reputations, and bottom lines suffer. A well-functioning model for team-based care can serve to increase efficiency, generate revenue, and ultimately reduce costs for a healthcare system.

The potential reduction of per capita healthcare costs as influenced by the presence of high-reliability teams occurs across several spheres of the healthcare system. The factor that distinguishes organizations with a robust model of team-based care in place from their peers is neither the frequency nor magnitude of adverse events. Rather, the presence of a high-reliability team promotes the recognition, acknowledgment, and discussion of opportunities for improvement in patient safety and advancement of quality standards, even when the patient outcome is expected or not particularly negative. Teams that are at once versatile and resilient understand that often the best lessons learned are not from directly harmful events but from the near-miss occurrences that only by chance do not go on to directly affect the patient. The insights gained by teams from participation in critical event review, debriefings, and strategic team-building activities surrounding adverse events cannot be replicated.

The difference in cost savings and revenue between healthcare facilities with strong teams in place versus those without this asset can be significant.[22] For example, team structures that encourage a questioning attitude by all team members often exhibit fewer adverse events; as a consequence, fewer resources must be allocated toward paying for mistakes. With reimbursement for healthcare now tied to performance, the stakes for teams to "make the grade" are even higher. System resource use is more efficient when all stakeholders share common goals, have standard metrics by which to guide practice, and endorse a culture of continuous quality improvement. Teams that have built redundancy and adaptability into their structure are more resilient to the inevitable human factors that may challenge their success.

Successful teams continue to reap many rewards of their efforts both at individual and system-wide level. Performance incentives may help to encourage clinical team success, but sustainability is cultivated through consistent and frequent positive reinforcement. Formal reviews, debriefings and quality-improvement sessions highlight opportunities for change and advancement. Acknowledgment of both individual and group achievements promotes maintenance of the core principles of accomplished medical teams. Team members who are motivated and supported within their institutions are more likely to remain loyal and committed "investors" in the healthcare system.

SUMMARY

Clearly, teams matter.

They matter to patients and their families, to populations and communities, and to health organizations and systems. Having acknowledged the inextricable connection between team-based care and the foundational components of our current healthcare paradigm, we may find it instructive to consider what truly defines best practice in team-based care. We propose that an enhanced model of values-based practice will best meet the needs of individuals, communities, and systems alike.

A New Framework for Team-Based Care: Values-Based Practice

Values-based medicine as defined by Bill Fulford's formative work in this conceptual framework is a "skills-based approach to *consistently* and *intentionally* incorporate patients' values into clinical decision making alongside best research evidence; it is a process to guide balanced decision making where complex [or] conflicting values are involved." [23] What most resonates from this enhanced

FIGURE 10.1 High-functioning teams are essential to good care

conceptual framework for healthcare delivery are the concepts of informed choice; shared, value-driven decision making between patients, families, and clinical teams; and mutual respect. In essence, teams in this proposed model should seek to manage symptoms and disease such that each *patient's* goals for care are met.

Optimal team composition places the patient and family squarely in the center of the healthcare structure with various surrounding and complementary spheres of care. Direct bedside care providers, clinical consultants, ancillary caregivers, and spiritual advisors are all part of the patient's team; the core team includes those individuals identified by the patient as primary caregivers or decision makers when necessary. Key measures for a successful team driven by values-based practice would include patient satisfaction, accuracy of the values elicited, and health outcomes.

Effective communication that is timely, accurate, and based in best scientific practice can significantly optimize the work of values-driven teams and the patient care experience. Strategies that may help teams maintain proficiency in achieving these goals include periodic training and simulated skill sessions, routine and formal feedback systems from patients, and self-reflection opportunities.

Operationalizing values-based practice requires a multifaceted and systematic approach to healthcare delivery redesign. This paradigm of practice fundamentally serves to enhance awareness of and promote individual reflection on values while maintaining care delivery standards consistent with the best scientific evidence. Teams must ensure that patients know the risks and benefits associated with various treatment choices as their values and preferences are incorporated into the plan of care. Implicit within this is a clear delineation of the roles and responsibilities of both patients are care providers alike within the healthcare team. Similarly, patients should be equipped with comprehensible information that enables them to describe the potential risks and benefits associated with their treatment choices; they should be encouraged to articulate uncertainty and assured that their decisions may be changed. Clinical teams engaged in shared and balanced decision making with patients must assess and affirm comprehension, clarity, and alignment throughout the care encounter.

Four Key Insights for Value-Based Practice by Teams

From the framework presented here, four key guiding insights emerge as team-based care evolves to further incorporate the values of patients. As Table 10.1 shows, we propose the following ideals to underlie the transformative process of engaging clinical teams as active partners in the practice of values-based medicine.

"TEAM AS FAMILY, FAMILY AS TEAM" Traditionally, even in most models of patient-centered care, the medical team has considered patients and families either in parallel with or as *part* of the medical team. In this enhanced framework for values-based care, we propose that the patient and family be considered at the core of the care team. The patient and family together formulate the values, beliefs, and practices that theoretically guide the patient care experience. Because as individuals we are linked inextricably to the culture, faith, and values that have shaped our life experiences, it would be seemingly unnatural to separate individuals from this foundation at the time in life when they are most vulnerable—that is, during periods of illness. With the philosophy of "Team as family, family as team" the team becomes simultaneous with family. Although conflicts will inevitably arise when the patient and his or her own family members either have differences in values between themselves or with the medical team, it is imperative to remember that it is the *patient's* values that ultimately and invariably underlie the goals of care.

TABLE 10.1 Fundamentals of Value-Based Teams

Team as family, family as team.	• Care model moves to patient and family and caregivers as the core. • Patient can define his or her core team members. • Patient's values serve as the foundation for goals of care.
We strive to manage symptoms and disease so that "your" goals are met.	• Providers must acknowledge that a patient's values and goals of care may differ from their own. • Shared decision making and value elicitation are skills that must be taught. • Consensus may be challenging and conflicts may arise; strive to balance patient's values with best scientific practice.
Error-free practice is the goal, but identification and mitigation of potential risks are equally important.	• Event review methodology is familiar and uses root cause and failure mode analyses. • Enhancements are needed in developing language surrounding apologies and near misses.
To be successful, team-based training must focus on interprofessional methods of collaboration.	• Historically, education and team development occurred within disciplines; for teams to work, education must be applicable across the continuum of clinical team members. • Interprofessional collaboration is likely to be required across multiple facets of the healthcare team to maintain professional competency.

MANAGING SYMPTOMS AND DISEASE TO MEET THE PATIENT'S GOALS Healthcare providers must acknowledge that patient's values and goals of care often differ from their own. How then does a practitioner strive to not allow cultural, religious, educational, social, or other disparities in thought and belief to influence his or her perception of the healthcare delivery experience?

The skill of value elicitation must be taught. With the ability to elicit a patient's values, teams are better equipped to consider the goals of care in the context of these ideals. Recognizing that there is rarely a single approach to most medical problems, clinical teams can strive to both consider and offer alternative choices to patients. The ability to do so requires confidence, empathy, and a healthy awareness of one's own biases and preconceptions. Consensus may be difficult to achieve and conflicts may arise, but ultimately teams must strive to attain the best possible balance of patient's values with best scientific practice.

ERROR-FREE PRACTICE MAY BE THE GOAL, BUT IDENTIFICATION AND MITIGATION OF POTENTIAL RISK ARE EQUALLY IMPORTANT Even the most reliable and best-performing teams make errors. Although never desirable, unplanned events will occur because systems are not completely resilient against human factors. Performance improvement is now considered a standard component of the healthcare delivery process; in fact, many teams now function within a culture of continuous quality improvement. Critical event review and analysis make up an important aspect of improving the performance of clinical teams; however, further enhancements are needed in developing language surrounding apology and disclosure of near-misses. These are challenging tasks for many clinical teams. The admission of errors often evokes fear in practitioners because they are uncertain as to how patients and families will react.[24,25] Similarly, many would rather forget that those potential adverse events that never affected the patient even occurred because "no harm" was actually done. When clinical teams succeed in maintaining sincere relationships with patients and families, they engender a sense of shared trust, empathy, and compassion.[26] In a values-based culture of medicine in which patients often cite such values as integrity, honesty, and mutual respect as central to the care process, the importance of transparency cannot be underscored any further.

SUCCESSFUL TEAM-BASED TRAINING MUST FOCUS ON INTERPROFESSIONAL COLLABORA-TION METHODS Historically, team development and education has occurred within disciplines. We now realize that for teams to work well and sustainably, this education must be applicable across the continuum of clinical team members and delivered in a means that is accessible, no matter the role of any team member.[27] In a system of values-based medical practice, it should no longer be acceptable for physicians to learn only with physicians or for nurses to receive instruction only through their peers. As team-based care evolves, it is time for health professionals to develop mutual understanding and respect for the roles of colleagues and to direct this collective expertise toward a values-driven system of healthcare delivery.

EDUCATION AND TRAINING: THE NEXT GENERATION OF CLINICAL TEAMS

Having defined an ideal framework for the next era of healthcare delivery, we need to equip medical teams with the right tools and skills to achieve this desired model. We need innovative and strategic educational methods to engage the next generation of clinical teams and leaders. As previously noted, at the cornerstone of these initiatives are collaborative, interdisciplinary learning experiences with emphasis on commonalities in the shared goals of care delivery rather than on differences in specific roles and responsibilities.

Interprofessional education is likely to be required across multiple facets of healthcare training in order to maintain professional competency. When integrated throughout the educational experience for all healthcare providers, such collaborative initiatives become natural and sustainable. Early introduction of interprofessional methods of education encourages learners from the beginning of their health professional training to be sensitive to the roles of their peers, to develop strategies for managing conflict, and to leverage strengths and weaknesses effectively.[28] Teams that collaborate both in learning and in practice are more effective, efficient, and productive in their work. Recent literature demonstrates the successful integration of interprofessional education across various disciplines, including health ethics, mental health, and graduate medical education in surgery.[29–31]

Even if clinical teams receive sufficient integrated education to inform their structure, function, and performance, without effective communication skills, they cannot fully engage patients in the care delivery process. Excellence in patient-centered and values-based medical care depends on clear, informative, and respectful communication throughout the healthcare continuum. Successful execution of such interactions requires the following:[32]

- consideration of the patient as a "whole" person with values, beliefs, and opinions that must be incorporated into the care experience;
- exploration of the disease through the individual's experience of illness;
- use of open-ended questions and enhanced listening and negotiation skills; and
- active engagement and commitment to finding common ground.

Tools such as the "ideas, concerns, expectations" (ICE) and "strength, aspirations, resources" (STAR) mnemonics are instruments of communication that have the potential to enhance understanding and cooperation between clinical teams and patients when consistently integrated into practice.[33,34] When combined with a culture of balanced and shared decision making, these principles will afford patients the greatest satisfaction and outcomes of their healthcare experience.

Finally, as we consider how to guide teams toward more satisfying and functional healthcare delivery experiences, we must be prepared to consider how our personal values, fears, and biases might influence our care encounters. We must put the patient and family squarely in the center of our work and strive to actively engage with every patient, even when there are no obvious areas of commonality. Being in touch with our own beliefs enables us to care compassionately and empathetically for patients and their families. Promotion of self-introspection and self-awareness through activities such as narrative reflection, shared storytelling, and reminiscence therapy support the development of healthy and mutually satisfying care provider and patient relationships.[35]

CONCLUSION

The benefit of a values-driven model for team-based care to patients and families, populations, and health is certain. We know also that the presence of high-performing teams is vital to ensuring the highest-quality healthcare experience for every patient, every time. Patients thrive when they feel integrated in the process of care delivery, believe that their values matter, and know *their* goals of care are being met. Healthier patients lead to healthier communities, which in turn leads to decreased costs and lessened disease burdens. *How* we will collectively move clinical teams toward this enhanced framework of healthcare delivery will require proactive engagement, integration, and collaboration between patients, communities, and systems so we can realize our fullest potential in healthcare delivery and practice.

REFERENCES

1. Dzau VJ. An IOM in transition: seizing the opportunity to shape the future. President's Address, October 20, 2014.

2. Coleman NE, Pon S. Quality: performance improvement, teamwork, information technology and protocols. *Crit Care Clin.* 2013;29(2):129–151.

3. Fulford KW. Values-based practice: Fulford's dangerous idea. *J Eval Clin Pract.* 2013;19(3):537–546.

4. Levinson W, Lesser CS, Epstein RM. Developing physician communication skills for patient-centered care. *Health Affair.* 2010;29(7):1310–1318.

5. Gittell JH, Beswick J, Goldmann D, Wallack SS. Teamwork methods for accountable care: relational coordination and TeamSTEPPS. *Health Care Manag Rev.* 2015; 40(2):116–125.

6. Rosen MA, Hunt EA, Pronovost PJ, Federowicz MA, Weaver SJ. In situ simulation in continuing education for health care professions: a systematic review. *J Cont Educ Health Prof.* 2012;32(4):243–254.

7. Braddock CH, Szaflarski N, Forsey L, Abel L, Hernandez-Boussard T, Morton J. The transform patient safety project: a microsystem approach to improving outcomes on inpatient units. *J Gen Intern Med.* 2014;30(4):425–433.

8. Harrison MI, Paez K, Carman K, Stephens J, Smeeding L, Devers KJ, Garfinkel S. Effects of organizational context on lean implementation in five hospitals. *Health Care Manag Rev.* 2016 (advanced electronic publication).

9. Provost SM, Lanham HJ, Leykum LK, McDaniel RR, Pugh J. Health care huddles: managing complexity to achieve high reliability. *Health Care Manag Rev.* 2015; 40(1);2–12.

10. Rudolph JW, Simon R, Dufresne MS, Raemer DB. There is no such thing as "nonjudgmental" debriefing: a theory and method for debriefing with good judgment. *Simulat Health Care.* 2006;1(1):49–55.

11. Berwick DM, Nolan TW, Whittington J. The triple aim: care, health, and cost. *Health Affair.* (Millwood) 2008;27(3):759–769.

12. Elf M, Fröst P, Lindahl G, Wijk H. Shared decision making in designing new healthcare environments—time to begin improving quality. *BMC Health Serv Res.* 2015; 15(1):114.

13. Fulford KWM, Peile E, Carroll H. *Essential Values-Based Practice: Clinical Stories Linking Science with People.* New York, NY: Cambridge University Press; 2012.

14. Coleman N, Lambert S, Slonim A. Collaborative care for children: essential models for integrating and optimizing team performance in pediatric medicine. In: Salas E, ed. *Improving Patient Safety through Teamwork and Team Training.* New York, NY: Oxford University Press; 2013.

15. Stewart M, Brown JB, Donner A, McWhinney IR, Oates J, Weston WW, Jordan J. The impact of patient-centered care on outcomes. *J Fam Pract.* 2000;49(9):796–804.

16. Picker Institute. Principles of patient-centered care. Available at http:// pickerinstitute.org/about/picker-principles/.

17. Kleefstra SM, Zandbelt LC, Hanneke JCJM, Kool RB. Trends in patient satisfaction in Dutch university medical centers: room for improvement for all. *BMC Health Serv Res.* 2015;15:112.

18. Kocher R, Emanuel EJ, Deparle NM. The ACA and the future of clinical medicine: the opportunities and challenges. *Ann Intern Med.* 2010:153:536–539.

19. Levinson W, Lesser CS, Epstein RM. *Health Affair.* 2010;29(7):1310–1318.

20. Hunter D, Perkins N. Partnership working in public health: the implications for governance of a systems approach. *J Health Serv Res Pol.* 2012;17(suppl 2):45–52.

21. Gawande A. Cowboys and pit crews. *The New Yorker.* May 26, 2011.

22. Mundt MP, Gilchrist VJ, Fleming MF, Zakletskaia LI, Tuan WJ, Beasley JW. Effects of primary care team social networks on quality of care and costs for patients with cardiovascular disease. *Ann Fam Med.* 2015 Mar;13(2):139–148.

23. Fulford KW. Bringing together values-based and evidence-based medicine: UK Department of Health initiatives in the "personalization" of care. *J Eval Clin Pract.* 2011;17(2):341–343.

24. Bell SK, White AA, Yi JC, Yi-Frazier JP, Gallagher TH. Transparency when things go wrong: physician attitudes about reporting medical errors to patients, peers, and institutions. *J Patient Saf.* 2015. Available at http://www.ncbi.nlm.nih.gov/pubmed/25706909.

25. McLennan SR, Diebold M, Rich LE, Elger BS. Nurses' perspectives regarding the disclosure of errors to patients: a qualitative study. *Int J Nurs Stud.* 2014;pii: S0020-7489(14)00259-4.

26. Wu AW, Boyle DJ, Wallace G, Mazor KM. Disclosure of adverse events in the United States and Canada: an update, and a proposed framework for improvement. *J Public Health Res.* 2013;2(3):e32.

27. Kirch DG, Ast C. Interprofessionalism: educating to meet patient needs. *Anat Sci Educ.* 2014;8(4):296–298.

28. Hagemeier NE, Hess R Jr, Hagen KS, Sorah EL. Impact of an interprofessional communication course on nursing, medical, and pharmacy students' communication skill self-efficacy beliefs. *Am J Pharm Educ.* 2014;78(10):186.

29. Heath O, Church E, Curran V, Hollett A, Cornish P, Callanan T, Bethune C, Younghusband LJ. Interprofessional mental health training in rural primary care: findings from a mixed methods study. *Interprof Care.* 2015;29(3):195–201.

30. Poirier TI, Hecht KA, Lynch JC, Otsuka AS, Shafer KJ, Wilhelm MJ. Health professions ethics rubric: validation of reliability in an interprofessional health ethics course. *J Dent Educ* 2015;79(4):424–431.

31. Nicksa GA, Anderson C, Fidler R, Stewart L. Innovative approach using interprofessional simulation to educate surgical residents in technical and nontechnical skills in high-risk clinical scenarios. *JAMA Surg.* 2015;150(3):201–207.

32. Steward M et al. *Patient-Centered Medicine: Transforming the Clinical Method.* Oxon, UK: Radcliffe Medical Press; 2003

33. Matthys J, Elwyn G, Van Nuland M, Van Maele G, De Sutter A, De Meyere M, Deveugele M. Patients' ideas, concerns, and expectations (ICE) in general practice: impact on prescribing. *Br J Gen Pract.* 2009;59(558):29–36.

34. St. Catherine's College, Oxford. The Collaborating Centre for Values-Based Practice in Health and Social Care. Available at www2.warwick.ac.uk/fac/med/study/research/vbp/teaching/teaching_framework.pdf.

35. Schwartz M, Abbott A. Storytelling: a clinical application for undergraduate nursing students. *Nurse Educ Pract.* 2007;7(3):181–186;epub 2006 Aug 22.

Medicine Unplugged: Can M-Health Transform Healthcare?

Ju Young Kim
Steven R. Steinhubl

Abstract

In a surprisingly short period of time, the world has become enormously connected and mobile, and this force will be transforming healthcare into a connected mobile health environment with healthcare consumers at the center.

Unobtrusive sensing and wireless connectivity enable not only real-time remote health monitoring but also immediate diagnostic tools, resources, and services to patients at their point of need. Empowered patient online communities and crowdsourcing clinical trials are transforming traditional patients into actively engaged partners in health practice as well as advancements in science.

The current health system is facing large challenges of an aging population, the increasing prevalence of chronic disease, and acute outbreaks of infectious diseases. Re-engineering the health system so that it fully adopts mobile health—m-health—technologies will be one of the most powerful solutions to these challenges.

Extraordinary advancements in mobile technology and connectivity over the last decade have provided the foundation needed to transform the way healthcare is practiced. Through the combination of ever-greater personal computational capabilities, innovative biosensors, and advanced microanalytics, much of healthcare previously relegated to the physician's office or the hospital can now—or soon will—be carried out within one's own home or just around the corner at the local drug store. At the same time, the wide availability of virtual e-communities can foster healthcare consumers' literacy and deepen their knowledge and understanding of specific diseases, conditions, and treatment options.[1] These newly empowered consumers—sometimes referred to as *e-patients*—have the ability, skills, and willingness to manage their own healthcare. This allows them to become more engaged as equal partners with their doctors in the healthcare process. There is growing evidence that these more actively engaged patients have better health outcomes and incur lower costs.[2]

The World Health Organization (WHO) defines mobile health (m-health)[3] as "medical and public health practice supported by mobile devices, such as mobile phones, patient monitoring devices, personal digital assistants and other wireless devices." Key features that enable m-health to be the main enabler for transforming healthcare are the convergence of four pervasive technologies: unobtrusive sensing, wireless connectivity, cloud computing, and social networking. Re-engineering the practice of medicine to take full advantage of these technologies can lead to a new healthcare ecosystem with healthcare consumers at the center.

In this chapter, we will provide a snapshot of a representative selection of m-health tools directed toward the healthcare consumer that are now or soon will be available. We highlight the remarkable capabilities these innovative technologies can bring to individuals to improve their awareness and engagement in their own health and wellness. By doing so, we aim to provide the basis for a vision of a new clinical paradigm that is focused first and foremost on the individualized needs of healthcare consumers.

M-HEALTH TECHNOLOGIES SHAPING THE FUTURE OF MEDICINE

Wireless Body Network Systems

The term *wireless body sensor network* (WBSN)[4] or wireless body area network is used to describe a network of devices connected wirelessly for communication on, in, and near the human body. The WBSN[5] facilitate continuous health monitoring of physiologic parameters and provide real-time feedback. This can enable improved diagnosis, modification of treatment, rehabilitation, and early detection of life-threatening events. With the advance of technology, WBSN can smartly sense, process, and communicate with sensor devices of all makes.

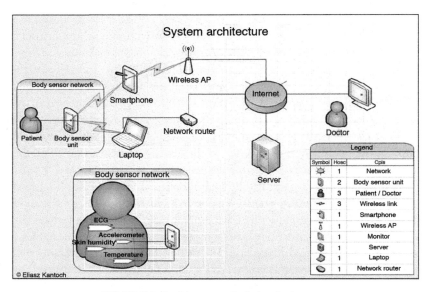

FIGURE 11.1 Architecture of wireless body sensor

Body sensor networks can be implantable or wearable, measuring different physiological parameters in a comfortable and user-friendly manner to monitor health status.

The combination of wireless body sensor networks with computing and artificial intelligence research[6] has a great potential for transforming healthcare. Wireless body sensor network systems can help monitor physiologic signals, daily activities, and behaviors in multiple chronic conditions, as well as respond to important acute changes in individuals or their environment. It carries the promise of improved quality of care across a wide variety of healthcare applications: screening, diagnosis, treatment, rehabilitation, and bi-directional communications.

Sensors may be worn on or even implanted in the body. They also can be embedded in furniture, rugs, television screens, and other parts of a patient's house. The ideal system of sensors is passive and as unobtrusive as possible. Other important characteristics are portability, low cost, low power, and high performance sensing that can be integrated through many types of wireless communication modes.[7] Another key characteristic of the most promising sensors is their ability to seamlessly track and transfer monitored biometric data into an actionable and informative data display that can be shared with a healthcare provider or others in a concise and meaningful manner.

TYPES OF SENSORS Biosensors[8] can be categorized into six different diagnostic types, depending on their use and physical location:

1. **Noninvasive sensors** use electromagnetic radiation to "see inside" or use smartphones or other connected devices to capture motion and activity.
2. **Electrochemical sensors** are used to analyze fluids outside the body such as sweat and saliva.
3. **Transcutaneous sensors** are devices placed on the skin that measure heart rhythms or many other important types of data.
4. **Ingested sensors** such as pills are swallowed to measure internal body temperature or visualize the colonic mucosa.
5. **Wearable sensors** can be incorporated into clothing such as hats, shirts, wrist bands, watches, glasses, or shoes.[8]
6. **Implanted sensors** are surgically implanted in the body and use near field communication (NFC) and medical body area networks.

WHEN AND HOW SENSORS ARE USED When monitoring health, sensors measure vital signs such as temperature, heart rate, blood pressure, blood oxygen saturation, and respiration. In addition, they can produce electrocardiograms (ECGs) and electroencephalograms (EEGs). These measurements can then undergo real-time processing and feedback to the wearer or medical staff and provide alerts when appropriate.

ACTIVITY MONITORING Currently, the greatest numbers of sensors have been developed in support of personal wellness. More than a dozen different monitors are commercially available to accurately quantitate activity; all of them work using fairly similar technology—a three-axis accelerometer that allows motion and sometimes its intensity to be sensed, reported, and tracked. Previous studies show that tracking step counts can lead to significant increases in daily activity, at least in the short term.[9] Activity monitors can also be used as individualized guidance in a variety of disease states as a real-world equivalent to a six-minute walk test. For example, activity monitoring can help guide safe hospital discharge following surgery.[10]

STRESS MEASUREMENT An especially innovative area of sensor development is the technology to track stress and anxiety levels through various measures of autonomic nervous system function. For example, electrodermal activity (EDA), a sensitive measure of sympathetic nervous system activity, can be

FIGURE 11.2 Wireless sensors collecting physiologic data to study mediation's effect

tracked long-term with wearable sensors.[11] An even wider variety of sensors are able to analyze and track heart rate variability (HRV), which is indicative of primarily parasympathetic or vagal tone.[12] Options for long-term tracking include adhesive patches that can be worn for days to weeks as well as wrist bands, shirts, and headbands that can be worn daily or as desired to monitor and report situational changes in HRV or EDA over time. With an unconscious stress response likely playing an underappreciated role in multiple mental and physical pathophysiologic states, having the capability to objectively monitor emotional status can allow individuals to discover and implement the tools best suited for them to minimize unhealthy responses to daily stressors.[13]

SLEEP MONITORING Disorders of sleep, especially obstructive sleep apnea, are increasingly common conditions that are underdiagnosed and thus ineffectively treated.[14] To allow individuals to better understand their sleep patterns and recognize potential issues, several home-based devices have been devised to track sleep quality.[15] Many activity monitors transmit via accelerometer actigraphy data to smartphones to report basic sleep metrics such as total sleep time, sleep latency, and awakenings; some devices derive a measure of "sleep quality" based on movements. Other simple and wearable devices with additional sensors have been compared favorably to polysomnography in their ability to identify the duration of various sleep stages such as rapid eye movement and light and heavy sleep.[16] Studies are underway to help demonstrate the best role for individual sensors or combinations of sensors in diagnosing and addressing sleep disorders.

CARDIOVASCULAR DISEASE A large number of mobile health devices have been developed to identify, track, and transmit details on multiple manifestations of cardiovascular disease and their risk factors. Although home blood pressure monitoring is not unique, several new devices build on their proven albeit minimal efficacy by allowing automated tracking and real-time connectivity with providers. This ability to foster improved patient engagement has been found to improve blood pressure control well beyond home monitoring alone.[17] Wearables that noninvasively but continuously track blood pressure are already approved for inpatient use.[18] Using similar technologies designed for the outpatient setting will substantially improve our understanding of hypertension, its individual variability, and eventually its optimal treatment for any individual.

Detecting infrequent symptoms that are potentially secondary to dysrhythmias as well as screening for asymptomatic but clinically important heart rhythms are especially well suited tasks for mobile sensor technology. Depending on the clinical need, wearable patch sensors can passively record a single-lead ECG for up to two weeks, shirts can track and record three-lead ECGs, and smartphone-connected devices that can record and transmit a 30-second rhythm strip whenever needed. Studies have found long-term monitoring to be more effective than 24-hour Holter monitoring in identifying arrhythmias.[19] Intermittent ECG screening can be done by no more than holding a smartphone; this has been found useful in identifying previously unrecognized atrial fibrillation.[20]

RESPIRATORY DISEASE The use of mobile health device can completely transform the care of individuals with respiratory diseases. Respiratory rate and activity levels can be tracked in real time during daily activities to help patients and providers identify potential early signs of exacerbations.[21] More specific evidence of changes in pulmonary function can be tracked at home with simple handheld spirometers, or potentially in the future by merely exhaling into the microphone of a standard smartphone.[22] When this information is overlaid on

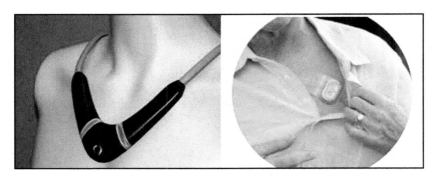

FIGURE 11.3 Multisensor device monitoring blood pressure, heart rate, and ECG

environmental data such as allergen counts and air quality, triggers can be identified. In addition, data from a population of users with these sensors can allow public health officials to collect real-time epidemiologic data to help better recognize and minimize controllable exposures.

MEDICATION ADHERENCE Many wireless solutions have been developed to address medication adherence.[23] Some are as simple as apps that allow for easier prescription refills, including automated reminders of when to do so, whereas other solutions include sensors embedded into medicine bottle caps or pill boxes that can remind, track, and report whether a medication was taken when scheduled.[24,25] The most technologically sophisticated solution that can be especially useful when a complete and continuous course of a medication is especially critical involves an ingestible and nearly invisible sensor embedded into the medication. Once activated in the acidic stomach environment, the sensor transmits a signal that confirms its ingestion, allowing for tracking and documentation of adherence.[26]

REHABILITATION Movement and activity patterns recordings using accelerometers, magnetometer-based apps, and photographic-based apps can be used for rehabilitation in knee injury.[27] Also a "SMART" arm[28] that provides functional electric stimulation of muscles can be used to improve the paralyzed arm after a stroke. Implantable devices can restore function after paralysis by bypassing damaged regions of the nervous system,[29] helping patients regain essential functions.

A wide range of other sensor technologies are available or are being developed to address almost every medical need. The very first mobile sensor technology deployed to improve patient outcomes—glucose monitoring—will be transformed from the need for repetitive, uncomfortable fingersticks to continuous noninvasive monitoring through wearables as unique as contact lenses.[30,31] Another range of wearable electrochemical sensors and biosensors has been developed for real-time noninvasive monitoring of electrolytes and metabolites in sweat, tears, and saliva as indicators of health status.[32] Measuring sweat makes it possible to collect rich information about the physiological condition of the person and could have a big impact on the field of sports and human performance as well as open new fields of research in the clinical setting.[33] Other sensors are available to track subclinical head trauma for sports and military use,[34] to measure gastrointestinal function,[35] track maternal–fetal wellness, or determine hemoglobin levels noninvasively.[36] These novel sensor technologies, and dozens of others not discussed here, are just the beginnings of personalized health solutions that can be enabled through the incorporation of mobile technologies into routine care.

Point-of-Need Testing

The processing power and connectivity made available from smartphone technologies allows for a wide range of testing to be taken out of the lab and brought directly to the individual. The combination of microfluidic (devices and processes that require just nano- or picoliter volumes of fluid) and microelectronic technologies allow for the digitization of sampled sweat, blood, saliva, urine, tears, breath, and more. These diagnostic capabilities go well beyond just improved convenience of testing. Rather, they offer the potential of entirely new diagnostic testing that also happens to be accessible virtually anytime, anywhere.

The ability to rapidly and reliably identify infectious pathogens in the home or community has remarkable healthcare implications. For example, point-of-care diagnostics of upper respiratory tract pathogens could substantially minimize the need for an acute office visit for cold symptoms, which is currently the most common reason for an urgent medical appointment.[37,38] Multiple mobile technologies are under development that utilize microfluidics to allow for portable pathogen diagnostics for a wide range of diseases that can aid in rapidly accelerated individual diagnostics and population screening.[39] Smartphone-linked mobile genetic diagnostics can enable rapid, accurate point-of-care diagnosis of a range of pathogens, along with future applications in multiple areas where rapid genetic diagnostics such as pharmacogenomics would be of benefit.[40,41]

The development of "electronic noses" that can be linked to smartphones also offer remarkable diagnostic abilities for a vast array of conditions.[42] Otherwise undetectable changes in skin odors or exhaled breath content can be actively sampled or passively collected when a patient talks on the smartphone, thus allowing noninvasive screening and detection. Using various technologies, extremely minute changes in volatile organic compounds can be identified that may prove to be the distinct signature for a pathologic state.[43] These changes can be used to identify the presence of infectious diseases[44] or to identify ketosis during fat burning that could help guide food intake in individuals attempting to lose weight.[45] In addition, markers in exhaled breath can aid in the identification of early signs of exacerbated chronic conditions such as heart failure and reactive airway disease.[46,47] Perhaps even more exciting is the possibility of using breath analysis to noninvasively screen for various cancers, therefore allowing individuals to forgo harmful radiation exposure or procedures such as colonoscopies.[48,49]

Once limited to specialized laboratories, many diagnostics tests can now be accomplished outside the routine healthcare setting when microfluidic technology is coupled with the optical capabilities found on smartphones. Micropatterned paper diagnostic tools can be used to diagnose thyroid-stimulating hormone (TSH), liver enzyme, protein, and cholesterol abnormalities from fingerstick blood, as well as a range of urinary, sweat, and salivary diagnostics with the smartphone camera for image capture and optical diagnostics.[50–53] Environmental toxins, food pathogens, and more can also be detected using the camera as a spectrometer, allowing for mobile biodetection nearly anywhere.[54]

Handheld ultrasound equipment, some directly connected to smartphones or tablets, can have a transformative impact on routine practice within and outside the hospital setting. Some medical schools are starting to teach students to use pocket ultrasounds as part of their routine physical exams.[55]

Cameras are among the most popular tools built into mobile phones. The high quality of smartphone lenses and their screen resolution allow their optical systems to be used for a wide range of medical applications, from medical-grade imaging to photometric diagnostics.

Eye health, especially visual impairment, is an area of tremendous need worldwide and one in which mobile, smartphone-based solutions could have a tremendous impact. An estimate of more than 700 million individuals worldwide are forced to live with uncorrected refractive errors.[56] One technology developed at the Massachusetts Institute of Technology allows for automated determination of refractive error just by having an individual look through a lens attached to a smartphone. By using the camera and flash, pediatric photoscreening for detecting amblyopia risk factors can be reliably carried out in large cohorts.[57] Other technology can turn a smartphone into an ophthalmoscope that allows for the diagnosis of retinal pathology remotely by the capture and transmission of images.[58]

Innovative designers have used smartphone optical systems to enable a wide range of other mobile medical-imaging instruments. Home diagnostics of inner ear infections are possible through a smartphone case with a scope attachment that allows the capturing and sharing of images.

Simplified, mobile cancer screening using smartphone-based systems can bring lifesaving care virtually anywhere. One such technology being studied is a smartphone-based multimodal colposcopy for cervical cancer identification.[59] Also, a screening tool developed at Stanford allows for panoramic imaging of the oral cavity with blue fluorescent light that highlights cancerous oral lesions. Another innovative design for a docking system provides for the coupling of a smartphone with most modern endoscopes.[60] By making the smartphone an integral component of all of these screening tools, health workers with focused training would be able to screen large populations in remote areas and transmit images for expert review.

Furthermore, early diagnosis of critical health changes could enable the prevention of fatal events. So point-of-care systems are expected not only to act as data collectors but also to automatically discover problem using advanced information algorithms.

PATIENT ONLINE COMMUNITY AND CROWDSOURCED CLINICAL TRIALS

The PatientsLikeMe[61] social networking platform, which has some 300,00 users with more than 2,300 different conditions, uses a crowdsourcing approach to elicit consumer's feedback and provide practical information. The company also has built a research exchange through which patients, clinicians, and researchers can collaborate to develop measures of patients' experiences and outcomes as drawn directly from patient reports. CureTogether is another example of a patient online community, recently acquired by 23andMe a personal genetics testing company, providing a combined genetic and phenotypic research platform.[62] Crowdsourced health research studies[63] illustrate how the convergence of citizen science, crowdsourcing, smartphone health applications, and personal health records can come together in innovative ways to advance our knowledge of health sciences. This type of participatory research model is becoming part of the public health ecosystem, with its rapid growth facilitated by the Internet and social networking influences.[64]

AUGMENTED REALITY AND VIRTUAL REALITY

Augmented reality[65] is a real-time view of a real-world environment that is enhanced by computer-generated sound, video, graphics, GPS data, and other inputs. Receiving information via devices such as Google Glass and digital contact lenses could improve the practice of medicine.

Some surgeons are already using Google Glass to stream their operations online, float medical images in their field of view, and hold video consultations with colleagues as they operate.[66] One exploratory study[67] found that wearing Google Glass throughout the day was well tolerated, although another study found that it caused a blind spot.[68] Hands-free photo and video documentation, making hands-free telephone calls, looking up billing codes, and Internet searches for unfamiliar medical terms were rated as useful applications.[69] Google Glass may also be a promising technology for augmented-reality disaster-response support to increase operators' performance, helping them make better choices in the field. The technology also represents an excellent option for professional education.[70]

Virtual reality (VR)[71] is a computer-simulated environment that can simulate physical presence in places in the real world or imagined worlds by re-creating sensory experiences, which include virtual taste, sight, smell, sound, and touch. Use of VR in a therapeutic role has been implemented in the treatment of various anxiety disorders,[72] in stroke rehabilitation, and in pain control. Recently, VR on mobile phones was shown to help reduce anxiety in outpatient surgery as well.[73] Use of VR in healthcare is expected to grow as it becomes more widely available.

M-HEALTH AND THE REVOLUTION OF HEALTHCARE DELIVERY

Health Consumers at the Center of the System

We are in a period of unique convergence with ubiquitous Internet availability, mobile devices, and social resources that can combine to provide the most disruptive set of factors to ever affect the provider–consumer relationship. Health consumers want to use mobile technology to better manage their healthcare and improve their access and connectivity to their health providers. According to one m-health roadmap,[74] health consumers can and should be involved in every aspect of their care—seeking information, accessing care, receiving care, selecting follow-up care, and managing their personal health and wellness—and they have the power to make their own care choices through every stage in the care continuum.

With an aging population, caregivers—including family members, friends, live-in nurses, and assisted living facilities—are more likely than others to use online social tools to acquire health-related information and are more active health consumers. Mobile technology and social media enable health consumers to seek out the levels of empowerment, convenience, and control that best fit their personal preferences. Health consumers will use mobile technology to seek healthcare information with more convenient tools that consolidate health information resources to help them better manage their healthcare. Those mobile tools will be offering symptom checkers, disease and medical condition information, emergency room wait times, physician and healthcare facility information, personal health records, healthcare cost information, and so on. These will all be linked to the next levels of action such as making appointments and accessing lab results.

In the future, health consumer's daily interactions with the healthcare system can be more simplified and straightforward and enabled by mobile technology, wireless unobtrusive sensors, and cloud computing embedded with real-time meaningful data analytic tools. Health consumers will have full access to their clinical and cost data through devices that provide meaningful feedback to them at the right place and the right time. They can take care

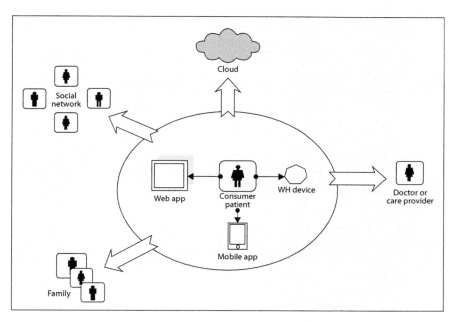

FIGURE 11.4 Wireless health ecosystem

of health tasks, self-support their behaviors, and be supported by family, friends, and social network systems. Healthcare providers are able to eliminate nonproductive parts of their current work and focus more on spending time with health consumers, helping them when they are sick, and coaching and educating them to get and stay healthy.

CHRONIC NONCOMMUNICABLE DISEASE

Chronic noncommunicable diseases (NCDs)[75] accounts for almost 60% of global mortality; 80% of deaths from NCDs occur in low- and middle-income countries. The major causes of NCD-attributable mortality are cardiovascular disease, cancer, chronic respiratory disease, and diabetes. These conditions share common behavioral risk factors, including diet, physical activity, smoking, and alcohol consumption. If the major risk factors for NCD were eliminated, around 75% of heart disease, strokes, and type 2 diabetes would be prevented, as would 40% of cancers.[75]

More than 9 million of all deaths attributed to NCDs occur before people turn 60, and they affect men and women equally as well as their dependents. Unlike acute episodic care, chronic NCDs can only be managed by reaching patients where they live; patients have to take responsibility and be actively engaged in their disease management. Mobile health can be a bridge that connects patients to healthcare providers through real-time monitoring, educational apps, and symptom trackers. Empowering health consumers with NCDs to better manage their health has been shown to prevent complications, improve outcomes, and reduce medical costs as well.[76,77] Sensors can create a stream of highly actionable clinical data by readily available cloud-embedded analytic tools, ranging from glucose monitoring and heart monitoring to asthma tools. Mobile health platforms offer new ways for patients to stay connected to clinicians and bridge barriers to adherence by delivering educational support and accessing real-time compliance regardless of physical distance. Many m-health tools also enable patients to get involved in online communities and get feedback by peer-to-peer interaction to help them manage their conditions and change behaviors.

Mobile healthcare can be a solution in lowering healthcare costs as well. One study has shown the possibility that e-health users had lower medical expenditure on lifestyle-related illnesses.[78] Mobile health technologies empower healthcare providers to improve engagement by prioritizing and setting patient-centered goals that allow patients to build sustainable health improvement.

ACUTE COMMUNICABLE DISEASE

Outbreaks of communicable disease often begin in pockets; when left unde-tected or undertreated, they can develop into epidemics. Disease- and epidemic-tracking m-health applications are being used in Peru, Rwanda, and India as early warning systems, allowing public health officials to monitor the spread of infectious diseases.[79] Wireless devices with mobile phones have been used when SARS (severe acute respiratory syndrome)[64] hit the world in 2002. Several tech-nology solutions were developed from a temperature-monitoring program in healthcare workers, as well as a service from a mobile phone operator that alerted subscribers if they were near buildings where cases of SARS had been documented.

Following the recent devastating outbreaks of Ebola in western Africa, trials are now using wearable health sensors, wireless vital sign monitoring platforms, and advanced analytics technology to monitor and analyze multiple vital signs

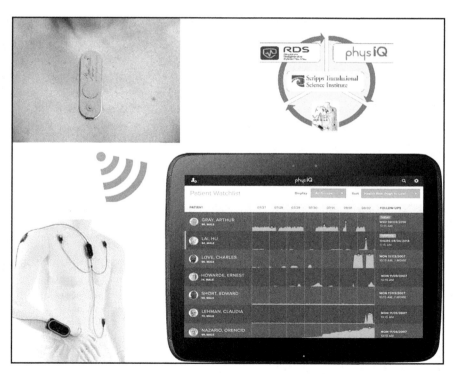

FIGURE 11.5 STAMP program

of patients either suspected or confirmed to be infected with the Ebola virus. This trial will be another step in transforming healthcare delivery in cases of acute infectious disease to identify warning signs early on when potentially life-saving care can be provided.

MOBILE TECHNOLOGIES FOR DEVELOPING COUNTRIES

People in the developing world have plentiful access to mobile phones even when other technologies and health infrastructure are scarce. This explosion of mobile phone usage has the potential to improve health service delivery on a massive scale. A growing number of developing countries are using mobile technology to address health needs.[79] The m-health field is remarkably dynamic, and the range of applications being designed is constantly expanding. The key applications for m-health in developing countries are as follows.

- *Education and awareness:* Short message service (SMS) texting offers a cost-effective, efficient, and scalable method of providing services for a wide array of health issues. SMS alerts have proven particularly effective in targeting hard-to-reach populations and rural areas where the absence of clinics, a lack of healthcare workers, and limited access to health-related information all too often prevent people from making informed decisions about their health. An SMS campaign promoting HIV and AIDS awareness resulted in nearly a tripling of call volume to a local HIV and AIDS helpline in South Africa. Also, an SMS-based HIV and AIDS awareness quiz led to an increase of 40% in the number of people coming in for free testing in Uganda.
- *Remote monitoring:* Monitoring patients at home for chronic conditions dramatically improves survival rates. And mobile phones are also used to increase medication adherence for diabetic patients, tuberculosis patients, and HIV patients.
- *Communication and training for healthcare workers:* Shortages of healthcare workers are a major challenge facing the health sectors in developing countries. Connecting health workers with sources of information via mobile technology is a strong basis for empowerment.

CONCLUSIONS

In a surprisingly short period of time, the world has become enormously connected and mobile. Monthly digital mobile traffic now exceeds an exabyte (a quintillion bytes or a billion gigabytes); in 2016, it is predicted to grow ten-fold.[80] Yet the mobile health environment is still in its early stages of development. A large number of innovative individuals, universities, and companies are focused on developing new technological solutions to address existing healthcare needs or refining proven technologies from the non-healthcare sector into new and powerful tools to help promote health and wellness. Most of the m-health technologies discussed here will likely seem as antiquated in several years as the early "brick" mobile phones do today. Mobile health technologies will continue to evolve and expand as the current generation of technologies is incorporated into a variety of existing and new systems of care.

Although there is tremendous interest and growth in m-health technology, its meaningful and evidence-based incorporation into clinical practice represents a much more nuanced challenge. Incremental incorporation of m-health into routine care is unlikely to be successful and will certainly not allow its full potential to be achieved. Instead, a near total re-engineering of healthcare that mandates a visionary collaboration between payers, providers, governments and industry is required. Unfortunately, *consumerism* is a term neither frequently taught in medical training nor emphasized in practice. And because m-health is at its core directed toward the healthcare consumer, its incorporation into current systems of care is far from straightforward. Empowering patients with their own medical data reverses the mostly one-way dynamic of today's healthcare system and instead places consumers at the center of their own care. Beyond convenience, m-health can help redefine the definition of what is considered normal: from a population-based perspective of comparing one individual to thousands of others to a time-based perspective comparing an individual to him- or herself prior before a symptom or sign appears.

TABLE 11.1 M-Health: A Rapidly Emerging Global Market

Headline	Source
Medical app revenues to grow 25% annually	MobiHealthNews, June 14, 2012
Global mobile health market worth $8 billion by 2018	MobiHealthNews, April 16, 2012
Global wireless health market forecast to reach $38.51 billion by 2016	Fast Market Research, April 13, 2012
Global revenue for m-health apps reaches $1.3 billion in 2012	Research2Guidance, January 25, 2012
44 million health app downloads in 2012	MobiHealthNews, November 30, 2011
13,000 iPhone consumer health apps in 2012	MobiHealthNews, September 22, 2011

REFERENCES

1. Meehan TP. Transforming patient to partner: the e-patient movement is a call to action. *Connecticut Med.* 2014;78(3):175–176.

2. Greene J, Hibbard JH, Sacks R, Overton V, Parrotta CD. When patient activation levels change, health outcomes and costs change, too. *Health Affair.* 2015;34(3):431–437.

3. WHO Global Observatory for eHealth. *New Horizons for Health through Mobile Technologies: Based on the Findings of the Second Global Survey on eHealth.* New York, NY: WHO Press; 2011.

4. Hao Y, Foster R. Wireless body sensor networks for health-monitoring applications. *Physiol Meas.* 2008;29(11):R27–56.

5. Kantoch E, Augustyniak P, Markiewicz M, Prusak D. *Monitoring Activities of Daily Living Based on Wearable Wireless Body Sensor Network.* Conference proceedings. Annual International Conference of the IEEE Engineering in Medicine and Biology Society. IEEE Engineering in Medicine and Biology Society. Annual Conference. 2014;2014: 586–589.

6. Darwish A, Hassanien AE. Wearable and implantable wireless sensor network solutions for healthcare monitoring. *Sensor.* 2011;11(6):5561–5595.

7. Kumar P, Lee SG, Lee HJ. E-SAP: Efficient-strong authentication protocol for healthcare applications using wireless medical sensor networks. *Sensor.* 2012;12(2): 1625–1647.

8. What's Next Workgroup. What is the role of biosensors in next generation health care? 2014. Available at http://www.himss.org/ResourceLibrary/genResourceFAQ.aspx ?ItemNumber=35996.

9. Bravata DM, Smith-Spangler C, Sundaram V, et al. Using pedometers to increase physical activity and improve health: a systematic review. *JAMA.* 2007;298(19): 2296–2304.

10. Cook DJ, Thompson JE, Prinsen SK, Dearani JA, Deschamps C. Functional recovery in the elderly after major surgery: assessment of mobility recovery using wire-less technology. *Ann Thorac Surg.* 2013;96(3):1057–1061.

11. Poh MZ, Swenson NC, Picard RW. A wearable sensor for unobtrusive, long-term assessment of electrodermal activity. *IEEE T Bio-Med Eng.* May 2010;57(5):1243–1252.

12. Appelhans BM, Luecken LJ. Heart rate variability as an index of regulated emo-tional responding. *Rev Gen Psych.* 2006;10(3):229–240.

13. Brosschot JF. Markers of chronic stress: prolonged physiological activation and (un) conscious perseverative cognition. *Neurosci Biobehav R.* 2010;35(1):46–50.

14. Punjabi NM. The epidemiology of adult obstructive sleep apnea. *Proc Am Thorac Soc.* 2008;5(2):136–143.

15. Kelly JM, Strecker RE, Bianchi MT. Recent developments in home sleep-monitoring devices. *ISRN Neurol.* 2012;768–794.

16. Patel S, Ahmed T, Lee J, Ruoff L, Unadkat T. Validation of basis science advanced sleep analysis: estimation of sleep stages and sleep duration; 2014. Available at http://www .mybasis.com/wp-content/uploads/2014/04/Validation-of-Basis-Science-Advanced -Sleep-Analysis.pdf.

17. Green BB, Cook AJ, Ralston JD, et al. Effectiveness of home blood pressure monitoring, web communication, and pharmacist care on hypertension control: a randomized controlled trial. *JAMA*. 2008;299(24):2857–2867.

18. Henry I, Bernstein D, Banet M, et al. Body-worn, non-invasive sensor for monitoring stroke volume, cardiac output and cardiovascular reserve. *Proceedings of the 2nd Conference on Wireless Health*; 2011; San Diego, CA.

19. Barrett PM, Komatireddy R, Haaser S, et al. Comparison of 24-hour Holter monitoring with 14-day novel adhesive patch electrocardiographic monitoring. *JAMA*. 2014;127(1):95.e11-97.

20. Lau JK, Lowres N, Neubeck L, et al. iPhone ECG application for community screening to detect silent atrial fibrillation: a novel technology to prevent stroke. *Int J Cardiol*. 2013;165(1):193–194.

21. McLean S, Nurmatov U, Liu JL, Pagliari C, Car J, Sheikh A. Telehealthcare for chronic obstructive pulmonary disease. *Cochrane Database System Rev*. 2011(7): Cd007718.

22. Wang W, Finkelstein SM, Hertz MI. Automatic event detection in lung transplant recipients based on home monitoring of spirometry and symptoms. *Telemed J & E-Health*. 2013;19(9):658–663.

23. Ho PM, Bryson CL, Rumsfeld JS. Medication adherence: its importance in cardiovascular outcomes. *Circ*. 2009;119(23):3028–3035.

24. Brath H, Morak J, Kastenbauer T, et al. Mobile health (mHealth) based medication adherence measurement—a pilot trial using electronic blisters in diabetes patients. *Brit J Clin Pharmacol*. 2013;76(suppl 1):47–55.

25. Lester RT, Ritvo P, Mills EJ, et al. Effects of a mobile phone short message service on antiretroviral treatment adherence in Kenya (WelTel Kenya1): a randomised trial. *Lancet*. 2010;376(9755):1838–1845.

26. Belknap R, Weis S, Brookens A, et al. Feasibility of an ingestible sensor-based system for monitoring adherence to tuberculosis therapy. *PLoS One*. 2013;8(1):e53373.

27. Milani P, Coccetta CA, Rabini A, Sciarra T, Massazza G, Ferriero G. Mobile smartphone applications for body position measurement in rehabilitation: a review of goniometric tools. *PM&R*. 2014;6(11):1038–1043.

28. Hayward KS, Barker RN, Brauer SG, Lloyd D, Horsley SA, Carson RG. SMART arm with outcome-triggered electrical stimulation: a pilot randomized clinical trial. *Top Stroke Rehab*. 2013;20(4):289–298.

29. Pancrazio JJ, Peckham PH. Neuroprosthetic devices: how far are we from recovering movement in paralyzed patients? *Expert Rev Neurotherap*. 2009;9(4):427–430.

30. Hu Y, Jiang X, Zhang L, Fan J, Wu W. Construction of near-infrared photonic crystal glucose-sensing materials for ratiometric sensing of glucose in tears. *Biosens Bioelectron*. 2013;48:94–99.

31. Goldman D. Google to make smart contact lenses. CNN Money, 2014. Accessed January 18, 2014, at http://money.cnn.com/2014/01/17/technology/innovation/google-contacts/.

32. Bandodkar AJ, Wang J. Non-invasive wearable electrochemical sensors: a review. *Trends Biotechnol*. 2014;32(7):363–371.

33. Coyle S, Lau KT, Moyna N, et al. BIOTEX—biosensing textiles for personalised healthcare management. *IEEE T Inf Technol Biomed.* 2010;14(2):364–370.

34. Eisenberg A. A wearable alert to head injuries in sports. *New York Times.* 2013. Accessed January 18, 2014, at http://www.nytimes.com/2013/06/16/business/a-wearable -alert-to-head-injuries-in-sports.html?_r=0.

35. Ye-Lin Y, Garcia-Casado J, Martinez-de-Juan JL, Prats-Boluda G, Ponce JL. The detection of intestinal spike activity on surface electroenterograms. *Phys Med Biol.* 2010; 55(3):663–680.

36. Shamir MY, Avramovich A, Smaka T. The current status of continuous noninvasive measurement of total, carboxy, and methemoglobin concentration. *Anesth Analg.* 2012;114(5):972–978.

37. Framework for Consumer Engagement Roadmap. Available at http://www .himss.org/ResourceLibrary/mHimssRoadmapContent.aspx?ItemNumber=30388 &navItemNumber=30069.

38. Cao Q, Mahalanabis M, Chang J, et al. Microfluidic chip for molecular amplification of Influenza A RNA in human respiratory specimens. *PLoS ONE.* 2012;7(3):e33176.

39. Foudeh AM, Fatanat Didar T, Veres T, Tabrizian M. Microfluidic designs and techniques using lab-on-a-chip devices for pathogen detection for point-of-care diagnostics. *Lab Chip.* 2012;12(18):3249–3266.

40. Ruano-Lopez JM, Agirregabiria M, Olabarria G, et al. The SmartBioPhone, a point of care vision under development through two European projects: OPTOLAB-CARD and LABONFOIL. *Lab Chip.* 2009;9(11):1495–1499.

41. Stedtfeld RD, Tourlousse DM, Seyrig G, et al. Gene-Z: a device for point of care genetic testing using a smartphone. *Lab Chip.* 2012;12(8):1454–1462.

42. Shirasu M, Touhara K. The scent of disease: volatile organic compounds of the human body related to disease and disorder. *J Biochem.* 2011;150(3):257–266.

43. Wilson AD, Baietto M. Advances in electronic-nose technologies developed for biomedical applications. *Sensor.* 2011;11(1):1105–1176.

44. Sethi S, Nanda R, Chakraborty T. Clinical application of volatile organic compound analysis for detecting infectious diseases. *Clin Microbiol Rev.* 2013;26(3):462–475.

45. Samudrala D, Lammers G, Mandon J, et al. Breath acetone to monitor life style interventions in field conditions: an exploratory study. *Obesity.* 2014;22:980–983

46. Sandrini A, Taylor DR, Thomas PS, Yates DH. Fractional exhaled nitric oxide in asthma: an update. *Respirol.* 2010;15(1):57–70.

47. Samara MA, Tang WH, Cikach F, Jr., et al. Single exhaled breath metabolomic analysis identifies unique breathprint in patients with acute decompensated heart failure. *J Amer Coll Cardiol.* 2013;61(13):1463–1464.

48. Dent AG, Sutedja TG, Zimmerman PV. Exhaled breath analysis for lung cancer. *J Thorac Dis.* 2013;5(suppl 5):S540–550.

49. Li J, Peng Y, Duan Y. Diagnosis of breast cancer based on breath analysis: an emerging method. *Critl Rev Oncol Hematol.* 2013;87(1):28–40.

50. Vella SJ, Beattie P, Cademartiri R, et al. Measuring markers of liver function using a micropatterned paper device designed for blood from a fingerstick. *Anal Chem.* 2012;84(6):2883–2891.

51. Oncescu V, O'Dell D, Erickson D. Smartphone based health accessory for colorimetric detection of biomarkers in sweat and saliva. *Lab Chip.* 2013;13(16):3232–3238.

52. Velikova M, Lucas PJ, Smeets RL, van Scheltinga TJ. *Fully Automated Interpretation of Biochemical Tests for Decision Support by Smartphones*; 2012. Paper presented at Computer-Based Medical Systems (CBMS), 25th International Symposium.

53. Oncescu V, Mancuso M, Erickson D. Cholesterol testing on a smartphone. *Lab Chip.* 2014;14(4):759–763.

54. Gallegos D, Long KD, Yu H, et al. Label-free biodetection using a smartphone. *Lab Chip.* 2013;13(11):2124–2132.

55. Greenberg R. Making waves: ultrasound use increases in medical education. 2012; Retrieved January 18, 2014, from https://www.aamc.org/newsroom/reporter/dec2012/323592/ultrasound.html.

56. Fricke TR, Holden BA, Wilson DA, et al. Global cost of correcting vision impairment from uncorrected refractive error. *Bull World Health Org.* 2012;90(10):728–738.

57. Vaughan J. *Photoscreening for Refractive Error and Strabismus with a Smartphone App*; 2013. Paper presented at 2013 AAP National Conference and Exhibition.

58. Maamari RN, Keenan JD, Fletcher DA, Margolis TP. A mobile phone-based retinal camera for portable wide field imaging. *Brit J Ophthalmol.* 2014;98(4):438–41

59. Webster M, Kumar VS. Picturing cervical cancer. *Clin Chem.* 2014;60:277–279.

60. Sohn W, Shreim S, Yoon R, et al. Endockscope: using mobile technology to create global point of service endoscopy. *J Endourol.* 2013;27(9):1154–1160.

61. Wicks P. Video Q&A: patients leading the direction of clinical research—an interview with Paul Wicks. *BMC Med.* 2014;12:118.

62. CureTogether Acquired by 23andMe; 2012. CureTogether Blog. Available at http://curetogether.com/blog/2012/07/15/curetogether-acquired-by-23andme/.

63. Swan M. Crowdsourced health research studies: an important emerging complement to clinical trials in the public health research ecosystem. *J Med Internet Res.* 2012; 14(2):e46.

64. Eysenbach G. SARS and population health technology. *J Med Internet Res.* 2003;5(2):e14.

65. Wikipedia. Augmented reality; 2015. Available at http://en.wikipedia.org/wiki/Augmented_reality.

66. Google Glass enters the operating room. *New York Times*; 2014. Available at http://well.blogs.nytimes.com/2014/06/01/google-glass-enters-the-operating-room/.

67. Schreinemacher MH, Graafland M, Schijven MP. Google Glass in surgery. *Surgical Innovat.* 2014;21(6):651–652.

68. Ianchulev T, Minckler DS, Hoskins HD, et al. Wearable technology with head-mounted displays and visual function. *JAMA.* 2014;312(17):1799–1801.

69. Muensterer OJ, Lacher M, Zoeller C, Bronstein M, Kubler J. Google Glass in pediatric surgery: an exploratory study. *Int J Surg.* 2014;12(4):281–289.

70. Carenzo L, Barra FL, Ingrassia PL, Colombo D, Costa A, Della Corte F. Disaster medicine through Google Glass. *Eur J Emergen Med.* 2015;22:222–225

71. Wikipedia. Virtual reality; 2015. Available at http://en.wikipedia.org/wiki/Virtual_reality.

72. Krijn M, Emmelkamp PM, Olafsson RP, Biemond R. Virtual reality exposure therapy of anxiety disorders: a review. *Clin Psychol Rev.* Jul 2004;24(3):259–281.

73. Mosso JL, Gorini A, De La Cerda G, et al. Virtual reality on mobile phones to reduce anxiety in outpatient surgery. *Stud Health Technol Inform.* 2009;142:195–200.

74. mHealth & Consumer Engagement. Framework for Consumer Engagement; 2015. Accessed March 24, 2015, at http://www.himss.org/ResourceLibrary/mHimss RoadmapContent.aspx?ItemNumber=30388&navItemNumber=30069.

75. World Health Organization. Ten facts on noncommunicable diseases; 2013. Available at http://www.who.int/features/factfiles/noncommunicable_diseases/facts/en/.

76. Greene J, Hibbard JH. Why does patient activation matter? an examination of the relationships between patient activation and health-related outcomes. *J Gen Intern Med.* 2012;27(5):520–526.

77. American Hospital Association. *Engaging Health Care Users: A Framework for Healthy Individuals and Communities.* 2013. Available at http://www.aha.org/research/cor/content /engaging_health_care_users.pdf.

78. Akematsu Y, Tsuji M. An empirical analysis of the reduction in medical expenditure by e-health users. *J Telemed Telecare.* 2009;15(3):109–111.

79. Vital Wave Consulting. mHealth for development: the opportunity of mobile technology for healthcare in the developing world; 2009. Available at http://www .globalproblems-globalsolutions-files.org/unf_website/assets/publications/technology /mhealth/mHealth_for_Development_full.pdf.

80. Peckham M. Mobile explosion: wireless traffic could reach 10.8 exabytes a month by 2016. PC World; 2012. Accessed January 26, 2014, at http://www.pcworld.com/article /249922/mobile_explosion_wireless_traffic_could_reach_10_8_exabytes_a_month_by _2016.html.

Telemedicine

VIRTUALLY REDEFINING THE DELIVERY OF CARE

Jason Gorevic

Abstract

Telemedicine—the virtual physician visit—is one of the most significant trends in healthcare today. By offering patients 24/7 access to physicians, telemedicine can reduce the costly use of emergency rooms and urgent care centers without any trade-off in quality. Access to care is a worsening problem as the U.S. population ages and more Americans gain insurance—and the supply of primary care physicians is shrinking.

Telemedicine eliminates geographic barriers and dynamically matches supply with demand in real time, changing the way market participants access and deliver healthcare. It eliminates traditional barriers and inefficiencies and enables participants to engage in a healthcare marketplace. Reduction in cost is realized by reducing overhead and administration.

Innovators in other industries have solved similar inefficiencies through on-demand business models that create new economies by connecting and empowering both consumers and businesses. Telemedicine similarly addresses the pervasive challenges of access, cost, and quality that face the U.S. healthcare system today.

Telemedicine has appeared on countless healthcare industry top trends lists in recent years, sometimes cited as an innovation in patient care, other times in the context of technology, and always as an area of substantial growth. Telemedicine has captured mindshare among industry experts for many good reasons, all pointing to the conclusion that telemedicine is an idea whose time has come after many decades.

Occupying a unique place in the shifting landscape of healthcare transformation, telemedicine offers practical solutions to current and near-term problems while also promising exciting future applications. We now have wristwatches capable of sensing heart rates and tracking physical activity, as well as prototype smartphones that produce electrocardiograms and monitor blood oxygen, temperature, respiration, and blood pressure through a user's fingers. We also have glucose monitoring via smartphone, and lung function monitoring is on the horizon. A smartphone-enabled otoscope attachment can capture and share medical-quality images of a patient's ear canal and ear drum. We have the technology—the microelectronics, nanosensors, imaging, and data analytics—to achieve all these things and the ability to integrate them into a single digital platform. Imagine a future in which both patient and physician can check just about everything in real time without an office visit. That is where the future is quickly headed.

Existing telemedicine services such as on-demand remote physician visits, however, have garnered much of the recent attention because they are already fundamentally reshaping ideas about how healthcare can and should be delivered. In fact, another trend list where telemedicine belongs might be "rate of adoption." In a field that historically has been slow to implement new solutions, primary care telemedicine is being adopted at an unprecedented pace, including a sizable share of employer-offered health plans that now provide it to their members. The virtual doctor visit has entered the mainstream.

A 2014 report from Deloitte Technology Media and Telecommunications (TMT), predicted that the number of telemedicine visits globally would reach 100 million by the end of 2014, with 75% of those in North America. Deloitte TMT calculated that growth as a 400-percent increase from 2012 levels, estimating global cost savings of $5 billion when compared with traditional in-person consults.[1]

To understand how and why telemedicine is changing the delivery of care, it is important to look at the constellation of factors leading to its surge in growth. On the consumer side, the popularity of mobile digital devices has played an important role, with smartphones in particular changing the way people interact and manage the tasks of everyday life. And telemedicine aligns with the steady democratization of healthcare, shifting from a paternalistic and provider-driven environment to a patient-driven one. On the provider side, the healthcare industry's continued focus on *increased access to care, improved*

The Virtual Doctor Is In: How Telemedicine Works

Services such as Teladoc are generally offered to people through their health insurance plans. People register and fill out their medical histories, and they can then request a consult by phone, mobile device, or computer. Certain common health issues such as upper respiratory infections and certain times such as weekends and evenings make telemedicine a logical choice. However, there are as many reasons why someone may need to consult a physician as there are people and problems:

- The son of a single mom comes home with a goose-egg hematoma that looks alarming; he seems lethargic. It's late in the day and her choices are limited: Pile the kids into the car and drive to an urgent care center or wait and watch.
- A man prone to allergic rashes develops one that is unusually severe. Should he tough it out with antihistamines or call for an appointment? Should he try his physician or a dermatologist? Can he even *get* an appointment?
- It's the weekend, and a dad with young children believes his inflamed eye is conjunctivitis—pink eye. He knows early diagnosis and treatment will help keep it from spreading to his family. There's no urgent care or walk-in clinic nearby, so an emergency room is his only option.
- A woman suspects a bladder infection; she's had them before. But making a doctor's appointment is problematic because she has to arrange for transportation and someone to cover for her at work. Maybe she'll wait to see if it resolves on its own.

These examples illustrate typical circumstances people face when considering what to do about a health problem, and all are candidates for telemedicine visits.

But what about bigger problems? Consider these two real-life examples of telemedicine consults that helped people with serious medical issues:

- A man in his 30s who was working unusually long hours and had little sleep or food was experiencing an erratic heartbeat. The earliest available appointment was in two days, but he wasn't sure it was serious enough to go to an emergency room. He called Teladoc and within minutes was speaking with a physician in his home state. The doctor not only determined that the man was in the early stages of a heart attack but also stayed with him on the phone until he got appropriate care.
- A couple whose teenage son was experiencing tingling and numbness for several days called for a weekend consult. A physician asked detailed

questions about the symptoms and advised them to go to an ER to rule out various possibilities, including multiple sclerosis—which turned out to be the eventual diagnosis. The parents credited the doctor with preparing them for the testing that took place in the following hours and the speed at which a definitive diagnosis was made. Later, in a parents' support group, they learned it is common for diagnosis to take up to a year because MS in children is rare.

In addition to efficiently providing care for routine medical problems, telemedicine can help people make better and more informed decisions, seek the appropriate level of care, and avoid delays in diagnosis and treatment.

quality, and *reduced cost* is driving growth in telemedicine because it offers real solutions to all of these pressing challenges.

TELEMEDICINE: BACKGROUND IN BRIEF

Telemedicine—or *telehealth* as it is sometimes called—is defined as the use of electronic communications to exchange medical information with the aim of improving patient health. Often these terms are used interchangeably, although some are defining telehealth more broadly to include education and advocacy in addition to patient care. In its simplest form, telemedicine is a virtual or remote visit between patient and clinician as opposed to an on-site visit. Technologies that enable those interactions include computers, tablets, smartphones, and traditional wired telephony, along with specialized freestanding kiosks.

Telemedicine is not a discrete medical specialty but the use of technology to deliver care that might otherwise be delivered on site. The federal government is increasingly adding Medicare and Medicaid codes eligible for reimbursement if services are provided via telemedicine and under the same fee structure as an on-site visit. A telemedicine option within a benefits plan might have a flat rate fee that is much lower than an average office visit; it is important to note, however, that even when the cost is dramatically lower, a telemedicine interaction is still a "real" physician visit and much more than a helpline. It is a real consultation with a state-licensed physician who can make diagnoses and prescribe medications.

Telemedicine has been around for many decades, primarily to provide healthcare access to people in rural and remote locations. Telemedicine grew with advancements in high-speed data communication, video conferencing, and digital imaging technology, but it remained at the margins for many years, randomly used in isolated or specific circumstances and not something most patients would ever expect to encounter.

Today, through companies such as Dallas-based Teladoc, telemedicine offers 24/7 access to networks of primary care physicians, helping to reduce the use of emergency rooms and urgent care centers without trading off quality and in some cases improving it. Given the healthcare industry's imperative for greater access to quality care at reduced cost, telemedicine is at the vanguard of exciting new services, solutions, and efficiencies and represents the best kind of "disruptive" innovation.

CHALLENGES DRIVING TELEMEDICINE'S GROWTH

Past discussions about access to healthcare have generally focused on uninsured or rural populations, but today even people with quality health plans can have difficulty getting the care they need when and where they need it. Access to care is a problem that is expected to worsen as millions of people are added to the pool of the insured. Numerous researchers, think tanks, and professional associations have warned about looming problems in access to primary care physicians—the backbone of the U.S. health system.

According to estimates by the U.S. Department of Health and Human Services, the Patient Protection and Affordable Care Act has already expanded coverage to 16.4 million of the 47 million previously uninsured Americans. That number is expected to increase over the next few years as a result of individual and employer mandates, premium subsidies, state insurance exchanges, and the ban on withholding coverage because of preexisting medical conditions.

However, this growing population of insured Americans has added more demand to a dwindling supply of primary care physicians, with shortages expected to worsen in the coming years. The National Association of Community Health Centers estimates that approximately 62 million people today have no or inadequate access to primary care as a result of physician shortages. The Association of American Medical Colleges estimates that by 2020 the nation will face a shortfall of 45,000 primary care physicians.[2] That projection is based on the aging physician workforce, the 15 million Americans who will become eligible for Medicare, and the many more millions who will become insured through the Affordable Care Act.

Although efforts have been made in recent years to lure more medical students into primary care, and especially family medicine, health advocates assert that the number of new primary care physicians is acutely insufficient and will not keep pace with current needs and future demands. The extent to which medical students have turned away from primary care in favor of better-paying specialties has been widely reported with corresponding alarm. General practitioners work the same or more hours but have among the lowest reimbursement rates and are buried by government and insurer paperwork.

Across the board, physicians face declining compensation and increasing administrative burdens. Medscape's 2014 *Physician Compensation Report* found that 50% of all physicians do not feel fairly compensated and 42% would not choose medicine as a career today.[3] In response to growing dissatisfaction, physicians are taking steps that unfortunately will result in further reductions to access. The 2014 *Survey of America's Physicians: Practice Patterns and Perspectives* from the Physicians Foundation indicated that 44% plan to limit their practices by cutting back on the number of patients seen, working part-time, closing practices to new patients, seeking nonclinical jobs, or retiring.[4]

CONSUMERS AFFECTED BY ACCESS AND COST

Without convenient access to primary care, people delay seeing physicians, forgo care entirely, or visit urgent care clinics and hospital emergency rooms (ERs), which are the most expensive and least efficient ways to provide non-urgent and nonemergent care. According to the Centers for Disease Control and Prevention (CDC), nearly 80% of ER visits not resulting in hospital admissions were because of a lack of access to an alternative provider. The estimated annual cost of unnecessary ER visits varies widely, but even the lowest figures are expressed in billions of dollars.

It does not appear that healthcare reform has improved the situation. A 2015 survey sponsored by the American College of Emergency Physicians found that emergency room volume has not leveled off as many hoped it would following the implementation of the Affordable Care Act.[5] Three-quarters of ER physicians in 2015 reported emergency visits going up, compared with less than half of them reporting an increase just one year earlier.

Timely access to care continues to be a problem for consumers, even for some who have a primary care physician and a "medical home." A 2014 study conducted by healthcare employment consultants Merritt Hawkins & Associates found the average wait time to see a primary care physician was 19 days across 15 metropolitan markets, and the wait was significantly more to see a specialist.[6] The report also pointed out that many of the urban centers included in the study have higher physician-to-population ratios than the national average.

Tellingly, Boston had the highest cumulative average wait time for all physician appointments at 45.4 days, according to the Merritt Hawkins study. The average wait time to see a family physician ranged from a high of 66 days in Boston, which has among the highest rates of insured adults, to a low of 5 days in Dallas, which has among the lowest. The Boston findings suggest that wider access to health insurance within a population adversely affects timely access to care because of demand stress, and this conclusion does not augur well for the national impact of the Affordable Care Act.

Although Massachusetts' healthcare reform—enacted in 2006 and well before the Affordable Care Act—has resulted in more adults statewide receiving preventive care services, about one in five residents report difficulty finding a physician, according to a 2012 Kaiser Family Foundation report.[7] And the state continues to struggle with escalating healthcare costs and high individual premiums.

Nationally, there is no question that healthcare costs have hit consumers' pocketbooks. Although premium cost increases have generally leveled off, many consumers with employer-offered health plans are now bearing the burden of higher deductibles and a larger share of the cost of premiums. In addition, a 2015 Harris Poll conducted on behalf of SCIO Analytics found that one in five insured Americans has avoided seeing a physician in the past year because of cost concerns.

Many experts also have warned that the nation's healthcare system is not fully prepared to meet the needs of a consumer population that is aging and living longer. In the past century, life expectancy has increased by nearly 30 years. According to a 2013 CDC report, *The State of Aging and Health in America*, by 2030, one in five Americans will be senior citizens, nearly double the 12% in 2000.[8] A 2015 report from the nonpartisan Congressional Budget Office also notes that of all the main factors contributing to increased Social Security and healthcare-related spending, including the Affordable Care Act, the aging population is the key driver of cost over the long term.[9]

TELEMEDICINE OFFERS SOLUTIONS AND EFFICIENCIES

One bright spot in this otherwise troubling picture of healthcare access is that telemedicine is expanding access to low-cost primary care—in multiple ways. Perhaps most obviously, 24/7 primary care availability through telemedicine is able to shift some patients from costly emergency or urgent care. There are clear bottom-line benefits to that, along with benefits to patients whose needs can be met with less hassle and interruption of their lives.

Telemedicine also offers a near-immediate response time as compared with the days, weeks, and even months that some patients must wait to secure an appointment with a family or general medicine practitioner. A faster resolution can also improve quality of care if it means getting a needed prescription more expeditiously or simply eliminating a delay in treatment.

In addition, telemedicine is an alternative for people who would otherwise not have sought care from any source because of logistical hassles, expected delays in securing a physician appointment, or other reasons that make people reluctant to seek professional care or face difficulty in pursuing care.

But access to care is not restricted only by physician availability; waste and inefficiencies within the healthcare system are not solely about supply and demand. Patients are limited by myriad factors that include cost of care, location of available services, and office hours in addition to wait times for appointments. Similarly, physicians have to contend with many obstacles that sap their productivity and efficiency, including burdensome administrative costs, cancellations, and unfilled appointment slots.

Using technology, telemedicine is able to eliminate geographic barriers and dynamically match supply with demand in real time. As a business model, this is similar to the "sharing economy" concept of pioneering companies such as Uber (transportation) and Airbnb (vacation properties). Telemedicine empowers physicians to provide their assets—time and clinical experience—at their own discretion and in whatever way is most efficient for them. Telemedicine bridges the supply-and-demand gap between physicians and patients by fundamentally changing the way market participants access and deliver healthcare. It eliminates traditional barriers and inefficiencies between participants and enables them to engage in a healthcare marketplace anytime and anywhere. Reductions in cost through telemedicine are also realized by eliminating overhead and administration.

Telemedicine networks allow participating physicians to be productive during office downtime or in the comfort of their homes, without overhead or administrative and paperwork burdens. At Teladoc, physicians are paid every two weeks via direct deposit and with no invoicing; record keeping is embedded in the technology platform. Physicians find this concept very appealing. They can generate additional income—many earn more than $100,000 annually through Teladoc—and make it fit their individual schedules and lifestyles. Many physicians have active office practices but find they have extra time in their schedules. Some have taken time off from a full-time practice to do other things such as additional academic work, pursuing other business interests, or raising children. And still others are winding down their practices and find telemedicine provides them with added flexibility in creating a perfect part-time schedule.

All this has the net effect of adding to physician availability—that is, the supply—without minting new physicians. Teladoc's own analysis shows that if every primary care physician in the United States performed about five telemedicine visits per day—a little more than an hour of time on average—it would essentially "create" 30,000 new physicians for the healthcare system and more than solve any shortfall.

According to the CDC, there are approximately 1.25 billion ambulatory care visits in the United States annually, including those at primary care offices, hospital emergency rooms, and outpatient clinics. It has been estimated that as many as one-third of those visits could be treated through telemedicine.

HOW TELEMEDICINE WORKS

There are different types of telemedicine solutions and different ways to provide on-demand care at a distance. A common misconception is that most telemedicine visits are live videoconferencing, with patient and physician interacting via a live video connection over a secure web portal. In fact, phone and mobile device interaction is far more prevalent. Another misconception is that visits always involve patient and physician interacting with one another live in real time—which is not true. Telemedicine has the great advantage of "asynchronous" interaction, meaning patients can transmit descriptions and images to be evaluated later by a physician or specialist, who then circles back and provides counsel to the patient. It is a highly efficient way to communicate, saving time and resources, and consumers today are already extremely comfortable with asynchronous mobile applications such as texting.

The most common telemedicine applications can be categorized as follows.

Synchronous: This involves live or real-time, two-way interaction between a patient and a physician using telecommunications technology, which may include videoconferencing, phone calls, mobile devices, or specialized kiosks.

Asynchronous: This includes any type of "store-and-forward" application involving electronic transmission of recorded information or images to be evaluated by physician or specialist. Data are captured, temporarily stored, and then forwarded to another location. This kind of asynchronous application is sometimes used in combination with a synchronous interaction. For example, in a specialty area such as dermatology, a patient can take a photo and upload it with a description for later evaluation by a specialist, who then responds in 24 to 48 hours and has a live consult with the patient.

Remote patient monitoring: This includes any kind of home-based or portable or wearable monitoring devices used by patients to collect health and medical data. Information is collected from an individual in one location and transmitted electronically to a clinician for the purpose of care. Applications include monitoring things such as glucose levels and blood pressure, and they are especially useful in treating chronic conditions.

When telemedicine is offered as part of a health plan through a provider such as Teladoc, members receive information about the service and register by entering their medical history information online. They can then request a visit using a mobile device, phone, or computer. The system finds an appropriate provider using automated complex routing, queuing, and scheduling. After successfully matching supply and demand, a "visit" is automatically arranged with a board-certified physician licensed to practice in the person's geographical location. Any needed prescription is sent directly to a local pharmacy. All payment and administrative functions are fully integrated. And, after the consultation, there is a follow-up within 72 hours to ensure the medical issue has been resolved.

Physician response is fast; Teladoc's median response time is less than 10 minutes. Physicians in the network are carefully selected and trained, and they follow proprietary evidence-based clinical guidelines. Prescribing frequency is similar to in-person office visits; antibiotics are limited to short durations, and no controlled substances or lifestyle drugs are permitted. In Teladoc's experience, plan members who use the service are extremely pleased—a documented 95-percent satisfaction rate; not a single malpractice claim has been filed against the company.

Certain health issues more commonly trigger telemedicine visits, including upper respiratory infections and skin problems. Certain instances also make telemedicine a logical choice such as evenings, weekends, and holidays; these make up half of all Teladoc consults. There are also many individual reasons why someone may need to consult a physician via telemedicine.

Telemedicine also responds to shifting household demographics—for example, more families now include two working parents and there are more single female heads of households. For many Americans, decisions about where and how to seek care are constrained by complex work schedules, transportation logistics, and child care issues.

When integrated as part of a health plan offering, telemedicine can even be used proactively to improve outcomes by identifying people who are high users of emergency rooms and urgent care centers and redirecting them to better and more efficient solutions.

Companies that have added telemedicine offerings to their health plans are realizing bottom-line savings, and some have commissioned proprietary, third-party studies to quantify the results. In 2014, an independent research firm was hired to evaluate the impact of Teladoc's services on a population of 150,000 individuals insured through a major U.S. retailer. By analyzing healthcare use data, the firm conducted a per-member, per-month analysis to evaluate resource use and spending before and after telemedicine was introduced; it then conducted an episode-based analysis to evaluate resource use and spending by telemedicine users compared to other beneficiaries receiving care for the same conditions in physicians' offices or ERs.

The study found that adding telemedicine as a health plan benefit resulted in an average saving per telemedicine visit of $1,157; an average reduction in per-member, per-month spending of $21.30 or 9.8%; and a return on investment of $9.10 for every dollar spent. They also found that 92% of medical issues were resolved with no follow-up required. Overall annual savings for this single employer were calculated at $5.4 million for 2014.

FIRST LARGE STUDY OF TELEMEDICINE

Now that telemedicine is reaching larger numbers of people, healthcare researchers also are eager to understand more about its effectiveness. In 2014, results were released from the first major assessment of telemedicine services offered to a large patient group.[10] Conducted by RAND Health, the nation's largest independent health policy research program, the study looked at a large sample of public employees in California who were offered new access to care through Teladoc. The California Public Employees' Retirement System (CalPERS), which manages pension and health benefits for more than 1.6 million members, began offering Teladoc services as a covered benefit to approximately 300,000 members enrolled in its Blue Shield of California plan. The RAND study looked at CalPERS enrollees' experience with Teladoc in the first eleven months of the program in 2012–13, evaluating 3,701 Teladoc visits by 2,718 children and adult enrollees and comparing them to traditional on-site visits.

Published in the February 2014 edition of the journal *Health Affairs,* the authors found that although telemedicine represented only a small portion of overall healthcare use, Teladoc's offerings provided a useful and potentially

TABLE 12.1 Leading Reasons for Teladoc Visits by Children and Adults

	Visits	
Condition	Number	Percent
Acute respiratory illnesses	1,151	31.1
Urinary tract infections and urinary symptoms	439	11.9
Skin problems	335	9.1
Abdominal pain, vomiting, and diarrhea	231	6.2
Back and joint problems	190	5.1
Influenza and general viral illnesses	172	4.7
General advice, counseling, and refills	169	4.6
Eye problems	138	3.7
Ear infections (internal and external)	137	3.7
All others	739	20.0

Data Source: RAND Corporation analysis of claims data from CalPERS, April 2012–February 2013.
Note: Percentages do not sum to 100 because of rounding.[10]

cost-effective service and was expanding access to healthcare in certain instances. RAND researchers looked at whether there was evidence to support concerns expressed by some providers that the limitations of telemedicine might lead to misdiagnoses and higher rates of follow-up visits. To the contrary, researchers found little evidence of treatment failure and less need for follow-up consults among the telemedicine patients.

The study also found Teladoc to be a potential entry point to the healthcare system for enrollees who had difficulty accessing a regular physician, including employees unable to take time off work to obtain care. More than one-third of Teladoc visits occurred on weekends and holidays, according to the study, and people used telemedicine for a "surprisingly diverse" set of conditions—395 distinct diagnosis codes overall. The top nine categories accounted for 80% of visits, and the three leading ones were acute respiratory illnesses, urinary tract infections and symptoms, and skin problems. RAND researchers concluded that telemedicine is an important area for further study, noting that "the shortage of primary care providers make it likely that telehealth will play an important role in healthcare delivery."

EMPLOYERS ADOPT TELEMEDICINE

The annual Towers Watson and National Business Group on Health (NBGH) survey is an important barometer of benefits decisions and trends among large U.S. companies, and the 2014 report illustrates how fast telemedicine is gaining traction.[11] The survey covers a wide range of topics related to health-

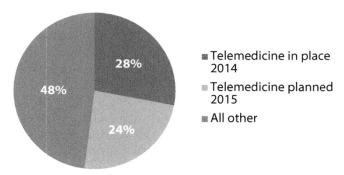

FIGURE 12.1 Large employer health plan telemedicine offerings. Data Source: Towers Watson.[11]

care benefits and focuses on companies with 1,000 or more employees, with special emphasis on the practices of best-performing companies that are healthcare trend leaders.

According to the report, telemedicine was adopted by 28% of large employers overall and nearly one-third of best performers. Significantly, another 24% of large employers and 29% of best-performing companies said they planned to add telemedicine to their offerings in 2015 for professional consultations. Although telemedicine accounts for only a small portion of the full range of healthcare benefits offered, the survey shows tremendous growth. More than half of large employers surveyed said they expect to have some type of telemedicine offering in place by the end of 2015.

The 2014 Towers Watson–NBGH survey also indicated substantial support for telemedicine as a way to expand access to care. More than half of all respondents said they foresaw healthcare becoming more accessible as a result of new technologies that provide additional access points. In addition, the report noted that although "telemedicine typically accounts for only incremental savings, it can be combined with other interventions to drive aggregate savings, and it provides a viable alternative to emergency room or physician office visits for nonemergency health issues." The survey found that best performers place more value on emerging strategies such as telemedicine, and the report advised looking at them for "a glimpse of where healthcare is headed."

TELEMEDICINE: AMERICA'S BEST HOPE?

The U.S. healthcare system's significant waste and inconsistency in access, cost, and quality of care has been well documented. A study published in the *Journal of American Medical Association* estimated that approximately $734 billion or 27% of all healthcare spending in 2011 was wasted because of factors such as the provision of unnecessary services, inefficient delivery of care, and inflated prices. When people are forced to seek treatment at inappropriate and more costly sites of care because they have no alternatives, those cost inefficiencies affect consumers, their health plans, and their employers.

The high costs and associated burdens on all participants in the healthcare system are only expected to escalate. The Centers for Medicare and Medicaid Services (CMS) projected U.S. national health expenditures to reach $3.1 trillion or approximately 18% of U.S. GDP in 2014 and approximately 20% of GDP by 2022. The 2013 Towers Watson–NBGH survey found that U.S. employers bear on average approximately two-thirds of their employees' healthcare costs, which translates to approximately $660 billion, according to CMS projections for 2015.[12] Despite this significant expenditure, U.S. healthcare outcomes remain inferior compared with those of many other countries.

The unsustainable levels of spending on healthcare and extreme inefficiencies in the system have resulted in greater focus by employers and health plan organizations to control costs. Governments, private insurance companies, and self-insured employers are implementing serious cost-containment measures, including shifting financial responsibility to patients through higher co-pays and deductibles, and delivering care through alternate but more cost-effective methods. This shift of financial responsibility to patients coupled with increasing pricing transparency has, in turn, heightened emphasis on care alternatives. According to a 2013 survey for Prudential Insurance by MRops Inc. and Oxygen Research Inc., 49% of employers are very or extremely likely to eventually offer only high-deductible health plans. As consumers take responsibility for a larger share of their healthcare costs and spend more on healthcare services, they are likely to demand higher-quality care, greater control in how and where they receive care, increased convenience, and more service for dollars spent.

Innovators in other industries have solved access, cost, and quality inefficiencies through business models that deliver products and services on demand and create new economies by connecting and empowering both consumers and businesses. Telemedicine is using the same approach to solve the pervasive access, cost, and quality challenges facing the current healthcare system.

Telemedicine may not be America's *only* hope for fixing the nation's healthcare problems, but it has vast potential to make an important impact.

REFERENCES

1. Deloitte Technology Media and Telecommunications. eVisits: the 21st century housecall. In; *Predictions 2014*. Available at http://www2.deloitte.com/content/dam /Deloitte/global/Documents/Technology-Media-Telecommunications/dttl_TMT _Predictions-2014-lc2.pdfl.

2. Association of American Medical Colleges. The complexities of physician supply and demand: projections from 2013 to 2025; 2015. Retrieved from https://http://www .aamc.org/download/426242/data/ihsreportdownload.pdf?cm_mmc=AAMC -_-ScientificAffairs-_-PDF-_-ihsreport.

3. Kane L, Peckham C. Medscape physician compensation report 2014. Medscape Business of Medicine, Art Science Code LLC. Available at http://www.medscape.com /features/slideshow/compensation/2014/public/overview.

4. The Physicians Foundation. Survey of America's physicians: practice patterns and perspectives. Available at http://www.physiciansfoundation.org/news/survey-of-20000 -us-physicians-shows-80-of-doctors-are-over-extended-or-at.

5. American College of Emergency Physicians. 2015 ACEP Poll Affordable Care Act research results; 2015 Available at http://www.scribd.com/doc/264530627/2015 -ACEP-Poll-Affordable-Care-Act-Research-Results-scribd.

6. Merritt Hawkins. Physician appointment wait times and Medicaid and Medicare acceptance rates; 2015. Available at http://www.merritthawkins.com/uploadedFiles /MerrittHawkings/Surveys/mha2014waitsurvPDF.pdf.

7. Kaiser Family Foundation. Massachusetts health care reform: six years later; 2015. Available at http://kff.org/health-costs/issue-brief/massachusetts-health-care-reform-six -years-later/.

8. Centers for Disease Control and Prevention. *The State of Aging and Health in America 2013*. Washington, DC: U.S. Department of Health and Human Services; 2013. Available at http://www.cdc.gov/features/agingandhealth/state_of_aging_and_health _in_america_2013.pdf.

9. Congressional Budget Office. The 2015 long-term budget outlook; 2015. Available at https://www.cbo.gov/publication/50250.

10. Uscher-Pines L., Mehrotra A. Analysis of Teladoc use seems to indicate expanded access to care for patients without prior connection to a provider. *Health Affair.* 2014; 33(2):258–264.

11. Towers Watson. 2013/2014 employer survey on purchasing value in health care—driving performance, connecting to value. 19th Annual Towers Watson/National Business Group on Health Employer Survey on Purchasing Value in Health Care; 2014. Available at http://www.towerswatson.com/en-US/Insights/IC-Types/Survey -Research-Results/2014/05/full-report-towers-watson-nbgh-2013-2014-employer -survey-on-purchasing-value-in-health-care.

12. Towers Watson. Employer Survey on Purchasing Value in Health Care; 2013. Available at http://www.towerswatson.com/en-US/Insights/IC-Types/Survey-Research -Results/2013/03/Towers-Watson-NBGH-Employer-Survey-on-Value-in-Purchasing -Health-Care.

Grand-Aides

LEVERAGING THE WORKFORCE FOR MORE
EFFECTIVE AND LESS EXPENSIVE CARE

Arthur Garson Jr.

Abstract

Grand-Aides provide an innovative healthcare delivery program with nurse extenders making home visits to develop a trusting relationship and use telemedicine with protocols that connect the patient and care team. Regardless of age, a Grand-Aide has the temperament of a good grandparent. These aides have had training in medical care (e.g., nurse aide or community health worker), take an added Grand-Aides curriculum, and are paid at the rate of a certified nursing assistant. Under nurse video supervision, Grand-Aides provide transitional and chronic disease management. They visit at least three times the first week but then decrease over the first month as determined by supervisors. As noted recently in *Health Affairs*, when Grand-Aides worked with heart failure patients at the University of Virginia, the patients had a 58% reduction in all-cause readmissions and a 91% medication adherence one month after discharge. This represents the best published data on readmissions in the last five years.

GRAND-AIDES: WHAT'S IN A NAME?

In the mid-1990s, the chair of family medicine of a well-respected medical school confided that he thought a large number of his patients could be taken care of by a "good grandmother." I stored this idea away. Several years later as the chair of a national workforce commission, I had a chance to revisit this idea as the conversation around a table brought hand wringing about the lack of physicians. I asked another venerable chair of family medicine what he thought about the idea I brought up several years before. "I'll go you one better," he said. "About 80% of the rest could be taken care of by a good nurse." Shortly thereafter, I was asked to address a large Chinese delegation in Beijing, so I put together the idea of the historical "barefoot doctors" with grandparents and suggested a "grandparent corps" to work as extenders for physicians and nurses.[1,2] The first two pilot programs were in Baotou in Inner Mongolia and in Shanghai. With a group of University of Virginia students, we demonstrated in Baotou that 53% of adults and 74% of children seen in either emergency rooms (ERs) or acute care clinics could have been cared for by a grandparent corps.[3] Trying to apply the concept here, we discovered that it is illegal to require anyone who wants to join such a corps to be a grandparent because it is discriminatory against individuals who have no grandchildren. Therefore, the name *Grand-Aides* was born. Grand-Aides are either in operation or in advanced stages of discussion in 62 U.S. locations and 17 countries.[4]

The concept of the "good grandparent" remains. No matter how old a Grand-Aide is, and we have many in their 30s, the hallmark is still "acting like a good grandparent," and most especially the ability to deliver "tough love."

THE GRAND-AIDES CONCEPT

Grand-Aides is an innovative healthcare delivery program in which caring and experienced nurse or physician extenders make home visits to develop a trusting relationship and use portable telemedicine with established protocols. They connect with the patient and care team quickly and cost effectively. Grand-Aides leverage the supervising nurse or physician with five Grand-Aides to one supervisor. In the United States, the supervisors are either registered nurses, advanced practice nurses, or physician assistants. Overseas, the supervisors are more often physicians.

Given that virtually every hospital, physician group, and health system is attacking problems such as readmissions in their own way, a major goal of the Grand-Aides program is to fit into and adapt to the current program. In some cases, especially when a care manager is trained to become a Grand-Aides supervisor, supervisors may spend half their time remaining as care managers (so they do not leave jobs they enjoy) and the other half supervising two or three Grand-Aides.

The major goal of the Grand-Aides program is to improve health and provide appropriate access to care while reducing unnecessary visits to ERs, clinics, and hospitals, thus reducing costs. To quantitate this goal, the reductions are expected to be between 25% and 50%.

A Grand-Aide is an individual with some medical training. Most commonly, a Grand-Aide is a certified nurse aide or medical assistant. As we soon discuss, Grand-Aides do not make decisions, and the training of certified nurse aides or medical assistants makes them particularly useful because they have already been taught to take instructions from nurses or physicians. They are taught not to "wing it" on the basis of their own experience. We have trained community health workers to become Grand-Aides, but it is important that they really want to help care for patients; many have worked in communities performing valuable functions such as enrolling families in Medicaid or functioning as social work extenders. Their training may not at all have been related to patient care. Therefore, we need to be certain through the interview process that a community health worker not only has the true desire to take care of patients but also has the capability of doing so.

We have occasionally trained laypeople with no previous medical experience to become Grand-Aides. This is most applicable where patients are in extremely rural settings and no one with medical training is available. In choosing laypeople, the same issues apply as for community health workers. Paradoxically, the original idea that grandparents could rely on their own experience does not apply because every Grand-Aide must follow the instructions of his or her supervisor to the letter. Nonetheless, the original idea of having the characteristics of a "good grandparent" most definitely apply in that much of the success of a Grand-Aide is his or her ability to have a close relationship with the patient, family, and other caregivers and to be accepting, warm, and yet tough when necessary. This is "tough love."

Depending on the type of patients (described later), a Grand-Aide can care for between 75 and 250 patients.[5,6] Therefore, a supervisor can care for between 375 and 1250 patients. Most often, Grand-Aides are paid. The rate is the same as a certified nurse aide; in the United States, the median payment is $12 per hour. It is possible in rare situations to use volunteers, although the requirement of daily visits is something that most volunteers are not able to commit to.

TYPES OF GRAND-AIDE PROGRAMS

Grand-Aide programs can be either disease-based or population-based and apply to both adults and children as the following listings show.

Disease-Based Grand-Aides Programs
- Transitional and chronic care
  - Examples: Heart failure, myocardial infarction, chronic obstructive pulmonary disease, asthma, diabetes, delirium, mental health (e.g., schizophrenia)
- Palliative care
- Primary care
  - Emergency department "hyperutilizers"
    - ○ Parents who use emergency departments (EDs) as clinics to care for their children with minor illnesses (e.g., colds)
    - ○ Adults who have drug abuse problems or mental illness issues
- Preventive treatment
  - ○ Examples: hypertension, diabetes, obesity
- Mother and infant care

Population-Based Grand-Aides Programs
- Medicare
- Medicaid
  - Children
  - New adult expansion
    - ○ Dual eligibles
    - ○ Children with medically complex conditions

The listing serves as an index for the types of programs we now discuss.

The Transitional and Chronic Care Grand-Aides

The goals of the transitional and chronic care Grand-Aides are as follow:

1. improve health process and outcome measures;
2. reduce 30-day readmissions by 25% to 50%;
3. reduce length of stay for all admissions (including readmissions); this is achieved by having a competent individual such as a Grand-Aide who can help care for a patient and bring about a discharge perhaps a day faster;
4. reduce costs; and
5. bring about high patient and family satisfaction.

FREQUENT VISITS For patients with chronic disease who are being discharged from the hospital, the process begins when a supervisor sees the patient and his or her family in the hospital. The Grand-Aide visits within 24 hours of discharge at least three times in the first week. This frequent visiting is a hallmark of the Grand-Aide program and has been shown to be necessary to create the sort of relationship on which Grand-Aides rely. Unfortunately, we have had programs in which the directors of the programs decided that they could "get away with" fewer visits, and the program did not achieve the necessary results.

After the first week, the supervisor determines the need for visits in consultation with the Grand-Aide, the patient, and the family. Usually, there are two visits in the second week, one to two visits in the third week, and one visit in the fourth week. After the fourth week, Grand-Aides continue to stay in touch with their patients, visiting approximately once per month and using the telephone as needed. The Grand-Aide becomes the first point of contact for the patient and family if the patient's condition worsens. In this case, it is extremely likely that the patient would be brought back into the clinic, and the number of Grand-Aide visits increased. Grand-Aides also can begin to care for patients who were not recently hospitalized—for example, extremely ill patients for whom medication adherence has been a problem. In this case, the procedure is the same in that the Grand-Aide needs to create a similar relationship.

HOME VISITS In the first home visit, the Grand-Aide has three specific functions, the first of which is medication reconciliation. The Grand-Aide takes all of the medications the patient was taking before hospital admission (emptying out all paper bags) and puts them on one side of a table; all of the new medications are put on the other side of the table. A video link through a mobile tablet is turned on so the nurse supervisor can do the actual reconciliation. The Grand-Aide operates the tablet and video software.

HIPAA-COMPLIANT VIDEO It is important that the video be compliant with the requirements of the Health Insurance Portability and Accountability Act (HIPAA). Each information technology department will have its own view of what is HIPAA-compliant. We have always managed to find an application that is acceptable. Common ones that have apps in Apple IOS or Android: Jabber from Cisco, Zoom, and Apple's FaceTime. The video uses the camera built into a tablet without any other modification needed. The tablet is also used to record data by the Grand-Aide and can be either an Apple or an Android brand.

Second, the Grand-Aide administers a questionnaire as part of a protocol. These questionnaires have yes or no answers that are personalized to the patient by the supervisor. The supervisor begins with a stock Grand-Aide protocol—for example, for heart failure. These protocols are tiered so that emergency questions are at the beginning of the questionnaire portion (e.g.

"The patient is gasping for air such that he or she cannot speak a sentence"), and the Grand-Aide is taught to stop and contact the supervisor if there is a "yes" in that part of the protocol. The supervisor may also add questions that are specific to the patient, especially if he or she has more than one disease. The protocol is then transmitted to a HIPAA-compliant server and the supervisor then can access the protocol. The supervisor then goes live with the patient and family, again with the Grand-Aide acting as video operator. The supervisor has the opportunity to observe the patient, as well as answer any questions from the patient and family. The supervisor may change the medical regimen, either immediately in the case of a nurse practitioner or after consultation with the physician. The third and final job of the Grand-Aide is likely the most important: explaining the entire medical regimen and then using every bit of the Grand-Aides' previous teaching to have the patient take his or her medication appropriately and to establish routines that will maximize the chance of adherence to medication schedules in the future. The contents of the visits in the future are similar with brief video contact (3–4 minutes), early symptom recognition, and continuing aim toward medication adherence.

At the end of the visit, the supervisor adds impressions and any changes in medical regimen to the protocol, which is then added to an electronic medical record, either directly or as a PDF attachment to a brief nursing note.

The Grand-Aide can also become the person who interfaces with technology. Many patients are sent home with electronic scales and blood pressure cuffs. The Grand-Aide not only can troubleshoot if one of the pieces of equipment seems to be malfunctioning but also check the patient's technique. For example, if the patient takes his or her own blood pressure and comes up with a number that is significantly different from the one the Grand-Aide gets, then the Grand-Aide can reteach the task to the patient. In addition, in many cases using telemedicine, the person sends a nurse to observe the patient directly. The Grand-Aide can become the "person on the ground" deployed by a telemedicine company so that a nurse does not have to make a visit.

Process and Outcome Measures

Grand-Aides USA has a minimum data set for input when a patient enters the program and then takes new data at 1, 3, 6, and 12 months. These consist of demographics, clinical characteristics, medication adherence, number of clinic visits, ED visits, and hospitalizations. Death is noted if it has occurred between these data-entry points. Grand-Aides USA also has optional forms that can be downloaded such as the condition of the home environment, a depression scale, and satisfaction with the program and the Grand-Aide.

Results of Transitional and Chronic Care Grand-Aides

The following data were recently published in *Health Affairs* based on data at 12 months from the University of Virginia.[6] Among 62 unselected Medicare patients with class III–IV heart failure, there was one heart failure 30-day readmission (1.6%) with one elective coronary artery bypass graft. There was an 8.1% all-cause readmission rate among patients in the Grand-Aide program compared with an 18.6% historical rate (university health system consortium patient-matched), a 58% reduction. The heart failure–related 30-day readmission rate was 3.2% compared to the historical of 6.8%, a 53% reduction. Medication adherence was 91% at 30 days in the Grand-Aide program. Early results in two programs, one randomized, showed similar data with reduction in heart failure readmissions of >55%.

The Palliative Care Grand-Aide

Part of the training of the chronic and transitional care Grand-Aide involves how to begin conversations on end-of-life care. Sometimes patients are discharged without an appropriate time for such conversations; after a patient has spent a few days at home, a Grand-Aide may be able to initiate such a conversation. In every case, Grand-Aides will be directed by supervisors to have these conversations. If a supervisor feels a talk is not necessary, the Grand-Aide will not initiate one.

In some cases, Grand-Aides may be attached to a palliative care service. The goals are improved symptom control and improved quality of life. Depending on the wishes of the patient and his or her family and care team, goals may also include reducing emergency department visits and intensive care unit admissions in the last days of life. In addition to routine visits, the Grand-Aide receives calls from the patient and family and then uses palliative care protocols that may relate to increased pain, constipation, nausea, depression, or family support.

The supervisor may then decide to have the Grand-Aide make a home visit and change medications. In cases where a Grand-Aide has been helping to care for a patient who then elects palliative care, the Grand-Aide remains in place; the supervisor may or may not change.

Primary Care Grand-Aide

In the case of children whose parents use EDs as clinics, the goal is to reduce unnecessary visits and to increase visits to primary care clinics and establish patient-centered medical homes. A Grand-Aide can meet a patient in a clinic, at home, or on "neutral territory" such as a grocery store or church after the supervisor has a referral from the ED. In cases where the ED will not notify the primary care physician, the physician will need to have a system for early notification either by the health system or by the payer. The Grand-Aide discusses with the parent the reason for taking the child to the ER and, in consultation with the nurse supervisor, reinforces the teaching about the specific condition (e.g. fever) and ways to deal with it, and then the Grand-Aide offers to become the contact for that parent when a child is ill, making a call to the Grand-Aide the first call whenever a child is ill. The Grand-Aide then completes a tiered questionnaire with yes and no answers that is made available to the supervisor who decides either to send the patient to the ER, send the patient to a clinic, have the patient stay home with specific instructions (e.g., take acetaminophen), or send the Grand-Aide to make a home visit. The Grand-Aide then follows up within 48 hours.

In the case of adults who overuse the emergency department, a combination of skills and protocols involving chronic care, primary care, and social work are used.

RESULTS OF PRIMARY CARE GRAND-AIDES As published in *Health Affairs*, the data from a drop-in clinic in a federally qualified health center caring for Medicaid children demonstrated that 62% of the visits could have been cared for by a Grand-Aide and supervisor, with the top diagnoses being rash, fever, congestion, earache, and cough. In that same paper, visits by Medicaid children to the ED showed that 74% of the visits fit one of the Grand-Aides protocols (earache, congestion, cough, rash, and pharyngitis). Similar results were obtained for dual-eligible Medicaid patients visiting the emergency department.[4]

The Prevention Grand-Aide (Hypertension, Diabetes, Obesity)

The goals of the prevention Grand-Aider are to have patients following their regimen. In the case of hypertension, this is medication adherence; in the case of diabetes, this is a combination of medication adherence and diet; and in the case of obesity, it is diet and exercise. The use concept for these Grand-Aides is the same as used in other conditions: create a relationship between Grand-Aide, patient, and family; make frequent visits; and continue educating and monitoring. Therefore, regardless of the condition, the Grand-Aide visits three to four times in the first week and then continues with intensive visits until there appears to be adherence with the regimen. At that point, the intensity of the visits can decrease, with more distant monitoring and an increase in visits as needed.

For all three conditions, there is a need to monitor and reduce caloric and sodium intake. Grand-Aides have rolls of food labels, each the size of a quarter; red represents 250 calories or 175 mg of sodium; yellow represents 140 calories or 150 mg of sodium (the number of calories in a sugared drink such as Coca-Cola); and green labels represent other amounts. The Grand-Aide helps the patient label all the food at home with the goal of creating a "shock value" in seeing that virtually all of the food is labeled red. The Grand-Aide will also go food shopping with the patient along with a red–yellow–green shopping list; the patient is taught to shop the "perimeter" of the store where all of the fresh food is kept. The Grand-Aide will also add red, yellow, and green labels to the menus of the patient's five favorite restaurants.

The Maternal–Infant Grand-Aide

The goals of the maternal–infant Grand-Aide are to reduce complications of pregnancy, reduce ED visits and hospital admissions, improve the outcomes of pregnancy with healthier babies, and improve neonatal outcomes such that mothers are as prepared as possible to care for their newborns and that there are reduced ED visits and readmissions for infants. The Grand-Aide meets a pregnant woman and her family as soon as possible after the woman learns she is pregnant. After delivery, the Grand-Aide again visits with decreasing frequency over the first 8 to 12 weeks. The maternal–infant Grand-Aide will then be ready to hand off to a primary care Grand-Aide who will provide ongoing connection of the family to the care team.

The Population-Based Grand-Aides

For populations such as Medicare, Medicaid (children as well as the newly eligible adults), dual eligibles, and children with medically complex conditions, the Grand-Aide curriculum uses combinations of the various disease-based Grand-Aides programs. For example, Medicare patients are likely to have one or more chronic diseases as well as primary care conditions such as colds. The Grand-Aides manual for the Medicare patient covers the primary care protocols and the most common chronic diseases, but not in as much depth as the disease-related manual.

REGULATIONS: WHAT A GRAND-AIDE CAN AND CANNOT DO

The job of a Grand-Aide fits entirely into what can be expected for those trained as certified nurse aides and medical assistants. The following list has been acceptable to both boards of nursing and unions.

1. There is *no assessment* by the Grand-Aide and *no delegation* of decision making.
2. The Grand-Aide is supervised directly by the nurse before *every* phone call is completed.
3. *Every* home visit connects the patient and the nurse on video.
4. The Grand-Aide asks yes–no questions and transmits them verbatim to the nurse.
5. The *Grand-Aide "observes, records, and reports and" reinforces* only what the nurse tells the patient to do.
6. At no time is the Grand-Aide involved in suggesting or dispensing prescription medication.
7. The nurse involves the physician in the same way as current practice.

TRAINING

A standardized curriculum has been developed for each type of Grand-Aide. Grand-Aides USA uses a train-the-trainer model. Grand-Aides USA teaches the supervisors, who then train the Grand-Aides. There are two important reasons for this. First, this is a highly efficient mechanism for scaling, in which Grand-Aides USA can train up to 15 supervisors and each supervisor can then train 5 Grand-Aides. It is important for Grand-Aides USA trainers to interact with the supervisors; the key to an outstanding Grand-Aides program is the supervisors, and the Grand-Aides USA trainers will be able to work with the supervisors to see who is outstanding. Second, the supervisors get to know their own trainees and decide who will and will not make the cut.

The train-the-trainers manual has won awards for the teaching of adults. After teaching about the Grand-Aides program, the remainder of the manual is concerned with how to teach adult learners. Each Grand-Aide manual has started as a Word document of 200 to 300 pages. All manuals have been modified with the best concepts of distance education such that the majority of learning is done electronically.

The train-the-trainers teaching is approximately three to four days, and the Grand-Aide teaching is two to three weeks. Much of this can be done at home.

GRAND-AIDES AND THE UNITED STATES

The need for Grand-Aides is based on population estimates and acceptance of the program. The total market demand for Grand-Aides is approximately 500,000.

Considering only Medicare readmissions, the impact on the United States is 1.84 million readmissions yearly at an expense of $24 billion.[7] Grand-Aides will

TABLE 13.1 Grand-Aides Projected Market

	% Population	Population	% Need GA	Pop. Need	GA Ratio (1:x)	GAs Needed
Medicare	0.15	45,916,500	0.30	13,774,950	100	137,750
Medicaid children	0.108	33,059,880	0.23	7,438,473	250	29,754
Medicaid pregnant	0.016	4,897,760	0.56	2,754,990	100	27,550
Medicaid adults	0.062	18,978,820	0.38	7,117,058	100	72.171
Insured adults <65	0.513	157,034,430	0.15	23,555,165	100	235,552
Insured children	0.066	20,203,260	0.08	1,515,245	100	15,152
Uninsured adults	0.071	21,733,810	0			
Total						516,828

prevent 25% to 50% of those, saving Medicare $6 billion to $12 billion at a cost of $2.21 billion for a net savings of $3.79 billion to $9.79 billion. In addition to the financial impact, from 460,000 to 920,000 patients and families will not have to undergo the wasted discomfort, time, and exposure to added disease of a readmission; hospitals will increase capacity by 2.3 million to 4.6 million bed days.

EMPLOYMENT AND FINANCES

There are two financial and employment models for Grand-Aides. In the first, Grand-Aides and supervisors are employed by an institution; the expense to the institution is for a Grand-Aide salary (similar to a certified nurse aide), a supervisor (allocated one-fifth to each Grand-Aide because a supervisor has five Grand-Aides), technology (e.g., tablet and wireless charges), and transportation because the Grand-Aides usually use their own automobiles. Second, the Grand-Aides and supervisors are employed by a home health agency that charges a fee to the institution for the Grand-Aides' and supervisors' services. Grand-Aides USA does not employ Grand-Aides; the payer, health system, hospital, or physician group or a home health agency employs the Grand-Aides.

Grand-Aides USA is paid a fee by the institution or home health agency for the first three years and then a maintenance fee is paid for annual certification. The expense of the Grand-Aide program is (U.S. median) per Grand-Aide: Grand-Aide $26,000; supervisor $17,000 ($85,000 allocated among five Grand-Aides for each supervisor); technology (tablet and Internet) $3,000; and transportation (gasoline or per-mile) $5,000 = $51,000.

In a year, a Grand-Aide can care for 100 chronically ill patients at $510 per patient per year or 250 relatively well Medicaid children (to reduce ED visits for colds) at $204 per child.

SCOPE OF WORK: WHAT DOES GRAND-AIDES USA DO?

Grand-Aides USA begins by determining both current and projected systems of workforce and workflow. On the basis of these determinations, the Grand-Aides program is customized to fit what an institution needs. The training materials are then developed and customized to fit the program.

Next, Grand-Aides USA works with the clinicians and the information technology department to create a web-based tool for data collection. This tool must be integrated into either current or projected electronic health records. Grand-Aides USA provides data analysis and reporting every three months. Several consortia exist around diseases and populations. Grand-Aides USA provides quarterly sharing of each consortium's data with identification removed and then posts webinars to share ideas, successes, and areas for improvement in the consortium.

Grand-Aides USA provides quality assessment and improvement of each program with frequent visits not only for teaching but also for monitoring implementation. There are weekly, then biweekly, and then monthly telephone follow-up calls. The first three months are critical, and there is a great deal of interaction between the institution and Grand-Aides USA during this period.

Finally, Grand-Aides USA provides initial certification of supervisors, Grand-Aides, and the entire program. Grand-Aides undergo a formal written evaluation at six months and then yearly recertification with a site visit based on tests, evaluations, and documentation of continuing education for each Grand-Aide and supervisor.

WHAT IS DIFFERENT ABOUT GRAND-AIDES?

Grand-Aides USA

1. The program is the "people answer" that fits into the armamentarium of physician groups, hospitals, and health plans.
   - Some patients do perfectly well with apps, whereas some can do well with an occasional nurse call, and some with telemedicine. Others do better with Grand-Aides.
2. Grand-Aides USA fits into current programs or replaces what an institution has tried and found either too expensive or ineffective.
3. The program leverages what physicians and nurses do not need to do by using five Grand-Aides to every one supervisor.
4. The program uses the least expensive personnel possible ($12/hour).

5. It relies on a highly personal relationship between the Grand-Aide, the patient, and his or her family.
6. Every visit is supervised directly by a nurse on video.
7. The program provides software that collects an institution's data and comparative data.
8. The program hosts ongoing improvement seminars.
9. The program brings more than five years of experience in manuals and curricula and an understanding of what does and does not work.
   • The program assembles a group of experienced people who are dedicated to the success of every institution and will continue until the program is successfully implemented.

HOW DO GRAND-AIDES COMPARE WITH OTHER TRANSITIONAL AND CHRONIC PROGRAMS?

Numerous approaches to decreasing hospital readmissions have been developed. The credit for recognizing the problem of readmissions and then creating an effective intervention goes to Dr Mary Naylor,[8] who published details about a randomized trial in 1999 that showed that home visits to elderly patients by nurse practitioners could reduce readmissions. The four most commonly used approaches are described in the following.

Transitional Care Model

Transitional care is the ongoing work of Dr Naylor, the centerpiece of which is a transitional care nurse who is a nurse practitioner.[9,10] The nurse makes home visits for approximately two months after a patient is discharged, with approximately four visits per month. The nurse is available to the patient seven days a week. These visits are in addition to excellent discharge planning; the nurse may accompany the patient to certain physician clinic visits.

Care Transitions Intervention

Care transitions continue the work of Dr Eric Coleman and uses a transition coach, who is either a nurse or social worker. The intervention lasts one month and includes one home visit and three phone calls.[11]

Project RED (for "re-engineered discharge") from Boston University has 12 components mainly aimed at the discharge process, with one post-discharge telephone call 3 days after discharge.[12] The components are as follow:

1. Ascertain the need for and obtain language assistance.
2. Make appointments for follow-up medical appointments and postdischarge tests or labs.
3. Plan to follow up on results from lab tests or studies that are pending at discharge.
4. Organize postdischarge outpatient services and medical equipment.
5. Identify the correct medicines and establish a plan for the patient to obtain and take them.
6. Reconcile the discharge plan with national guidelines.
7. Teach a written discharge plan the patient understands.
8. Educate the patient about his or her diagnosis.
9. Assess the patient in understanding the discharge plan.
10. Review with the patient what to do if a problem arises.
11. Expedite transmission of the discharge summary to clinicians who accept care of the patient.
12. Provide telephone reinforcement of the discharge plan.

Project BOOST from Dr Eric Coleman and Dr Mark Williams is a program that focuses on outstanding preparation for discharge, with each of eight "P's" assigned to an individual for teaching before discharge.[13,14] The teaching uses a "teach back" method, explaining in the patient's own words what was just taught, not just using the words of the teacher. The eight P's are:

1. problems with medications (especially with patients with polypharmacy— that is, more than 10 routine medications);
2. psychological (patients who screen positive for depression or who have a history of depression);
3. principal diagnosis (patients with a principal diagnosis or reason for hospitalization related to cancer, stroke, diabetic complications, COPD, or heart failure);
4. physical limitations (patients with frailty, deconditioning, or other physical limitations that impair or limit their ability to significantly participate in their own care—for example, performing the activities of daily living, medication administration, and participation in posthospital care);
5. poor health literacy (patients who are unable to demonstrate adequate understanding of their care plan as demonstrated by their inability to successfully complete teach back instruction);

6. poor social support (when there is no reliable caregiver to assist with the discharge process and assist with care after the patient is discharged and where social isolation is a problem);

7. prior hospitalization (unplanned hospitalization in the six months before the current hospitalization); and

8. palliative care (whether or not the patient should be in palliative care or in hospice).

Telehealth

The data on telehealth helping to prevent readmissions are quite variable, most likely because of the level of support given. If the telehealth monitors vital signs only, the likelihood of preventing readmissions from medication nonadherence is low. However, the more that a telehealth operator acts like a coach, the better the likely results.[15–17]

COMPARATIVE DATA ON REDUCTION IN READMISSIONS   Table 13.2 shows the type of intervention, the percent reduction in readmissions, and references.[18–23] These were all from adult patients, mainly those on Medicare, taken the last five years. Review of these data show that, in keeping with the Grand-Aides model, the interventions with the greatest effects are those using people such as nurses and Grand-Aides, with Grand-Aides showing the best reduction in readmissions. (I want to restate my potential conflict of interest: I am the chair of Grand-Aides USA and did the literature review. I would be pleased to receive references that contradict the current conclusions.)

The paper from Bradley et al demonstrates that keeping people healthy and out of the hospital requires a multipronged approach from discharge planning through support at home.[24]

The editorial from Katz[25] about the Stauffer paper[26] concludes that although intense visits by a nurse are effective, they are also expensive at $1,100 per patient, whereas the data show that the Grand-Aide program is exactly 50% the cost.

WHERE DOES GRAND-AIDES "FIT" INTO THE ARMAMENTARIUM TO REDUCE READMISSIONS?

We know that different people require different types and levels of support. Some patients may be fine with getting support only from caring family and friends. Some may be fine with the increasing number of apps that help patients and families to manage themselves.[27,28] Some require only low levels of support by nurse calls, and some will only need telemonitoring. Those who require

TABLE 13.2 Literature on Reduction In Admissions

Intervention	% Reduction in Readmissions	% Reduction in Readmissions							Ref No.
		0	1–10	11–20	21–30	31–40	41–50	51–60	
Community health workers	0	X							18
Single nurse call	0	X							19
	0	X							20
Care at hand (app) + community health workers	6		X						21
Boost	40					X			22
	2		X						13
	14			X					14
	30				X				13
Project Red	28				X				12
Transitional care model	25				X				9
	36					X			10
Nurse weekly calls	33					X			23
Peer support	15			X					24
Care transitions intervention	12			X					11
	17			X					11
	30				X				11
	39					X			11
	48						X		11
Telehealth	0	X							15
	0	X							15
	13			X					16
	21				X				16
	23				X				17
Frequent nurse visits	48						X		27
Grand-Aides	58							X	6

behavioral changes beyond just occasional reminders are more likely to need Grand-Aides. We need to create studies that identify which specific patients in say, a population of 1,000 patients, will get the best result from the least expensive intervention rather than comparing intervention A with intervention B.

CONCLUSION: GRAND-AIDES AND THE TRANSFORMATION OF HEALTHCARE

A few years ago, Chris McGoff posted an online video that went viral.[29] His topic was the distinction between *change* and *transformation*. In change, one looks at the past and attempts to improve the current condition, making it better, faster, smarter, and so on. In transformation, one looks to the future (not at past), mapping out a vision of what needs to be and then working out how to get there. We have been called transformational. This seemed a bit much at first, but after viewing the video, I have concluded that the idea of leveraging well-trained people to do what professionals currently do is indeed transformational. This may explain why such a seemingly simple idea may require several people in an organization to adopt it. More than the positions are different; what is truly different is that at all levels of the organization, people need to view their own jobs as made up of what they must do and what—regardless of previous assumptions—they can easily transfer to others, thus making their own jobs potentially more interesting. In the case of Grand-Aides, this means making patient care better and less expensive.

REFERENCES

1. Garson A. Leveraging the health care workforce: what do we need and what educational system will get us there? *Acad Med.* 2011;86:1448–1453.

2. Garson A. New systems of care can leverage the health care workforce: how many doctors do we really need? *Acad Med.* 2013;88:1233–1237.

3. White C, Bowles ES, Carver GM, Compton FB, Eschenroeder TA, Van Meter MM, Marquardt M, Garson A. The Grand-Aides program in Baotou, Inner Mongolia: a revolutionary health care workforce. *Int Public Health J.* 2013;5:333–340.

4. A Garson, Green DM, Rodriguez L, Beech R, Nye C. Innovation profile: a new corps of trained Grand-Aides has the potential to extend reach of primary care and save money. *Health Aff* 2012;31:1016–1021.

5. Thomas C. A structured home visit program by non-licensed healthcare personnel can make a difference in the management and readmission of heart failure patients. *J Hosp Admin.* 2014;3:1–6.

6. Garson A. Grand-Aides and health policy: reducing readmissions cost-effectively. *Health Aff. Blog* 2014, October 29:1–4.

7. Shinkman R. Readmissions lead to $41.3B in additional hospital costs. 2014. Retrieved from http://www.fiercehealthfinance.com/story/readmissions-lead-413b -additional-hospital-costs/2014-04-20.

8. Naylor MD, Brooten D, Campbell R, Jaconsen BS, Mezey MD, Pauly MV, Schwartz S. Comprehensive discharge planning and home follow-up of hospitalized elders: a randomized clinical trial. *JAMA* 1999;281:613–620.

9. Hostetter M, Klein S. Avoiding preventable hospital readmissions by filling in gaps in care: the community-based care transitions program. Retrieved from http:// www.commonwealthfund.org/publications/newsletters/quality-matters/2012/august -sept/in-focus.

10. Voss R, Gardner R, Baier R, Butterfield K, Lehrman S, Gravenstein S. The care transitions intervention: translating from efficacy to effectiveness. *Jama Int Med.* 2011;171(14). Retrieved from http://archinte.jamanetwork.com/article.aspx?articleid=1105851.

11. Medicaring.org. CCTP success—will we know it when we see it? Retrieved from http://medicaring.org/tag/coleman-model/.

12. Paasche-Orlow M. Project RED: reengineering the discharge process; 2011. Retrieved from http://www.avoidreadmissions.com/wwwroot/userfiles/documents /40/arcredmkpo.pdf.

13. James J. Medicare hospital readmissions reduction program. *Health Aff.*; 2013. Retrieved from http://www.healthaffairs.org/healthpolicybriefs/brief.php?brief_id =102,202015.

14. Bird J. Mentoring project reduces 30 day rehospitalizations; 2013. Retrieved from http://www.fiercehealthcare.com/story/mentoring-project-reduces-30-day -rehospitalizations-136/2013-07-22.

15. Desai AS. Home monitoring heart failure care does not improve patient outcomes. *Circ.*; 2012. Retrieved from http://circ.ahajournals.org/content/125/6/828.full.

16. Tietze M, Reeves M, Horton D, Wolfe R. Telehealth for heart failure patients: an evolving strategy to reduce readmissions; 2013. Retrieved from http://nurse-practitioners -and-physician-assistants.advanceweb.com/Features/Articles/Telehealth-for-Heart -Failure-Patients.aspx.

17. Hall SD. Geisinger finds telemedicine cuts readmissions, costs for heart failure patients; 2014. Retrieved from http://www.achp.org/member-news/geisinger-finds -telemedicine-cuts-readmissions-costs-heart-failure-patients-2/.

18. Burns ME, Galbraith AA, Ross-Degnan D, Balaban RB. Feasibility and evaluation of a pilot community health worker intervention to reduce hospital readmissions. *Int J Qual Health Care.* 2014;26(4):358–365. Retrieved from http://www.ncbi.nlm.nih.gov /pubmed/24744082.

19. Penn Medicine. Penn's innovative community health worker model improves outcomes for high-risk patients; 2014. Retrieved from http://www.uphs.upenn.edu/news /News_Releases/2014/02/kangovi/.

20. MacDonald I. Nurse-led intervention program didn't improve readmission rates or reduce ER visits; 2014. Retrieved from http://www.fiercehealthcare.com/story

/nurse-led-intervention-program-didnt-improvement-readmission-rates-or-reduc /2014-10-08.

21. Ostrovsky A. Care at hand: a health coaching tool for patients; 2015. Retrieved from http://www.fiercemobilehealthcare.com/special-reports/care-hand-health-coaching -tool-patients.

22. Rowe C. Health coaches use care at hand tablet app to reduce readmissions; 2014. Retrieved from http://blogs.oliverwyman.com/healthcare/2014/08/06/health-coaches -use-care-at-hand-tablet-app-to-reduce-readmissions/.

23. Velicer C. Peer supporters as transition coaches for reducing hospital readmissions; 2013. Retrieved from http://peersforprogress.org/pfp_blog/peer-supporters-as-transition -coaches-for-reducing-hospital-readmissions/.

24. Bradley EH, Curry L, Horwitz LI, Sipsma H, Wang Y, Walsh M, Goldmann D, White N, Pina IL, Krumholz H. Hospital strategies associated with 30-day readmission rates for patients with heart failure. *Circ Cardiovasc Qual Outcomes.* 2013;6(4):444–450. Retrieved from http://www.ncbi.nlm.nih.gov/pubmed/23861483.

25. Katz M. Interventions to decrease hospital readmission rates: who saves? who pays? *Jama Int Med.* 2011. Retrieved from http://archinte.jamanetwork.com/article.aspx?articleid =1105805.

26. Stauffer BD, Fullerton C, Fleming N, Ogola G, Herrin J, Stafford PM, Ballard DJ. Effectiveness and cost of a transitional care program for heart failure: a prospective study with concurrent controls. *Arch Intern Med.* 2011;171(14):1238–1243. Retrieved from http://www.ncbi.nlm.nih.gov/pubmed/21788541.

27. Lee J. Preventing readmissions: is there an app for that? *Mod Healthc.* 2014;44(28):18–20. Retrieved from http://www.ncbi.nlm.nih.gov/pubmed/25134241.

28. Accardi K. Eight apps that can reduce readmissions; 2014. Ankota Healthcare Delivery Management Blog. Retrieved from http://www.ankota.com/blog/8-apps-that -can-reduce-readmissions.

29. McGoff C. Change vs transformation; 2010. Retrieved from http://vimeo.com /14002728.

CHAPTER 14

Convenience Care and the Rise of Retail Clinics

Tine Hansen-Turton
Kenneth W. Patric
Janet J. Teske

Abstract

In just over a decade, the notion of convenient care has evolved from nothing more than an intriguing idea and untested business model to an established, viable industry with tangible effects on healthcare delivery in the United States and beyond. This chapter examines the convenient care industry's history and evolution, its business model, and its growing popularity, and it offers some ideas as to why it is working. Since their inception, retail-based convenient care clinics (CCCs), also known as *retail clinics*, have established themselves as providers of affordable and accessible quality healthcare to consumers who may otherwise wait hours, days, or even weeks for basic primary care to become consumer favorites. Industry experts share insights into how a relative young but exiting journey of a new model has revolutionized healthcare as we know it and made it consumer driven.

HISTORY

Healthcare driven by consumer demand is the bedrock of the convenient care industry (CCI). Since their inception, retail–based convenient care clinics (CCCs) have established themselves as providers of affordable, accessible, and quality healthcare to consumers who may otherwise wait hours, days, or even weeks for basic primary care. In short, they have become consumer favorites with more than 35 million patient visits to CCCs to date (www.ccaclinics.org). The predicted growth of such clinic locations will enable them to treat millions more.

CCCs also became media favorites early on because they challenged the status quo in healthcare delivery. Hence, CCCs naturally raised concerns among many in the medical establishment, which resulted in articles that highlighted a medical community at odds with these new market entrants.[1]

Despite apparently opposing views, journalists have consistently reported on the expectation that retail health clinics will "profoundly affect healthcare delivery by providing an alternative site for basic medical care."[2] CCCs have been referred to as a "disruptive innovation," a term coined by Clayton Christensen, a professor at Harvard University and a *New York Times* bestselling author, because they represent a new interpretation of an aging and inefficient system. Instead, CCCs are consumer driven and provide an alternative for patients who "are frustrated with the conventional healthcare delivery system," which struggles with providing appropriate and timely access to basic healthcare services.[3]

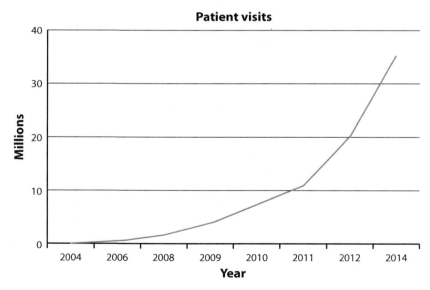

FIGURE 14.1 Patient visits

The creators of these clinics recognized that the existing primary care infrastructure was not meeting the basic healthcare needs of a significant number of people. This spurred the first convenient care clinic, operated by QuickMedx (which later became MinuteClinic and is now owned by CVS Health), to open its doors in 2000 in the Minneapolis–St. Paul area. Over the next six years, new market entrants began to emerge in other retail settings, many with financial backing from venture capital companies. Today a variety of institutions across the country manage CCCs, including private not-for-profit organizations, for-profit companies, hospital systems, and even some healthcare insurers. Current leading clinic operators include MinuteClinic, owned and operated by CVS Health; Healthcare Clinic, owned and operated by Walgreens; The Little Clinic, owned and operated by Kroger Co.; RediClinic, owned and operated by Rite Aid; and Target. Walmart serves as a landlord for a number of CCCs that are generally hospital owned; the company has also begun piloting its own clinics.

NONPHYSICIAN PROVIDERS IN PRIMARY CARE

The convenient care industry has relied heavily on the restructuring of primary care, which started in 1965 with the establishment of two new provider groups, nurse practitioners (NPs) and physician assistants (PAs). Nurse practitioners are the largest single group of primary care providers (PCPs) currently working in the CCI.

Nurse-managed care is not new to healthcare; this manner of treatment has traditionally developed in settings where there were few or no physicians (e.g., rural and urban health).[4] Nursing education opportunities exploded following World War II as nurses who had practiced in the war could subsequently pursue advanced education through the GI Bill and then begin working in all areas of the United States.[4] Later, when Medicare and Medicaid legislation passed in the 1960s, there was a new demand for services and an almost immediate shortage of physicians to fill this growing demand. This became the impetus for the expansion of other professions into primary care and the development of new types of providers, including NPs and PAs.[4] In 1965, Professor Loretta Ford and pediatrician Henry Silver established the first nurse practitioner program at the University of Colorado, and it was quite popular from the start.[4]

Other programs were soon instituted, attracting nurses and other health workers to pursue advanced degrees. Also in 1965, Dr Eugene Stead founded the nation's first PA program at Duke University. This platform was initially only available in the military, but eventually civilian programs were established at universities across the United States.[5] One such program is the MEDEX primary care training program at the University of Washington's School of Medicine, established in 1968 with a federal grant. Another example is the combined NP and PA program at the University of California, Davis. This master's of science nurse practitioner and physician assistant dual-track course is a unique arrangement originally administered by the Department of Family Practice in the UCD School of Medicine; since 2013, it has been administered by the UC Davis Betty Irene Moore School of Nursing, and it remains a combined NP and PA program.

The responsibilities of the NP and PA have grown substantially since the mid-1980s, and in 1994 these were boosted when the Institute of Medicine's Committee on the Future of Primary Care broadly defined primary care as "the provision of integrated, accessible healthcare services by clinicians who are accountable for addressing a large majority of personal healthcare needs, developing a sustained partnership with patients, and practicing in the context of family and community."[6] As of 2010, the Agency for Healthcare Research and Quality estimated there were more than 106,000 nurse practitioners and 70,000 physician assistants in practice at that time.[7]

In 2015, more than 5,000 nurse practitioners and physician assistants were working in the CCI. The need for more NPs and PAs is only likely to grow as the industry evolves and expands in response to consumer demand and the growing numbers of recently insured patients entering the healthcare system.

THE RETAIL-BASED CONVENIENT CARE CLINIC MODEL

The CCC model continues to develop and adapt based on the needs of consumers and as changes in the healthcare industry. During the first five years of operation, a limited number of illnesses were treated in the clinics. QuickMedx (now MinuteClinic), for example, treated only seven conditions: strep throat, mononucleosis, flu, pregnancy testing, and bladder, ear, and sinus infections. The clinics were offered as cost-effective alternatives to basic episodic care, thus removing the need for expensive emergency room visits for relatively simple medical issues. QuickMedx founders Rick Krieger and Douglas Smith wanted to establish a model of care delivery that permitted patients to receive efficient and effective treatment without the delays and high costs associated with the traditional healthcare system. To meet that need, the first clinics accepted only cash for services, and other market entrants quickly modeled themselves after QuickMedx. However, it soon became clear that minor tweaks in the process could make it even more beneficial. Clinicians believed that additional services could be added to the menu and that the cash model was limiting the clinics' ability to grow and scale.

Consumers were fans of convenient care clinics right from the start. Mothers with young children were among the first to embrace convenient care, recognizing its value in providing basic treatment to children when primary pediatricians were unavailable, especially on weekends, during evening and night, and whenever traditional primary care offices were closed.

Consumers were also integral to the clinics' early success by encouraging their employers and insurers to offer contracts to the clinics. Today, all clinic operators have contracts and therefore can accept most health insurance. Some insurers even provide incentives for their members to use the clinics for non-emergency care. Based on provider and consumer feedback, the scope of services has significantly expanded and today includes a broader range of acute care, preventive services, and even chronic disease management, the latter of which is usually offered in partnership with major healthcare systems.

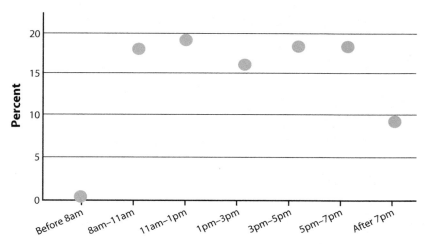

FIGURE 14.2 Percent of weekday visits to retail clinic visits by time of day, 2007–09

Notes: Each data point represents the fraction of weekday (Monday through Friday) retail clinic visits in our data that occurred during that time period. Data on day of week were not available for one of the three retail clinic companies, so data from that company were not included here. Source: Authors' analysis. Graph adapted from Mehrota, Lave.[8]

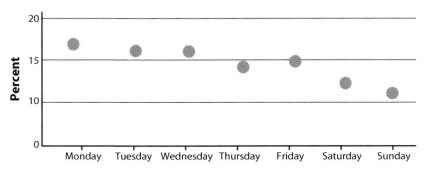

FIGURE 14.3 Percent of visits to retail clinics by day of week, 2007–09

Notes: Each data point represents the fraction of weekday retail clinic visits in our data that occurred on that day. Data on day of week were not available for one of the three retail clinic companies, so data from that company were not included here.

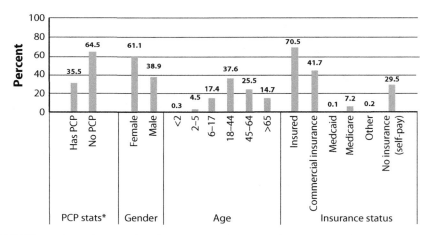

FIGURE 14.4 Sociodemographic characteristics of patients who visited retail clinics (2007–09)

*PCP = primary care physician

*Information source adapted from Mehrota, Lave.[8]

Convenient Care Clinic Description

By definition, CCCs are generally located in a wide array of retail locations such as drugstores, food stores, and other retail settings usually with in-house pharmacies. CCCs thus provide easy accessibility and are convenient for patients, who can get needed prescriptions filled on-site. The clinics range in size from single exam rooms to multiple rooms, complete with sinks and traditional exam tables. Though the clinics are small, typically occupying only 250 to 500 square feet, they are outfitted with all the provisions of any other outpatient healthcare office. Federal laws require that clinic owners and operators rent any retail space at fair market value as assessed by an appraiser. The providers, nurse practitioners, and physician assistants who staff the CCCs usually work for the operators of the clinics and typically have a collegial relationship with the associated retail pharmacy staff.

Given their retail location and focus, most of the clinics are open 7 days a week (typically 12 hours a day during the week and 8 hours on weekends). These operational hours are generally more accommodating than traditional doctors' offices, and nearly half of convenient care clinic visits occur in the off-hours of customary clinicians.[8,9] The majority of clinics see patients 18 months of age and older, and visits generally only take 15 to 25 minutes for both diagnosis and treatment.[8] CCC clinicians can diagnose, treat, and write prescriptions for all common illnesses (e.g., pinkeye, strep throat, skin conditions such as poison ivy and ringworm, and nose, ear, throat, and bladder infections). In addition, most common vaccinations are offered (e.g., flu, pneumonia, pertussis, hepatitis, measles, mumps, and rubella). CCC clinicians also may treat minor injuries and joint sprains. Finally, most now offer routine lab tests and a wide range of wellness and nonemergent services, including sports physicals, smoking cessation, TB testing, and preventative services for those with diabetes, high cholesterol, high blood pressure, and asthma.

The CCI has strongly supported transparency of medical costs. All major CCC operators clearly post their services and rates physically at the clinic, on the clinic's website, or via a brochure or other mechanism.

Since the industry's inception, the clinics have relied on a minimum number of employees who serve in multiple roles. Clinic staff is typically a nurse practitioner or physician assistant and in some cases medical assistants with both clinical and nonclinical duties. "Collaborating physicians" will provide consults for the clinics' providers as needed and as required by state law and regulation. Maintaining a limited number of employees means that clinicians often carry out some or most of the administrative functions of the clinic and aid with patient flow as well. Electronic health records (EHRs) are generally used to ensure coordination and continuity of care in concert with a patients' primary care providers, if they have one. Every clinic also has established guidelines or protocols available to assist the providers with medical decision making to ensure the highest level of patient care and satisfaction possible.

Patient flow in the convenient care clinic is designed to do just that—flow. The typical visit to a CCC starts like any other physician visit with patient registration, but unlike most traditional physician visits it typically involves a user-friendly, touch-screen computer similar to that of an airline self-check-in kiosk. To sign in, the patient supplies basic demographic information and reason for the visit; this automatically initiates a personal health record for the patient. There is often either assistance in the store or a phone number on hand to reach technical support should a patient require help. The patient's information is captured at the kiosk, transmitted electronically to a computer terminal inside the patient's designated treatment room, and a clinician is then notified of a patient waiting to be seen. The patient is escorted to the exam room, where the provider validates the information provided at check-in and enters any additional information regarding symptoms, conditions, and relevant medical history. To determine diagnosis and treatment, providers then perform a physical exam and may perform CLIA-waived lab tests. These tests—known as Clinical Laboratory Improvement Amendments—are accurate and useful but are considered simple enough as to not require the services of a certified laboratory technician. As part of the clinician's recommended treatment, they may write prescriptions that can be transmitted electronically to any pharmacy the patient chooses. If the pharmacy does not accept e-prescribing, then the clinician may write or print a prescription for the patient to hand carry. With the patients' consent, their visit records can be shared with their primary care provider, thus guaranteeing continuity of care.

With an estimated 40–50% of people visiting CCCs that do not have existing medical homes and up to 60% of patients reporting that they also do not have regular primary care providers,[10] CCCs have become valuable partners with local medical communities, referring their patients to PCPs who still accept patients. Aurora QuickCare Clinic referrals have resulted in a significant number of conversions of patients into the health system, thus establishing a primary care provider relationship with Aurora Health providers.

Founding of the Industry and the Convenient Care Association

In 2006, Hal Rosenbluth, founder of Take Care Health Systems, which is now the Healthcare Clinic at Walgreens, held a meeting for interested stakeholders to introduce themselves and the network with the idea of designing the blueprint for the future of the new industry. Participants included a diverse cross-section of interested parties: clinic operators, providers, nurse practitioner leaders, medical and physician assistant representatives, and other stakeholders. Two overarching concerns quickly became apparent: (1) the need to ensure that quality was at the forefront of the convenient care model and

(2) the importance of emphasizing that just one clinic operator not adhering to quality standards could put the entire nascent industry at risk. Donna Shalala, former secretary of the U.S. Department of Health and Human Services, suggested that the stakeholders form a more permanent association, and her recommendation initiated the birth of the CCC trade association, the Convenient Care Association (CCA). The CCA organized with the support and leadership of founding members and retail clinic operators Hal Rosenbluth and Web Golinkin and clinic consultant Tine Hansen-Turton.

The Convenient Care Association was officially incorporated in October 2006. CCA was thus operational and had begun to focus on implementing the recommendations made at the meeting to create a mechanism that would ensure quality above all else. In November 2006, CCA held its first board meeting of the retail clinic operators at that time and outlined the plans to establish quality and safety standards for the new industry. The goal was to have the criteria approved in spring 2007 and include a certification program that would ensure the highest quality standards.

From the very beginning the CCA has positioned itself as a nationally recognized organization. In only a few short years, the industry has enjoyed many significant accomplishments. The CCA was instrumental in developing and adopting industry quality and safety standards, including implementing third-party certification; advocating successfully against legislation and regulations that would reduce consumer access to high-quality, affordable healthcare; providing continuing education to thousands of convenient care practitioners; establishing CCA as a reliable media source; and creating the National Convenient Care Clinic Week.

Both 2006 and 2007 were notable for several important industry restructurings and acquisitions. In July 2006, CVS Health announced that it would acquire Minneapolis-based MinuteClinic (formerly QuickMedx), establishing MinuteClinic as a wholly owned subsidiary. In May 2007, Walgreens acquired Take Care Health Systems of Conshohocken, Pennsylvania. One year later, Kroger and The Little Clinic announced a partnership whereby Kroger became a shareholder; in April 2010, Kroger bought out the remaining shares in The Little Clinic and became the company's sole owner.

The onset of the 2008 recession presented significant challenges for the CCI. A slumping economy combined with the nascence of the industry and the low profit margins initially associated with the business model all contributed to the closings of some smaller industry operators and individual clinics belonging to larger operators. However, this temporary downsizing presented an opportunity for existing providers to expand their clinic services and fine-tune their overall operations, which ultimately resulted in a stronger industry that today boasts more than 1,900 clinics and continues to grow.

Initial Challenges from the Medical Establishment and Public Skepticism

As with any emerging industry, there was initial uncertainty about the need for convenient care clinics. In light of the small number of clinics nationwide and questions about the viability of the business model, the founding of the CCA was initially considered by some to be premature. However, it would soon prove prescient when large industry opponents delivered the first formal challenges to convenient care.

The American Medical Association (AMA), American Academy of Family Physicians (AAFP) and American Academy of Pediatrics (AAP) were among the first to publicly question the value and efficacy of retail-based convenient care.[8] Skepticism regarding the convenient care model focused on three specific issues: quality of care, continuity of care, and potential conflicts of interest related to the ownership model of the clinics. Critics felt that adequate quality standards and positive care outcomes could not possibly be upheld without regular on-site physician oversight. Allegations of poor quality suggested that a healthcare practice under the principal direction of nurse practitioners and physician assistants was completely insufficient for the tasks at hand. As to continuity of care, detractors feared that treatment based largely around acute, episodic interactions with patients would result in missed opportunities for key care, such as preventive health counseling and important vaccinations. The conflict-of-interest argument supposed that a healthcare practice owned by and situated inside a for-profit retail setting would be unable to provide purely objective service. As an example, a clinic might over-prescribe medications simply to drive business to the retail host's in-house pharmacy.

The CCC industry worked with third-party research groups and collected and disseminated data to combat the skepticism. Research has repeatedly shown that the clinics provide high-quality healthcare services. Quality scores and rates of preventive care at CCCs have been found to be superior to other ambulatory care delivery settings such as urgent care centers and emergency departments.[11,12] In addition, CCCs have a 92.72% compliance with quality measures for appropriate testing of children with pharyngitis versus the Health Plan Employer Data and Information Set (HEDIS) average of 74.7% and 88.35% compliance score for appropriate testing of children with upper respiratory infections versus the HEDIS average of 83.5%.[13]

The initial response of the public to convenient care was tepid, at best. Early demand for access and word-of-mouth advertising proved inadequate to increase patient volume, demonstrating that more direct marketing efforts would be required to drive the numbers of patient visits necessary to sustain the business model. These start-up speed bumps ironically helped to shape and streamline the clinics currently in operation, and these changes came largely and directly from provider and patient feedback. Today there is high acceptance of the clinics from the public, as well as high patient satisfaction.

Increasing Involvement with Hospitals and Health Systems

As the convenient care industry has grown and advanced, one of the most striking changes over time has been the vastly increased involvement of provider groups. Although traditional healthcare providers may have initially felt threatened by a disruptive newcomer to the medical field, today nearly all the major CCC operators have strategic partnerships with more than 60 hospitals or major medical groups (Table 14.1).

These partnerships facilitate bidirectional referral channels; service expansion opportunities, including chronic disease management and maintenance; and quality monitoring and improvement programs. Although a few large health systems were early adopters of retail-based healthcare and were among the founding members of the CCA (e.g., Aurora Health Care, Geisinger, Sutter), the majority of the first CCC operators were private corporations. Over the last few years, larger numbers of health systems have partnered with retail-based healthcare in two main capacities: (1) They serve as direct operators of the clinics in tandem with retail host stores or (2) they may join as partners with another CCC operator to provide collaborative physicians and allow a smoother transition of patient care from purely episodic to more involved continuity of care. In this manner, CCCs actually facilitate appropriate access to the often cumbersome and confusing U.S. healthcare system.

COMMITMENTS TO QUALITY

Under the leadership umbrella of the CCA, the CCI made a strong commitment to high quality of care from the outset. To achieve and maintain this commitment, the CCA first set out to design a set of quality and safety standards to which all members would be required to adhere.

TABLE 14.1 Strategic Partnerships Between CCC Operators and Other Healthcare Delivery Organizations

MinuteClinic
Dignity Health (AZ)
Sharp Healthcare (CA)
St. Joseph Health (CA)
UCLA Health System (CA)
Baptist Health Care (FL)
Cleveland Clinic Florida (FL)
St. Vincent's HealthCare (FL)
Florida Hospital Medical Group (FL)
Emory Healthcare (GA)
Indiana University Health (IN)
UMASS Memorial Health Care (MA)
Henry Ford Health System (MI)
Allina Health (MN)
St. Rose Dominican Hospitals (NV)
Dartmouth-Hitchcock (NH)
North Shore—LIJ (NY)
Atlantic Health System (NJ)
Barnabas Health (NJ)
Hackensack University Health
    Network (NJ)
Robert Wood Johnson (NJ)
Virtua (NJ)
Carolinas HealthCare System (NC)
Cleveland Clinic (OH)
Ohio Health (OH)
OU Physicians (OK)
Main Line Health (PA)
Greenville Hospital System (SC)
TriStar Health (TN)
Parkridge Health Systems (TN)
UT Medicine San Antonio (TX)
Inova Health System (VA)
University of Maryland (MD)
Houston Methodist (TX)

Healthcare Clinic in Select Walgreens
Centura Health (CO)
Orlando Health (FL)
Memorial Health (FL)
WellStar (GA)
Eastside (GA)
Community Health Network (IN)

Kentucky One Health (KY)
Ochsner Health System (LA)
Nevada Primary Care Network (NV)
Johns Hopkins (MD)
SSM Healthcare (MO)
HCA (MO)
The Valley Health System (NV)
Summa Health (OH)
Baptist Memorial (TN)
Baylor Health System (TX)

Target Clinics
Kaiser Permanente (CA)
Duke Medicine (NC)
Texas Health Physicians Group/Texas
    HealthResources (TX)

Rite Aid/RediClinic
Memorial Hermann Health System (TX)
Seton Healthcare Family (TX)
Methodist Healthcare System (TX)

The Little Clinic
University of Colorado Health
    Partners (CO)
University of Louisville Physicians (KY)
The Ohio State University Wexner Medical
    Center (OH)
UC Health (OH)

FastCare
St. Francis Hospital and Medical
    Center (CT)
Norwalk Hospital (CT)
Wheaton Franciscan
    HealthCare-Iowa (IA)
Anne Arundel Medical Center (MD)
Bronson Medical Group (MI)
Aria Health (PA)
Pinnacle Health Hospitals (PA)
Bon Secours Richmond Health
    System (VA)
Aspirus Medford (WI)

The CCA leaders understood that the establishment of quality standards for the entire industry would be critical to ensuring the safety and delivery of the highest quality care in CCCs.

To that end, industry leaders, clinicians, and operators all agreed to support the following industry-wide, consumer-driven, patient care performance standards:

- Use of national evidence-based guidelines for each condition treated
- Achieve measurable high patient satisfaction
- Set a minimum standard for wait times
- Track numbers of patient visits to the clinic
- Establish a healthcare provider referral system in all markets that allows for timely treatment of conditions beyond the center's scope of practice
- Establish cost transparency for patients
- Adhere to Occupational Safety and Health Administration and CLIA standards
- Establish quality-monitoring and quality-improvement programs
- Establish corporate compliance programs
- Establish emergency response plans and emergency equipment available at each site
- Establish postvisit access plans
- Provide discharge instructions and educational materials for each patient
- Establish minimum age for pediatric patients
- Use EHR with embedded evidence-based protocols from key national organizations

The next step in quality assurance was to organize a clinical advisory board consisting of representatives of clinic operators and national medical, nursing, and accreditation organizations who were responsible for developing the first quality and safety protocols for the CCI. To continue its dedication to industry and health quality, in 2010 the CCA revised its standards to reflect maturation in the industry.

Even before the quality and safety standards had been defined, CCA leadership recognized the importance of providing members with an accessible path to third-party certification. Some clinic operators elected early on to pursue accreditation with The Joint Commission, and the CCA has a partnership with the Health Care Improvement Foundation to administer a certification developed specifically for members of CCA. The certification has been well received and has proven a useful tool for clinic operators negotiating contracts with third-party payers.

The most important factor for clinics and patients is quality. Quality assurance is critical to the long-term survival of the convenient care industry. To assist in the clinical decision-making process at most convenient care clinics, standardized protocols have been developed to help NPs decide which treatment path to follow. It is important to note that these protocols are guidelines and are not intended to replace the critical judgment of providers but enhance and aid in decision making. The leading CCCs' practices are grounded in evidence-based medicine and follow guidelines published by major medical bodies such as the AAP and AAFP. The clinics incorporate strict quality assessments into their evaluative structures, including chart reviews by collaborating physicians and CCC clinician peers. Chart reviews consistently demonstrate adherence to evidence-based protocols and no excessive prescribing of antibiotics. In addition, most clinic operators use standard coding audits. Provider credentials are primary source-verified, and work histories are reviewed, ensuring that those who work in these independent roles have adequate education and experience. CCCs strive to establish a referral base with physicians and other healthcare providers to support the best interests of patients and providers and maintain the continuity of healthcare within the entire community. The CCI is dedicated to ensuring that all of its clinicians abide by all state laws and regulations.

In addition to quality, patient satisfaction is a priority for CCCs. According to a 2010 Gallup Poll, the Take Care Clinic fared well with patients:

> Take Care Clinic's (now Healthcare Clinic at Walgreens) customer-engagement results that have been collected thus far are in the top 10% of all organizations that Gallup has measured since 2003. To put this level of performance in some kind of context, the typical company in Gallup's database strongly engages [fewer than one in five of their customers]; Take Care Clinic strongly engages more than [three out of every four]. Moreover, more than [9 out of every 10] patients strongly feel that the nurse practitioner or physician assistant spends enough time with them, and a similar number strongly feels that the nurse practitioner or physician assistant carefully listens to them and explains things in a way that is easy to understand.[14]

FUTURE DIRECTIONS

Over time and through feedback from patients who visited the CCCs in the early years of the industry, the scope of services offered in the convenient care setting has steadily expanded. However, even with a broader range of services and procedures now available, clinic operators have basically adhered to their original model by staying within a range of treatments that do not require expensive large-scale diagnostics and can be carried out in 15–20 minute intervals. This model has been successful and is unlikely to change dramatically in the foreseeable future.

CCI operators will also remain focused on quality, convenience, and consumer choice. Convenient care clinics have set the bar high for themselves in an effort to promote the best possible patient care in the retail setting by establishing clear standards, employing efficient and well-educated clinicians committing to the use of evidenced-based guidelines, and continually updating medical skills for ongoing quality improvement.

Potential Future Challenges and Opportunities

Because of the CCI's history as a disruptive innovation and its success with providing accessible, affordable high-quality healthcare, the industry has started using technology to expand services and increase access to affordable healthcare for more patients. There has been a rapid growth of telehealth service companies, platforms, and products. Patients are making as many as 300 million telehealth visits per year, and patients, payers, and providers are embracing technology as a viable mode for healthcare delivery.[15] Moreover, Anthem recently announced it would offer telehealth visits without co-pays to its Medicare Advantage members in 12 states; approximately 37% of employers were planning to offer their employees telemedicine consultations in 2015.[15] Some clinic operators have started to expand their scope of services through the use of technology; through this expansion, CCCs are able to increase access to care for many more patients who would otherwise not have it.

The challenge with telehealth is not an unfamiliar one to the CCI as there are numerous legislative telehealth proposals in every state. The industry had begun its efforts to offer a unified voice by identifying telehealth principles for CCCs to use as guidance. Those principles include: (1) Quality and privacy are central principles in the provision of telehealthcare, (2) telehealth as defined in the law should ensure access to care, and (3) payment for telehealth services should be encouraged through the law.

Quality and Privacy

Services delivered through telehealth should be provided through means that uphold the highest standards of patient care and the protection of patients' private health information.

Telehealth is a method of healthcare delivery by which a licensed healthcare professional uses information and communication technologies to deliver diagnoses, consultation, and treatment to patients. To maintain optimal standards of quality, members of the Convenient Care Association believe that:

- Telehealth services must be provided with the use of advanced telecommunications technology, not just mechanisms such as telephone, e-mail, and text messages and facsimile transmissions.
- Telehealth services must be provided in conjunction with electronic patient data collection that excels in maintaining security and confidentiality and meets all relevant privacy standards.

Telehealth Definitions in the Law

A definition for telehealth should be written broadly to allow services delivered through telehealth to be provided across settings through appropriate providers.

Across the nation, states are defining telehealth in law. However, the definitions are often drafted using language that restricts access to care by inappropriately limiting delivery settings and eligible providers.

- To maximize access to care, state laws should define telehealth in a way that allows all licensed nurse practitioners and physician assistants to provide services through telehealth up to their scope of practice. Further, no new telehealth-specific supervision requirements of licensed NPs and PAs should be imposed.
- Definitions should be written carefully to ensure access to those delivery settings and mechanisms in which quality telehealthcare can be provided; doing otherwise will hinder the use of telehealth and restrict access to care.

Payment for Telehealth Services

State law should strongly encourage payment for telehealth services to improve healthcare access.

State lawmakers may define telehealth in law, but if insurance companies do not reimburse for services delivered through telehealth, then patients will not be able to use them.

- To encourage adoption of telehealth by providers, state law should encourage private insurers to reimburse for services provided through telehealth.

• State law should ensure that telehealth services are reimbursed at an appropriate rate for the service provided. If telehealth services are not reimbursed at a reasonable rate, it is much less likely that the necessary services will be available through telehealth.

The CCI, having identified the need for change early, set out to bridge the chasm of access to high-quality, affordable primary care. The industry has successfully shown how that chasm can be bridged, and it will continue to grow and remain an essential and important piece to solving the U.S. healthcare puzzle.

The U.S. Supreme Court's summer 2012 decision to uphold the Affordable Care Act guaranteed that the large numbers of newly insured patients would be able to keep their access to affordable quality healthcare; as such, the need for CCCs has never been greater. Equally great is the value proposition of the retail-based CCC model of care, and the industry is poised, ready, and able for future success.

REFERENCES

1. Riff J, Ryan SF, Hansen-Turton T. *Convenient Care Clinics: The Essential Guide to Clinicians, Managers and Educators.* New York, NY: Springer; 2013.

2. Malvery D, Fottler MD. The retail revolution in health care: who will win and who will lost? *Health Care Manage R.* 2006;31:168–178.

3. Christensen C, Grossman J, Hwang J. *The Innovator's Prescription: A Disruptive Solution for Health Care.* New York, NY: McGraw-Hill; 2009.

4. Mezey MD, McGivern DO, Sullivan-Marx EM, Greensberg SA. *Nurse Practitioners: Evolution of Advanced Practice.* 4th ed. New York, NY: Springer; 2003.

5. Vorvik LJ. Physician assistant profession (PA). *MedlinePlus* 2001. Retrieved April 16, 2015, from http://www.nlm.nih.gov/medlineplus/ency/article/001935.htm.

6. Donaldson M, Yordy K, Vanselow N. *Defining Primary Care: An Interim Report.* Washington, DC: National Academies Press, 1994.

7. Agency for Healthcare Research and Quality. The number of nurse practitioners and physician assistants practicing primary care in the United States: primary care workforce facts and stats no. 2. Rockville, MD: AHRQ; 2014. Retrieved April 16, 2015, from http://www.ahrq.gov/research/findings/factsheets/primary/pcwork2/index.html.

8. Mehrota A, Lave JR. Visits to retail clinics grew fourfold from 2007 to 2009, although their share of overall outpatient visits remains low. *Health Affair.* 2012;31,1–7.

9. Hansen-Turton T, Ridgeway CG, Ryan SF, Nash DB. Convenient care clinics: the future of accessible health care—the formation years 2006–2008. *Pop Health Manag.* 2009;12,5:231–240.

10. Patwardhan A, Davis J, Murphy P, Ryan SF. After-hours access of convenient care clinics and cost savings associated with avoidance of higher-cost sites of care. *J Primary Care Comm Health.* 2012;3(4):243–245.

11. Mehrota A, Liu H, Adams JL, et al. Comparing costs and quality of care at retail clinics with that of other medical settings for 3 common illnesses. *Ann Int Med.* 2009; 151,5:321–328.

12. Shrank WH, Krumme AA, Tong AY., et al. Quality of care at retail clinics for 3 common conditions. *Amer J Manag C.* 2014;20,10:794–801.

13. Jacoby R, Crawford AG, Chaudhari P, Goldfarb NI. Quality of care for 2 common pediatric conditions treated by convenient care providers. *Am J Med Qual.* 2010; 26:53–58.

14. Frazee SG, Fleming J, Ozan-Rafferty M. Elevating the patient experience to a new level at take care clinics. *Retail Clinician;* 2010.

15. Tahir D. Telehealth services surging. *Mod Healthcare.* 2015;45,8:18–20.

III

EMERGING PARADIGMS IN THE PRACTICE OF MEDICINE

Using Guideline-Based Medicine to Improve Patient Care

Kunal N. Karmali
Philip Greenland

Abstract

Clinical practice guidelines are an integral component of the effort to improve healthcare quality and outcomes. They systematically appraise and summarize scientific evidence and provide evidence-based practice recommendations to guide healthcare decisions on a specific clinical topic. Clinical practice guidelines set a reference standard for evidence-based practice that can be used by clinicians, third-party payers, and governments as a benchmark for quality to improve patient care. This chapter describes the rationale, use, and standards of trustworthy clinical practice guidelines as established by the Institute of Medicine. It also highlights the critical role of implementation science in bringing guideline-concordant care into clinical practice to improve patient care and healthcare quality.

RATIONALE FOR GUIDELINES

Clinicians and patients face difficult management decisions every day. Choosing the right diagnostic test or therapeutic intervention is a routine part of clinical encounters. Ideally, the best available medical evidence should inform these decisions. However, the pace of biomedical science is rapid and the extent of published literature is vast. In 2013 alone, more than 730,000 new citations were added to MEDLINE, bringing the total citation count to nearly 20.7 million.[1] Assessments of healthcare quality in the United States suggest that clinicians are unable to keep up with this volume of medical literature because only 50% of U.S. adults receive recommended care and 20% to 30% receive contraindicated care.[2] Studies have also exposed significant regional variations in practice that further highlight that many individuals in the United States are not receiving evidence-based care. In the field of cardiovascular disease, for example, national surveys have demonstrated dramatic regional differences in treatment of myocardial infarction and cardiovascular diagnostic testing that are not explained by case-mix differences.[3,4]

Clinical practice guidelines represent an effort to promote evidence-based practice by gathering, appraising, and synthesizing this vast medical knowledge into a convenient and usable format. The Institute of Medicine (IOM) defines clinical practice guidelines as "statements that include recommendations, intended to optimize patient care, that are informed by a systematic review of evidence, and an assessment of the benefits and harms of alternative care options."[5] Thus, guidelines are designed to enhance clinician and patient decision making by translating research findings into discrete management recommendations and providing evidence-based reasoning behind these recommendations. Guidelines aim to facilitate evidence-based practice, reduce regional practice variability, and direct care toward therapies of known benefit while minimizing therapies of uncertain benefit or harm.[5]

GUIDELINE DEVELOPERS

Several agencies have taken on the responsibility of formulating guidelines to direct clinical practice. Professional societies such as the American College of Cardiology (ACC) and the American Heart Association (AHA) have long histories and established procedures for guideline development and continuing medical education for their members.[6] Government agencies in the United States such as the United States Preventive Services Task Force (USPSTF) and the Centers for Disease Control and Prevention (CDC) have also issued several guidelines focusing on preventive care practices and public health policy.[5] In the United Kingdom, the National Institute for Health and Clinical Excellence (NICE) develops guidelines to advise the National Health Service (NHS), the publicly funded healthcare system.[7] To some extent, guidelines may be influenced by the specific agency that produces them. This fact is important to keep in mind when trying to understand how different guidelines on the same topic might reach differing recommendations.

GUIDELINE USERS

Clinical practice guidelines serve their users through two principal means. First, guidelines serve as *professional guides*. By summarizing the current state of knowledge in a specific topic area and providing evidence-based recommendations, guidelines can inform clinicians and patients in clinical decision making. They direct care toward interventions of known benefit while minimizing interventions of uncertain benefit or harm. Guidelines present best-available evidence for a given condition to foster shared decision making with patients and can be used in continuing medical education to help clinicians stay abreast of an ever-expanding knowledge base.

Second, stakeholders within the healthcare system can use guidelines as means of *external control*. Recommendations within guidelines can be translated into performance indicators to measure hospital and clinician quality of care. Insurers and administrators can also use guidelines to determine insurance coverage and reimbursement policies. The Affordable Care Act, for example, has explicit legislation that new private health plans and insurance policies must cover preventive services that are rated "strongly recommended" or "recommended" by USPSTF guidelines.[8] Government agencies frequently use guidelines in policy making and public health interventions. Guidelines also have important medico-legal implications as lawyers can use them to define "standard" medical practice in malpractice litigation. This practice is particularly concerning when different guidelines conflict in their recommendations.[9]

Outside of the healthcare system, scientific researchers and research funders can use the gaps identified by guidelines to direct efforts and funding toward areas of uncertainty to promote scientific discovery and knowledge generation.[10] Table 15.1 summarizes several common benefits and pitfalls of clinical practice guidelines.

GUIDELINES IN QUALITY IMPROVEMENT

The past two decades have seen a rapid growth in quality-improvement initiatives. Guidelines directly serve such efforts by summarizing scientific evidence of effective patient care. Thus, many guideline recommendations have been

TABLE 15.1 Potential Benefits and Limitations of Guidelines

Potential Benefits	Potential Limitations
Summarize and appraise research findings	Reduce individualized care for patients with special circumstances
Increase consistency of care	May misinterpret evidence or provide misleading recommendations
Empower patients to make informed healthcare choices	Professional resistance
Provide external accountability and efficiency	Concern for legal consequences
Summarize best-practice for clinicians and patients	Misuse by governmental authorities and health insurance industry
Influence public policy and set research priorities	Uncertainty about cost-effectiveness
Support quality-improvement activities	

translated by professional societies, hospitals, and regulatory agencies into *performance measures* and *appropriate use criteria* (AUC) to measure and quantify healthcare quality to facilitate quality improvement.

Performance Measures

Performance measures are quantitative tools to measure the quality of medical care. Operationally, guidelines directly feed into the development of performance measures by identifying actions that are supported by such high-quality evidence that failure to perform them reduces the likelihood of optimal patient outcomes. The ACC and AHA outline key criteria of evidence-based guidelines that produce optimal performance measures, specifically recommendations that are measureable, actionable, address a gap, and are associated with improved outcomes.[11] Consumers, insurers, and regulatory agencies can then use performance measures to determine the quality of different healthcare providers and healthcare systems. For example, a number of the ACC and AHA performance measures—including those for management of acute myocardial infarction and heart failure—have been adopted by national programs such as the Centers for Medicare and Medicaid Services (CMS) and the National Quality Forum to rate and compare hospitals and clinical practices on healthcare quality.[5]

Appropriate Use Criteria

Appropriate use criteria are another derivative of clinical practice guidelines that supplement guideline recommendations by rating the "appropriateness" of various medical interventions for a range of commonly encountered clinical scenarios. Professional societies such as the ACC, American Society of Nuclear Cardiology, and American College of Radiology have developed AUC in response to concerns from third parties about the growth of healthcare costs, variations in healthcare delivery, and concerns about overuse and misuse of medical interventions.[12,13] AUC cover a broad array of clinical scenarios, including clinical situations where evidence is lacking or where management is highly dependent on the specific clinical characteristics. Panels of specialty experts rate the "appropriateness" of a given medical intervention based on the clinical scenario and thereby illustrate how specific recommendations in guidelines might be implemented in practice. In cardiovascular disease, the ACC has developed AUC for a variety of cardiovascular imaging tests and interventional procedures.[12]

Taken together clinical practice guidelines, performance measures, and AUC help define evidence-based practice, measure how consistently these processes are implemented in patient care, and provide benchmarks to facilitate quality improvement and promote safe, effective, and cost-effective patient care. Figure 15.1 demonstrates the relationship between scientific evidence, guideline development, guideline implementation, performance measures, and improved patient outcomes.

EFFECTIVENESS OF GUIDELINES

Even when guidelines represent the best synthesis of evidence and expert opinion, real-world analyses are still required to validate their effect on improving patient outcome. Because it is difficult to randomize patients against evidence-based practices that are already recommended by experts, much of the validation of guideline recommendations is based on observational studies.

In cardiovascular disease, the Can Rapid Risk Stratification of Unstable Angina Patients Suppress Adverse Outcomes with Early Implementation (CRUSADE) registry for non-ST-segment elevation acute coronary syndromes provides face validity for class I recommendations in the ACC and AHA guidelines. Analyses from CRUSADE demonstrated a significant association between guideline adherence to nine class I recommendations and in-hospital mortality. Every 10% increase in composite adherence to the ACC and AHA guidelines was associated with a 10% reduction in in-hospital mortality (adjusted OR 0.90, 95% CI 0.84–0.97; $p < 0.001$). Hospitals in the highest quartile of guideline adherence had a lower mortality rate compared to hospitals in the

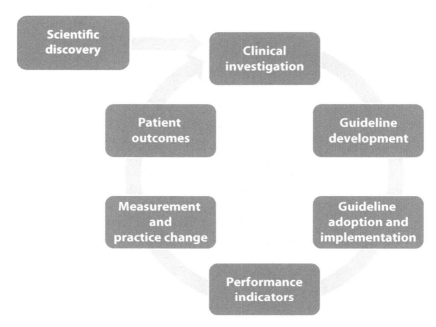

FIGURE 15.1 Improving patient outcomes through clinical practice guideline development and implementation. Adapted from Jones et al.[55]

lowest quartile of guideline adherence (4.15% versus 6.31%, $p < 0.001$).[14] Similarly, in the Mahler study, a multicenter observational study in six European countries, Komajda et al demonstrated that adherence to beta-blockers, ACE inhibitors, and spironolactone as outlined in heart failure management guidelines predicted a lower risk of heart failure and cardiovascular hospitalization (HR 0.64, 95% CI 0.41–1.00; $p = 0.048$).[15]

Guideline adherence has also been associated with improved patient outcomes for noncardiovascular conditions. In an analysis of adults in community and tertiary care hospitals treated for community-acquired pneumonia, adherence to joint guidelines from the Infectious Disease Society of America (IDSA) and American Thoracic Society was associated with decreased in-hospital mortality after adjusting for potential confounders (OR 0.70, 95% CI 0.63–0.77).[16] Similar improvements in outcomes have also been shown for guideline-concordant treatment for depression and trauma surgery.[17,18]

Supporting these observational analyses, Grimshaw et al completed a systematic review of trials that evaluated the effectiveness of guidelines.[19] Of the 59 trials identified that met predefined criteria for scientific rigor (balanced incomplete block, randomized crossover, simple randomized, controlled before and after, and interrupted time series), 55 of them found improved process of care activities. Only 11 trials reported outcomes of care, and 9 of them demonstrated significant improvements in outcomes of care. An updated search in 2004 similarly demonstrated improvements in process of care measures with guideline adherence, but only 26 of 235 trials reported patient outcomes.[20]

ENSURING GUIDELINE QUALITY

The past two decades have seen an increase both in the number and influence of clinical practice guidelines. In the face of such an expansion, many have come to question the validity and quality of guidelines. Guideline developers often do not follow the standards for guideline development that were initially established by the IOM in 1992, and there has been little change in the guideline development process over the years.[21,22] Concerns highlighted by these studies include conflicting recommendations from different guidelines, low-quality evidence underlying recommendations, conflicts of interest among guideline writers, and a lack of transparency when outlining the derivation of treatment recommendations.

The growth of professional societies in healthcare has led to a surge of guideline documents. By the beginning of 2015, the National Guideline Clearinghouse sponsored by the Agency for Healthcare Research and Quality (AHRQ) had archived more than 2,400 clinical practice guidelines while the Guidelines International Network (GIN) had archived more than 6,400 guidelines.[23,24] The explosive growth in guidelines development can lead to conflicting recommendations from different medical societies. For breast cancer screening, the American College of Radiology, the American Cancer Society, the USPSTF, and the American College of Obstetrics and Gynecology all provide different recommendations about the appropriate interval for screening mammography and clinical breast exams in women aged 40 to 74 years.[9] Conflicting guidelines like these can defeat the very purpose of guidelines by leading to greater confusion for clinicians as well as the lay public.

Examination of the evidence behind guidelines has also demonstrated that many guideline recommendations are developed from lower levels of evidence or expert opinion. In a review of guidelines from the IDSA, only 14% of the 4,000 guideline recommendations were supported by randomized clinical trials.[25] Similarly, in a study of ACC and AHA guidelines, Tricoci et al found that 48% of recommendations in the guidelines were developed from the lowest levels of evidence, and only 11% of recommendations were supported by high-quality evidence, a finding of significant concern given the frequency with which ACC and AHA guidelines are used to benchmark hospital quality and determine reimbursement.[26]

These studies highlight opportunities for improving scientific research, but the reliance on low-quality evidence and the inherent subjectivity of "expert opinion" have led many people to criticize the vagueness behind the derivation of recommendations and the possibility that conflicts of interest among panel members may unduly influence recommendations.[27,28] A cross-sectional survey of 192 authors from 44 different clinical practice guidelines between 1991 and 1999 demonstrated considerable contact between guideline writers and the pharmaceutical industry; 87% of guideline writers had some form of interaction with the industry, and 58% received financial support.[29] The frequency of pharmaceutical contact during the guideline development process threatens the credibility of a given guideline among practitioners. This is illustrated by the controversy with sepsis-treatment guidelines in which Eli Lilly played a prominent role in funding the guideline committee and had multiple relationships with guideline panel members; treatment recommendations ultimately featured a novel sepsis drug manufactured by Eli Lilly.[30] The frequency with which guidelines incompletely describe methods used to identify studies, the rationale behind recommendations, and rating schemes to denote the strength of recommendation has led many people to call for fundamental changes in the composition and dynamics of guideline development.[28]

PRINCIPLES OF TRUSTWORTHY GUIDELINES

In response to these concerns, through the Medicare Improvements for Patients and Providers Act of 2008, the U.S. Congress charged the IOM with developing standards for objective, scientifically valid, and consistent approaches for developing clinical practice guidelines. The report—*Clinical Practice Guidelines We Can Trust*—established a new definition for clinical practice guidelines as "statements that include recommendations, intended to optimize patient care, that are informed by a systematic review of evidence and an assessment of the benefits and harms of alternative care options."[5] The revised definition emphasizes two essential features of trustworthy guidelines: (1) the role of systematic reviews as the foundation of the evidence–based guideline and (2) the importance of structuring recommendations around a benefits and harms assessment.

In *Clinical Practice Guidelines We Can Trust*, the IOM proposed eight standards of trustworthy clinical practice guidelines that addressed transparency, management of conflicts of interest, composition of the guideline development group, the intersection between systematic reviews and guidelines, grading

TABLE 15.2 Institute of Medicine (IOM) Standards for Trustworthy Clinical Practice Guidelines: 2011[5]

Standards	IOM Recommendations
Transparency	The process and funding of guideline development should be detailed and publicly accessible.
Conflicts of interest	Writing group members should openly declare conflicts of interest, including commercial, institutional, professional, and intellectual. Members should divest from any financial investment that could be affected by guideline recommendations. The committee chair and co-chair, who are responsible for directing guideline priorities and discussions, should have no conflict of interest relevant to the guideline topic.
Group composition	The writing group should be a multidisciplinary panel, including clinicians, methodological experts, stakeholder representatives, and affected populations.
Systematic review of evidence	Guidelines should be based on rigorous systematic evidence review and consider quality, quantity, and consistency of the available evidence.
Grading strength of recommendations	Guidelines should summarize evidence (and evidence gaps), potential benefits and harms relevant to each recommendation, and level of confidence underpinning each recommendation.
Articulation of recommendations	Recommendations should be clearly stated and actionable. Wording should facilitate implementation in clinical practice and external surveillance.
External review	The draft guidelines should be externally reviewed by a full spectrum of stakeholders and include an open period for public comment.
Updating	Guidelines should be updated when new evidence should result in modifying the recommendations.

CLASS (STRENGTH) OF RECOMMENDATION

CLASS I (STRONG)   Benefit >>> Risk

Suggested phrases for writing recommendations:
- Is recommended
- Is indicated/useful/effective/beneficial
- Should be performed/administered/other
- Comparative-Effectiveness Phrases†:
  - Treatment/strategy A is recommended/indicated in preference to treatment B
  - Treatment A should be chosen over treatment B

CLASS IIa (MODERATE)   Benefit >> Risk

Suggested phrases for writing recommendations:
- Is reasonable
- Can be useful/effective/beneficial
- Comparative-Effectiveness Phrases†:
  - Treatment/strategy A is probably recommended/indicated in preference to treatment B
  - It is reasonable to choose treatment A over treatment B

CLASS IIb (WEAK)   Benefit ≥ Risk

Suggested phrases for writing recommendations:
- May/might be reasonable
- May/might be considered
- Usefulness/effectiveness is unknown/unclear/uncertain or not well established

CLASS III: No Benefit (MODERATE)   Benefit = Risk
(Generally, LOE A or B use only)

Suggested phrases for writing recommendations:
- Is not recommended
- Is not indicated/useful/effective/beneficial
- Should not be performed/administered/other

CLASS III: Harm (STRONG)   Risk > Benefit

Suggested phrases for writing recommendations:
- Potentially harmful
- Causes harm
- Associated with excess morbidity/mortality
- Should not be performed/administered/other

LEVEL (QUALITY) OF EVIDENCE‡

LEVEL A

- High-quality evidence‡ from more than 1 RCTs
- Meta-analyses of high-quality RCTs
- One or more RCTs corroborated by high-quality registry studies

LEVEL B-R   (Randomized)

- Moderate-quality evidence‡ from 1 or more RCTs
- Meta-analyses of moderate-quality RCTs

LEVEL B-NR   (Nonrandomized)

- Moderate-quality evidence‡ from 1 or more well-designed, well-executed nonrandomized studies, observational studies, or registry studies
- Meta-analyses of such studies

LEVEL C

- Randomized or nonrandomized observational or registry studies with limitations of design or execution
- Meta-analyses of such studies
- Physiological or mechanistic studies in human subjects

LEVEL E

Consensus of expert opinion based on clinical experience when evidence is insufficient, vague, or conflicting

COR and LOE are determined independently (any COR may be paired with any LOE).

A recommendation with LOE C or E does not imply that the recommendation is weak. Many important clinical questions addressed in guidelines do not lend themselves to clinical trials. Although RCTs are unavailable, there may be a very clear clinical consensus that a particular test or therapy is useful or effective.

* The outcome or result of the intervention should be specified (an improved clinical outcome or increased diagnostic accuracy or incremental prognostic information).

† For comparative-effectiveness recommendations (COR I and IIa; LOE A and B only), studies that support the use of comparator verbs should involve direct comparisons of the treatments or strategies being evaluated.

‡ The method of assessing quality is evolving, including the application of standardized, widely used, and preferably validated evidence grading tools; and for systematic reviews, the incorporation of an Evidence Review Committee.

COR indicates Class of Recommendation; LOE, Level of Evidence; NR, nonrandomized; R, randomized; and RCT, randomized controlled trial.

FIGURE 15.2 Classification scheme used by the American College of Cardiology (ACC) and the American Heart Association (AHA) to provide strength of recommendation and level of evidence. From Jacobs.[6]

strength of recommendations, articulating recommendations, external review, and updating guidelines.

The adoption of structured language to denote the strength of a recommendation and the quality of evidence informing that judgment was also emphasized. An example of the classification scheme used in ACC/AHA guidelines, adapted by many other guideline developers, is shown in Figure 15.2.

Similar quality standards for clinical practice guidelines have also been developed by organizations such as GIN, a network that represents 44 countries and 93 organizations.[31] This consensus document proposed a set of minimal standards for guideline development, including panel composition, decision-making processes, conflicts of interest, guideline objectives, development methods, evidence review, basis of recommendations, ratings of evidence and recommendations, guideline reviews, updating processes, and funding.

The IOM and GIN reports have been applauded for promoting the development of high-quality guidelines to foster effective and evidence-based patient care, but they have also been criticized for their complexity and the difficulty of implementing the long list of proposed standards.[32]

EVIDENCE: PRACTICE GAPS AND
BARRIERS TO GUIDELINE USE

Standards for ensuring the trustworthiness of guidelines are an important component of the mission to fulfill the promise of guidelines. However, to actually have an impact on patient outcomes, guidelines require deliberate implementation.

Despite the accessibility of clinical practice guidelines, health services research is awash with examples of the gap between *recommended care* and *actual care* delivered to patients. In 2003, an analysis of 6,712 randomly sampled adults living in the United States demonstrated that only 54.9% (95% CI 54.3 to 55.5) of adults received recommended care with marked variation in care quality, depending on their medical conditions.[33] Another overview of systematic reviews examining the quality of care delivered in the United States demonstrated evidence-practice gaps in all three phases of healthcare: preventive, acute, and chronic. Further, there was evidence of "underuse" of effective therapies and "overuse" of nonbeneficial and potentially harmful care.[2] For chronic conditions, approximately 60% of patients received recommended care, whereas 20% received contraindicated care.[2] Similarly, for acute conditions, 70% of patients received recommended care while 30% received contraindicated care. Taken together, these findings illustrate the unrealized health gains by inadequate and inappropriate translation of medical evidence into clinical practice. For example, one study estimated that if clinicians in the United States followed six heart failure guideline recommendations, nearly 68,000 deaths per year could be prevented.[34]

Reasons for guideline adherence and nonadherence among clinicians are varied. Systematic reviews examining physicians' barriers to guidelines have identified physicians' lack of awareness, lack of familiarity, and lack of agreement with guidelines as the principle barriers to guideline adoption.[35]

Other studies have shown that attributes of guidelines that promote adoption include strong supporting evidence, simple treatment decision algorithms, relevance to practice, congruence with existing norms and values, and not requiring new skills or changes in practice routine.[36]

Thus, mere publication of guidelines does not guarantee dissemination, acceptance, or routine use, particularly when guidelines are complex, present new knowledge, or require a change in practice. The need for a guideline implementation strategy to healthcare quality and outcomes has led to the emergence of "implementation science." The discipline of implementation science, also known by the names *knowledge translation*, *knowledge utilization*, *dissemination research*, and *health services research*, describes the "scientific study of methods to promote the systematic uptake of clinical research findings and other evidence-based practice into routine practice to improve the quality and effectiveness of healthcare."[37] It provides a conceptual framework for studying guideline implementation and describes the process of guideline adoption as an interplay between guideline characteristics and factors at the patient, clinician, and healthcare systems levels.

The Cochrane Effective Practice and Organization of Care (EPOC) group of the Cochrane Collaboration has compiled and evaluated the evidence supporting an ever-growing list of interventions to improve implementation of guidelines. At the patient level, decision aids are effective means to involve patients in the decision-making process and have been shown to improve patients' knowledge of different treatment options and decision quality. At the clinician level, audit and feedback is a process of continually measuring performance, compiling data into reports, and providing that information back to clinicians to improve evidence-based care. At the healthcare systems level, financial incentives such as the "pay for performance" programs instituted by CMS for treatment of common medical conditions such as heart failure and pneumonia encourage guideline-concordant care by linking physician and hospital payment to quality measures.[38] Table 15.3 summarizes several other examples of implementation strategies at the patient, clinician, and system level

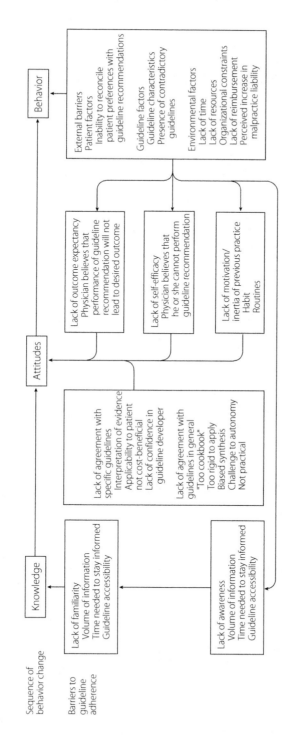

FIGURE 15.3 Conceptual framework to explain barriers to physician adherence to clinical practice guidelines. From Cabana.[34]

TABLE 15.3 Effective Interventions to Increase Guideline Adherence at the Patient, Clinician, and Healthcare System Level as Compiled by the Cochrane Collaboration

Intervention	Description	Effect
Patient level		
Decision aids	Tools that help people become involved in the decision-making process by providing information about the options and outcomes of a treatment and clarifying personal values	Increased knowledge (mean difference 13.34, 95% CI 11.17–15.51) Increased accuracy of risk perception (RR 1.82, 95% CI 1.52–2.16) Increased value congruence (RR 1.51, 95% CI 1.17–1.96) Decreased decisional conflict (mean difference 7.26, 95% CI 9.73-4.78)[39]
Personalized risk information	Providing information based on unique, individual characteristics	OR 1.15 (95% CI 1.02–1.29) for increase in uptake of screening test but low quality of evidence[40]
Provider-level interventions		
Continuing education meetings	Conferences, lectures, workshops, seminars, symposia, and courses for healthcare professionals	Median absolute increase in recommended care 6.0% (IQR 1.8–15.9)[41]
Audit and feedback	Any summary of clinical performance over a specified period of time, given in a written, electronic, or verbal format	Median absolute increase in compliance with desired practice 4.3% (IQR 0.5–16)[42]
Local opinion leaders	Health-care professionals considered by colleagues as educational influential disseminating and implementing "best evidence"	Median absolute increase in uptake of desired practice of 12.0% (IQR 6–14.5)[43]
Computerized reminders	Electronic reminders embedded into the electronic health record and delivered at the point of care	Median absolute increase in process adherence of 4.2% (IQR 0.8–16.8)[44]
Organizational or system-level interventions		
Clinical pathways	Structured multidisciplinary care plans used by health services to detail essential steps in the care of patients with a specified clinical problem	Reduction of in-hospital complications for patients undergoing an intervention, primarily surgery (OR=0.58, 95% CI 0.36–0.94), and improvement in documentation in medical record (OR=11.95, 95%CI 4.72–30.30)[45]
Financial incentives	Financial reward for professionals or systems for affecting a behavior	Potential improvement in process measures but insufficient evidence to support effects on patient outcomes[46,47]

drawn from systematic reviews conducted by the Cochrane EPOC and Consumer & Communications Groups.[39–47] The reviews demonstrate that each strategy has a small to moderate improvement in care when used in isolation but can potentially have an enhanced effect when combined in multiple strategies and tailored to specific clinical contexts.[48]

SUCCESSFUL STRATEGIES

The Kaiser Permanente Northern California (KPNC) hypertension quality-improvement program demonstrates the dramatic improvements in blood pressure control rates that can occur after implementation of a multifactorial, multilevel intervention. Based on data from the KPNC hypertension registry, which included 349,937 adults in 2001 and 652,763 adults in 2009, Jaffe et al reported that hypertension control rates within KPNC increased from 44% in 2001 to 80% in 2009 after implementation of the hypertension program.[49] In comparison, hypertension control rates during the same period in California and the nation increased only modestly from 63% to 69% and 55% to 64%, respectively. Features of the KPNC quality-improvement program included the following: (1) a systemwide internal registry to identify hypertensive patients and an electronic health record to provide immediate access to blood pressure readings, (2) audit and feedback to identify best practices in high-performing centers and dissemination of these reports to all other centers, (3) development of an internal evidence-based practice guideline with widespread distribution, (4) use of medical assistants for follow-up visits and medication adjustments, and (5) use of generic combination pills. Improvements in healthcare quality have also been demonstrated by the Veterans Health Administration, another integrated health system that has implemented widespread and multilevel interventions to facilitate guideline-concordant care.[50,51]

Professional societies have also employed complex, multifactorial interventions to facilitate guideline implementation. In cardiovascular disease, two notable programs are the Guidelines Applied in Practice (GAP) project from the ACC and the Get with the Guidelines (GWTG) program from the AHA.[52,53] The GAP initiative was performed in acute-care hospitals in southeast Michigan and created customized, guideline-oriented tool kits (standardized order sets, pocket guides, critical pathways, patient information sheets, discharge forms, hospital performance charts, and patient stickers) to facilitate adherence to recommended medications, tests, and counseling measures. Implementation of GAP was associated with significant reductions in 30-day mortality (16.7%

versus 21.6%, adjusted OR 0.74, 95% CI 0.59–0.94) and 1-year mortality (33.2% versus 38.3%, adjusted OR 0.78, 95% CI 0.64–0.95).[54]

AHA's counterpart to GAP is the GWTG program, a similar implementation tool kit that includes order sets; clinical pathways; and a web-based patient-management tool that provides patient-specific guideline recommendations, allows real-time data validation, and generates reports to allow each institution to track its adherence to guidelines individually and against national benchmarks. Pre- and postanalysis of hospitals in the GWTG coronary artery disease (CAD) registry have demonstrated rapid and significant improvements in 10 of 11 evidence-based acute care and secondary prevention interventions for CAD. Observational analyses that used the publicly available Centers for Medicare and Medicaid "Hospitals Compare" database to compare hospitals participating in the GWTG CAD registry with hospitals that were not participants demonstrated higher "Hospital Compare" composite scores [mean (SD), 89.7% (10.0%) versus 85.0% (15.0%); $p < 0.001$]. Adherence to the GWTG CAD performance measures was also higher [89.5% (11.0%) versus 83.0% (18.0%); $p < 0.001$] in GWTG CAD hospitals.[55] Currently, three different GWTG modules address CAD, heart failure, and stroke.[56]

FUTURE DIRECTIONS IN GUIDELINES

Using clinical practice guidelines is one strategy for providing high-quality, state of the art, and evidence-based care to patients. Efforts to formalize the guideline-development process and expand the discipline of implementation science are important steps in realizing the promise of guidelines. However, stakeholders also recognize the need for continued evolution of clinical practice guidelines to increase their relevance for patients, clinicians, and the healthcare system.

A common criticism of guidelines is that they are narrowly focused on single diseases and do not take into account patients who have multiple comorbidities. An analysis by Boyd et al demonstrated that if applicable clinical practice guidelines were blindly followed, a hypothetical older patient with several commonly seen comorbidities could be prescribed 12 guideline-directed medications with significant financial burden and risk of drug–drug interactions.[57] The integration of different guidelines to address individuals with multiple comorbidities will be increasingly important in an aging population.[6]

The rise of multivariable prediction models that estimate absolute risk of clinically relevant events also provide an opportunity to develop risk-stratified treatment guidelines. This principle has been adopted by cardiovascular prevention guidelines such as those addressing aspirin and cholesterol management to direct medical therapy to groups at highest risk that would have the greatest expected benefit from treatment.[58,59] Modeling analyses comparing "individualized" guidelines that are tailored to a patient's expected treatment benefit versus traditional guidelines have shown that individualized guidelines could prevent more events and lead to fewer patients requiring treatment compared with traditional guidelines.[60]

The attempt to individualize guidelines and incorporate risk–benefit assessments into the guideline process also extends to the goal of integrating this information with each patient's unique preferences to foster shared decision making. This motivation arises from the acknowledgement that several evidence-based treatment options exist, each with its own set of advantages (expected health gains) and disadvantages (expected health losses). Because the relative importance of achieving or avoiding a given clinical outcome can vary substantially between patients, many experts have called for guideline developers to incorporate patient preferences and shared decision making into guideline recommendations.[61] Strategies to facilitate shared decision making in clinical practice guidelines include structuring the presentation of healthcare options to make clinicians and patients aware of the multiple different evidence-based management strategies; structuring the shared decision-making process between clinicians and patients; and providing relevant support tools embedded at the point of care to facilitate this discussion.[62]

A key attribute of clinical practice guidelines is that they can summarize state-of-the-art medical care for busy clinicians. However, a study of guidelines sponsored by the AHRQ demonstrated that more than three-fourths of guidelines required updating.[63] Responding to a rapidly expanding evidence base in a timely manner while maintaining a rigorous guideline-development process remains a challenge. Guideline developers such as the ACC and AHA in the United States and NICE in the United Kingdom have developed formal processes to monitor medical literature for new, potentially relevant evidence and mechanisms to rapidly update recommendations to reflect the new evidence.[5]

The increased adoption of electronic health records and clinical decision support tools offer additional opportunities to rapidly translate knowledge from scientific literature into clinical practice at the point of care. Although the use of electronic health records in many medical practices is still in its infancy, its maturation provides an opportunity to establish "learning health systems," to continuously integrate scientific evidence into practice, and to evaluate its outcome for further scientific investigation.[64]

Finally, the concepts of value and cost-effectiveness have traditionally not factored into guideline recommendations. However, in an era of rising costs and limited resources in healthcare, this practice has been reevaluated. Guideline developers such as NICE have started to include cost-effectiveness analyses and value judgments to supplement guideline recommendations, a development that has also made its way toward U.S. guidelines.[7]

CONCLUSIONS

Patients rely on clinicians for quality healthcare and expect that their clinicians have the knowledge and expertise to provide sound medical recommendations. Clinical practice guidelines aid clinicians and patients alike by summarizing the current state of knowledge and providing recommendations on the best treatment options for a particular disease or condition. There may always be uncertainty in clinical practice, but trustworthy guidelines support clinicians and patients by ensuring that the best medical evidence can be incorporated into decision making. In that way, creating trustworthy guidelines hold the promise of improving healthcare quality and outcomes. Guideline development, however, is not an isolated activity, and implementation into practice is the final essential step to bring guideline-concordant care into clinical practice and improve patient care and healthcare quality.

REFERENCES

1. U.S. National Library of Medicine. Detailed indexing statistics: 1965–2013; 2015. Retrieved January 11, 2015, from http://www.nlm.nih.gov/bsd/index_stats_comp.html.

2. Schuster MA, McGlynn EA, Brook RH. How good is the quality of health care in the United States? *Milbank Q* 1998;76(4):517–563,509.

3. Ko DT, Krumholz HM, Wang Y, et al. Regional differences in process of care and outcomes for older acute myocardial infarction patients in the United States and Ontario, Canada. *Circ.* 2007;115(2):196–203.

4. Song Y, Skinner J, Bynum J, Sutherland J, Wennberg JE, Fisher ES. Regional variations in diagnostic practices. *N Engl J Med.* 2010;363(1):45–53.

5. Institute of Medicine. *Clinical Practice Guidelines We Can Trust.* Washington, DC: National Academy Press; 2011.

6. Jacobs AK, Anderson JL, Halperin JL, et al. The evolution and future of ACC/AHA clinical practice guidelines: a 30-year journey: a report of the American College of Cardiology/American Heart Association Task Force on Practice Guidelines. *Circ.* 2014; 130(14):1208–1217.

7. Peterson PN, Rumsfeld JS. The evolving story of guidelines and health care: does being nice help? *Ann Intern Med.* 2011;155(4):269–271.

8. Koh HK, Sebelius KG. Promoting prevention through the Affordable Care Act. *N Engl J Med.* 2010;363(14):1296–1299.

9. Kachalia A, Mello MM. Breast cancer screening: conflicting guidelines and medicolegal risk. *JAMA.* 2013;309(24):2555–2556.

10. Gibbons GH, Shurin SB, Mensah GA, Lauer MS. Refocusing the agenda on cardiovascular guidelines: an announcement from the National Heart, Lung, and Blood Institute. *Circ.* 2013;128(15):1713–1715.

11. Spertus JA, Eagle KA, Krumholz HM, Mitchell KR, Normand SL. American College of Cardiology and American Heart Association methodology for the selection and creation of performance measures for quantifying the quality of cardiovascular care. *Circ.* 2005;111(13):1703–1712.

12. Antman EM, Peterson ED. Tools for guiding clinical practice from the American Heart Association and the American College of Cardiology: what are they and how should clinicians use them? *Circ.* 2009;119(9):1180–1185.

13. Blackmore CC, Medina LS. Evidence-based radiology and the ACR appropriateness criteria. *J Am College Radiol.* 2006;3(7):505–509.

14. Peterson ED, Roe MT, Mulgund J, et al. Association between hospital process performance and outcomes among patients with acute coronary syndromes. *JAMA.* 2006;295 (16):1912–1920.

15. Komajda M, Lapuerta P, Hermans N, et al. Adherence to guidelines is a predictor of outcome in chronic heart failure: the Mahler survey. *Eur Heart J.* 2005; 26(16):1653–1659.

16. McCabe C, Kirchner C, Zhang H, Daley J, Fisman DN. Guideline-concordant therapy and reduced mortality and length of stay in adults with community-acquired pneumonia: playing by the rules. *Arch Intern Med.* 2009;169(16):1525–31.

17. Hepner KA, Rowe M, Rost K, et al. The effect of adherence to practice guidelines on depression outcomes. *Ann Intern Med.* 2007;147(5):320–329.

18. Glance LG, Dick AW, Mukamel DB, Osler TM. Association between trauma quality indicators and outcomes for injured patients. *Arch Surg.* 2012;147(4):308–315.

19. Grimshaw JM, Russell IT. Effect of clinical guidelines on medical practice: a systematic review of rigorous evaluations. *Lancet.* 1993;342(8883):1317–1322.

20. Grimshaw JM, Thomas RE, MacLennan G, et al. Effectiveness and efficiency of guideline dissemination and implementation strategies. *Health Technol Assess.* 2004; 8(6):iii–iv,1–72.

21. Kung J, Miller RR, Mackowiak PA. Failure of clinical practice guidelines to meet institute of medicine standards: two more decades of little, if any, progress. *Arch Intern Med.* 2012;172(21):1628–1633.

22. Shaneyfelt TM, Mayo-Smith MF, Rothwangl J. Are guidelines following guidelines? the methodological quality of clinical practice guidelines in the peer-reviewed medical literature. *JAMA.* 1999;281(20):1900–1905.

23. Agency for Healthcare Research and Quality. National guideline clearinghouse guideline index; 2015. Retrieved from http://www.guideline.gov/browse/index.aspx.

24. Guidelines International Network. International guideline library; 2015. Retrieved from http://www.g-i-n.net/library/international-guidelines-library/.

25. Lee DH, Vielemeyer O. Analysis of overall level of evidence behind Infectious Diseases Society of America practice guidelines. *Arch Intern Med.* 2011;171(1):18–22.

26. Tricoci P, Allen JM, Kramer JM, Califf RM, Smith SC Jr. Scientific evidence underlying the ACC/AHA clinical practice guidelines. *JAMA.* 2009;301(8):831–841.

27. Mendelson TB, Meltzer M, Campbell EG, Caplan AL, Kirkpatrick JN. Conflicts of interest in cardiovascular clinical practice guidelines. *Arch Intern Med.* 2011; 171(6):577–584.

28. Nissen SE. Can we trust cardiovascular practice guidelines? comment on "Conflicts of interest in cardiovascular clinical practice guidelines." *Arch Intern Med.* 2011; 171(6):584–585.

29. Choudhry NK, Stelfox HT, Detsky AS. Relationships between authors of clinical practice guidelines and the pharmaceutical industry. *JAMA.* 2002;287(5):612–617.

30. Eichacker PQ, Natanson C, Danner RL. Surviving sepsis—practice guidelines, marketing campaigns, and Eli Lilly. *N Engl J Med.* 2006;355(16):1640–1642.

31. Qaseem A, Forland F, Macbeth F, Ollenschlager G, Phillips S, van der Wees P. Guidelines International Network: toward international standards for clinical practice guidelines. *Ann Intern Med.* 2012;156(7):525–531.

32. Kuehn BM. IOM sets out "gold standard" practices for creating guidelines, systematic reviews. *JAMA.* 2011;305(18):1846–1848.

33. McGlynn EA, Asch SM, Adams J, et al. The quality of health care delivered to adults in the United States. *N Engl J Med.* 2003;348(26):2635–2645.

34. Fonarow GC, Yancy CW, Hernandez AF, Peterson ED, Spertus JA, Heidenreich PA. Potential impact of optimal implementation of evidence-based heart failure therapies on mortality. *Am Heart J.* 2011;161(6):1024–1030.e1023.

35. Cabana MD, Rand CS, Powe NR, et al. Why don't physicians follow clinical practice guidelines? a framework for improvement. *JAMA.* 1999;282(15):1458–1465.

36. Burgers JS, Grol RP, Zaat JO, Spies TH, van der Bij AK, Mokkink HG. Characteristics of effective clinical guidelines for general practice. *Br J Gen Pract.* 2003;53(486): 15–19.

37. Damschroder LJ, Aron DC, Keith RE, Kirsh SR, Alexander JA, Lowery JC. Fostering implementation of health services research findings into practice: a consolidated framework for advancing implementation science. *Implement Sci.* 2009;4:50.

38. Jha AK, Joynt KE, Orav EJ, Epstein AM. The long-term effect of premier pay for performance on patient outcomes. *N Engl J Med.* 2012;366(17):1606–1615.

39. Stacey D, Legare F, Col NF, et al. Decision aids for people facing health treatment or screening decisions. *Cochrane Database Syst Rev.* 2014;1:Cd001431.

40. Edwards AG, Naik G, Ahmed H, et al. Personalized risk communication for informed decision making about taking screening tests. *Cochrane Database Syst Rev.* 2013;2:Cd001865.

41. Forsetlund L, Bjorndal A, Rashidian A, et al. Continuing education meetings and workshops: effects on professional practice and health care outcomes. *Cochrane Database Syst Rev.* 2009(2):Cd003030.

42. Ivers N, Jamtvedt G, Flottorp S, et al. Audit and feedback: effects on professional practice and healthcare outcomes. *Cochrane Database Syst Rev.* 2012;6:Cd000259.

43. Flodgren G, Parmelli E, Doumit G, et al. Local opinion leaders: effects on professional practice and health care outcomes. *Cochrane Database Syst Rev.* 2011(8):Cd000125.

44. Shojania KG, Jennings A, Mayhew A, Ramsay CR, Eccles MP, Grimshaw J. The effects of on-screen, point of care computer reminders on processes and outcomes of care. *Cochrane Database Syst Rev.* 2009(3):Cd001096.

45. Rotter T, Kinsman L, James E, et al. Clinical pathways: effects on professional practice, patient outcomes, length of stay and hospital costs. *Cochrane Database Syst Rev.* 2010(3):Cd006632.

46. Flodgren G, Eccles MP, Shepperd S, Scott A, Parmelli E, Beyer FR. An overview of reviews evaluating the effectiveness of financial incentives in changing healthcare professional behaviors and patient outcomes. *Cochrane Database Syst Rev.* 2011(7): Cd009255.

47. Scott A, Sivey P, Ait Ouakrim D, et al. The effect of financial incentives on the quality of health care provided by primary care physicians. *Cochrane Database Syst Rev.* 2011(9):Cd008451.

48. Boaz A, Baeza J, Fraser A. Effective implementation of research into practice: an overview of systematic reviews of the health literature. *BMC Res Notes.* 2011;4:212.

49. Jaffe MG, Lee GA, Young JD, Sidney S, Go AS. Improved blood pressure control associated with a large-scale hypertension program. *JAMA.* 2013;310(7):699–705.

50. Hysong SJ, Best RG, Pugh JA. Clinical practice guideline implementation strategy patterns in Veterans Affairs primary care clinics. *Health Serv Res.* 2007;42(1 Pt 1):84–103.

51. Jha AK, Perlin JB, Kizer KW, Dudley RA. Effect of the transformation of the Veterans Affairs health care system on the quality of care. *N Engl J Med.* 2003;348(22): 2218–2227.

52. LaBresh KA, Ellrodt AG, Gliklich R, Liljestrand J, Peto R. Get with the guidelines for cardiovascular secondary prevention: pilot results. *Arch Intern Med.* 2004; 164(2):203–209.

53. Mehta RH, Montoye CK, Gallogly M, et al. Improving quality of care for acute myocardial infarction: the Guidelines Applied in Practice (Gap) initiative. *JAMA.* 2002;287(10):1269–1276.

54. Eagle KA, Montoye CK, Riba AL, et al. Guideline-based standardized care is associated with substantially lower mortality in Medicare patients with acute myocardial infarction: the American College of Cardiology's Guidelines Applied in Practice (Gap) projects in Michigan. *J Am Coll Cardiol.* 2005, Oct 4;46(7):1242–1248.

55. Lewis WR, Peterson ED, Cannon CP, et al. An organized approach to improvement in guideline adherence for acute myocardial infarction: results with the Get with the Guidelines quality improvement program. *Arch Intern Med.* 2008, Sep 8;168(16): 1813–1819.

56. Jones DW, Peterson ED, Bonow RO, et al. Translating research into practice for healthcare providers: the American Heart Association's strategy for building healthier lives, free of cardiovascular diseases and stroke. *Circ.* 2008, Aug 5;118(6):687–696.

57. Boyd CM, Darer J, Boult C, Fried LP, Boult L, Wu AW. Clinical practice guidelines and quality of care for older patients with multiple comorbid diseases: implications for pay for performance. *JAMA.* 2005;294(6):716–724.

58. Wolff T, Miller T, Ko S. Aspirin for the primary prevention of cardiovascular events: an update of the evidence for the U.S. Preventive Services Task Force. *Ann Intern Med.* 2009;150(6):405–410.

59. Stone NJ, Robinson JG, Lichtenstein AH, et al. 2013 ACC/AHA guideline on the treatment of blood cholesterol to reduce atherosclerotic cardiovascular risk in adults: a report of the American College of Cardiology/American Heart Association Task Force on Practice Guidelines. *Circ.* 2014;129(25)(suppl 2):S1–45.

60. Eddy DM, Adler J, Patterson B, Lucas D, Smith KA, Morris M. Individualized guidelines: the potential for increasing quality and reducing costs. *Ann Intern Med.* 2011;154(9):627–634.

61. Montori VM, Brito JP, Murad MH. The optimal practice of evidence-based medicine: incorporating patient preferences in practice guidelines. *JAMA.* 2013;310(23): 2503–2504.

62. van der Weijden T, Pieterse AH, Koelewijn-van Loon MS, et al. How can clinical practice guidelines be adapted to facilitate shared decision making? a qualitative key-informant study. *BMJ Qual & Safety.* 2013;22(10):855–863.

63. Shekelle PG. Updating practice guidelines. *JAMA.* 2014;311(20):2072–2073.

64. Krumholz HM. Big data and new knowledge in medicine: the thinking, training, and tools needed for a learning health system. *Health Aff.* (Millwood) 2014;33(7): 1163–1170.

Precision Medicine

EXPANDED AND TRANSLATIONAL

Hanh H. Hoang
Mauro Ferrari

Abstract

Precision medicine is an emerging concept that emphasizes the individual patient rather than a generalized approach when treating a medical condition. Genomics has served as the basis of several platforms for precision medicine; however, with the advent of additional technologies and platforms in recent years, other "omics" of molecular biology and medicine—such as bioinformatics, nanotechnologies, and imaging modalities—have provided complementary approaches. Here we examine the basic framework for precision medicine in the context of tumor heterogeneity (as it relates to cancer, the main clinical example in this chapter); prevention, risk assessment, and diagnostics; the limitations of current disease taxonomies; platform technologies beyond genomics; considerations for regulatory and developmental pathways to the clinic; the role of research and multidisciplinary education; and, ultimately, the need for precision medicine if we are to make transformational inroads toward the cure for some of the most complex diseases.

BASIC CONCEPTS AND FRAMEWORK

The term *precision medicine* refers to the notion that all healthcare-related procedures, including therapeutics, diagnostics, screening, and prevention, can be optimized to reflect differences between individual patients, even with respect to nominally identical medical conditions.[1,2] Although this rather obvious concept has been embodied since the dawn of the practice of medicine, only in recent times have the scientific foundations emerged to provide a firm approach to the identification of interpatient differences within broad classes of individuals affected by or at risk for individual pathologies of interest. These foundations are largely reflective of advances in molecular genetics and have been pursued dominantly in the domain of oncology, at least initially.[3] However, expansion of basic notions and approaches to a vast spectrum of different pathologies rapidly followed, and currently virtually every aspect of medicine is studied under a genetic foundation framework, including cardiovascular disease,[4-6] neurological disease,[7,8] and sepsis [response to traumatic and burn injury[9]], to name just a few.

The basic notion of precision medicine is that every patient responds differently to medical intervention even if affected by a nominally identical disease; these differences in response are reflective of both the specific genetic alterations present in their form of the disease and the individual patient's genetic makeup. Pharmacological sciences have thus joined forces with molecular oncology to identify classes of molecularly targeted drugs that have exceptional specificity for signaling pathways, processes, and pathological manifestations associated with individual genetic mutations found in a specific presentation of a cancer type as determined by biopsy of the cancer mass.[10,11] How the patient's individual genetic makeup is involved in the response to therapy, beyond the mutations present in their cancer, is a more recent frontier of precision medicine, one that basically addresses the flip side of the concept of therapeutic index in a medical treatment—that is, the adverse effect denominator complementing the efficacy numerator embodied in the search for specificity of treatment. Thus, interpatient differences in response to therapies are often related to individual genetic differences, say, in the ability to transport, biodistribute, or metabolize a therapeutic molecule or in susceptibility to cross-reactions.

Precision Medicine and Tumor Heterogeneity

Focusing attention on oncology naturally brings up additional considerations that are common to oncology and broader domains of medicine. First, there is the notion of intra- versus interpatient or tumor heterogeneity, even within the confines of a nominally identical disease. Cancer is inherently characterized by genetic instability, so it is not surprising that cancer lesions in patients evolve their genetic profiles over time or with response to therapy, as in the example of genetic evolution as a function of tumor progression in a set of patients presenting with chronic lymphocytic leukemia.[12,13] In particular, metastases from an individual primary tumor in the same patient are genetically different[14–16] even when they present in the same metastatic site or organ, as demonstrated in a study of axillary lymph node metastases in patients with breast cancer.[14] Thus, the genetic signature of a cancer varies in the same patient, even presents with differences in different lesions, or at times even within the same primary or metastatic lesion, as demonstrated by studies in renal carcinoma and glioblastoma.[15–17] On these grounds, the term *precision medicine* is perhaps preferable to "individualized, or personalized, medicine" which is frequently used to point to the same general concept of tailoring intervention to individual patients. It may be noted that the intrapatient genetic variability of cancer tissues is a cause of the emergence of therapeutic resistance to treatment, which is the unsolved frontier of medical oncology.

In a recent study focusing on resistance to RAF- and MEK-targeted therapies in non–small cell lung cancer (NSCLC) and melanoma, Lin et al determined that patients whose tumors expressed a specific gene variant of the protein kinase BRAF and had increased levels of the Hippo effector YAP exhibited worse responses to treatment and a higher proclivity toward resistance.[18] At the same time, though, the individual genetic makeup of the patients and their import in adverse reactions to and maldistributions of therapeutic agents are also fundamentally important for determining individual responses and selecting optimal regimens.[19] Terms for these areas of research and clinical application include *pharmacogenetics* and *pharmagenomics*, depending on the depth of analysis. In addition to many applications in oncology,[20–25] pharmacogenetics and pharmacogenomics have also been extended to other areas of medicine, as demonstrated in the following selected examples in cardiovascular disease, asthma, neurological disorders, and pain management. Pharmacogenetics have been applied as a strategy for better treatment of hypertension[26] and for designing therapeutic regimens in the aftermath of myocardial infarctions.[27] In a targeted pharmacogenetics study that spanned 12 years and included analysis of 259 patients treated with clopidogrel (after surviving a first myocardial infarction), investigators found that the cytochrome P450 CYP2C19 genetic variant played a major role in determining the likelihood of the patient having another coronary event.[27]

In the treatment of type 2 diabetes, the standard clinical guidelines recommend metformin as a first-line therapy, and, much like other clinical indications, considerations for the individual patient have spawned an explosion of pharmacogenetics and pharmacogenomics studies to determine the optimal regimen for this antihyperglycemic drug.[28,29] As part of a systematic, multiyear study of 2,896 patients with type 2 diabetes, Zhou and colleagues identified a single-nucleotide polymorphism (SNP), rs11212617 (from more than 700,000 SNPs analyzed) within a locus that includes the atacia telangiectasia mutated (ATM) gene involved in DNA repair and cell cycle control.[28] They concluded that the rs11212617 genetic variant led to improved treatment efficacy as measured by a level of glycosylated hemoglobin (HbA1c) below 7%. Asthma affects hundreds of millions of people worldwide, but patients' responses to treatment vary broadly, with nearly half of patients categorized as nonresponders to therapy. Tantisira et al conducted a genome-wide association study that examined the effect of interpatient variability on lung function and response to treatment with inhaled glucocorticoids, the most common therapy for patients with asthma.[30] The investigators analyzed nearly 1,000 patients from several clinical trials and characterized in depth a SNP (from among 534,290 SNPs identified) in the glucocorticoid-induced transcript 1 gene (GLCCI1). In particular, the GLCCI1 rs37973 variant correlated with poor lung function and response to inhaled glucocorticoid treatment.

Studying the pharmacogenetics of neurological disorders such as schizophrenia has also been the subject of intense research for the past couple of decades.[31] Much focus has been on the genetic variances of the class of cytochrome P450 enzymes (e.g., CYP1A2 and CYP2D6), which are major metabolizers of antipsychosis drugs, and of known drug targets including neurotransmitter receptors (of dopamine and serotonin). Whether a functional correlation exists for the role of the CYP family in cardiovascular and neurological diseases is unknown, however.

Pain management extends to many clinical areas and is arguably one of the most difficult barriers against implementation of a comprehensive and consistent pharmacogenetics strategy, owing to the lack of clear and quantitative measures of pain and largely variable phenotypic displays among patients.[32,33] Despite these challenges, many groups have continued the search for underlying genetic explanations for the (in)effectiveness of certain analgesics, particularly opioids, although pharmacogenetics analyses have helped to expand the list to other analgesics, including ones that target various ion channels, signaling pathways, and receptors.[33] However, given the complexity of certain clinical indications, the pharmacogenetics and pharmacogenomics approach to pain management does not always yield satisfactory results, which argues for additional studies and recognition of possible limitations of this strategy toward precision medicine. As a case in point, Klepstad and colleagues examined genetic variability as a factor for differences in individual responses to opioid pain treatment in 2,294 adult cancer patients from 17 centers across 11 European countries in a genetic association study that classified 112 SNPs in 25 candidate genes.[32] In contrast to previous studies referenced in their publication, the investigators did not find significant correlation between efficacy of opioid dosing or type to clinical outcome and individual genetic variability.

Precision Medicine and Prevention, Risk Assessment, Diagnostics, and Quality-of-Life Concerns

While precision medicine has been dominantly focused on medical therapeutics—that is, the identification of molecularly targeted therapies that are specific to individual genetic presentations—similar concepts readily extend to prevention, screening or risk assessment, diagnostics, and quality-of-life concerns. In a study that examines the familial patterns and hereditary link to predisposition toward pancreatic cancer, Roberts et al conducted a series of whole-genome and whole-exome sequencing experiments in patients with familial pancreatic cancer (plus spousal controls). The researchers identified variant alleles in the ATM gene as a predisposition factor for pancreatic ductal adenocarcinoma.[34]

More recently, Zhang and colleagues explored the role of genetic variability in influencing energy homeostasis and how this affects a patient's risk for pancreatic cancer. After examining 173 patients from several hospital sites and 476 controls in the general population, the authors determined that gene variants in the neuropeptide Y (NPY) gene were associated with a lower risk of cancer, whereas variants in the adrenoceptor beta 2 (ADRB2) gene correlated with increased risk.[35] In other instances, there has been less optimism for the focus on genetic variances as a predictor of risk, especially for the use of single-gene alleles rather than a combination of several susceptibility alleles as discussed by Pharoah et al.[36]

In a different approach, Wacholder and colleagues set out to assess the performance of several genetic variants identified through genome-wide association studies in order to ascertain whether the genetic information added value to a standard clinical breast-cancer risk model (the Breast Cancer Risk Assessment Tool, commonly known as the Gail Model).[37] They examined 5,590 subjects diagnosed with breast cancer and 5,998 control subjects, genotyping each for 10 SNPs previously determined to be associated with breast cancer. The authors concluded that the genetic information provided only a modest gain in knowledge about a patient's risk for developing breast cancer.

Precision medicine as an approach toward prevention and risk assessment has been applied in other clinical indications including asthma (onset and progression[38]) and Alzheimer's disease (AD).[39–41] Studies of genetic variants of proinflammatory cytokines and other immunological mediators (e.g., interleukins, tumor necrosis factor) identified particular polymorphisms, which can be used to stratify patients according to risk profiles for the development of AD.

Precision Medicine and the Limitations of Current Taxonomies

The emergence of precision medicine makes it painfully clear that the current taxonomies used in medicine require rapid and thorough overhaul. In oncology, we continue to use a site-of-origin classification for cancer that is literally centuries old. This classification system does not reflect the possibility that the genetic profiles of two cancers in different organs of two different patients may be much more similar, and therefore amenable to the same therapeutic regimen, than two cancers of the same organ in two different patients. Taxonomy and classifications are still fundamental as they drive the practice of medicine, regulatory approval, and the entire organization of healthcare. However, novel taxonomies are required in order to take full advantage of the revolution of precision medicine. There are probably no two cancer cases that are fully identical from a genetic perspective. How to bring rational order to this collection of metaphorical malignant snowflakes remains an extremely complex challenge, but it is a necessity that over time may make itself just as urgent and essential in domains of medicine beyond oncology.

Precision Medicine and Delving Beyond Genetic Information

Genetic information may be insufficient or not available for the treatment of an individual patient at any given time. Therefore, epigenetics and epigenomics are now major factors involved in understanding the fundamental pathogenesis and individual responses to treatment of cancer[42–45] and other clinical indications such as cardiovascular disease,[46] inflammatory bowel diseases,[47] neurological disorders,[48] and others.[49] Further molecular "omic" information (i.e., proteomics, peptidomics, metabolomics, transcriptomics, etc.) are emerging to be just as fundamental for precision medicine as the original gene-based approaches to it. Proteomics and peptidomics approaches have been widely applied in investigations of cancer[50] and other diseases as disparate as alcoholism,[51] AD,[52] and asthma and chronic obstructive pulmonary disease (COPD).[53] Such information can also supplement transcriptomic[54–59] or metabolomic[60–65] analyses for a more comprehensive understanding of patient stratification and individual-specific clinical management of symptoms and drug effect in a broad range of diseases.

On the point of availability of genetic information, it is obviously impossible to perform a full genetic analysis of each cancer lesion (and its surrounding microenvironment) in each patient at any given time for the purpose of optimizing therapy. Therefore, recourse must be made to surrogate evidences that can be used to infer information to optimize treatment. These may arise from advances in radiological imaging of any modality, with or without molecular recognition. They may also arise from transdisciplinary approaches such as systems medicine,[66,67] nanotechnology,[68,69] and transport oncophysics.[19] The next section of this chapter is dedicated to these novel frontiers of precision medicine.

Precision Medicine and Regulatory and Developmental Pathways

Precision medicine will necessarily engender a fundamental reconstruction of the product development and regulatory approval pathways for drugs, biologics, and broad classes of medical products.[70,71] From the perspective of the pharmaceutical industry, for instance, the current paradigm focusing on "blockbuster drugs" for large patient populations may be untenable given the development of individualized care and products. For the developers of medical products, the transdisciplinary nature of precision medicine requires the (highly challenging) establishment of entirely novel and unexpected but tightly interwoven skill domains in their industries. From the perspective of the regulatory approval framework, how can clinical trials be re-envisioned so they provide sufficient safety and efficacy information when every "trial" could be as small as $n = 1$? These connected issues are discussed later in this chapter.

Precision Medicine and Research and Education

The world of precision medicine is inherently inter-, trans-, and multidisciplinary, which in turn requires a redesign of the research and educational enterprises.

Precision Medicine as an Absolute Necessity

Terrifyingly daunting as those challenges previously listed may be, precision medicine is an absolute need. Metastatic cancers remain virtually incurable today, with only modest improvements in survival over the past several decades.[72] Only in testicular cancer have we been able to achieve cure rates as high as 92% for the good-prognosis group.[73,74] No decisive progress toward curative approaches against metastatic disease will be achieved without precision medicine approaches. We suspect that similar considerations might apply to broad expanses of medicine beyond cancer. This chapter is written with the desire to provide a broad summary of the key challenges in precision medicine and with the hope of assisting those who might be interested in helping to address them and usher in a new era of medical advances.

BEYOND THE GENES

As summarized earlier in this chapter, information databases that have broadened the boundaries and capabilities of precision medicine have not been limited to what can be deduced from the genes or even to the realm of the "omics." In the exposition that follows, we will expand on just a few examples from the vast volumes of literature for the other "omics"—nanomedicine, precision surgery, molecular imaging, transport oncophysics, and systems medicine as they pertain to the rubric of precision medicine.

Epigenomics and Epigenetics

As we discussed previously, it is now hard to find an area in which epigenomic or epigenetic factors are not explored as a main or underlying reason for disease and patient-specific disease progressions and responses to therapy. Epigenomics and epigenetics in their current terminology and use refer to the study of heritable changes in gene expression that do not depend on the DNA sequence. Such changes include DNA methylation and histone deacetylation, with accompanying drugs that inhibit these activities, some of which are approved for use in patients with myelodysplastic syndrome or T-cell lymphoma.

In an effort to recapitulate some of the successes seen in preclinical models using combinatorial administration of inhibitors of DNA methylation and histone deacetylase (HDAC), Juergens et al conducted a phase I and II trial of combinatorial therapy consisting of azacitidine (a DNA methyltransferase inhibitor) and entinostat (an HDAC inhibitor) at concentrations much below the maximally tolerated doses.[45] The authors treated a total of 45 pretreated patients with recurrent, metastatic non–small cell lung cancer and monitored them for cytotoxicity, pharmacokinetics, efficacy, and DNA methylation status as biomarkers. As expected, patients had varying responses to treatment, with the median survival of 6.4 months; however, one patient had a complete response, and another had a partial response with no evidence of relapse up to two years after cessation of therapy.

Transcriptomics

Transcriptomics involves the examination of genome-wide changes in gene expression under varying environments and disease conditions, and this field has also expanded into the domain of precision medicine, where many expect it to help optimize patient care strategies. Making transcriptomics even more powerful has been the advent of RNA sequencing technologies, where hundreds of millions of reads can be obtained in a single experiment. In a clinical examination of tumor tissues from 17 individuals diagnosed with triple-negative breast cancer (TNBC), non-TNBC, and HER2-positive breast cancer, Eswaran et al used mRNA sequencing to obtain all 17 transcriptomes at high resolution for comprehensive comparative analyses.[54] The authors not only identified differentially expressed transcripts in the three patient cohorts but also pinpointed several previously unidentified transcripts that seem to play a significant role in disease. Before the development of RNA-sequencing techniques, some researchers exploited microarray chips to conduct transcriptional profiling. Although encumbered with several technical limitations, the use of microarrays has nonetheless been widespread, yielding vast volumes of information for diseases beyond cancer. Desire and colleagues conducted a phase IIa trial with 20 patients diagnosed with mild to moderate AD (and subtyped with poor or good prognosis) and given EHT 0202 as an adjuvant, which is a new compound that could have therapeutic potential.[58] The researchers conducted genome-wide transcriptional profiling (via microarray analysis) of blood samples taken from the 40 patients (with 20 for placebo) before and after treatment, and they found that in responders to EHT 0202, pathways related to disorders of the central nervous system, diabetes, inflammation, and autoimmunity were activated.

Proteomics and Peptidomics

Comprehensive analyses of the proteome and peptidome (of blood, tumor, and other experimental samples) in many disease areas have complemented genomics and other "omics" studies and have offered a more detailed understanding of post-transcriptional factors that drive disease. These studies typically rely on the resolution of mass spectrometry (MS) coupled to a chromatographic or other size-selection or filtering procedure. In a small cohort study for biomarkers of AD, Holtta et al used a quantitative MS approach to analyze the proteomic and peptidomic profiles of cerebrospinal fluid samples from eight patients with positive diagnosis (against eight nondemented individuals).[52] The investigators identified several proteins and peptides associated with AD. Many similar studies in oncology and other clinical indications as varied as asthma and alcoholism have been conducted, necessitating further clinical validation and implementation of multidisciplinary strategies including biostatistics, engineering, and systems biology.

Metabolomics

Recent years have seen a surge in the number of studies that use metabolomics information, either singly or in combination with other approaches, to identify patient-specific disease signatures or to monitor treatment efficacy. Metabolomics is based on the identification and quantification of metabolites, usually by MS coupled to various chromatography methods and high-proton nuclear magnetic resonance. This strategy was used by Zhu and colleagues to examine the metabolic profiles of sera from three patient groups (66 patients with colorectal cancer or CRC, 76 patients with polyps only, and 92 healthy volunteers) in order to establish potential biomarkers of CRC.[60] They identified 158 metabolites that classified to 25 different metabolic pathways. Similarly, Miller et al used metabolic profiling to determine the changes in 39 patients with breast cancer who had been given limonene, a substance found in citrus peels.[61] All of the patients were diagnosed with early-stage breast cancer and had not undergone surgical resection. Their plasma samples were analyzed by MS before and after intervention, and 72 metabolites appeared significantly affected by administration of limonene. Such strategies have extended to studies beyond cancer, as in the case of Cassol and coworkers, where the authors examined the cerebral fluids of 46 HIV patients who were on antiretroviral therapy (with 54 HIV-negative controls) for signatures of disease-related neurocognitive impairment.[64] The authors also compared the metabolic profiles to those from plasma samples of the same patient cohorts. They demonstrated that there are indeed metabolite signatures specific to HIV-associated neurocognitive disorders, which map to pathways involved in neurotransmitter production, mitochondrial activity, oxidative stress, and metabolic waste.

Nanomedicine

The introduction of nanotechnology has accompanied many novel designs and uses of nanoparticles for imaging modalities and therapeutics, as well as for oncology and other domains of medicine such as cardiovascular disease, neurology, and regenerative medicine.[68,69] Mulder et al discussed several applications for nanotechnology with particular regard to popular imaging techniques (intravital microscopy, magnetic resonance imaging or MRI, positron emission tomography or PET, computed tomography or CT, fluorescence

imaging) for cardiovascular medicine (specifically, atherosclerosis) to identify vulnerable plaques and areas of inflammation as part of preventive measures. However, the authors do not limit discussion to cardiovascular nanomedicine from a purely diagnostic perspective; for example, studies have used
different types of nanoparticles to target the atherosclerotic plaques or inhibit
inflammation of the arteries. Cancer nanomedicine has been a dominant area
of nanotechnology, bringing many discoveries closer to clinical application than
ever before.[68] Shen et al used a multistage vector (MSV) platform, comprised
of nanoporous silicon microparticles, to deliver liposomal EphA2 (encoding
an epithelial cell receptor kinase involved in tumorigenesis), siRNA, and
docetaxel to chemo-resistant metastatic tumors in a murine model of ovarian
cancer.[75] The authors demonstrated significant decrease in tumor growth and
burden in the otherwise chemo-resistant animals, with effective accumulation
of the MSV–EphA2 siRNA at tumor sites as a function of the shape, size, and
surface chemistry of the MSV.

Precision Surgery

With the advent of imaging technologies and sophisticated software for three-
dimensional (3-D) rendering of scans, especially in the past couple of decades,
surgeons are able to perform difficult procedures or access deep masses with
greater accuracy than ever before and with more positive outcomes[76] in what
is commonly referred to as *image-guided interventions*. Patient-specific information for preoperative planning guide complex interventions or enable more precise visualization of the patient's anatomy or that of the pathology (e.g., tumor
margins), both pre- and postoperatively. Nemec and coworkers[77] conducted a
small validation study with 10 patients who had benign or malignant orbital
tumors that examined the usefulness and accuracy of multidetector computed
tomography (MDCT) and MRI modalities that were coupled to a navigation
system for surgical planning, intraoperative guidance, navigation, and performance. Data sets from the study techniques (MDCT–MRI fusion images of
the tumor lesions) compared to standard-of-care histopathology analyses were
70% concordant (7 of 10 patients). The intraoperative navigation accuracy had
a mean value of 1.35 mm, and complete tumor resection was achieved in all
cases, with 6 of the 10 patients showing complete regression. These types of
image-guided navigation techniques can be further enhanced with laser
guidance for more precise alignment of surgical instruments[78] or 3-D reconstruction for visualization of internal anatomical structures and hidden tumor
masses and their associated vascular networks.[79] Ukimura et al created a 3-D
reconstruction from 0.5-mm thickness CT scans that takes into consideration

three anatomical features of the kidneys (in this case) for precise surgical planning and visualization in four patients with central completely intrarenal hilar masses. In a remarkable demonstration of true precision surgery, the surgeons were able to identify tumor-specific arterial branches and thus avoid unnecessary ischemia in a partial nephrectomy to remove the masses that had been invisible even through laparoscopic view.

Molecular Imaging

Pre-, intra-, and postoperative procedures and diagnostic measures in oncology, neurology, and cardiovascular diseases, for instance, have been greatly aided by the introduction of molecular imaging modalities (CT, MRI, PET, single-photon emission computed tomography or SPECT, etc.) and the development of specific radioactive, fluorescent, or multimodal agents. In a proof-of-concept clinical study of prostate cancer, van der Poel and colleagues injected the tracer indocyanine green (ICG)-^{99m}Tc-NanoColl into the prostates of 11 patients who were slated for a robot-assisted laparoscopic prostatectomy prior to imaging via SPECT and CT to identify the sentinel lymph nodes.[80] During surgery, a fluorescence laparoscope was used to confirm the visualization of the nodes, and with the SPECT and CT imaging the surgeon was able to optimize preoperative planning for sentinel lymph node dissection and intraoperative visualization of the nodes.

Transport Oncophysics

It is becoming abundantly clear that the transport of mass (e.g., drugs, imaging agents) differs fundamentally in cancer compared to surrounding healthy tissues,[19] likely as a result of differences in pathological modifications of multiple biological barriers (vascular, stromal, and cellular) in the former. Thus, the emerging field of transport oncophysics takes into consideration the mass transport differentials when designing diagnostics and therapeutics. Koay et al demonstrated this concept in a clinical study of pancreatic cancer and the effect of physical properties and how they are altered during disease or during gemcitabine treatment and uptake into the tumors.[81] Using CT scans of 176 human pancreatic ductal adenocarcinoma tumors, the investigators developed a model in which they can derive measurements of mass transport properties, and they correlated these surrogate markers to patient outcomes. They demonstrated that drug uptake and incorporation into DNA within tumors varied markedly according to the CT-derived transport properties of the cancer and in an interpatient manner. Together, the surrogate markers can be correlated to pathological response and patient survival.

Systems Medicine

Single gene or protein approaches may still be useful and necessary in some instances, but advancement of the many "omics" and computational and modeling technologies and the generation of "big data" have pushed the frontiers of the field of systems medicine and its applications in precision medicine.[66] Systems medicine often combines data from multiple approaches and integrates them into a knowledge-based prediction model for individual therapeutic response or mechanisms of pathology. In a recent study to identify genetic drivers of tumorigenesis from a vast amount of genomics data, Bertand et al presented a data-integration algorithm and framework referred to as OncoI-IMPACT, which is based on in silico predictions and in vitro and clinical validations.[67] The authors identified patient-specific driver genes from large public data sets of several cancer subtypes. They then applied OncoIMPACT to 1,000 patient tumor samples to compile lists of additional patient-specific driver genes in five different cancer subtypes to identify modes of synergistic action and as an approach to patient stratification and prognosis.

Although still quite powerful as singular approaches, it has become evident (as seen in some of the studies described above) that true achievement in precision medicine, and ultimate optimal outcomes for patients, requires the tandem and interconnected application of several or all of the above approaches.

CONSIDERATIONS ON THE CLINICAL TRANSLATION OF PRECISION MEDICINE

The approval of novel therapeutic agents is delegated to the Food and Drug Administration, which requires a regulatory pathway involving preclinical data obtained with current Good Manufacturing Practices and animal experimentation in the Good Laboratory Practice mode. Following approval of an Investigational New Drug, the novel therapeutic agent may enter various phases of clinical trial validation, resulting in approval (registration) or regulatory rejection. The fundamental steps of clinical trial validation are phase I (primarily focused on safety), phase II (mechanism of efficacy), and phase III (comparative superiority with respect to current treatments). The full theory of clinical trials is based on rigorous statistical approaches, which require a large number of patients, especially in phase III (typically thousands to tens of thousands), to be able to yield scientifically significant results. This approach remains largely current for many diseases and has evolved from the times in which there is simply not enough information on patients, beyond their nominal health concern, to ascertain the best therapeutic option needed.

Improvements in the broad nominal categorization of diseases have been substantial. Not four decades ago, all breast cancers would have been considered one and the same; now it is well established that breast cancers that are hormone sensitive differ greatly from those that express HER2/Neu molecular pathologies, and both types differ from those that are generically listed as "triple-negative." Further differentiations are warranted based on the stage of the disease and additional considerations of prior therapy and its response. This approach is most certainly justified and downright indispensable in the times preceding precision medicine. However, if it is truly desired that medicine enter the era of personalization, this methodology is paradoxical as the only number that matters is $n = 1$. Medicine in the times of $n = 1$ may be significantly different from what it is today because each patient's treatment coordinates will be defined through an interdisciplinary set of parameter biomarkers, including gene profiles, a variety of "omics" profile signatures, and radiological imaging results (including molecular distributions and mass-transport characteristics) that are all entered in computational algorithms to define the patient's unique "state." This evolution of medicine will engender transformations that are extraordinary and probably unimaginable at this time. The most immediate considerations will be the evolution of the approval processes to accommodate for registration of treatment for extremely small patient groups without conventional "controls" and possibly for single individuals. Such changes will require the regulatory approval of biomarkers of individuality, which are based on biomolecular medicine ("omics") and other approaches such as imaging and transport physics. Furthermore, the "individualization algorithms" will have to be formulated and approved. Finally, the methods for addressing these individualities will have to enter the main modes of medicine and regulatory approval. These will probably involve not only molecularly targeted biological therapies but also their transport counterparts, nano- and other localization-enhancing vectors.

CONSIDERATIONS ON BASIC RESEARCH IN PRECISION MEDICINE

On January 30, 2015, the Obama administration launched its Precision Medicine Initiative, which added $215 million to the president's 2016 budget.[82] Of this amount, $130 million will be allocated to the National Institutes of Health (NIH) to develop a voluntary national cohort of volunteer subjects for research, and $70 million will go to the National Cancer Institute for studies to identify genetic drivers of cancer. Although these are key programs with national recognition and coordination, the NIH is not (and should not) be alone in the effort to drive basic research toward application in precision medicine. All across the nation and the globe, research groups will continue to explore what we believe are three of the major research foci for precision medicine in the years to come: (1) identifying targets and biomarkers of disease, (2) applying trans- and multidisciplinary approaches toward mechanistic studies and molecular characterizations of disease models that can inform clinical decisions, and (3) systematically organizing and integrating data and access to the volumes of data sets.

Identifying biomarkers of disease is an ongoing task for scientists because they will enable the development of companion diagnostics for prognosis, disease staging, and therapeutic monitoring. With the advent of technologies and development of new platforms for research and clinical application, we are no longer confined to extensively invasive methods (tumor biopsies) of detection and identification of disease biomarkers. A case in point: To identify and characterize blood-based (soluble) biomarkers for early detection of breast cancer, Li and coworkers analyzed the circulating proteolytic products catalyzed by carboxypeptidase N (CPN) via a nanopore-based platform coupled to MS analysis of plasma samples from animal models and histopathology analysis of patient tissues (at different stages of disease).[50] They correlated the changes in CPN-catalyzed peptides with the activity of tumor-resident CPN, as well as the expression of CPN in stage-specific human tumor tissues, which support further investigation into the use of CPN-catalyzed peptides as biomarkers of early-stage breast cancer.

In a different approach, but one that also seeks to establish and analyze biomarkers of breast cancer, Dawson et al compared the use of circulating tumor-specific DNA (by digital polymerase chain reaction or sequencing), the known cancer antigen CA 15-3 (by immunoassay), and circulating tumor cells (by cell counting) for therapeutic monitoring in 30 metastatic breast cancer patients undergoing systemic treatment over two years.[83] Of the three methods, detection of circulating tumor DNA proved to be the most sensitive and accurate, had the greatest dynamic range, and correlated most readily with treatment response seen in CT imaging scans and assessments of tumor burden and disease progression.

To make sound, patient-specific clinical decisions, we need to understand the fundamental biological processes underlying the pathology. Given obvious ethical and some technological constraints, these studies must largely stay within the confines of basic, albeit translational, research before proceeding toward clinical validation for safety and efficacy. Therefore, we anticipate basic and translational research into the mechanisms of disease to remain an ever critical factor in the success of precision medicine. It must be stressed that no longer will a singular approach or discipline be sufficient to identify and dissect the multitude of biological factors that play a role in the disease, but trans- and multidisciplinary strategies will be crucial to the achievement and feasibility of precision medicine. Widespread collaboration and data sharing (also discussed later) will be prudent, even necessary, to fully maximize the use of knowledge, time, and resources. This inevitable breakdown of research silos should provide a strong impetus for us to rethink and reshape the current research paradigm of the single-laboratory teams.

One of the biggest challenges for precision medicine is the organization, integration, and sharing of the massive amounts of research and clinical data generated by various initiatives and programs. Part of the 2016 budget for President Obama's Precision Medicine Initiative include $5 million for the Office of the National Coordinator for Health Information Technology to establish standards for data privacy and secure exchange of data. Already, the Mayo Clinic Biobank at its Center for Individualized Medicine has amassed a collection of genetic and health information on 50,000 individuals for clinical and research uses.[84] Whether or how these clinical databases can be integrated is currently unknown, but from the outset designing and implementing a nationwide data repository for research information may be less straightforward. The National Center for Biotechnology Information hosts several databases such as the Database of Genotypes and Phenotypes and Gene,[85] where researchers can access and contribute genetic information. How these and other disparate but similar information repositories can be expanded, maintained, or even integrated to keep pace with the explosion of research data that will certainly culminate in the years to come, particularly for the purposes of precision medicine, is a question that remains unanswered.

CONSIDERATIONS ON EDUCATION IN PRECISION MEDICINE

For precision medicine to truly become the clinical reality, we must recognize the critical need to educate all stakeholders—healthcare providers, patients, policy makers, insurance providers, educators at academic medical institutions and hospitals to name a few—who must achieve their specific but integrated roles. For instance, clinicians who are on the front lines of healthcare may find themselves ill prepared for the numerous implications of genetic-based diagnosis and treatment.[86] In fact, of those clinicians surveyed, only 1.7% considered themselves "experts" in applying family history and genetic information to interpret risk and to make recommendations for care. Patients and advocates have virtually the highest stakes in the success (or failure) of precision medicine. In addition to keeping current on the latest news, policies, and technologies, they must be willing to fully engage in research and clinical programs and initiatives, and encourage the next generation of patient advocates to participate in such. It is also imperative that policy makers and insurance providers understand both the power and limitations of precision medicine and work to establish laws and strategies that protect patients and sustain the cost and quality of care. Last, but certainly not the least trivial, academic research and clinical institutions have an obligation to develop and implement nuanced educational programs to train the next wave of researchers and clinicians in the multidisciplinary approaches to precision medicine. As mentioned at the beginning of this chapter, precision medicine will likely lead to the development of new taxonomies of disease and thus necessitate a similar overhaul of current curriculums in universities and medical schools and even research institutions. The Duke Center for Personalized and Precision Medicine[87] and the Weill Cornell Medical College Institute for Precision Medicine[88] are two of several leading institutions that are investing significant effort in educating trainees and the public about the latest developments in precision medicine.

CONCLUSION

Precision medicine is necessary to conquer currently incurable diseases such as metastatic cancer. Precision medicine encompasses a broad variety of synergistic platforms, which all together offer the promise of truly individualized approaches from risk assessment to screening, prevention, diagnostics, therapeutics, and quality-of-life or end-of-life considerations. The groundbreaking platforms for precision medicine were genetics and genomics, which remain essential tools for the determination of susceptibility to specific diseases and optimized, molecularly targeted interventions. Additional synergistic modalities enabling precision medicine include the so-called "omics" of molecular biology and medicine, including proteomics, peptidomics, transcriptomics, metabolomics, transcriptomics, glycomics, and others. These complement genomics in the sense that they provide a basis for the assessment of the disease state and its evolution over time, together with possible indications of the ideal therapeutic options.

Just like microtechnology was an essential platform for the development of genomics and its reduction to medical practice through the advances in sequencing modalities, nanotechnology is the necessary platform for the additional "omics," which require a much greater information density and processing power. Advances in bioinformatics are similarly required to conquer the much greater computational and data management complexities of the postgenomic era. Nanotechnology offers additional opportunities to personalize medicine because nanovectors can be used to deliver therapeutic agents to specific locations in the body. The transport of all mass, including drugs, biological molecules, cells, and vectors, differs among patients even with the same nominal disease. Transport oncophysics, the discipline that studies these differences, is an example of a novel frontier and interdisciplinary science that arose to serve the cause of precision medicine. Transport oncophysics is based on imaging, mathematics, physics, biology, and pharmaceutical and clinical sciences. It may be expected that many new disciplines will similarly arise, which will be based on truly multidisciplinary foundations. On these bases, it may be argued that deeply interdisciplinary educational paradigms will be required in order to optimize advances in precision medicine research and its deployment.

The regulatory protocols currently employed for the approval of novel treatments are based on clinical trials approaches, which require large cohorts of carefully selected patients to demonstrate or disprove the superiority of a novel treatment with respect to current ones. These trials are accompanied by sufficient statistical analyses and control for a suitably small set of variables. This approach inherently contradicts precision medicine, where each treatment course is by definition for $n=1$ patient. The contradiction could be solved if each "personalized" variable such as a specific genetic variation in cancer was found to be prevalent in a sufficiently large number of patients with diseases that would now be considered different, such as lung, ovarian, and brain cancer. In such cases, the current regulatory protocols and clinical trial modalities in phases I–III (or even 0–IV) could remain viable. Otherwise, a major overhaul in the regulatory establishment will be required.

REFERENCES

1. Hollebecque A, Massard C, Soria JC. Implementing precision medicine initiatives in the clinic: a new paradigm in drug development. *Curr Opin Oncol*. 2014;26:340–346.

2. Intlekofer AM, Younes A. Precision therapy for lymphoma—current state and future directions. *Nat Rev Clin Oncol*. 2014;11:585–596.

3. Wheeler DA, Wang L. From human genome to cancer genome: the first decade. *Genome Res.* 2013;23:1054–1062.

4. Kittleson MM, Hare JM. Molecular signature analysis: using the myocardial transcriptome as a biomarker in cardiovascular disease. *Trends Cardiovas Med.* 2005; 15:130–138.

5. Damani SB, Topol EJ. Emerging genomic applications in coronary artery disease. *JACC Cardiovas Interven.* 2011;4:473–482.

6. Loth DW, Artigas MS, Gharib SA, et al. Genome-wide association analysis identifies six new loci associated with forced vital capacity. *Nat Genet.* 2014;46:669–677.

7. Boone PM, Wiszniewski W, Lupski JR. Genomic medicine and neurological disease. *Hum Genet.* 2011;130:103–121.

8. Cirulli ET, Lasseigne BN, Petrovski S, et al. Exome sequencing in amyotrophic lateral sclerosis identifies risk genes and pathways. *Science.* 2015;347(6229):1436–1441.

9. Feezor RJ, Cheng A, Paddock HN, Baker HV, Moldawer LL. Functional genomics and gene expression profiling in sepsis: beyond class prediction. *Clin Infect Dis.* 2005; 41(suppl 7):S427–435.

10. Thomas A, Rajan A, Lopez-Chavez A, Wang Y, Giaccone G. From targets to targeted therapies and molecular profiling in non-small cell lung carcinoma. *Ann Oncol.* 2013;24:577–585.

11. Thomas F, Desmedt C, Aftimos P, Awada A. Impact of tumor sequencing on the use of anticancer drugs. *Curr Opin Oncol.* 2014;26:347–356.

12. Burrell RA, McGranahan N, Bartek J, Swanton C. The causes and consequences of genetic heterogeneity in cancer evolution. *Nature.* 2013;501:338–345.

13. Landau DA, Carter SL, Stojanov P, et al. Evolution and impact of subclonal mutations in chronic lymphocytic leukemia. *Cell.* 2013;152:714–726.

14. Poplawski AB, Jankowski M, Erickson SW, et al. Frequent genetic differences between matched primary and metastatic breast cancer provide an approach to identification of biomarkers for disease progression. *Eur J Hum Genet.* 2010;18:560–568.

15. Vogelstein B, Papadopoulos N, Velculescu VE, Zhou S, Diaz LA, Jr., Kinzler KW. Cancer genome landscapes. *Science.* 2013;339:1546–1558.

16. Almendro V, Kim HJ, Cheng YK, et al. Genetic and phenotypic diversity in breast tumor metastases. *Cancer Res.* 2014;74:1338–1348.

17. Martinez P, Birkbak NJ, Gerlinger M, et al. Parallel evolution of tumour subclones mimics diversity between tumours. *J Pathol.* 2013;230:356–364.

18. Lin L, Sabnis AJ, Chan E, et al. The Hippo effector YAP promotes resistance to RAF- and MEK-targeted cancer therapies. *Nat Genet.* 2015;47:250–256.

19. Ferrari M. Frontiers in cancer nanomedicine: directing mass transport through biological barriers. *Trends Biotechnol.* 2010;28:181–188.

20. McLeod HL, Sargent DJ, Marsh S, et al. Pharmacogenetic predictors of adverse events and response to chemotherapy in metastatic colorectal cancer: results from North American Gastrointestinal Intergroup Trial N9741. *J Clin Oncol.* 2010;28:3227–3233.

21. Bray J, Sludden J, Griffin MJ, et al. Influence of pharmacogenetics on response and toxicity in breast cancer patients treated with doxorubicin and cyclophosphamide. *Brit J Cancer.* 2010;102:1003–1009.

22. Kitzmiller JP, Groen DK, Phelps MA, Sadee W. Pharmacogenomic testing: relevance in medical practice: why drugs work in some patients but not in others. *Cleve Clin J Med.* 2011;78:243–257.

23. Savonarola A, Palmirotta R, Guadagni F, Silvestris F. Pharmacogenetics and pharmacogenomics: role of mutational analysis in anti-cancer targeted therapy. *Pharmacogenom J.* 2012;12:277–286.

24. Wheeler HE, Maitland ML, Dolan ME, Cox NJ, Ratain MJ. Cancer pharmacogenomics: strategies and challenges. *Nature Rev Genet.* 2013;14:23–34.

25. Fernandez-Rozadilla C, Cazier JB, Moreno V, et al. Pharmacogenomics in colorectal cancer: a genome-wide association study to predict toxicity after 5-fluorouracil or FOLFOX administration. *Pharmacogenom J.* 2013;13:209–217.

26. Fontana V, Luizon MR, Sandrim VC. An update on the pharmacogenetics of treating hypertension. *J Human Hypertens.* 2015; 29:283–291.

27. Collet JP, Hulot JS, Pena A, et al. Cytochrome P450 2C19 polymorphism in young patients treated with clopidogrel after myocardial infarction: a cohort study. *Lancet.* 2009;373:309–317.

28. GoDarts, Group UDPS, Wellcome Trust Case Control C, et al. Common variants near ATM are associated with glycemic response to metformin in type 2 diabetes. *Nat Genet.* 2011;43:117–120.

29. Amblee A. Patient profiling in diabetes and role of canagliflozin. *Pharmacogenom Personal Med.* 2014;7:367–377.

30. Tantisira KG, Lasky-Su J, Harada M, et al. Genomewide association between GLCCI1 and response to glucocorticoid therapy in asthma. *N Engl J Med.* 2011;365:1173–1183.

31. Pouget JG, Shams TA, Tiwari AK, Muller DJ. Pharmacogenetics and outcome with antipsychotic drugs. *Dialog Clin Neurosci.* 2014;16:555–566.

32. Klepstad P, Fladvad T, Skorpen F, et al. Influence from genetic variability on opioid use for cancer pain: a European genetic association study of 2294 cancer pain patients. *Pain.* 2011;152:1139–1145.

33. Lotsch J, Geisslinger G. Pharmacogenetics of new analgesics. *Brit J Pharmacol.* 2011;163:447–460.

34. Roberts NJ, Jiao Y, Yu J, et al. ATM mutations in patients with hereditary pancreatic cancer. *Cancer Disc.* 2012;2:41–46.

35. Zhang J, Dhakal IB, Zhang X, Prizment AE, Anderson KE. Genetic variability in energy balance and pancreatic cancer risk in a population-based case-control study in Minnesota. *Pancreas.* 2014;43:281–286.

36. Pharoah PD, Antoniou AC, Easton DF, Ponder BA. Polygenes, risk prediction, and targeted prevention of breast cancer. *N Engl J Med.* 2008;358:2796–2803.

37. Wacholder S, Hartge P, Prentice R, et al. Performance of common genetic variants in breast-cancer risk models. *N Engl J Med.* 2010;362:986–993.

38. Holloway JW, Yang IA, Holgate ST. Interpatient variability in rates of asthma progression: can genetics provide an answer? *J Allergy Clin Immun.* 2008;121:573–579.

39. Lio D, Licastro F, Scola L, et al. Interleukin-10 promoter polymorphism in sporadic Alzheimer's disease. *Gene Immun.* 2003;4:234–238.

40. Licastro F, Porcellini E, Caruso C, Lio D, Corder EH. Genetic risk profiles for Alzheimer's disease: integration of APOE genotype and variants that up-regulate inflammation. *Neurobiol Aging.* 2007;28:1637–1643.

41. Vasto S, Candore G, Duro G, Lio D, Grimaldi MP, Caruso C. Alzheimer's disease and genetics of inflammation: a pharmacogenomic vision. *Pharmacogenomics.* 2007;8: 1735–1745.

42. Rodriguez-Paredes M, Esteller M. Cancer epigenetics reaches mainstream oncology. *Nat Med.* 2011;17:330–339.

43. Heyn H, Esteller M. DNA methylation profiling in the clinic: applications and challenges. *Nat Rev Genetics.* 2012;13:679–692.

44. Mummaneni P, Shord SS. Epigenetics and oncology. *Pharmacotherapy.* 2014; 34:495–505.

45. Juergens RA, Wrangle J, Vendetti FP, et al. Combination epigenetic therapy has efficacy in patients with refractory advanced non-small cell lung cancer. *Cancer Disc.* 2011;1:598–607.

46. Abi Khalil C. The emerging role of epigenetics in cardiovascular disease. *Ther Adv Chron Dis.* 2014;5:178–187.

47. Ventham NT, Kennedy NA, Nimmo ER, Satsangi J. Beyond gene discovery in inflammatory bowel disease: the emerging role of epigenetics. *Gastroenterol.* 2013;145: 293–308.

48. Urdinguio RG, Sanchez-Mut JV, Esteller M. Epigenetic mechanisms in neurological diseases: genes, syndromes, and therapies. *Lancet Neurol.* 2009;8:1056–1072.

49. Handel AE, Ebers GC, Ramagopalan SV. Epigenetics: molecular mechanisms and implications for disease. *Trends Molec Med.* 2010;16:7–16.

50. Li Y, Li Y, Chen T, et al. Circulating proteolytic products of carboxypeptidase N for early detection of breast cancer. *Clin Chem.* 2014;60:233–242.

51. Gorini G, Harris RA, Mayfield RD. Proteomic approaches and identification of novel therapeutic targets for alcoholism. *Neuropsychopharmacol.* 2014;39:104–130.

52. Holtta M, Minthon L, Hansson O, et al. An integrated workflow for multiplex CSF proteomics and peptidomics-identification of candidate cerebrospinal fluid biomarkers of Alzheimer's disease. *J Proteome Res.* 2015;14:654–663.

53. Terracciano R, Pelaia G, Preiano M, Savino R. Asthma and COPD proteomics: current approaches and future directions. *Proteomics Clinical App.* 2015;9: 203–220.

54. Eswaran J, Cyanam D, Mudvari P, et al. Transcriptomic landscape of breast cancers through mRNA sequencing. *Sci Rep.* 2012;2:264.

55. Wyatt AW, Mo F, Wang K, et al. Heterogeneity in the inter-tumor transcriptome of high risk prostate cancer. *Genome Biol.* 2014;15:426.

56. Ichikawa H, Yoshida A, Kanda T, et al. Prognostic significance of promyelocytic leukemia expression in gastrointestinal stromal tumor; integrated proteomic and transcriptomic analysis. *Cancer Sci.* 2015;106:115–124.

57. Malheiros D, Panepucci RA, Roselino AM, Araujo AG, Zago MA, Petzl-Erler ML. Genome-wide gene expression profiling reveals unsuspected molecular alterations in pemphigus foliaceus. *Immunology.* 2014;143:381–395.

58. Desire L, Blondiaux E, Carriere J, et al. Blood transcriptomic biomarkers of Alzheimer's disease patients treated with EHT 0202. *J Alzheimer's Dis.* 2013;34:469–483.

59. Smith PJ, Levine AP, Dunne J, et al. Mucosal transcriptomics implicates under expression of BRINP3 in the pathogenesis of ulcerative colitis. *Inflamm Bowel Dis.* 2014;20:1802–1812.

60. Zhu J, Djukovic D, Deng L, et al. Colorectal cancer detection using targeted serum metabolic profiling. *J Proteome Res.* 2014;13:4120–4130.

61. Miller JA, Pappan K, Thompson PA, et al. Plasma metabolomic profiles of breast cancer patients after short-term limonene intervention. *Cancer Prev Res.* 2015;8:86–93.

62. Ke C, Hou Y, Zhang H, et al. Large-scale profiling of metabolic dysregulation in ovarian cancer. *Int J Cancer.* 2015;136:516–526.

63. Xiang J, Liu L, Wang W, et al. Metabolic tumor burden: a new promising way to reach precise personalized therapy in PDAC. *Cancer Lett.* 2015;359:165–168.

64. Cassol E, Misra V, Dutta A, Morgello S, Gabuzda D. Cerebrospinal fluid metabolomics reveals altered waste clearance and accelerated aging in HIV patients with neurocognitive impairment. *AIDS.* 2014;28:1579–1591.

65. Kang J, Zhu L, Lu J, Zhang X. Application of metabolomics in autoimmune diseases: insight into biomarkers and pathology. *J Neuroimmunol.* 2015;279:25–32.

66. Hansen J, Iyengar R. Computation as the mechanistic bridge between precision medicine and systems therapeutics. *Clin Pharmacol Therapeut.* 2013;93:117–128.

67. Bertrand D, Chng KR, Sherbaf FG, et al. Patient-specific driver gene prediction and risk assessment through integrated network analysis of cancer omics profiles. *Nucleic Acids Res.* 2015;43(7):44.

68. Ferrari M. Cancer nanotechnology: opportunities and challenges. *Nat Rev Cancer.* 2005;5:161–171.

69. Mulder WJ, Jaffer FA, Fayad ZA, Nahrendorf M. Imaging and nanomedicine in inflammatory atherosclerosis. *Sci Translational Med.* 2014;6:239sr1.

70. Greenbaum D. Regulation and the fate of personalized medicine. *Virtual Mentor.* 2012;14:645–652.

71. Food and Drug Administration. *Paving the Way for Personalized Medicine: FDA's Role in a New Era of Medical Product Development.* 2013. Washington, DC: U.S. Department of Health and Human Services.

72. Dubecz A, Gall I, Solymosi N, et al. Temporal trends in long-term survival and cure rates in esophageal cancer: a SEER database analysis. *J Thorac Oncol.* 2012; 7:443–447.

73. Rodriguez-Vida A, Chowdhury S. Diagnosis and management of testicular cancers. *Trends Urology Men's Health.* 2013;4:25–30.

74. Hanna N, Einhorn LH. Testicular cancer: a reflection on 50 years of discovery. *J Clin Oncol.* 2014;32:3085–3092.

75. Shen H, Rodriguez-Aguayo C, Xu R, et al. Enhancing chemotherapy response with sustained EphA2 silencing using multistage vector delivery. *Clin Cancer Res.* 2013; 19:1806–1815.

76. Cleary K, Peters TM. Image-guided interventions: technology review and clinical applications. *Ann Rev Biomed Eng.* 2010;12:119–142.

77. Nemec SF, Peloschek P, Schmook MT, et al. CT-MR image data fusion for computer-assisted navigated surgery of orbital tumors. *Eur J Radiol.* 2010;73:224–229.

78. Liao H, Ishihara H, Tran HH, Masamune K, Sakuma I, Dohi T. Precision-guided surgical navigation system using laser guidance and 3D autostereoscopic image overlay. *Comput Med Imag Grap.* 2010;34:46–54.

79. Ukimura O, Nakamoto M, Gill IS. Three-dimensional reconstruction of reno-vascular-tumor anatomy to facilitate zero-ischemia partial nephrectomy. *Eur Urol.* 2012; 61:211–217.

80. van der Poel HG, Buckle T, Brouwer OR, Valdes Olmos RA, van Leeuwen FW. Intraoperative laparoscopic fluorescence guidance to the sentinel lymph node in prostate cancer patients: clinical proof of concept of an integrated functional imaging approach using a multimodal tracer. *Eur Urol.* 2011;60:826–833.

81. Koay EJ, Truty MJ, Cristini V, et al. Transport properties of pancreatic cancer describe gemcitabine delivery and response. *J Clin Invest.* 2014;124:1525–1536.

82. Fact Sheet: President Obama's Precision Medicine Initiative. Accessed March 2, 2015, at https://www.whitehouse.gov/the-press-office/2015/01/30/fact-sheet-president-obama-s-precision-medicine-initiative.

83. Dawson SJ, Tsui DW, Murtaza M, et al. Analysis of circulating tumor DNA to monitor metastatic breast cancer. *N Engl J Med.* 2013;368:1199–1209.

84. Mayo Clinic Biobank. Accessed April 9, 2015, at http://www.mayo.edu/research/centers-programs/mayo-clinic-biobank/about/resources.

85. NCBI Genetics and Medicine. Accessed April 9, 2015, at http://www.ncbi.nlm.nih.gov/guide/genetics-medicine/#databases_.

86. Sussner KM, Jandorf L, Valdimarsdottir HB. Educational needs about cancer family history and genetic counseling for cancer risk among frontline healthcare clinicians in New York City. *Genet Med.* 2011;13:785–793.

87. Duke Center for Personalized and Precision Medicine. Accessed April 9, 2015, at http://dukepersonalizedmedicine.org/home.

88. Institute for Precision Medicine at Weill Cornell Medical College. Accessed April 9, 2015, at http://ipm.weill.cornell.edu/.

CHAPTER 17

Evidence-Based Medicine and Shared Decision Making

Kasey R. Boehmer
Victor M. Montori
Henry H. Ting

Abstract

Evidence-based medicine (EBM) encompasses three important principles: (1) Clinicians should consider the best available evidence when making clinical decisions; (2) some evidence warrants greater confidence than other evidence; and (3) the evidence alone is never enough to fully inform clinical decisions without considering patient values, preferences, and context. To practice the third principle, EBM requires the incorporation of shared decision making (SDM), where the patient and the clinician will deliberate together and arrive at a decision collaboratively. SDM requires an empathic "dance" across decision-making models, which are discussed in this chapter. We also discuss the importance of SDM for the translation of evidence into clinical practice, the evidence to support the practice of SDM, and how clinicians can practice SDM, as well as the future of SDM in the context of challenges of implementation, measurement, policy, and research.

EVIDENCE-BASED MEDICINE

Evidence-based medicine (EBM) is the practice of medicine based on three fundamental principles. The first principle states that clinicians should use systematic summaries of the pertinent body of research when making clinical decisions.[1] The second principle requires the recognition that some research

262

TABLE 17.1 Factors That Weaken Confidence in the Evidence

Factor	Effect
Risk of bias	Systematic error: variability not resulting from chance
Imprecision	Random error: variability from chance
Inconsistency	The degree to which the relative treatment effects differ from differences in populations, interventions, outcomes, or risk of biases
Indirectness	The applicability of the evidence to the clinical situation under consideration
Publication bias	The selective publication of studies that show a statistically significant effect

results warrant more confidence as compared with other research.[1] According to these two principles, the best source of evidence about the relative efficacy and safety of treatment options would be a systematic review of multiple high-quality, precise, homogeneous, and directly relevant randomized trials. Clinical decisions informed by this level of evidence would be made with more confidence than when the available evidence is sparse, biased, imprecise, inconsistent, and indirectly related to the patients or outcomes of interest. Experts such as the GRADE Working Group have proposed criteria for determining the degree of confidence in the evidence: assess bias, precision, consistency, directness, and completeness of reporting and publication of the body of evidence to inform clinicians' confidence in the estimates of benefits and harms.[2] Such criteria are most pertinent in the context of specific treatment choices by individual patients. For example, consider the randomized trials of statins versus placebos for primary and secondary prevention. These trials confer a high level of confidence in their estimates of short-term efficacy and safety. However, estimates of their long-term effects may warrant less confidence when advising patients about using these agents for a lifetime.

The Third Principle of EBM

The third principle of EBM is that the research evidence alone is not sufficient to fully inform clinical decisions. Such decisions require consideration of individual, informed patient preferences, as well as the specific context and circumstances of the patient. Although recognized early on, this principle is often neglected from discussions and recommendations from EBM.[3] Without this principle, however, EBM could be characterized as evidence tyranny: the indiscriminate application of research evidence to every patient, regardless of what the patient may want if he or she knew what the clinician knew.[4] To

FIGURE 17. 1 Evidence-based medicine requires the consideration of research evidence, patient values and preferences, and context.

fully translate research evidence into clinical practice, patient preferences and context must be considered before the values and preferences of the clinician or population. It also requires clinician expertise to ensure that the patient's preferences are correctly diagnosed and the proposed treatments fit the patient's context. The incorporation of patients' preferences and context into clinical decision making requires that both parties—patient and clinician—bring their unique knowledge into a conversation about treatment options.

Requirements for Effective EBM

Paramount to practicing EBM, the first principle of EBM requires that clinicians consider the entire body of evidence rather than selectively focus on the most salient or recent study. Important reasons for this practice include the desirable outcomes to (1) calibrate our confidence in the point estimates of efficacy by demonstrating consistency with other studies and by improving their precision by pooling them with other studies, (2) avoid premature conclusions about the magnitude of effect or the potential lack of usefulness of an intervention, and (3) increase the usefulness to clinicians with the results that come from studies conducted in multiple settings and patients.[5] Paramount to producing evidence that is consistent with the principles of EBM and therefore most useful to clinicians and patients is the generation of evidence protected from bias or systematic deviations from the truth.[6] To mitigate bias, strategies can be used for studies of therapeutic interventions such as randomization, blinding of patients and investigators, following the intention-to-treat principle to optimize the complete analysis of participants as randomized, and completing studies as initially planned rather than stopping early for benefit.[7,8] Furthermore, the full publication of studies regardless of a positive or negative result is of critical importance to facilitate the practice of EBM.[9]

Finally, to be most useful to patients and clinicians, it is important to directly measure the impact of alternative courses of action on outcomes that matter to patients. Patient-important outcomes are those that patients believe would affect their lives and what these patients wish to achieve or avoid—such as quality of life, mortality, and adverse outcomes rather than intermediate clinical outcomes such as imaging or blood test results.[10] For example, when considering a study of the effects of a new medication versus placebo for patients with diabetes, one might consider comparing its effect on hemoglobin A_1c. However, patients value cardiovascular outcomes more than hemoglobin A_1c.[11] Further, patients may place a higher value on the frequency of testing blood sugars and the occurrence of low blood sugars.[12] Evidence about the effects of interventions on outcomes that matter to patients are key in the decision-making process. Indeed, paramount to the third principle of EBM is the ability to engage in the process of making fateful decisions. Patient participation in making decisions helps realize this third principle and promote the patient-centered implementation of EBM.[4]

DECISION-MAKING MODELS

Charles et al has described the spectrum of decision-making models that incorporate patient values and preferences to varying extents.[13] The oldest of these models, referred to as paternalistic, refers to clinicians making decisions without deliberating with the patient and their family. The patient is simply asked to provide consent. This type of decision making in the realm of EBM should be reserved for technical decisions in which the patient values and preferences would have no impact on the decision, such as in the context of emergency care or when a cardiologist chooses to implant an 11mm or 13mm length coronary stent. Patients assume such decisions represent the majority of clinical decisions. Consequently, patients may respond to invitations for an

TABLE 17.2 Decision-Making Models

	Parental	Clinician as Perfect Agent	Shared Decision Making	Informed
Options	Informed consent		Clinician ↔ Patient	
Deliberation	Clinician	Clinician after discussion	Joint	Patient (after discussion)
Decision	Clinician orders	Clinician recommends	Consensus	Patient requests

Modified from Charles, Gafni, Whelan.[13]

active role in decision making by suggesting that the party that attended medical school make the decision.

The remaining decision-making models attempt to incorporate the patient's views to varying extents.[13] In the *physician-as-agent model*, the clinician engages the patient in conversation to understand and incorporate the patient's values, preferences, and context. The clinician deliberates independently, taking this information and research evidence into account and then making a recommendation to the patient.

On the other end of this gradient is the *informed decision-making model*. Here the patient obtains information from the clinician and other sources, considers the alternatives, and requests the treatment option he or she wants. Between the physician as agent and informed decision making is *shared decision making* (SDM). In this model, the patient and clinician engage in conversation, deliberate together about the evidence, the patient's values and preferences, and the context to jointly arrive at a mutual consensus decision.

In many cases, SDM is an ideal decision-making model, accounting for the current decision facing the patient; the relevant options for treatment, including no treatment; and individual patient values, preferences, and context. In practice, these decision-making models are not mutually exclusive, and clinicians and patients will engage in an empathic dance across these models, with the clinician carrying the responsibility to lead and tailor the decision-making approach most relevant to each decision and for each patient.

To illustrate this "dance," let's consider an example. Joan has multiple chronic conditions, including chronic obstructive pulmonary disease. This condition causes fatigue for her daily activities, but during severe exacerbations she must go to the hospital for treatment. Her clinician has come to know her well and has a good relationship with her. When reviewing her treatment plan or considering new treatments, she and her clinician work together, using SDM during their visits. When Joan is managing at home, she sometimes needs to make minor modifications to her treatment and self-management routines. In these cases, she calls on her clinician when needed but primarily directs her own care and requests any modifications she needs—in a process akin to using the informed decision-making model. In the most severe instances, when she is in the hospital, she prefers her clinician to take the knowledge about her life from their ongoing relationship, deliberate independently and with colleagues, and make recommendations to Joan, acting as her agent. It is this dance across models, built on a foundation of a long-term and trusting clinician–patient relationship that is the hallmark of patient-centered care. While we advocate for the application of this flexible and empathic decision-making model, we will use the more common moniker of SDM to represent these participatory forms of decision making that invite patient values, preferences, and context into making a clinical decision.

SHARED DECISION MAKING

In its most basic form, SDM involves, at a minimum, the patient and clinician dyad deliberating as equal partners during the decision-making process.[13] Clinicians share the best research evidence and personal clinical experience about the decision at hand, and patients share their individual and unique values, preferences, and context. At the end of this exchange, the dyad agrees to the arrived-at decision for treatment among all relevant alternatives, including no treatment.

Patients seek to make the best decision for themselves and their families, whereas clinicians contribute medical knowledge and experience. Such deliberation takes time and purposeful effort. Decision aids (DAs) are tools created to facilitate the process of SDM and to encourage clinicians to invite patients to participate in decision making during the encounter. DAs intended for use during a clinical encounter have specific functional requirements. First, they do not require complex logistical solutions to identify the appropriate patients to receive the material before a visit as do pre-encounter educational materials.[14] They do not require patients to review material in advance, which can cause confusion during the visit when clinicians assume the review, or even a decision, has already taken place.[14] They avoid patients feeling as if they may be judged as difficult if they bring individual values, preferences, or concerns to the clinical encounter.[14] Finally, they enhance clinician self-efficacy to engage in a discussion of the best evidence and the estimated benefits and harms for each alternative treatment as applied to individual patients rather than a population estimate of efficacy.

The International Patient Decision Aid Standards (IPDAS) collaboration has developed a four-step criteria for developing DAs:

1. Understand the decision, including what the evidence says about the risks, benefits, and impact on patient-important factors (i.e., cost, regimen, etc.), and in what context the DA will be used.
2. Develop a first draft of the DA.
3. Iteratively modify the DA with potential users.
4. Test the DA in real-world settings.[15]

Encounter DA development includes a specific methodology, particularly in the first three steps, which has been described by Breslin et al.[16,17] To understand the decision, developers conduct an evidence synthesis and an experience synthesis. The evidence synthesis is a systematic review of the literature either extant or newly conducted for the decision at hand. The experience synthesis is a process by which the developers use the principles of user-centered design, combining observations of the clinical setting where the DAs will be used and discussions with relevant stakeholders—that is, patients, their caregivers, and clinicians. After the first prototype is developed, it is piloted in real clinical encounters, using direct observation or video-recorded observation. Prototypes are continuously iterated until patient and clinician conversations emerge from their use; hallmarks of a successful prototype are characterized by patients expressing why they value the different pieces of evidence presented and beginning to "try on" the treatment options to discover what those different options would look like in their own lives and context.

DAs are not the only tools available to support patient involvement in decision making. Many groups have developed patient education materials such as pamphlets and videos that are distributed before or after a clinical encounter for patients to review on their own or with family to facilitate knowledge transfer. The assumption that such education materials enhance decision making presumes that an informed patient will be able to break down the power–distance gradients between him- or herself and the clinician and actively participate in decision making during the clinical encounter. There is, however, scant evidence that this is true—and some evidence that it is not.[18,19]

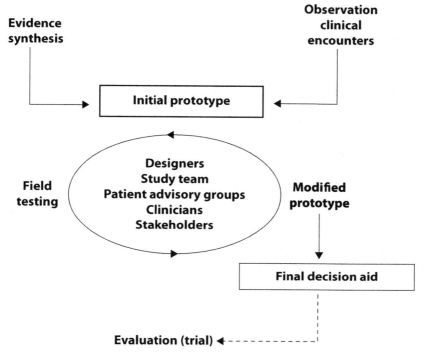

FIGURE 17.2 Decision aid development process

Why Is SDM Important?

Beyond our limited ability to practice EBM without integrating the patient's values, preferences, and context, there are other reasons for which SDM is critically important. The efficiency of translating research evidence into routine clinical practice has been shown to be problematic across health disciplines, with only 55% of eligible patients receiving EBM-recommended treatments for conditions such as cancer and atrial fibrillation.[20] In an era when evidence is being generated at a rate of 560,000 new articles per year, clinicians struggle to uptake and apply this evidence into routine clinical practice.[21] Translating evidence into clinical practice requires that clinicians become aware of it, accept it, and find it applicable and available. They then must be able to apply it to the individual patient they are seeing and act on the information synthesized in the previous steps.[21] Making sense of and acting on evidence is challenging and has been the focus of quality-improvement efforts. Yet even more challenging,

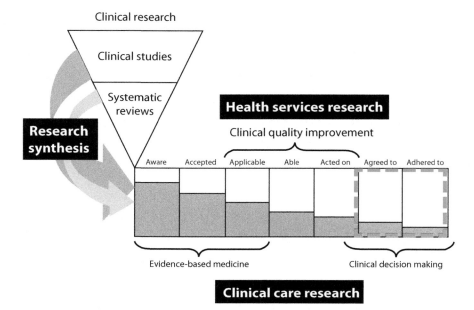

FIGURE 17.3 The challenge of translating evidence into clinical practice. Adapted from Glasziou, Haynes.[21]

the patient must then agree to that intervention and adhere, which is particularly relevant for interventions used for prevention and treatment of chronic conditions.[21] Conversation is required to synthesize evidence for patients and for them to consider whether agreement and adherence to the plans presented fit within their preferences, values, and context. For such conversations, SDM is useful to clinicians, lest patients leave the clinic visit with prescriptions they never intend to fill (primary nonadherence) or end up filling prescriptions they never intend to take over the long term (secondary nonadherence).

There are also important justifications for SDM in the policy environment. Healthcare reformers have called for the Triple Aim: improve the individual patient experience, improve the health of populations, and reduce the per capita costs of care.[22] SDM is integral to improving the individual patient experience of care, making it both evidence based and patient centered. Furthermore, without SDM, patient preferences may be misdiagnosed. Although misdiagnoses of patients' conditions or prescribed treatments are recognized for their consequences related to patient safety and emotional well-being, the misdiagnosis of patient preferences is often silent but can have similar negative consequences.[23]

What Is the Evidence of Value for SDM?

There is a growing body of evidence regarding SDM for treatment and screening decisions. The most recent Cochrane systematic review of SDM interventions included 115 studies. In summary, compared to usual care, DAs increased patient participation in decision making by 34% and patient knowledge about their available options by 13%.[24] They also reduced the conflict that patients felt about their decision by 7% and reduced the proportion of patients that remained undecided about the choice at hand by approximately 41%.[24] On average, DAs were found to increase the time of a consultation by 2.6 minutes.[24] This review found no consistent effect of DAs on patient adherence to the selected option, cost or resource use, general health outcomes, or condition-specific health outcomes—in part because of limited power to detect such differences and the variability in the reporting of these outcomes across studies. This review has a central limitation: It indirectly applies to the encounter DAs that are known to promote SDM. When looking at encounter DAs specifically, they have similar effects in terms of increased patient participation and patient knowledge, except that for these tools patient participation has been directly observed rather than assumed. Also, use of these tools during the encounter adds the same average time to the consultation as that estimated in studies of patient education materials.[25] An exciting development is the finding that encounter DAs are effective for patients with low education and socioeconomic status, perhaps mitigating healthcare disparities.[25]

How Does One Do SDM?

Consider the following scenario described by Montori et al:[26]

A 65-year-old woman with no [cardiovascular disease] risk factors has average blood pressure readings of 135/80 mm Hg, an LDL cholesterol level of 200 mg/dL, high-density lipoprotein (HDL) cholesterol of 30 mg/dL, and a total cholesterol level of 300 mg/dL, which did not change much with diet. She has been unable to tolerate atorvastatin because of gastrointestinal distress and muscle discomfort and returns to discuss treatment options with her physician. Following ATP III guidelines, the physician would prescribe rosuvastatin to reduce her LDL cholesterol level to lower than 160 mg/dL. The new [American College of Cardiology and American Heart Association] guidelines give a class I recommendation to use moderate- to high-intensity statin therapy in persons with LDL levels of 190 mg/dL or greater. Rather than merely prescribe statins for this patient, the physician used a decision aid (http://statindecisionaid.mayoclinic.org) to discuss the value of reducing 10-year risk

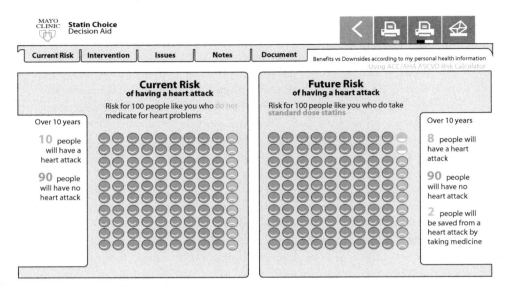

FIGURE 17.4 Statin choice decision aid case

from 10% to [8]% in the context of the patient's known issues with statins. This patient considered her options and chose not to use statin therapy, judging that neither aspirin nor statins would provide her with sufficient benefits to justify their use. It is important to recognize, as should the physician, that another patient may have chosen to try an alternative statin or to use aspirin alone.[26]

Additional cases, to which SDM can be applied, exist for patients facing the decision to take statin therapy for primary prevention under a variety of other circumstances.[26]

THE FUTURE OF SDM

Despite the evidence of the efficacy of DAs to facilitate SDM, positively influence patients' participation and knowledge, and reduce patients' decisional conflict, there are significant implementation challenges. Take for example, the recent 2013 change by the American College of Cardiology (ACA) and American Heart Association (AHA) of their guidelines for assessing the risk of cardiovascular disease and the treatment for risk prevention. In the new version of their guidelines, the ACA and AHA shift focus from measurement and lowering of LDL cholesterol and focus on measuring and lowering cardiovascular risk, which represents a "major shift in preventive cardiology."[26] Shortly after the change in guidelines, the Center for Medicare and Medicaid Services removed its quality measures for the measurement of LDL cholesterol and treatment of LDL with statin medications.[27] Although the new guidelines have called for statin therapy for patients with an absolute risk of 7.5% or greater, quality measures have yet to follow, suggesting uncertainty around such a cutoff.[27] Others have argued for a more patient-centered approach to replace the cutoff—such as SDM.[26]

The Statin Choice Decision Aid offers a solution to that call—as a tool that can create a SDM conversation between patient and clinician and illustrates individualized patient benefits and risks. The tool can document the patient's choice regarding statin therapy in the electronic health record (EHR), yet it has not been integrated into EHRs across the country. The value of such integration for the benefit of patients and clinicians has recently been highlighted.[27] Integration into EHRs and clinical workflows must be done in a way that preserves the quality of the SDM activity and represents a major challenge.

Training and the extent to which it is needed are also important factors to consider for future implementation. For encounter DAs, clinicians have been able to use them with minimal training and with 58% fidelity to the intended use of the tool, as determined by video review.[28] It remains uncertain what added effect on fidelity to the intended delivery additional training would have and what, if any, additional benefit to outcomes such as patient knowledge, involvement, and decision certainty would result or whether its value would warrant the additional resources it might require.

Measurement Challenges

As we move toward larger implementation of SDM, documenting that an SDM process has occurred and measuring its quality poses challenges. Measuring that SDM actually occurred with enough fidelity to its principles is important so that SDM does not become merely a checklist similar to what informed consent has become. Past studies looking at encounter DAs have relied on videographic study with standardized scales to answer questions of fidelity and SDM,[29–32] which are not feasible beyond small-scale efficacy studies. For future implementation, it is important to measure and document that the SDM experience demonstrated in research studies continues to be replicated across real-world practice settings.

Policy Challenges

To date, SDM has received its fair share of coverage in the policy arena, both at a federal and state level, primarily motivated by proposing SDM as a means to reduce unwarranted variation in practices regionally and to reduce cost. As already discussed, the available evidence does not suggest consistent effects in either area. Federally, the Patient Protection and Affordable Care Act (ACA) in section 3506 established a call for shared decision-making national resource centers and the provision for standards for certification of DAs, as well as grants to support these implementation efforts.[33] However, this section of the ACA has thus far gone unfunded. At the state level, attempts have been made to mandate SDM for specific conditions such as in Minnesota in 2011, where it was ultimately never passed. Other states such as Washington, Maine, and Vermont have passed legislation to set up SDM demonstration projects, whereas others have incorporated SDM as part of their requirements for certification of healthcare home initiatives.[33] Although these legislative efforts, particularly when funded, may be helpful to advance the implementation and study of SDM, they pose unique challenges. If SDM is proposed in policy as a mechanism by which variation and cost can be modified, which is not supported by current evidence, there is a risk policy makers will become disinterested in its implementation if demonstration projects echo the lack of consistent effect on cost and variation. In addition, the focus on cost and variation generally disinterests clinicians and may even deter them from SDM.[34]

Pending Research in SDM

As the example of the Statin Choice Decision Aid illustrates, understanding the way in which SDM is implemented into EHRs and clinical workflows effectively and efficiently remains an important research question. Second, high-quality, evidence-based DAs do not exist for most healthcare conditions. The Ottawa Registry of Decision Aids has been suggested as a resource to reference before embarking on any new DA development.[14] However, complete and comprehensive participation in the Ottawa Registry remains elusive. Before embarking on development, one must consider if a decision for a proposed DA warrants an SDM discussion in which the patient's values, preferences, and context are likely to be of importance to the deliberation and outcome and that there is high quality-evidence available to support such a DA. Another resource to consider for researchers that seek to develop encounter DAs is the Mayo Clinic Shared Decision Making National Resource Center (http://shareddecisions.mayoclinic.org/). Finally, currently untested DAs and new DAs deserve efficacy testing to ensure only DAs with proven efficacy progress toward implementation.

THE ROLE OF SDM IN EBM

We began by discussing the third principle of EBM, and we conclude that EBM is not possible without SDM. Because the best research evidence alone is never enough and clinicians must also take into account the patient's values, preferences, and context, SDM offers one tactic to adhere to this principle. Likewise, we should acknowledge that there is no SDM without EBM. SDM requires careful deliberation between patient and clinician about the best evidence. Therefore, SDM requires syntheses of the body of evidence, the ability to assess the level of confidence one should have in the evidence at hand, and evidence related to the interventions' impact on outcomes that matter most to patients. Therefore, just like EBM cannot be practiced with SDM, SDM cannot be practiced without EBM. The result of the evidence appraisal may yield high confidence in the estimates of benefits and risks of alternative options. In this circumstance, if the options are closely matched, SDM is ideally poised to help identify the best choice for individual patients. When the body of evidence warrants less confidence in the estimates about the merits of the options, deliberation is perhaps harder and filled with greater uncertainty. Patient preferences, clinician expertise, and careful attention to the context and circumstances will then play a major role in arriving at the best option. In both cases, careful appraisal of the body of evidence precedes the effort of SDM.

Finally, we should consider a key EBM "product": clinical practice guidelines. Guidelines may give strong recommendations or conditional recommendations. Where strong recommendations ("should be . . .") are formulated, quality metrics may be appropriate to determine to what extent clinicians are adhering to this recommendation. Where guidelines give conditional recommendations ("may be considered . . ."), SDM almost always should logically follow in order to incorporate the patient's preferences and context in arriving at the best decision for this patient. However, even in the case of strong recommendations, caution is important in creating and assessing quality metrics without first considering the variability in patient values, preferences, and context in light of the evidence. For example, SDM may be appropriate despite a strong recommendation—such as the recommendation for statin therapy in all patients with diabetes.[35] In such cases, quality metrics are particularly problematic because clinicians who rightly wish to engage in SDM must continually document that their patients "refused" treatment in light of their informed values and preferences discussed with their clinician. Such scenarios, the result of inappropriately strong recommendations[36] make it much easier for clinicians to promote treatment to patients instead of engaging in SDM.

CONCLUSION

Evidence-based medicine is the practice of medicine that encompasses three important principles: (1) Clinicians should consider the best available evidence, ideally summarized systematically from the entire body of research, when making clinical decisions; (2) some evidence warrants greater confidence than other evidence; and (3) the evidence alone is never enough to fully inform clinical decisions.

To practice this third principle, EBM requires the incorporation of SDM. Likewise, SDM requires EBM for patients and clinicians to be able to deliberate the pros and cons, with their nature and likelihood illuminated by the body of research evidence available. SDM requires an empathic "dance" across decision-making models to find the right model for this patient facing this decision at this point in time. When applied, SDM often means that the patient and the clinician will deliberate and arrive at a decision collaboratively. SDM has been shown to improve patients' knowledge and decrease decisional uncertainty and conflict.

Finally, challenges in SDM include the ability to undertake large-scale dissemination and implementation in routine clinical practice, to measure that shared decision making occurred when implemented broadly, and to continue the pursuit of SDM in clinical practice in a policy environment that places high emphasis on cost and clinical outcomes, where evidence to support beneficial effects of SDM related to those outcomes does not exist. Much work remains to be done—innovation to advance the practice of SDM, measurement to determine its full impact, and implementation to understand its benefits across diverse clinical practices. Continued research in the pursuit of EBM and SDM and their synergies should seek to overcome these challenges for the advancement of patient-centered care.

REFERENCES

1. Djulbegovic B, Guyatt G. Evidence-based medicine and the theory of knowledge. In: Guyatt G, Rennie D, Meade M, Cook D, eds. *Users' Guides to the Medical Literature.* 3rd ed. New York, NY: McGraw Hill Education; 2015.

2. Guyatt GH, Oxman AD, Schunemann HJ, Tugwell P, Knottnerus A. GRADE guidelines: a new series of articles in the *Journal of Clinical Epidemiology. J Clin Epidemiol.* 2011;64(4):380–382.

3. Murad MH, Montori VM, Guyatt GH. Incorporating patient preferences in evidence-based medicine. *JAMA.* 2008;300(21):2483;author reply 2483–2484.

4. Hoffmann TC, Montori VM, Del Mar C. The connection between evidence-based medicine and shared decision making. *JAMA.* 2014;312(13):1295–1296.

5. Murad MH, Montori VM. Synthesizing evidence: shifting the focus from individual studies to the body of evidence. *JAMA.* 2013;309(21):2217–2218.

6. Guyatt G, Jaeschke R, Meade M. Why study results mislead: bias and random error. In: Guyatt G, Rennie D, Meade M, Cook D, eds. *Users' Guides to the Medical Literature.* 3rd ed. New York, NY: McGraw Hill Education; 2015.

7. Bassler D, Briel M, Montori VM, et al. Stopping randomized trials early for benefit and estimation of treatment effects: systematic review and meta-regression analysis. *JAMA.* 2010;303(12):1180–1187.

8. Montori VM, Devereaux PJ, Adhikari NK, et al. Randomized trials stopped early for benefit: a systematic review. *JAMA.* 2005;294(17):2203–2209.

9. Brown T. It's time for all trials registered and reported. *Cochrane Database Syst Rev.* 2013;4:ED000057.

10. Guyatt G, Montori V, Devereaux PJ, Schunemann H, Bhandari M. Patients at the center: in our practice, and in our use of language. *ACP J Club.* 2004;140(1):A11–12.

11. Gandhi GY, Murad MH, Fujiyoshi A, et al. Patient-important outcomes in registered diabetes trials. *JAMA.* 2008;299(21):2543–2549.

12. Lipska KJ, Krumholz HM. Comparing diabetes medications: where do we set the bar? *JAMA Intern Med.* 2014;174(3):317–318.

13. Charles C, Gafni A, Whelan T. Shared decision-making in the medical encounter: what does it mean? (or it takes at least two to tango). *Soc Sci Med.* 1997;44(5):681–692.

14. Hess EP, Coylewright M, Frosch DL, Shah ND. Implementation of shared decision making in cardiovascular care: past, present, and future. *Circ Cardiovasc Qual Outcomes.* 2014;7(5):797–803.

15. Matlock DD, Spatz ES. Design and testing of tools for shared decision making. *Circ Cardiovasc Qual Outcomes.* 2014;7(3):487–492.

16. Montori VM, Breslin M, Maleska M, Weymiller AJ. Creating a conversation: insights from the development of a decision aid. *PLoS Med.* 2007;4(8):e233.

17. Breslin M, Mullan RJ, Montori VM. The design of a decision aid about diabetes medications for use during the consultation with patients with type 2 diabetes. *Patient Educ Couns.* 2008;73(3):465–472.

18. Joseph-Williams N, Elwyn G, Edwards A. Knowledge is not power for patients: a systematic review and thematic synthesis of patient-reported barriers and facilitators to shared decision making. *Patient Educ Couns.* 2014;94(3):291–309.

19. Frosch DL, Legare F, Mangione CM. Using decision aids in community-based primary care: a theory-driven evaluation with ethnically diverse patients. *Patient Educ Couns.* 2008;73(3):490–496.

20. McGlynn EA, Asch SM, Adams J, et al. The quality of health care delivered to adults in the United States. *N Engl J Med*. 2003;348(26):2635–2645.

21. Glasziou P, Haynes B. The paths from research to improved health outcomes. *ACP J Club*. 2005;142(2):A8–10.

22. Berwick DM, Nolan TW, Whittington J. The Triple Aim: care, health, and cost. *Health Affair* (Millwood). 2008;27(3):759–769.

23. Mulley AG, Trimble C, Elwyn G. Stop the silent misdiagnosis: patients' preferences matter. *BMJ*. 2012;345:e6572.

24. Stacey D, Legare F, Col NF, et al. Decision aids for people facing health treatment or screening decisions. *Cochrane Database Syst Rev*. 2014;1:CD001431.

25. Coylewright M, Branda M, Inselman JW, et al. Impact of sociodemographic patient characteristics on the efficacy of decision AIDS: a patient-level meta-analysis of 7 randomized trials. *Circ Cardiovasc Qual Outcomes*. 2014;7(3):360–367.

26. Montori VM, Brito JP, Ting HH. Patient-centered and practical application of new high cholesterol guidelines to prevent cardiovascular disease. *JAMA*. 2014; 311(5):465–466.

27. Stine NW, Chokshi DA. Elimination of lipid levels from quality measures: implications and alternatives. *JAMA*. 2014;312(19):1971–1972.

28. Wyatt KD, Branda ME, Anderson RT, et al. Peering into the black box: a meta-analysis of how clinicians use decision aids during clinical encounters. *Implement Sci*. 2014;9:26.

29. Abadie R, Weymiller AJ, Tilburt J, et al. Clinician's use of the Statin Choice decision aid in patients with diabetes: a videographic study nested in a randomized trial. *J Eval Clin Pract*. 2009;15(3):492–497.

30. Hess EP, Knoedler MA, Shah ND, et al. The chest pain choice decision aid: a randomized trial. *Circ Cardiovasc Qual Outcomes*. 2012;5(3):251–259.

31. Mullan RJ, Montori VM, Shah ND, et al. The diabetes mellitus medication choice decision aid: a randomized trial. *Arch Intern Med*. 2009;169(17):1560–1568.

32. Nannenga MR, Montori VM, Weymiller AJ, et al. A treatment decision aid may increase patient trust in the diabetes specialist. The Statin Choice randomized trial. *Health Expect*. 2009;12(1):38–44.

33. Alston C, Berger ZD, Brownlee S, Elwyn G, Fowler FJ, Hall LK, et al. *Shared Decision-Making Strategies for Best Care: Patient Decision Aids*; 2014. Washington, DC: Institute of Medicine.

34. Shafir A, Rosenthal J. *Shared Decision Making: Advancing Patient-Centered Care Through State and Federal Implementation*; 2012. Washington, DC: National Academy for State Health Policy.

35. Stone NJ, Robinson JG, Lichtenstein AH, et al. 2013 ACC/AHA guideline on the treatment of blood cholesterol to reduce atherosclerotic cardiovascular risk in adults: a report of the American College of Cardiology/American Heart Association Task Force on Practice Guidelines. *Circ*. 2014;129(25)(suppl 2):S1–45.

36. Brito JP, Domecq JP, Murad MH, Guyatt GH, Montori VM. The Endocrine Society guidelines: when the confidence cart goes before the evidence horse. *J Clin Endocrinol Metab*. 2013;98(8):3246–3252.

IV HEALTHCARE REFORM AND NEW PAYMENT METHODS

The Rise of Consumerism and How Insurance Reform Will Drive Healthcare Delivery Reform

James L. Field

Abstract

The lofty ambition of the Affordable Care Act (ACA) is to transform the U.S. healthcare system into a new and improved model. The first part of the law addresses insurance reform and expanding healthcare benefits to more Americans. Unknown to the vast majority of the public, the rest of the ACA is directed at revamping the established structure for delivering healthcare. The purpose of this chapter is not to concentrate on one component of the ACA or the other, but to link the two together and explain how insurance reform will drive delivery reform on a massive scale.

Insurance reform is transforming passive patients into active consumers, and these consumers will seek out and demand a different type of healthcare, effectively commanding the creation of a new delivery model that will operate according to a different set of metrics. Thus, the important question is not whether U.S. healthcare will undergo seismic change, but rather how quickly and in what physical forms, and whether constituents will be better or worse off.

By any measure, the Affordable Care Act (ACA) is a monumental piece of federal legislation. The statute itself is a tome—roughly 1,000 pages long—that has required an army of technocrats (reportedly issuing 20,000 pages of regulations to date—to translate its contents into tangible initiatives. The ambition of the ACA is breathtakingly grand: to transform the entirety of the U.S. health-care system—how it is structured, financed, and operated—into a new and improved model.

Did the drafters of the law truly appreciate the breadth of the potential implications? Certainly, no evidence suggests they had a concrete idea of what an alternative model should look like. The law provides a high-level blueprint without directions for assembly. Today, there is not a single person who can legitimately claim to know what U.S. healthcare will look like in a decade. The backdrop portends a high-stakes and tortured transition: national spending on healthcare exceeds $2.5 trillion each year, making it one of the largest sectors of the economy. Historically, it has been a sector doggedly resistant to change. Despite this uncertainty, what can be said with absolute confidence is that there is zero probability of going back to the system that has brought us this far. We have committed to change, albeit with only a vague notion for how things will evolve.

The law divides into two parts. The first addresses insurance reform and the expansion of healthcare benefits to more Americans. The second part (the focus of this chapter) seeks to overhaul the system and the way it delivers care, although many Americans were unaware of this intention. Before the ACA, the market for health insurance purchased by individuals was fraught with obstacles and land mines. Policies were expensive and beyond the means of average wage earners. Those with preexisting conditions, regardless of financial means, were denied coverage. Insurers could unilaterally modify or cancel policies for any reason. As a remedy, the ACA eliminated discriminatory coverage practices and established state-level exchanges where consumers could shop for policies in an organized marketplace. Each exchange offers dozens of insurance policy options grouped into tiers with colors corresponding to metals. At the top of the pyramid, platinum policies offer the broadest provider networks and lowest annual deductibles but with the trade-off of the highest premiums. At the bottom, bronze plans have the lowest premiums but impose narrow provider networks, restrictions on certain services, and high annual deductibles and co-payments. Policies listed on an exchange detail prices and distinguishing features, empowering consumers to comparison shop. Beyond coverage reform, the ACA expanded the ranks of the insured by (1) offering income-based subsidies to offset premium prices for policies purchased on the exchanges and (2) additional new dollars (fully offsetting incremental costs) to states that broadened Medicaid qualifications. This set of initiatives held special importance for the Democratic Party, furthering long-held aspirations to achieve universal healthcare coverage. Notably, nearly all of the national discussion and debate over the ACA's content and passage focused on this one component of the larger law.

Unknown to 99% of the public, the rest of the ACA was directed at over-hauling the established "system" for delivering healthcare to the American populace. This would affect all major constituents: insurers, hospitals, physicians, and the medical device and pharmaceutical industries. An overarching objective was to replace the existing fee-for-service model with alternative payment schemes that would transfer financial "risk" to providers. Ideally, payment incentives would prioritize wellness and prevention over treating acute illness, transition much of hospital-based care to ambulatory settings, and replace physician-centric episodic care with team-based management of patients across the care continuum. Investment in a new type of infrastructure would make all this possible: electronic medical records, patient-centered medical homes, accountable care organizations (ACOs), clinically integrated (CI) physician networks, and a care-management workforce, among others. Tactically, the federal government would lead the way with states and private insurers following in its wake. Some providers and markets have embraced this New World vision and undertaken major steps to start this transition, while others have adopted a more conservative "wait and see" posture. Although the Republican Party remains committed to repealing the ACA, its resistance centers on the first part—insurance coverage and subsidies—with scant attention paid to the statute's provisions for restructuring the delivery base.

In analyzing where U.S. healthcare is headed, a conventional approach has been to focus on one or another component of the ACA. The purpose of this chapter, however, is to link the two together and present a narrative describing how insurance reform will drive delivery reform—inevitably, irreversibly, and on a massive scale. Stepping back, it would seem only logical that major changes to the way Americans access healthcare insurance, and the form this insurance takes, would have a profound effect on the design and behavior of the delivery system. How could it be otherwise? A key takeaway insight is that insurance reform is transforming passive patients into active consumers, and these consumers will seek out and demand a different type of healthcare, necessitating the standup of a new delivery model that operates according to a different set of metrics. Thus, for the reader, the important question is not whether U.S. healthcare will undergo seismic change but rather how quickly, in what physical forms, and leaving which constituents better or worse off.

ESSENTIAL TERMINOLOGY: "CONSUMERS" AND "RETAIL" MEDICINE

Until recently, speaking of patients as consumers was frowned on in the provider community. To do so was tantamount to degrading their humanity and cheapening the importance of their illness through association with bargain hunters roaming malls. Rather, patients are afforded special status and respect, an elevated standing extended to whoever occupies the hospital bed. Physicians *serve* patients and, as their primary advocates, ensure that they receive the best care possible. Above all else, patient and family desires are respected and carried out to the letter (". . . nothing too good for our loved one"). The governing ethic among clinicians has been to separate medical decision making from cost considerations so as to minimize the potential for finances to bias recommendations based on scientific evidence. Paradoxically, although we honor the patient, we do not serve the *individual* before us, focusing instead on a chart containing clinical data. Waiting in each exam room is not a person but a puzzle to solve or a problem to fix. In reality if not by intention, we attend to the medical half of a patient without delving into his or her personal half. We have not been accountable if a chosen care path amounts to futile care, cannot be continued after discharge, or ends up bankrupting the recipient.

Today, thinking of patients as consumers is considered a prerequisite for understanding and succeeding in the emerging healthcare environment. Using this label in no way suggests a lessening of commitment to patients and medicine's larger mission; it is assumed we are able to navigate this crosswalk. But consumerism in healthcare is reality, not a concept to kick around, because changes in insurance coverage and, specifically, how patients gain access to providers and under what financial conditions, will direct patients to seek healthcare in ways that we have traditionally associated with purchasing general goods and services. Throughout our lifetimes, we have required patients to fit into a healthcare model organized by and around providers. We have required them to travel to the main hospital campus. We have trained them to bear any indignity to see the talented physician. We have led them by the hand and told them what do. We have not expected them to understand the labyrinth they have involuntarily entered. We have viewed patients not as care partners but as quasi-victims assigned temporarily to our charge. We have not woven healthcare into the fabric of their lives, aligning it to their financial resources and other conditions that govern their lives.

Judging by market forces currently in play, however, this model has obsolescence stamped all over it. Motivated consumers armed with information and options simply will not tolerate it. Consumerism and patient-centered healthcare, a long-standing over-the-horizon aspiration that never materialized under fee-for-service incentives, are synonymous. Today, the arrival of consumer empowerment, which ultimately will drive which patients are channeled to which providers, will finally force a major redesign of the healthcare system.

Besides consumerism, a second important concept to emerge on the scene—indeed, the current hot topic—is "retail" medicine. Mostly commonly, the term is taken literally and associated with nurse-run clinics located in Walgreens, CVS, and similar outlets. Walmart, the penultimate retail franchise, has announced its goal of becoming a dominant primary care provider.[1] Beyond this narrow usage, however, the term is applied more expansively—and powerfully—to refer to the reconfiguration of healthcare to meet the needs of patients-as-consumers. Used in this way, "retail" is not a setting—a storefront per se—but an approach to delivering healthcare in ways that align with how patients-as-consumers make other choices for products and services, important and mundane, in their lives.

So, if the tables have turned and consumers now occupy the high ground, then it is "game on" for providers to turn their delivery models inside out. In due time, providers who are able to make this transition—those with vision, capital, leadership, skilled managers, and a sense of urgency—will thrive in the New World, and those who fall short will disappear. It is that simple and clear. Consumers love retail; good retail attracts and retains consumers. The two are inseparable.

SETTING THE BASELINE: HOW THINGS WORK TODAY

The structure of the U.S. healthcare sector has not changed for decades. To understand where healthcare is headed, it is useful to baseline the point of departure. For this discussion, we will focus on four key constituents (omitting others) and review, using a broad brush, how they fit together (Figure 18.1).

Beginning the chain, payers feed dollars into the system. One of these—a big one—is the federal government, which finances Medicare and partners with states to fund Medicaid. Commercial payers provide insurance products (and services) to companies offering health benefits and to individuals buying their own insurance. To set premiums, commercial payers forecast costs and add in margin. Should costs go up, companies, as well as federal and state governments, contribute more dollars (a need that routinely occurs). Beneficiaries are granted access to a network of providers, who are remunerated for services rendered.

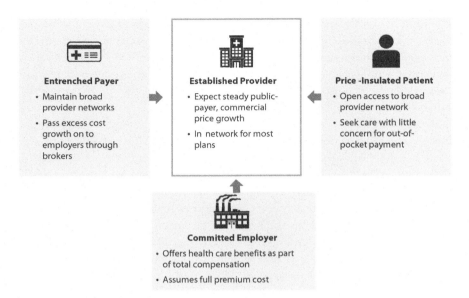

FIGURE 18.1 Conventional roles and relationships. ©2014 The advisory board company

Most plans (except health maintenance organizations, a small subset) include almost every area provider in their networks, reflecting unwavering beneficiary demand for unlimited choice.

The provider community encompasses different types of hospitals, the physician workforce, and a mix of subacute facilities and services (e.g., urgent care centers, nursing homes, home health). Each of these providers expects to be included in every payer network, which is largely standard practice. They also expect reimbursement levels to track changes in costs, which has not consistently happened. Still, physician compensation is attractive, and recent hospital margins have been good for most, inadequate for some, and lavish for a large minority.

Employers provide health insurance for roughly two-thirds of workers under 65 years of age. Historically, and unique to the United States, health insurance accompanies employment, and employers use this benefit to attract and retain top-notch employees. Unquestionably, rising healthcare costs have blunted company financial performance, and efforts to control these costs have proven unsuccessful. Employers play another unique role by paying inflated premiums to insurers to offset insufficient provider reimbursement from Medicare and Medicaid.

Finally, we have contemporary patients. They expect access to a broad network of providers, and through their employer coverage overwhelmingly select preferred provider organization (PPO) plans. Until very recently, deductibles and co-payments have been minimal, isolating them from the true costs of the healthcare Americans use. Notably, health insurance is unlike insurance purchased for homes and cars, which typically carry high deductibles. Instead, patients consider $50 co-pays expensive, and many seniors purchase supplemental insurance to cover Medicare-deductible requirements.

DEPICTING THE FUTURE: A WORK IN PROGRESS

The ACA is often characterized as a government "takeover" of U.S. healthcare. A fairer description is that the statute employs government interventions to incentivize the private sector to create a value-driven healthcare system. "Value" has various definitions, but the simplest is "to deliver maximum (beneficial) outcomes per dollar of investment." Currently, the general consensus is that we pay too much for the outcomes-enhancing healthcare we receive, which is partly explained by our obsession with expensive therapies delivering marginal, no, or unknown benefits. The ACA's insurance reform represents a boon for commercial insurers, expanding the pool of potential enrollees (many supported by government subsidies). Notably, many large health systems have jumped into this market, offering their own products. On the delivery end, the ACA-induced market chaos and left the provider community to sort it out. To be sure, the federal government has erected directional guideposts by imposing pay-for-performance standards and announcing, just recently, ambitious (audacious) goals to transform the bulk (90% by 2018) of government reimbursement from fee for service to unspecified payment schemes tied to "quality and value."[2] Also stated was that ACOs and bundled payment schemes will play a central role in this shift. It cannot go unnoticed that providers now have a billboard-sized road sign from the government suggesting the general type of delivery systems it might want to create. If we look at our own healthcare market where we live, we are witnessing, in real time, a large sector of our economy disassembling and reconstructing itself.

What follows is a description of how ACA insurance reform begets consumerism and retail medicine. Note the domino effect taking place: One change causes another, which causes another, and so on. On the receiving end, the private sector—the free market—is reacting, innovating, trying to keep up, for better or maybe worse. The clock is ticking.

Exchanges

The state-based exchanges are functioning and proving to be effective mechanisms for expanding health insurance coverage. Admittedly, their launch has been painful to watch. (Did we really expect perfection given the inherent complexities?) Still, the numbers speak for themselves. Since the first open enrollment period in October 2013, 14.1 million uninsured people ages 18 to 64 have secured insurance. Another 2.3 million young adults were allowed to remain on their parents' plans.[3] This 16.4 million total represents a reduction of adults without insurance from 20.3% to 13.2%, the largest change in 40 years. By 2018, this number is expected to hit 25 million. Consumers log in and search for policies that meet their criteria. Most state exchanges offered plenty of choice. For the 2013 period, roughly 250 insurers participated (this number is expected to grow in the following years). Few shoppers chose platinum and gold plans; 65% bought silver and 20% bought bronze. Of policies offered within these metal levels, 63% chose either the lowest- or second-lowest plan. Factors most influencing choice of metal level were size of deductible, co-pays, and out-of-pocket maximums.[4] The level of descriptive information provided to allow comparison shopping was poor, but ongoing efforts will bring improvements over time.

Private exchanges are an equally important innovation. Benefits companies are offering employers a portfolio of plans tailored to their employee bases. In this role, they have inserted themselves between traditional payer–employer relationships. The value proposition is to craft better insurance choices—for example, plans with lower premiums, top-tier quality providers, and red-carpet access features. As of October 2014, there were 172 private exchange operators. Enrollee growth has been explosive, with estimates of 40 million individuals accessing insurance through private exchanges by 2018.[5]

The advent of exchanges has channeled millions of people into brand new marketplaces to shop for insurance—just like going on Amazon. They have selection, pricing data, and comparative information. Most important, the duration of policies is a *single year*, meaning they can change plans every 12 months with the click of a mouse. Perhaps managed Medicare and Medicaid enrollees will funnel through these exchanges in the future. Perhaps employers will exit the healthcare benefits business, instead giving employees stipends to shop on the exchanges.

For providers, the exchanges raise many questions and potential challenges. Where are you represented on the exchanges? How do consumers find you?

Can you influence this and at what level—the plan or the consumer? How do you make consumers stay with you, year over year, if they can switch plans and networks freely and effortlessly?

Cost Sharing and Price Sensitivity

For years, experts have preached that patients need to have "skin in the game" if healthcare utilization and costs are ever to be controlled. When something is free, we tend to use unlimited amounts. In recent years, skin in the game has finally become a reality—with pros and cons attached. Employers are now asking employees to pick up a portion of their annual premium, an amount that has risen over time to become a significant contribution. For these same employees, deductibles and out-of-pocket expenses have also escalated. Should employees never see their contribution amounts—money is automatically with-held, so they do not take it out of their paychecks themselves—this sharing of costs may not effect utilization appreciably. However, this is not the case on the exchanges. We have seen that consumers are purchasing plans with the low-est premiums. To get these lower premiums, the trade-off is to assume higher deductible and co-payment amounts (an inverse relationship). Data for 2014 show annual deductibles across state exchanges ranging from $2,500 (median) to $6,250 (max). Further, roughly 30% of enrollees have a deductible between $3,000 and $5,999, and 40% in excess of $6,000.[6] All of which tells us what we already know: that American consumers are tightwads, explained in part by the fact that a large segment of the population has limited financial means. Thus, even with the help of federal subsidies, health insurance is a financial stretch for them. This newly introduced price sensitivity across a growing proportion of the insured is expected to have an enormous dampening effect on utiliza-tion and prices—perhaps the single most powerful force inflecting historical trends. Whereas insured patients have been largely sheltered from costs—$1,200 MRIs, $500 diagnostic panels, $50,000 elective procedures—and passive recipients of whatever doctors ordered, they will almost certainly question necessity when on the hook for a large payment. Carried beyond a certain point, escalating deductibles convert health insurance as we know it into cata-strophic coverage, equivalent to what we purchase for homes and cars. We often choose not to fix dents and scratches. Similarly, experts now worry that thrifty patients with high deductibles will choose to forgo necessary care—screenings, corrective procedures, drugs—which defeats the larger ambitions of coverage expansion.

How will cost-bearing patients affect providers? For starters, to the extent newly insured patients with high deductibles lack money to cover their obligations, coverage expansion will not provide a solution, as advertised, for the burden of patient-driven bad debt. If price now strongly influences patient behavior, how should providers set prices for services, and where should these prices be posted? In setting price, is the goal to cover fully allocated costs, marginal costs, or match what is offered by the competition? If prices need to be reduced to compete more effectively, will this incite price deflation across the market? At the clinical level, how should physicians address the price of treatments with patients, and how should price be factored—ethically, equitably, and consistently—into care decisions?

Narrow Networks

Insurers are now offering policies with limited, or "narrow," networks of providers. They do this is to lower their cost of care, allowing them to set low premiums (while still maintaining margins). Low premiums appeal to price-sensitive shoppers who dominate the exchanges. Low premiums may also attract employers looking to cut health insurance expenses. Coming full circle, the way insurers are able to reduce the cost of care is by reducing payment levels to providers (yes, there is always a catch.) The concept of narrow networks would appear to run counter to consumer demand for choice, which was confirmed in the years following the introduction of HMOs and ultimately led to their unpopularity. However, that was then—when patients were insulated from costs—and this is now—when patients are bearing a meaningful proportion of these costs. In short, price trumps choice in today's economy. That said, limited choice is not a shortcoming if only top-tier providers are included in the network. By identifying and channeling patients to only the best, narrow networks instead offer the potential to improve care and at the same time lower premiums. Thus consumers reap double benefits. Even the included providers receiving lower reimbursement can be made whole, assuming they see sufficient incremental volume to offset discounts. Recent survey data indicate that more than half of small employers would opt for narrow networks in exchange for a 5% reduction in premiums, increasing to 80% for a 20% lower premium. Consumer polls reflect similar inclinations. For some, the appearance of narrow networks runs counter to the ACA's intent, which was to broaden both coverage and access to providers. Currently, these opponents are encouraging the federal government to regulate this market-driven innovation.

The potential threats for providers excluded from networks are obvious. Again, there is an imperative for providers to deeply understand exchange dynamics.

Network Assemblers

The rise of narrow networks points to the importance of network assemblers—various entities making decisions on which patients get to see which providers, and vice versa. In the past, insurers created networks designed for different policies, although these networks were often similar, including virtually all area providers. Other insurers did the same thing, eliminating the potential for differentiation based on which providers enrollees could see. In contrast, today there can be any number of network assemblers. There are the private exchange operators building highly customized networks for employer clients. Alternatively, hands-on self-insured employers can select their own network. Then there are pure-play companies specializing in this, assembling local networks, multistate networks, or even national networks for the largest firms. The criteria used by assemblers to select providers overlap and prioritize a core set of attributes. One is geographic coverage and alignment of assets to enrollee clusters. Another is range of clinical services—trauma, transplant, procedure mix, and so on. Then, reducing the pool considerably, only those providers (e.g., top quartile performers) who meet designated thresholds on clinical metrics are included. And for those making this cut, a final screening can be made predicated on per capita cost of care, care utilization rates, and the existence of care experience programs.

Of all these metrics—each important in its own right—provider costs are particularly important, being one factor influencing an assembler's ability to set competitive premiums. It is important that provider costs are examined two ways. The first is the ability to deliver low unit prices today. The second is the ability to control cost growth in the future. The latter in part is determined by provider commitment to and investment in care-management capabilities—for example, data analytics, care manager, alignment structures (e.g., ACOs, CI networks)—which down the road may facilitate risk-based contracting. Early evidence suggests that assemblers are forcefully exercising their discriminatory powers. One narrow network, for example, excluded nearly 40% of PPO specialists.[7] In a sample of 20 urban markets, "narrow" networks excluded six of the 20 largest hospitals, and "ultranarrow" networks excluded 14 of the largest 20 hospitals. A median 25% premium reduction was attributed directly to network narrowing.[8]

The phenomenon of narrow networks is laden with implications for provider executives. Whereas insurers have been the sole buyer of provider services, this list now includes private exchange operators, custom network builders, employers themselves, and, ultimately, autonomous consumers.

How should a provider engage each of these entities to make a case for inclusion? Transparency facilitates differentiation: principled grounds for inclusion or exclusion. As metrics proliferate, become more rigorous, and gain greater visibility, reputational medicine will lose its veneer. This will punish poor performers, reshaping the provider community into a meritocracy. Do C-suite executives know what their externally reported metrics look like, and how these numbers are determined? Finally, provider cost structures matter. Bloated provider costs drive inflated premium rates and are unsustainable in an era of flat or declining reimbursement. Alternatively, low costs—in tandem with high quality—open doors to network inclusion and attract price-sensitive patients seeking services. There is simply no place in tomorrow's healthcare model for expensive but mediocre providers.

Access and Patient Experience

In the new healthcare market, maintaining and expanding market share is a three-step process. First, a provider must be included in networks at the discretion of assemblers. Second, consumers shopping on an exchange must select from dozens of options a health plan whose network includes the provider. Third, the provider is chosen by the consumer at the point of sale—that is, when selecting a service, whether an urgent care visit, a prescription, a CT scan, or hip replacement. In a consumer-driven model, the importance of this point-of-care decision cannot be overstated. Indeed, it is the ground where provider fortunes will be made or lost. This is where healthcare confronts true "retail" market dynamics—think electronics, clothing, furniture—and retail can be a rough-and-tumble undertaking.

We state what we know from our own experience: American consumers are highly intolerant of anything that strikes them as "wrong," and they have opinions and memories. Long lines, banker hours, missing paperwork, inattentive staff, nonsensical prices—a laundry list of flashpoints drives dissatisfaction. Unfortunately, if you apply these shortcomings to healthcare encounters, they apply far too often. Regrettably, some would say they typify patient experiences. A recent survey asked consumers to select preferences by three categories: access and convenience, cost, and service. Six of the top ten features aligned to access and convenience.[9]

Truth be told, many (educated) individuals don't want to see physicians for fear of overtreatment. The government has deemed annual physicals for asymptomatic people unnecessary. And when care is needed, the first person seen no longer has to be a physician—nurse practitioners are fine.

To satisfy consumers, provider facilities need to be nearby and open long hours. Wait times need to be minimized, guaranteed, or even eliminated. Just to be in the game, providers must offer sophisticated online portals where patients can go to see test results, schedule appointments, fill prescriptions, find educational materials, and, more commonly now, access images and clinical notes. Similar to what other businesses do (e.g., chain restaurants and hotels), there has to be a standardized approach to managing patients regardless of their point of access. And then there needs to be a total revamping of how care providers listen to and interact with patients. We know that patients, for example, retain a fraction of what we teach them—but what are we doing about it? This will need to be solved if we hope (need) to engage patients in their care.

To be fair, many providers have gotten this message and are committed to change. That said, there is the risk that the magnitude of the task and its importance will be underappreciated. A consumer-oriented healthcare system will require a complete rewiring of current practices. In the best of hands, it will be an immense undertaking.

CONCLUSION

Retail medicine and consumerism are seeping into healthcare, and their impact is likely to force historic changes (Figure 18.2).

Both are complementary with patient-centered care and may be necessary prerequisites. Cost growth in healthcare has been a runaway train—impossible

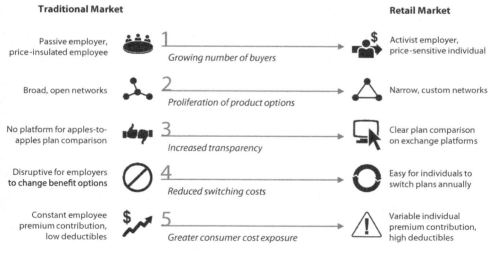

Traditional Market   **Retail Market**

Passive employer, price-insulated employee	1 Growing number of buyers	Activist employer, price-sensitive individual
Broad, open networks	2 Proliferation of product options	Narrow, custom networks
No platform for apples-to-apples plan comparison	3 Increased transparency	Clear plan comparison on exchange platforms
Disruptive for employers to change benefit options	4 Reduced switching costs	Easy for individuals to switch plans annually
Constant employee premium contribution, low deductibles	5 Greater consumer cost exposure	Variable individual premium contribution, high deductibles

FIGURE 18.2 Characteristics of traditional versus retail market.
©2014 The advisory board company

to control. Consumerism as a lone breaking mechanism may not to stop the train, but it is certain to slow its rate of progression. The thread is clear: Consumers, now with payment obligations, are demanding affordable healthcare; premiums must be aggressively priced to secure sufficient enrollment; only low cost—and high quality—providers can be included in networks to make the financing go round; consumers shopping for services will gravitate toward less-expensive options. It would seem right to move away from blank-check medicine, which is a root cause of many illogical, excessive, and sometimes harmful practices. Similarly, it would seem right for patients to exercise greater control over their healthcare and for providers to deliver services aligned to the total needs of *individuals*—not patients.

REFERENCES

1. Abrams R. In ambitious bid, Walmart seeks foothold in primary care services. *New York Times*; 2014:B1.

2. Health and Human Services. Better, smarter, healthier. In: *Historic Announcement, HHS Sets Clear Goals and Timeline for Shifting Medicare Reimbursements from Volume to Value* (Press Release); 2015, 26 Jan. Available at http://www.hhs.gov/about/news/2015/01/26/better-smarter-healthier-in-historic-announcement-hhs-sets-clear-goals-and-timeline-for-shifting-medicare-reimbursements-from-volume-to-value.html.

3. Pear R. Data on health law shows largest drop in uninsured in 4 decades, the U.S. says. *New York Times*; 2015:A12.

4. Health and Human Services. *Health Insurance Marketplace: Summary Enrollment Report for the Initial Annual Open Enrollment Period*; 2104, May 1. Available at https://aspe.hhs.gov/pdf-report/health-insurance-marketplace-summary-enrollment-report-initial-annual-open-enrollment-period.

5. Accenture. Are you ready? Private health insurance exchanges are looming; 2013. Available at https://www.accenture.com/us-en/insight-private-health-insurance-exchanges-looming-summary.aspx.

6. Robert Wood Johnson Foundation. Eight million and counting: a deeper look at premiums, cost sharing, and benefit design in the new health insurance marketplaces; 2014. Available at http://www.rwjf.org/content/dam/farm/reports/issue_briefs/2014/rwjf412878.

7. Gottlieb S. Hard data on trouble you'll have finding doctors in Obamacare. *Forbes*; 2014. Available at http://www.forbes.com/sites/scottgottlieb/2014/03/08/now-the-hard-data-on-the-trouble-youll-have-finding-specialist-doctors-in-obamacare/.

8. McKinsey & Company. *Hospital Networks: Configurations on the Exchange and Their Impact on Premiums*; 2013.

9. The Advisory Board Company. *What Do Consumers Want From Primary Care?* 2014.

CHAPTER 19

Creating the Healthcare Transformation from Volume to Value

Nikhil G. Thaker
Thomas W. Feeley

Abstract

The transformation from a volume-based to value-based healthcare delivery system will require the development of a patient-centric framework for healthcare reform. Providers will first need to create integrated and coordinated practice units that measure and publicly report outcomes that truly matter to patients. Providers will also need to understand their true costs of delivering care over the full care cycle. As providers deepen their expertise in specific service lines, currently broad service line strategies will need to give way to more focused, highly performing, and integrated units that seamlessly communicate between multiple geographically expanded sites of care. Rather than being a solution itself, health information technology systems will enable this transformation. Finally, shifting away from traditional reimbursement models, such as fee for service, capitation, and global provider budgeting systems, and toward bundled payments for the full care cycle will galvanize value-based competition among all healthcare stakeholders, ultimately improving outcomes and decreasing costs.

Healthcare spending in the United States has increased from 7% of the gross domestic product in 1970 to more than 17% in 2013.[1,2] Despite this steep increase in cost and an overall expenditure that exceeds any other country by a wide margin,[3–5] there has been no consistent rise in quality.[6–8] At the core of these higher expenditures is a system that incentivizes the volume of health-care services through a fee-for-service (FFS) reimbursement system rather than for the outcomes achieved. Providers are compensated for delivering a greater number of units of care (e.g., procedures, consultations, and medications) rather than delivering a higher quality of outcome.[9] Fragments of the current system have attempted to instead reimburse providers through a capitation or global provider budgeting model, both of which incentivize less care at the potential expense of quality of outcomes.

To improve outcomes and decrease costs, the U.S. healthcare system will require fundamental restructuring to shift its goal from volume to value:[10,11]

$$Value = \frac{\text{Health outcomes over the full cycle of care}}{\text{Costs over the full cycle of care}}$$

This strategic transformation will require substantial reform of the current legacy system toward a system of value-based competition that incentivizes higher-quality, patient-centered outcomes at lower costs. Patients want high-quality care at the best possible cost, not low quality at low cost.[12] Value-based healthcare delivery (VBHCD) will move away from paying for single proce-dures or capitated care to paying for the true costs of care delivery over the full care cycle. Because value is represented by both a numerator and a denomina-tor, providers will need to understand the relationship between both outcomes and costs in order to improve value.

In this chapter, we will define the key components of the value agenda, summarize the shortcomings of current payment systems, and describe new payment models that will better unite the interests of all healthcare stakehold-ers, including patients, providers, payers, and policy makers.

THE VALUE AGENDA

Restructuring care from the current legacy system to one of value-based com-petition that incentivizes improved outcomes at lower costs will require the engagement of all stakeholders. Porter and Lee have recently defined the stra-tegic agenda for transformation from the current legacy system to a VBHCD system (Figure 19.1).[13]

Although better outcomes at lower costs can be achieved, movement toward a value-based system has been slowed by inefficient provider organizations, an absence of information on outcomes and costs, reimbursement methods that reward volume over value, fragmented multisite healthcare systems, and poor interoperability of health information technology (IT).

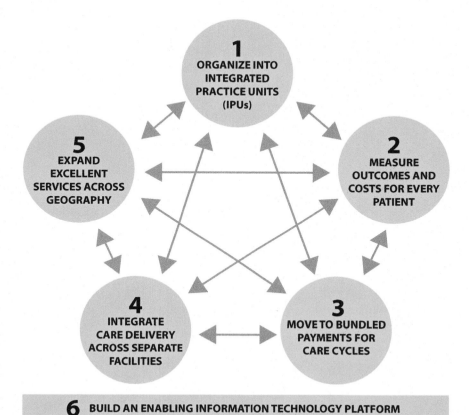

FIGURE 19.1 The value agenda. The strategic agenda for moving to a high-value healthcare delivery system has six components. They are interdependent and mutually reinforcing. Progress will be greatest if multiple components are advenced together. Reprinted by permission of Harvard Business Review. From "The Strategy That Will Fix Health Care" by Michael E. Porter and Thomas H. Lee, October 2013. Copyright © 2013 by Harvard Business Publishing; all rights reserved.

ORGANIZE CARE AROUND THE MEDICAL CONDITION

Providers have traditionally been organized around specialties and departments, which are staffed by independent practitioners from a single specialty.[11] Under this current system, a patient with a specific medical condition will require treatment by several providers who perform discrete services in separate departments (such as surgery, internal medicine, or radiology) in separate locations. This type of organization creates silos between providers, leads to fragmented and uncoordinated healthcare services, and focuses provider attention on discrete interventions rather than the full medical condition.

In VBHCD, providers are organized in integrated practice units (IPUs) around the patient's medical condition over the full care cycle.[13] Care is delivered by a dedicated, multidisciplinary team[14] that integrates patient education, adherence and compliance, and follow-up into the continuum of care. Rather than being in disparate silos, care is co-located in dedicated facilities and coordinated among teams that meet formally or informally to discuss patient care, operations, and quality improvement (QI). The IPU measures and accepts accountability of patient outcomes and costs.

MEASURE OUTCOMES AND COSTS FOR EVERY PATIENT

Measuring Outcomes

In the current system, true outcomes are rarely measured; when measurement is done, it does not go beyond departmental or hospital-wide indicators such as 30-day mortality, readmission, or infection rates. Most measures today are process measures and not true outcome measures. On the other end, outcomes should not be measured solely by procedure or intervention. Outcomes need to be measured by individual medical conditions and over the full care cycle. For each medical condition, payers and providers will need to define a standardized set of relevant outcomes and the metrics used to measure them (Figure 19.2).

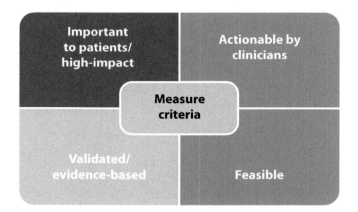

FIGURE 19.2 The outcomes framework. Outcome metrics will need to be important and impactful to patients, actionable by clinicians, validated and evidence-based, and feasibly executed throughout the institution.

FIGURE 19.3 The outcomes hierarchy. For each medical condition, patients, providers, and payers will need to identify the outcomes that matter most to patients. Porter has described a three-tier framework that captures short-term (tier 1), functional (tier 2), and long-term (tier 3) outcomes.

From *The New England Journal of Medicine*, Michael E. Porter, What Is Value in Health Care?, Volume 363, Page 2479, Copyright © (2010) Massachusetts Medical Society. Reprinted with permission from Massachusetts Medical Society.

These measures will need to include each patient's comorbidities and risk factors to allow for case-based risk adjustment. Outcomes will need to be multidimensional and those that matter most to patients rather than indicators that signify process, structure, compliance, or other easy-to-measure items. Outcomes should be tiered into short-term measures (tier 1), functional measures of recovery (tier 2), and long-term measures (tier 3) (Figure 19.3).[10,11]

Rather than broader measures, fewer but higher-level measures should focus on quality. Ideally, 5 to 10 outcome measures (within the various outcome tiers), should be measured, including patient-reported outcomes.

Measuring Costs

Cost accounting in most organizations is flawed because it is based on charges. Charge-based accounting systems have become inaccurate because of the tremendous cost shifting that has occurred in healthcare over the past 30 years. Hospital and outpatient costs are typically measured using a relative value unit (RVU) system (or the resource-based relative value scale, RBRVS), which aggregates costs for departments or for the whole hospital rather than at the level of the patient's medical condition.[15,16] The RVU system allocates costs in a top-down manner. General ledger costs are allocated to reimbursable processes, and all other costs are allocated into overhead pools. In most systems, cost accounting is led and updated by financial teams with little to no coordination with clinical teams.

Because of this approach, the price of specific processes may not be related to the actual resource cost of delivering the service. For instance, RVU-based cost may undervalue an endocrinologist's evaluation and management of a thyroid cancer patient by assigning a lower cost than the actual resources required to deliver that care. Costs therefore are not simply reimbursements or billed charges but are the actual expense of patient care. Although the RVU-based system allows for easy reconciliation of costs, a modified approach to estimating patient-specific costs, and how those costs compare to outcomes, would be a helpful tool in understanding the value of delivered care.

Time-driven activity-based costing (TDABC) is a promising bottom-up cost accounting tool that measures costs at the medical condition level by tracking expenses for all resources involved in treating a patient's medical condition over the full cycle of care.[17,18] TDABC is an application of the traditional cost–accounting equation:

Resource cost = (Quantity of resource units) × (Price per unit for the resource)

TDABC costs reflect both direct and indirect costs. Direct costs include actual resources involved in a patient's care such as personnel, facilities, supplies, and support services. Indirect or "overhead" costs are also associated with patient-facing resources that support these direct services such as IT, billing, human resources, and other space or facilities. TDABC cost calculations initially require clinical teams to create and update clinical and administrative process maps of the full cycle workflow for a medical condition. Each activity in the process map is associated with a resource (personnel, equipment, or facilities) and a time estimate (in minutes) for completing each step (Figure 19.4).[17,19]

Each resource's capacity cost rate (CCR) is calculated by determining the costs per unit time for a resource to be available for patient-specific work:[9]

$$\textit{Capacity cost rate} = \frac{\text{Expenses attributable to resource}}{\text{Available resource capacity in hours or minutes}}$$

The resource CCR is multiplied by the time (in minutes or hours) for conducting each activity in a process map; costs at each activity step are integrated

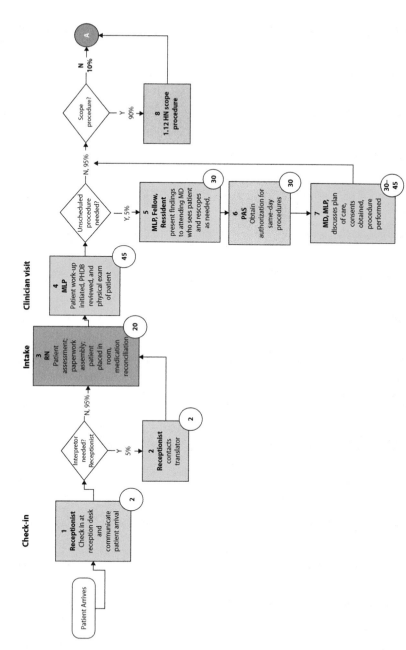

FIGURE 19.4 A sample process map with activity times (in minutes) of the patient consult process. Process maps are created of each component of care over the full medical condition and are used as inputs to calculate the TDABC costs of care.

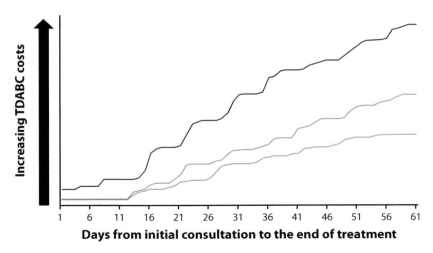

Days from initial consultation to the end of treatment

FIGURE 19.5 Full-Cycle TDABC Costs for Three Sample Patients with the Same Diagnosis Who Were Treated with the Same Overall Treatment Plan. TDABC costs varied among patients based on differential toxicities and complications of therapy. TDABC can capture patient-specific variations in cost with more granularity than traditional RVU systems and can be used to develop a bundle payment for specific medical conditions.

over the full care cycle to measure costs at the medical condition level. This methodology uniquely integrates hospital and physician costs and requires the coordinated and undivided inputs of clinicians, financial analysts, and administrators. This tool also allows aggregation of costs across multiple sites of care because many patients will require outpatient and inpatient care during the care cycle.[20] Figure 19.5 illustrates how TDABC can be used to measure variations in true patient-specific costs over the full care cycle.

Table 19.1 describes several major applications of TDABC in the healthcare setting.[18,19,21,22]

REIMBURSING VALUE IN HEALTHCARE

Current Payment Methods

Improving the method of paying for care delivery is ultimately the central component of the value agenda. Provider reimbursements need to be better linked to patient-centered value.[10,11,23] However, current reimbursement methods do not incentivize and sometimes negatively incentivize VBHCD. Current reimbursement methods include traditional fee for service, capitation, and global

TABLE 19.1 Value-Added Opportunities for TDABC

Value-Added Opportunities for TDABC	Description
Reduce full care cycle costs	• Eliminate low- or non–value added services or tests. • Increase cost awareness in clinical teams. • Optimize process steps to improve total care cycle cost versus lowering costs of individual service lines. • Identify processes for which initially higher costs may ultimately reduce costs over the long-term care cycle.
Improve outcomes	• Elimination of non–value added activities may improve outcome dimensions such as patient's experience, time away from work, time from diagnosis to the end of treatment, wait times, and others.
Reduce cycle time	• Identify and eliminate non–value added process and workflow inefficiencies to reduce cycle times across the full care cycle. • Increase throughput (i.e., higher volume) through a more efficient system.
Reduce process variation	• Reduce and eliminate process variations that lower efficiency and increase waste without improving outcomes.
Reorganize and rationalize resource use	• Rationalize redundant clinical, administrative, and financial units. • Improve capacity use of expensive physicians, staff, clinical space, and facilities by reducing duplication and service fragmentation. • Measure unused resource capacity. • Minimize use of costly physician and skilled staff time for less skilled activities. • Allow physicians and skilled staff to work at the "top of their license." • Identify opportunities to substitute lower-cost resources for higher-cost resources when appropriate.
Rationalize service lines	• Provide the right services at the right locations with the right resources. • Move routine or uncomplicated services out of highly-resourced facilities. • Benchmark costs and efficiency of care delivery for a specific medical condition across multiple sites.
Improve provider coordination	• Integrate clinical, administrative, and financial teams to better understand workflows and costs shared across the organization. • Support transparency of clinical and financial prices and workflows.
Conduct QI initiatives	• Integrate TDABC into lean and QI initiatives to understand their effect on overall resource use. • Use TDABC to predict the future effect of QI initiatives. • Eliminate administrative and clinical processes and process variations that do not improve outcomes.
Estimate clinical trial, research, or technology costs	• Use TDABC to quantify the cost impact of adding a new protocols to an existing workflow.
Conduct comparative effectiveness studies	• Measure differential TDABC costs and outcomes between competing treatment modalities (i.e. surgery vs. radiation therapy).

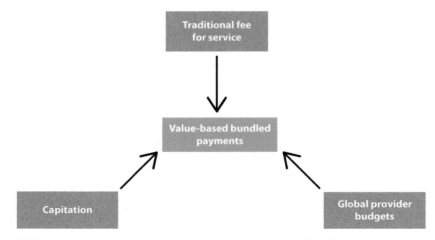

FIGURE 19.6 Transformation from current patient systems such as global capitation, global provider budgets, and traditional fee for service to value-based bundled payments

provider budgets. New payment models will need to move toward value-based bundled payments (Figure 19.6).

FEE FOR SERVICE Fee for service is the most common payment method in the United States and in many other countries—and it is a significant barrier to value transformation. FFS payments are directly linked to the volume and intensity of services such as treatments, procedures, medications, and hospital admissions rather than the quality of outcomes or appropriateness of care. Medical errors can even translate into higher revenue through generation of more services. Because each service requires generation of an insurance claim, the non–value added administration cost is substantial to both providers and payers. The result for patients can be higher out-of-pocket costs and reduced access to costly treatments. Fees also vary substantially between providers, regions of the country, and even the care setting (such as hospital or outpatient) for the same service. These FFS variations do not necessarily reflect better or worse outcomes or costs. Furthermore, FFS reimbursements are not tied to the complexity or intensity of resources required to provide service. For instance, imaging services have higher reimbursements (with a greater margin) than more poorly reimbursing services such as consultations or counseling performed by primary care providers (PCPs). Care coordination is rarely if ever reimbursed, which further aggravates fragmentation and poor integration of patient care within the system.

When reimbursements do not reflect the true underlying cost of providing needed services, providers rely on cross-subsidies from higher-margin to lower-margin (or negative) service lines. Providers may also invest more in top-line, higher-margin service lines, which can produce supply-driven care, excess system capacity, and overuse. Conversely, services that are reimbursed poorly but are of high value may be undersupported and underused even if the services decrease downstream complications and costs. Payers may also attempt to limit high-cost but high-value services by requiring exhaustive preauthorizations or peer-to-peer evaluations. Thus, patients, providers, payers, and policy makers all have varying and sometimes directly conflicting incentives that lead to a zero-sum competition of resources. These negative incentives inherent to the FFS system could be realigned if payment methods were to shift focus toward care that created value (i.e., better outcomes at lower costs) over the full care cycle.[24]

GLOBAL PROVIDER BUDGETS Global provider budgeting is another current method of reimbursement under which the payer provides a fixed yearly reimbursement to each provider based on the projected mix of services and risk-adjusted patient volumes. Reimbursement of the Veterans Administration system is predominantly under this arrangement.[25] Payers have predictable yearly expenditures and can control overall growth of spending at a systems level. However, global budgets would need to cover the provider's true costs of delivering all healthcare services to all patients. If the volume, complexity, or demand of services outpaces the provider's infrastructure for delivering care, then care may ultimately be rationed and wait times may increase substantially to meet demands.[26,27] More acute services such as emergency room and operating room procedures may be prioritized over value-added services such as preventative or primary care services. Providers may also underinvest in costly yet effective technologies or services because costs would need to be absorbed within an annual budget. Although this model of payment may control short-term costs, it may stifle long-term innovation and lead to rationing, increased wait times, reduced patient access, and significant financial risk for providers.

CAPITATION Given the limitations of global budgeting for the treatment of a patient population, capitation has emerged as a potential alternative. Under this model, providers receive a specific reimbursement per patient per unit of time (e.g., per year). All of that patient's care would need to be covered under this set amount, which ideally would incentivize providers to improve efficiency and lower cost. For instance, providers could invest more in preventive and primary care services rather than in acute, costly, and preventable conditions. However, because patient outcomes are not routinely measured or reported, capitation can incentivize providers to provider a lower *amount* of care in an attempt to reduce their costs. Costly services that lead to better outcomes in the long run may be rationed. Providers may preferentially take on healthier patients if risk-adjusted payments for complex patients do not cover the full cost of care. Service lines may therefore broaden to capture more volume rather than focusing on medical condition-specific IPUs that can deliver high-value care.

New Payment Models

Current reimbursement methods (noted earlier) have incentivized providers to deliver volume rather than value.[9,17,19] New payment methods will need to align quality and patient-centered care with the interests of patients, providers, payers, policy makers, government, and industry vendors. Several initiatives are currently underway to pay for value and enhance quality innovation in healthcare. Although a detailed discussion of these models is beyond the scope of this chapter, this section will introduce several programs and discuss their important advantages and limitations.

VALUE-BASED PURCHASING PROGRAMS Value-based purchasing aims to standardize outcome measures, improve public reporting of outcome measures, create innovative payment models, and improve consumer-driven healthcare choices—thereby improving *value* for the patient.[28] In *pay for performance* (P4P), providers are rewarded for delivering high-value and cost-effective care or penalized for not reaching benchmarks. P4P programs—such as those in Medicaid, health maintenance organizations, and Medicare programs—can reward providers financially or through a public reporting mechanism to increase provider recognition of clinical benchmarks. These programs better align the interests of providers and payers around the delivery of high-quality care through incentives. However, despite offering financial incentives, results of P4P programs have to date suggested only a modest effect on outcomes and costs.[29] Incentivizes in these programs are tied to mostly process compliance rather than improvement of true outcomes.[30] Financial rewards are typically in the form of FFS incentive payments that are grounded in service delivery and process adherence rather than delivery of integrated care and high-quality outcomes. Because penalties are modest for falling below clinical benchmarks, providers have little financial risk in this model. P4P can also lead to "cherry-picking" of low-risk patients, gaming of nonincentivized process measures, and decreased provider satisfaction and motivation.[31]

Value-based insurance design (VBID) attempts to lower costs and improve outcomes by focusing on patient rather than provider choices.[32] Payers increase incentives for patients to access services, treatments, or medications that are of high value by reducing co-payments or shifting costly but effective services into more basic benefit tiers. Such programs focus on general population health or the health of specific patient groups with complex, costly, or chronic medical conditions. Initial reductions in co-payments for patients is projected to be offset by future savings from better preventive services or more effective up-front interventions.

ACCOUNTABLE CARE ORGANIZATIONS AND PATIENT-CENTERED MEDICAL HOMES Recent models, including accountable care organizations (ACOs) and patient-centered medical homes (PCMHs), have been introduced to improve care coordination. The ACO model creates a contractually bound group of providers—PCPs, specialists, hospitals, and others—to coordinate care and share in the financial risk and reward for caring for a population of patients. The aims are to reform payments, increase accountability of care, and coordinate across the full cycle of care through support systems that integrate IT, practice design, and administrative efforts.[33] ACOs can take multiple forms—from small provider groups to multispecialty groups to large healthcare systems. The Centers for Medicare and Medicaid Services has instituted the Pioneer ACO model, Medicare Shared Savings Program, and the Advance Payment ACO model. Early demonstrations of this model have shown both cost savings and improvements in quality measure scores.[34] Challenges to this model include physician engagement, patient willingness to be treated solely within the ACO structure, appropriate payment approaches, and administrative and infrastructure barriers to transform from the current fragmented system to a more integrated coordinated system.

PCMHs similarly coordinate the efforts of multiple groups of providers but differ from ACOs in that a single PCP leads the effort in continuously coordinating, communicating, and engaging with the patient and any specialists.[35] In addition to those challenges for ACOs, challenges to PCMHs include substantial initial investment from PCP and specialist practices.

The Department of Health and Human Services (HHS) has also unveiled goals of transforming 30% of traditional Medicare FFS payments to quality or value through ACOs or bundled payments by the end of 2016 and 50% by 2018.[36] HHS will also tie 85% of Medicare payments to quality or value by 2016 and 90% by 2018 through hospital value-based purchasing and hospital readmissions reduction programs.[36] However, FFS and global capitated payments continue to be reimbursement methods for ACOs and other value-based purchasing arrangements. As providers, payers, and government stakeholders work toward transforming from volume to value, alternative payment models will need to continue to be defined.

VALUE-BASED BUNDLED PAYMENTS Bundled payments are a promising alternative payment model that further aligns the interests of all healthcare stakeholders, fosters care coordination, moves away from traditional reimbursement methods, and elevates value-based competition[9] (Figure 19.6). A bundled payment covers the cost of all procedures, tests, drugs, devices, and services involved in inpatient and outpatient (including rehabilitative) care for the full cycle of a patient's medical condition.[11,37] The payment includes care for common complications and comorbidities but excludes treatments for unrelated medical conditions.[11,13] A bundled payment would include a single price covering the full care cycle for an acute medical condition such as knee replacements[38] or time-based reimbursement for care of a chronic condition or for primary or preventative care.[39] However, the bundled payment needs to be tied to achieving a specific quality of outcome, with the provider bearing financial responsibility for preventable poor outcomes. Bundled payments therefore reward the *value* of the care delivered rather than the *volume* of services delivered.

According to Porter and Kaplan,[9–11,19,40] properly constructed bundled payments can successfully integrate all of the various inter-related components of the value agenda (Figure 19.1). Creating a bundled payment first begins with organizing a group of clinical providers, finance specialists, and administrators (Figure 19.7).

The beginning and end of the bundled payment episode is then defined for a specific medical condition. For instance, a bundled payment for a head and neck cancer patient may cover services from initial consultation to one year after treatment. Ideally, the medical condition pertains to a relatively homogenous patient population for which risk adjustment, risk stratification, and payment stratification can be achieved by disease stage and comorbidity. All services pertaining to the medical condition would be covered under the sin-

FIGURE 19.7 Bundled payment team structure

gle payment and would include guarantees for treatment of complications within the specified time period. Standardized outcome metrics would be defined and measured as described (Figures 19.2 and 19.3).

Before negotiating a price for the bundle, providers will need to understand their true baseline costs of delivering care and the cost of expected but potentially preventable complications. As previously described, TDABC is a highly effective tool for measuring true provider costs over the full cycle of care—even in cases where the patient requires treatment at multiple locations.[19] This approach can also measure variations in cost for delivering care to patients with a specific medical condition (Figure 19.5) and the impact of disease stage and risk factors to overall cost. Understanding the range of costs is important for determining the overall actuarial risk to the provider when negotiating a bundle price. Once the baseline cost is estimated, providers can undergo process improvement to further lower costs and improve efficiency and outcomes (Table 19.1). Such efforts can lower costs by 30% to 40% over the full care cycle without worsening outcomes, and they can ensure that payments are based on efficient, effective, and optimal care rather than historical aggregated charges.

Because some outlier patients may require intense resources for a catastrophic event during treatment, providers will need to develop stop-loss triggers to limit financial and actuarial liability of high-cost patients over whom they have little control. Once a predefined stop-loss threshold has been reached (such as two to three standard deviations above the mean), the provider should contractually bind the payer to provide additional payments through FFS[41] or another reinsurance mechanism.

Providers will then work with payers to negotiate a price that ideally maintains margins but not historical revenues. Ideally, the negotiated bundled price would be in effect for multiple years, which would further incentivize providers to improve process efficiency and maximize outcomes during a period of price stability before renegotiation. A challenge of the bundled reimbursement will be dividing, or "unbundling," the bundle among all involved providers. Traditional FFS has reimbursed each provider or department individually, whereas in a bundled reimbursement, the IPU will likely receive the payment. A possible mechanism for dividing reimbursement may be to allocate a fixed amount for providers (based on intensity of resources and traditional costs) with financial incentives for better outcomes at lower costs. Residual reimbursements can be distributed globally or used internally for process and infrastructure redesign. As more provider organizations move to bundled payments, more equitable mechanisms of dividing reimbursement may be discovered. Finally, to promote joint accountability for outcomes, each provider would be incentivized to publicly report risk-adjusted outcomes.

Moving toward bundled payments presents several challenges. Both provider and payer finance teams, who are accustomed to the traditional reimbursement system approach of FFS or capitation, will need to apply new methods of cost accounting. Current methods, such as the ratio of costs to charges,[42] do not reflect the true patient-specific cost of delivering care over a full care cycle. Movement toward a TDABC approach, however, will require unprecedented coordination between clinical, financial, and administrative teams (Figure 19.8) and a sizable effort to create and continuously update process maps. Policy makers, payers, and providers will need to identify fail-safe mechanisms to adequately mitigate the actuarial risk that will be shifted to providers. In systems that are not currently in IPUs, provider groups will need to determine how single bundled reimbursements can be distributed to all involved providers.

INTEGRATING SERVICE LINES ACROSS FACILITIES AND EXPANDING SERVICES GEOGRAPHICALLY

Delivering the right care at the right location in a multisite care delivery system is another key challenge.[11,43] To integrate care effectively, providers will need to redefine the scope of services at each facility and rationalize the added value of each site as a component of the whole organization. For instance, high-cost and highly resourced downtown medical campuses may be better suited for complex medical conditions, whereas regional care centers may be better suited for lower acuity, more routine, and higher-volume services.[44–46] This strategy will allow concentration of volume by medical condition to fewer locations. Several studies have shown that technically difficult procedures such as surgeries have been associated with higher mortality in lower-volume settings as compared with care received at higher-experience facilities.[47–49] Although volume is not the immediate goal, volume for complex therapies can be a proxy for value and needs to be considered when integrating and rationalizing service lines.

Subsequently, high-value, medical condition-specific IPUs need to expand geographically rather than continue competing only locally or regionally. Value

University of Texas MD Anderson Cancer Center
Houston, TX

CERTIFIED MEMBERS

Community Health Network
Indianapolis, IN

Covenant Health Care
Saginaw, MI

DCH Regional Medical Center
Tuscaloosa, AL

East Jefferson General Hospital
Metairie, LA

Ellis Fischel Cancer Center
Columbia, MO

OhioHealth
Columbus, OH

Piedmont Health System
Atlanata, GA

Providence Hospital
Mobile, AL

Sacred Heart Health System
Pensacola, FL

Saint Francis Medical Center
Cape Girardeau, MO

Spartanburg Regional Medical Center
Spartanburg, SC

St. John Health System
Tulsa, OK

St. Vincent's Medical Center
Bridgeport, CT

PARTNER MEMBERS ✪

Banner MD Anderson Cancer Center
Phoenix, AZ

Cooper MD Anderson Cancer Center
Camden, NJ

SINGLE DISCIPLINE PARTNER

Presbyterian Hospital
Albuquerque, NM

FIGURE 19.8 MD Anderson Cancer Network. The network includes the main center, regional care centers, partner affiliates, certified member affiliates, associate affiliates, specialty affiliates, and international sister institutions (not shown in this figure).

will increase exponentially when superior providers serve more patients through strategic expansion rather than through the purchase of full-service hospitals.[13,23] Expansion can occur through a hub-and-spoke model of satellite clinics or through clinical affiliations with existing providers. Several premier organizations have already begun this geographic expansion. The University of Texas MD Anderson Cancer Center, for instance, has geographically expanded through an MD Anderson Cancer network (Figure 19.8) that includes regional care centers, partner institutions, certified member community affiliate sites, and several other types of affiliations.[45]

BUILDING HEALTH IT SYSTEMS

IT is an essential tool to enable a VBHCD system but is not itself a solution to low-value care. To date, health IT has been siloed with regards to its functions, services, and interoperability. Overall per capita investment in health IT has also lagged behind other industries.[11] Although recent emphasis on "meaningful use" of IT has expanded the health IT industry, its functionality has been limited to mostly process measures. The transformation to a VBHCD system

TABLE 19.2 Value-Enhancing Elements of Information Technology Systems

Value-Enhancing Elements of IT Systems	Description
1. Focus on patients.	• Follows patients over the full cycle of care, including multisite inpatient care, outpatient care, and overall interventions. • Data are summarized by patient rather than by hospital, location, or department.
2. Uses common data definitions.	• Standardize data elements such as diagnosis, labs, interventions, hospitalizations, and all other data fields. • Standardize measurements, metrics, and methods of collection to allow for data exchange through the whole system.
3. Encompass all types of patient data.	• Combine all types of data (e.g., notes, images, medication orders, lab orders) for each patient. • Store all data in one location.
4. Allow access and communication among all stakeholders involved in care.	• Enable data exchange and aggregation among the different provider organizations involved with each patient. • Make accessible to referring physicians and patients.
5. Include templates and expert systems for each medical condition.	• Provide views and templates by medical condition to enhance data entry, search functionality, input of standard order sets. • Incorporate expert systems that facilitate evidence-based care, guideline concordance, decision support, and follow-up of clinical alerts (such as labs, drug interactions, allergies, and others).
6. Makes it easy to extract and report information.	• Allows seamless measurement and capture of patient-specific outcomes, process measures, costs (such as TDABC), and medical risk factors (such as comorbidities). • Incorporates structured data sets (rather than free text) and uses natural language processing to decrease need for manual data abstraction and hiring of staff specific for data abstraction.[50] • Builds outcome and cost measurements into electronic medical record for meaningful use criteria. • Uses timestamp data, where available, to automatically incorporate patient-specific transaction times. • Automates public reporting of outcomes and costs.

will require outcomes and cost measurements and reporting. According to Porter and Lee,[13] value-enhancing IT platforms have six key elements, which are outlined and described in Table 19.2. Providers, IT vendors, policy makers, and payers will need to coordinate and integrate efforts to accelerate value-added deployment of IT in healthcare.

CONCLUSIONS

Transformation to a VBHCD system will provide an essential patient-centric framework for healthcare reform. Providers will need to create integrated and coordinated practice units that measure and publicly report outcomes that truly matter to patients. Providers will also need to understand their true costs of delivering care over the full care cycle. As providers deepen their expertise in specific service lines, current broad service-line strategies will give way to more focused, highly performing IPUs that are integrated between multiple sites of care and that have expanded geographically. Health IT systems will enable this transformation rather than being solutions themselves. Finally, shifting away from the traditional FFS, capitation, and global provider budgeting systems toward bundled payments for the full care cycle will galvanize value-based competition among all healthcare stakeholders, ultimately improving outcomes and decreasing costs.

REFERENCES

1. Center for Medicare and Medicaid Services. NHE Fact Sheet; 2014. Available at http://www.cms.gov/Research-Statistics-Data-and-Systems/Statistics-Trends-and-Reports/NationalHealthExpendData/NHE-Fact-Sheet.html.

2. *Delivering Affordable Cancer Care in the 21st Century: Workshop Summary*; 2013. Washington, DC: National Academy Press.

3. Newhouse JP. An iconoclastic view of health cost containment. *Health Affair* (Millwood). 1993;12(suppl):152–171.

4. Squires DA. Explaining high health care spending in the United States: an international comparison of supply, utilization, prices, and quality. *Issue Brief* (Commonwealth Fund). 2012;10:1–14.

5. Pauly MV. Competition and new technology. *Health Affair* (Millwood). 2005;24(6): 1523–1535.

6. Chen AB et al. Provider case volume and outcomes following prostate brachytherapy. *J Urol.* 2009;181(1):113–118.

7. Begg CB et al. Variations in morbidity after radical prostatectomy. *N Engl J Med.* 2002;346(15):1138–1144.

8. Nolte E, McKee CM. In amenable mortality—deaths avoidable through health care—progress in the U.S. lags that of three European countries. *Health Affair* (Millwood). 2012;31(9): 2114–2222.

9. Kaplan RS, Porter ME. How to solve the cost crisis in health care. *Harv Bus Rev.* 2011;89(9):46–52,54,56–61.

10. Porter ME. What is value in health care? *N Engl J Med.* 2010;363(26): 2477–2481.

11. Porter ME, Teisberg EO. *Redefining Health Care*; 2006, Boston, MA: Harvard Business School Press.

12. National Quality Forum. *Measuring Affordability from the Patient's Perspective*; 2014. Washington, DC: National Quality Forum.

13. Porter ME, Lee TH. The strategy that will fix health care. *Harv Bus Rev.* 2013;91(10):50–70.

14. Pollock RE. Value-based health care: the MD Anderson experience. *Ann Surg.* 2008;248(4):510–518.

15. Cooper R, Kramer TR. RBRVS costing: the inaccurate wolf in expensive sheep's clothing. *J Health Care Finance.* 2008;34(3):6–18.

16. Berlin MF, Smith TH. Evaluation of activity-based costing versus resource-based relative value costing. *J Med Pract Manage.* 2004;19(4):219–227.

17. Kaplan RS, Anderson SR. Time-driven activity-based costing. *Harv Bus Rev.* 2004;82(11):131–138,150.

18. Kaplan RS et al. Using time-driven activity-based costing to identify value improvement opportunities in healthcare. *J Healthc Manag.* 2014;59(6):399–412.

19. Kaplan RS. Improving value with TDABC. *Healthc Financ Manage.* 2014;68(6): 76–83.

20. Thaker N et al. Defining the value of proton therapy in an evolving healthcare system using time-driven activity-based costing. *Oncology Payers, Policy Makers, and Prescribers.* 2014;1(1): 22–28.

21. McLaughlin N et al. Time-driven activity-based costing: a driver for provider engagement in costing activities and redesign initiatives. *Neurosurg Focus.* 2014;37(5): E3.

22. Donovan CJ et al. How Cleveland Clinic used TDABC to improve value. *Healthc Financ Manage.* 2014;68(6):84–88.

23. Porter ME. A strategy for health care reform—toward a value-based system. *N Engl J Med.* 2009;361(2):109–112.

24. Srinivasan M, Schwartz MD. Do we get what we pay for? transitioning physician payments towards value and efficiency. *J Gen Intern Med.* 2014;29(5):691–692.

25. Lehner LA, Burgess JF Jr, Stefos T. Hospital staffing adjustments under global budgeting. *Hosp Health Serv Adm.* 1995;40(4):509–523.

26. Duquette S et al. Decreased wait times after institution of office-based hand surgery in a veterans administration setting. *JAMA Surg.* 2015;150(2):182–183.

27. Department of Veterans Affairs. Expanded access to non-VA care through the Veterans Choice Program. Interim final rule. *Fed Regist.* 2014;79(214):65571–65587.

28. National Business Coalition on Health. *Value-Based Purchasing: A Definition*; 2011. Available at http://www.nbch.org/Value-based-Purchasing-A-Definition.

29. Ryan AM, Blustein J. The effect of the MassHealth hospital pay-for-performance program on quality. *Health Serv Res.* 2011;46(3):712–728.

30. Larkin DJ, Swanson RC, Fuller S, Cortese DA. The Affordable Care Act: a case study for understanding and applying complexity concepts to health care reform. *J Eval Clin Pract.* 2014, Nov 4:1–8.

31. Eijkenaar F. et al. Effects of pay for performance in health care: a systematic review of systematic reviews. *Health Policy* 2013;110(2–3):115–130.

32. Fendrick AM, Edlin M. *Value-Based Insurance Design Landscape Digest;* 2009. Available at http://www.npcnow.org/publication/value-based-insurance-design-landscape-digest-0.

33. Agency for Healthcare Research and Quality. The state of accountable care organizations; 2013 Available at https://innovations.ahrq.gov/perspectives/state-accountable-care-organizations.

34. Kocot SL, White R, Katikaneni P, McClellan MB. A more complete picture of pioneer ACO results; 2014. Available at http://www.brookings.edu/blogs/up-front/posts/2014/10/09-pioneer-aco-results-mcclellan#recent_rr/.

35. American Hospital Association. *AHA Research Synthesis Report: Patient-Centered Medical Home (PCMH);* 2010. Available at http://www.aha.org/research/cor/content/patient-centered-medical-home.pdf.

36. U.S. Department of Health and Human Services. Better, smarter, healthier: in historic announcement, HHS sets clear goals and timeline for shifting Medicare reimbursements from volume to value; 2015. Available at http://www.hhs.gov/news/press/2015pres/01/20150126a.html.

37. Tsai TC et al. Medicare's bundled payment initiative: most hospitals are focused on a few high-volume conditions. *Health Affair* (Millwood); 2015;34(3):371–380.

38. Porter M, Marks C, Landman Z. *OrthoChoice: Bundled Payments in the County of Stockholm.* Cambridge, MA: Harvard Business School Publishing; 2014;714–725

39. Porter ME, Pabo EA, Lee TH. Redesigning primary care: a strategic vision to improve value by organizing around patients' needs. *Health Affair* (Millwood); 2013;32(3):516–525.

40. Porter ME, Kaplan RS. How Should We Pay for Health Care? Working Paper; 2015.

41. Edmonds C, Hallman GL. Cardiovascular care providers. a pioneer in bundled services, shared risk, and single payment. *Tex Heart Inst J.* 1995;22(1):72–76.

42. Shwartz M, Young DW, Siegrist R. The ratio of costs to charges: how good a basis for estimating costs? *Inquiry* 1995;32(4): 476–481.

43. Porter ME, Teisberg EO. Redefining competition in health care. *Harv Bus Rev.* 2004;82(6): 64–76, 136.

44. Ballo MT et al. Prospective peer review quality assurance for outpatient radiation therapy. *Pract Radiat Oncol.* 2014;4(5):279–284.

45. Simeone WJ Jr. et al. Quality assessment across a national cancer network. *J Oncol Pract.* 2013;9(3):165–168.

46. Porter ME, Teisberg EO. Cleveland Clinic: growth strategy 2014. *Harv Bu School Case.* 2009;709–732.

47. Luft HS. The relation between surgical volume and mortality: an exploration of causal factors and alternative models. *Med Care.* 1980;18(9):940–959.

48. Hughes RG, Hunt SS, Luft HS. Effects of surgeon volume and hospital volume on quality of care in hospitals. *Med Care.* 1987;25(6):489–503.

49. Vernooij F et al. Specialized and high-volume care leads to better outcomes of ovarian cancer treatment in the Netherlands. *Gynecol Oncol.* 2009;112(3):455–461.

50. Walters RS et al. Developing a system to track meaningful outcome measures in head and neck cancer treatment. *Head Neck.* 2014;36(2):226–230.

V PATIENT EXPERIENCE, ENGAGEMENT, AND SERVICES

Innovations in Patient Experience

Deirdre Mylod
Thomas H. Lee
Sharyl Wojciechowski

Abstract

The strategic imperative to create value in healthcare by measuring unmet patient needs and improving performance to better meet those needs has never been greater. Caregivers are rediscovering a central purpose of medicine—the reduction of patient suffering—and finding that it is the right thing to do and good strategy. This chapter discusses innovations being rapidly adopted by pioneering organizations to reduce patient suffering, create value, and reengage the workforce in fulfilling the mission of healthcare. Advances in health information systems and communications technology have led to improvements in four major patient experience areas: (1) the type of data collected, (2) the methods of data collection, (3) the volume of data collected, and (4) the use of the data. These innovations allow organizations to take actions that can increase their market share, enhance their ability to meet their patients' needs and reduce suffering, and make true care transformation possible.

We are living in a time of spectacular medical progress—enjoying its benefits but also having to adjust to some of its side effects. Previously fatal diseases such as HIV and AIDS have become controllable chronic conditions. Testing and treatment options exist for illnesses that had none until recently. Specialized clinical expertise makes state–of–the–art care possible for medically complex patients at teaching institutions known for research as well as at community hospitals.[1] These and other advancements allow clinicians to affirm their mission to heal, something can almost always be done for even the sickest of those in their care.

Although much good has resulted from this progress, needed advances in patient experience have lagged behind. In fact, increases in the complexity of healthcare often come at the expense of how patients experience those care processes. However, healthcare reform is now pushing organizations to shift their focus from clinician activities to improving value, which from the patient's perspective means meeting patients' needs as efficiently as possible.[2] Before this new focus can be adopted, important questions must be addressed: What are we trying to accomplish in healthcare? Are we meeting all of our patients' needs? What is the best way to evaluate our progress?

Measuring "hard" clinical outcomes alone will not provide the answers. Nor will checking off boxes on a list of evidence-based medicine practices; there is more that patients seek from healthcare. Meeting patients' needs requires a focus on reducing suffering—from both the burden of disease and the dysfunction of the delivery system.[3] Whether we are doing a good job of reducing patients' suffering or not can only be measured by asking patients directly.

The Hospital Consumer Assessment of Healthcare Providers and Systems (HCAHPS) survey from the Centers for Medicare and Medicaid Services (CMS) has served as a catalyst for increased attention to patient experience. Figure 20.1 shows that, with each new HCAHPS mandate—measurement,

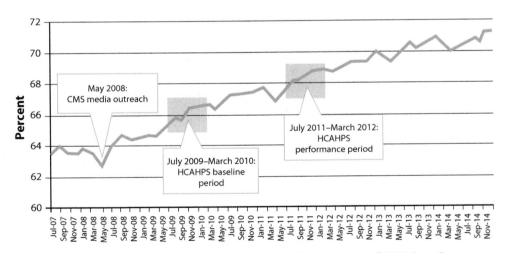

FIGURE 20.1 National "Rate This Hospital" average top box percentage. © 2015 Press Ganey Associated, Inc.

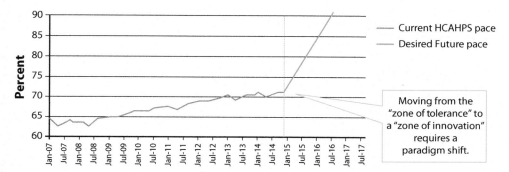

FIGURE 20.2 Current HCAHPS "Rate This Hospital" average top box percentage improvement pace versus desired future improvement pace. © 2015 Press Ganey Associated, Inc.

public reporting, reimbursement—providers have boosted their efforts to listen and respond to the patient voice, resulting in corresponding gains in the patient experience.

Although there have been incremental improvements in patient experience precipitated by external industry events (e.g., HCAHPS mandates), progress has been slow. Top box analyses on all hospitals using HCAHPS between January 1, 2013, and June 30, 2014, show that—almost a decade after HCAHPS was introduced—only 20% of patients report that 100% of their needs were met. Nationwide, hospital inpatients report HCAHPS items at the individual attribute level as optimal only between 49% and 89% of the time.

Tolerating the current pace of improvement will have consequences; optimal levels of patient experience performance will not be achieved for decades. Disrupting the "zone of tolerance" and inciting healthcare providers to move into a "zone of innovation" requires a paradigm shift (Figure 20.2). To drive this shift, an innovative performance framework is needed that fully captures the extent to which patients' needs are being met. This framework must deconstruct suffering by breaking it down into meaningful categories that reflect the experience of patients and help caregivers identify opportunities to reduce it.

Taking a comprehensive approach to measuring and reducing patient suffering is not just an ethical obligation—it is a strategic imperative. In an evolving healthcare marketplace, financial survival depends on patient loyalty.[4] Those institutions that can accurately categorize, measure, and mitigate their patients' suffering most effectively will reap greater market share as well as the loyalty and retention of clinicians and other personnel. These personnel will take pride in and be motivated by the shared purpose of reducing suffering—more than is possible with financially driven goals alone.

The goal of reducing patient suffering is consistent with most organizational mission statements and many healthcare professionals' motivations for choosing their careers. Use of the term *suffering* is being invoked with increasing frequency by healthcare providers to remind the entire patient care team to have empathy for the anxiety, confusion, and uncertainty that patients bear. Cleveland Clinic's video "Empathy: The Human Connection to Patient Care" has been viewed by millions around the world. It asks, "If you could stand in someone else's shoes. . . . Hear what they hear. See what they see. Feel what they feel. Would you treat them differently?"[5] The video is a compelling example of how healthcare organizations are finding new ways to help clinicians and other personnel tune in to the suffering that patients and their families endure. We are in a new era where improving patient experience goes beyond efforts to improve scores or individual elements of care with service initiatives. There is a new focus on improving holistically, taking the full context of patient needs into account and redesigning care to better meet those needs.

In this context, organizations are rapidly adopting innovations in patient experience to help them reduce patient suffering. Advances in health information systems and communications technology increasingly allow data to be collected from patients at low costs. It is now also possible for patient data to be segmented into groups with similar needs and thus similar outcomes of interest. Those patients can be followed over time so that their outcomes can be measured, analyzed, and improved. These technology and communications advances enable healthcare organizations to innovate in four major patient experience areas: (1) the types of data collected, (2) the methods of data collection, (3) the volume of data collected, and (4) the use of the data.[6]

INNOVATIONS IN DATA TYPE

Forward-thinking healthcare organizations are embracing an innovative performance framework that enables them to improve care by translating patient data into categories of unmet patient needs. Unmet needs are a reflection of patient suffering and an opportunity to better respond to what is important to patients to improve care. Just as medical science has broken down patients' clinical needs and created corresponding specialties, the framework identifies meaningful and measureable categories of patient suffering so that providers can organize themselves to address suffering more effectively.

TABLE 20.1 Deconstructing Suffering: Sources and Examples

Inherent Suffering (Providers' Goal: Mitigate)		Avoidable Suffering (Providers' Goal: Eliminate)
Suffering Associated with Diagnosis	Suffering Associated with Treatment	Suffering Associated with Healthcare Delivery System Dysfunction
Symptoms of disease, including pain	Postoperative pain	Unnecessary pain resulting from failure to identify and treat the source
Loss of functioning (temporary or permanent)	Loss of functioning (temporary or permanent)	Undesirable outcomes, such as hospital-acquired conditions and readmission because of failure to follow evidence-based practice
	Side effects	Misdiagnosis; delay in diagnosis
Fear or anxiety arising from the implications of the diagnosis for health and functioning	Fear or anxiety regarding outcome of treatment	Fear or anxiety because of poor coordination and teamwork, lack of respect shown to patient, and loss of trust in providers
	Fear or anxiety because of unfamiliar processes, disruption in daily life, and loss of control	Unnecessary waits and delays in treatment
		Poor adherence to discharge instructions and medication regimens resulting from inadequate communications and coordination

Patient suffering can be categorized as "inherent" to the patient's medical condition and associated treatment or as "avoidable" and the result of dysfunction in the care delivery process (Table 20.1).[7,8]

The inherent suffering patients experience before and after receiving their diagnoses may be unavoidable because of their specific medical condition, although it should be considered addressable as part of patient care. The condition may cause pain, other symptoms, and temporary or permanent loss of functioning. Further, a diagnosis itself can give rise to patient anxiety about the future, fear that life plans will be altered, or a feeling of loss of control.

Inherent suffering also encompasses the effects of medical treatment for the patient's condition. Treatment itself can be frightening, often causing side effects, pain, discomfort, and loss of functioning even when it ultimately leads to recovery. Patients may also feel overwhelmed by having to navigate a complex care delivery system.

Some pain cannot be eliminated. Some procedures will always be uncomfortable. And some degree of anxiety will always be present as patients move along their healthcare journeys. However, the goal of medicine must be to mitigate inherent suffering and to acknowledge that the act of alleviating patient suffering is crucial to the healing process.

Conversely, dysfunction in healthcare delivery is avoidable. Poor coordination of care, excessive waits for appointments, uncertainty about what will happen next, and ineffective care transitions all erode patient trust and lead to anxiety, frustration, and fear. Each example of dysfunction is preventable and within the control of the healthcare organization.

Collecting data that distinguish between inherent and avoidable sources of suffering allows organizations to understand where patient needs have not been met and provide a rich understanding of what steps need to be taken to close that gap. Current patient experience measures do not directly ask patients about their level of suffering. However, they do point to where patients view their care as optimal versus less than optimal. Suboptimal experiences are clear opportunities to reduce suffering.

HCAHPS survey items ask patients to report how often events occurred during their inpatient stays, and measures on Press Ganey's inpatient experience survey ask patients to evaluate the quality of the care they received. These combined insights reflect an understanding of patient needs as they relate to suffering.

Table 20.2 organizes the measures into needs that stem from both inherent and avoidable suffering. Although the examples relate to the inpatient setting, the constructs are relevant to all patient care settings.

For example, patients have an inherent need for information. In an inpatient setting, this need encompasses the seven survey items depicted in Figure 20.3. Although each construct may be measured with different survey items in other settings, the need is universal.[9] When patients report less-than-optimal experiences, it should serve as a cue to healthcare providers that patient needs are not being fully met and an opportunity to reduce suffering exists.

Collecting and organizing patient data in this way also allows care providers to better understand the needs of clinical subsets of patients. For example, congestive heart failure (CHF) patients endure a chronic, progressive, and unpredictable disease course that results in different needs for information compared to patients with other diagnoses. Being aware of differing needs can help

TABLE 20.2

Inherent Patient Needs Arising from Disease and Treatment	Patient Needs That Stem from Dysfunction in Care Delivery
As part of having a health condition or receiving treatment, patients have a need for: • pain control • skilled care providers • preparation for discharge • information • personalization • empathy • choice • privacy • responsiveness	When dysfunction exists, patients develop a need for: • courteous and respectful interactions • reduced wait times • comfortable environments • adequate amenities • service recovery • teamwork among care providers

© 2015 Press Ganey Associated, Inc.

Need for Information

Physician kept you informed

Nurses kept you informed

Doctors explained things in a way you could understand

Nurses explained things in a way you could understand

Explanations regarding tests or treatments

Staff described new medication side effects

Staff told you what new medication was for

FIGURE 20.3 Need for information (inpatient setting).
© 2015 Press Ganey Associated, Inc.

clinicians communicate more effectively with CHF patients to help them better understand their diagnosis and care plans.

Obtaining data on subsets of patients also enables clinicians to redesign care to reduce suffering for specific patient groups. For example, Yale-New Haven Hospital in New Haven, Connecticut, saw an opportunity to alleviate avoidable suffering for patients treated on the general medical unit who have conditions that do not require clinical intervention during the night. Interventions such as administering medication, monitoring vitals, and blood draws during nighttime hours interrupt patients' much-needed sleep. Poor sleep adds to the stress of being hospitalized and stands in the way of the healing and recovery process.

The organization identified patients for whom nighttime interventions were medically unnecessary, created a protocol for how those patients would receive care, and ensured a process existed for modifying the protocol if nighttime interventions became necessary. The new protocol, "clustered care," bundled routine aspects of care during waking hours to avoid disturbing patients between 11 pm and 6 am.

After piloting the care redesign program, Yale-New Haven found that its HCAHPS performance on the environmental measure "During this hospital stay, how often was the area around your room quiet at night" dramatically improved without any additional efforts to reduce noise on the unit; scores rose from a 16% "Always" score to a 47% "Always" score.[10] The success of the program prompted the organization to implement it on all medical units as well as the obstetrics unit.

To create value in healthcare, it is essential to collect data that measure what matters to patients. Successfully competing in today's complex and evolving healthcare marketplace requires being able to reduce patient suffering by meeting patients' unmet needs. Organizations that drive improvement in this way will attract and retain patients, engage their workforce, and support the mission of healthcare.

INNOVATIONS IN DATA COLLECTION

Robust amounts of timely data are needed to identify unmet patient needs and reduce suffering, especially at the clinical subset level. Just mailing questionnaires or conducting telephone surveys cannot capture the volume of data required to drive performance improvement in a competitive healthcare environment. Further, the protracted turnaround time for collecting data via traditional methods is increasingly problematic; organizations are striving to shorten their improvement cycles. To reach more patients faster and more efficiently, organizations are supplementing paper and telephone surveys with e-mail and other electronic methods such as point-of-care surveys using mobile devices.

The timeliness of e-mail surveys maximizes the value that organizations can obtain from their patient experience data. Organizations that employ e-mail surveys report significant reductions in improvement cycle times. As shown in Figure 20.4, survey turnaround times for e-surveys are faster than traditional surveys, meaning that organizations can take action more quickly.

Typically, e-surveys are sent the day after a patient's visit or discharge and returned within a day of receipt. The ongoing, near real-time feedback con-

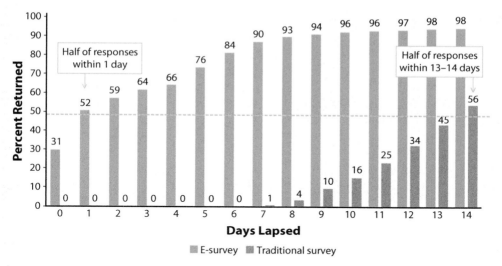

FIGURE 20.4 Percent of total returned surveys by days lapsed.
© 2015 Press Ganey Associated, Inc.

nected with e-surveys leads to more effective improvement efforts, providing organizations with numerous incremental opportunities to validate, monitor, course correct, and enhance initiatives. The immediacy of the data also makes the e-survey feedback more meaningful for caregivers because they can readily recall the events and experiences described by their patients.

The success of collecting data electronically depends on an organization's active integration of e-mail capture into its operation. Those organizations that have been effective at e-mail collection have embedded the process into their operations and have made it a clear priority with their staff. They are also committed to training their front line operations staff on collecting e-mail addresses and addressing concerns about the process.

The University of Utah Health Care in Salt Lake City, Utah, is a pioneer when it comes to successfully capturing patient e-mail addresses and implementing electronic patient experience surveys. When Utah made the decision to convert from paper surveys to electronic surveys, it did not have a single patient e-mail address. Its computer system did not even contain a field for e-mail addresses.

New practice management technology allowed staff to begin entering patient e-mail addresses on registration. Managers also created a frequently asked questions document for registration desk staff and scheduled weekly huddles with Utah's director of strategic initiatives to assess progress and work through issues. Leadership support was essential to convey the message that innovations in patient communication and data collection were organizational priorities.

The rapid turnaround time experienced with e-mail surveys has been transformative for the University of Utah. The organization was able to reduce its improvement cycle time by 83% (from 12 weeks to 2 weeks) after implementing e-surveys. This allows Utah to determine, close to real time, if improvement initiatives are working. Whether it is waiting-room rounding or a new greeting at the front desk, administrators can see quantitative and qualitative results almost immediately.

Under value-based purchasing (VBP), hospitals have a portion of their annual Medicare payment based in part on their performance on HCAHPS measures. To maximize VBP incentive payments, reduce patient suffering, and achieve patient loyalty in a highly competitive healthcare market, healthcare providers must have the ability to respond to patient experience feedback as quickly as possible. Electronic data collection shortens improvement cycles and enables organizations to promptly react to opportunities to address unmet patient needs.

INNOVATIONS IN DATA VOLUME

Innovations in electronic data collection also make it possible for organizations to capture more of the patient voice to better understand where suffering can be reduced. Larger amounts of data are needed for analyses at the levels where true accountability lies and where true improvement can occur. To identify the key drivers of patient experience unique to a specific patient population, an organization must have access to data with enough depth and breadth to fully capture the experiences of those patients.[11] Small facility-level sample sizes are adequate for assessing performance and meeting regulatory requirements at that level. However, these global views of performance cannot provide a clear picture of unmet patient needs at a granular level.

Research shows that organizations that try to capture more patient feedback tend to perform better because their data can be fully leveraged for quality-improvement purposes. As depicted in Figure 20.5, regardless of hospital size, those organizations that surveyed more than 81% of their patient populations see a higher average top box percentile ranking on the overall hospital rating HCAHPS survey question than those hospitals that surveyed fewer.

Instead of surveying samples of patients, increasing numbers of organizations are employing census-based surveying of all eligible patients after discharge and

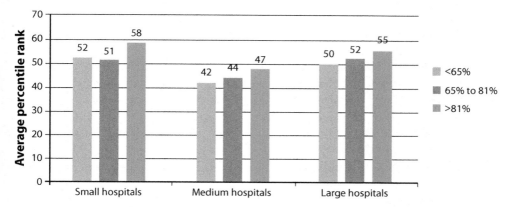

Greater sampling increases the utility of the data by providing sample sizes needed to have better performance measures at smaller breakouts levels.

FIGURE 20.5 Average percentile ranks by hospital size and sampling rate.
© 2015 Press Ganey Associated, Inc.

every outpatient encounter. This allows organizations to dramatically increase the volume of usable data for quality improvement.

Kaiser Permanente Northwest in Portland, Oregon, experienced a 300% increase in survey returns after implementing census-based surveying. Similarly, before implementing census-based electronic surveys, Utah had an annual volume of 14,822 returned surveys. In the year after adopting census-based surveying, Utah received 62,359 completed patient surveys—a 320% survey increase in patient feedback.

Utah also saw an increase in the number and detail of patient comments. When using only mailed surveys, it received approximately 380 comments per week with an average of 12 words per comment. After implementing census-based surveying, it began receiving approximately 1,700 patient comments per week with an average of 54 words per comment, more than quadrupling the number of comments per week.

An increased number of survey returns permits drilling down to a lower level of analysis while maintaining stable, credible sample sizes. Patient experience data can be integrated with operational, clinical, and financial data to leverage the relationships among all aspects of performance that shape the patient experience. In this way, patient experience data can become a vital management tool that a chief executive officer can use to increase the profile of the organization in the community and with employees, the chief nursing officer can use to commend performance or intervene in nursing performance issues, and the chief operating officer can use to drive accountability at all levels.

Having more data also reduces concerns about data validity. Physicians are pivotal to the patient experience, but they have historically challenged survey data. Larger sample sizes mitigate the concerns regarding margin of error and allow data to be effectively segmented for physician specific feedback.

With data they can trust—or at least not ignore—physicians are quickly becoming committed partners in developing meaningful and sustainable improvement initiatives. For example, the University of Pittsburgh Medical Center (UPMC) in Pittsburgh, Pennsylvania, operates approximately 450 medical practices with 2,800 physicians. After complementing its mail surveys with e-surveys, UPMC reported that "we have so much data that people are no longer saying, 'There's not enough data in the sample size.' We have completely mitigated that argument. So now the conversation has shifted to 'What are we going to do about this?' "

The increased survey and comment volume also has been instrumental in driving physician engagement at Utah. Originally, only 137 physicians received enough patient responses to obtain reports. Implementing census-based surveying through electronic surveys allowed the system to increase that number to 394 almost immediately. In 2013, the number of physicians receiving individualized reports grew again to 431. Physicians no longer debate the statistical validity of the data and instead focus on how they can improve the patient experience.

Collecting more data significantly expands the patient voice and affords deeper insights into unmet patient needs. It bolsters trust in the data and fosters physician commitment to performance improvement—driving higher VBP scores, optimizing reimbursements, and enabling organizations to thrive in a competitive marketplace. Most important, it equips healthcare organizations with the means to develop targeted improvement strategies to reduce suffering for every patient population it serves.

INNOVATIONS IN DATA USAGE

In addition to innovations in how data are being defined and collected, organizations are rapidly adopting innovations in how patient experience data are used. Data are no longer tapped simply to assess whether care is adequate but to act as a catalyst for performance improvement.

Transparency is one of the primary data usage innovations causing this shift, having been sparked by the proliferation of online consumer review websites.

A 2013 Pew Research Center study determined that 72% of adult Internet users searched online for information about health issues in the previous 12 months.[12] Further, the *Journal of the American Medical Association* reported that 59% of American adults strongly consider online ratings when choosing a physician. More than one-third of individuals using online reviews chose their physician based on positive reviews, and 37% avoided doctors with negative reviews.[13]

Unfortunately, some reviews that individuals rely on are probably deceptive. Researchers from MIT and Northwestern University examined 325,869 online consumer reviews and found that 4.8% were submitted by customers with no confirmed transaction. These questionable reviews also included a significantly higher proportion of negative comments.[14]

Patients' reliance on online physician ratings is concerning to many providers. Small numbers of reviews on these sites, as well as potentially fraudulent reviews, can lead to an inaccurate portrayal of quality of care. In many cases, patient-confidentiality regulations under the Health Insurance Portability and Accountability Act limit providers' ability to address false claims of substandard care.

To ensure that patients have valid, reliable data on which to base their care decisions, a growing number of organizations are using their own find-a-doctor websites as platforms for publishing their physicians' quantitative and qualitative patient experience performance data. The strategy allows them more control over the data that appear online about their physicians. It also ensures that patients are getting an accurate picture of quality of care provided by the organization.[15]

In December 2012, Utah became the first healthcare system in the country to share all patient ratings and comments on the Internet. Piedmont Healthcare in Atlanta, Georgia, and Wake Forest Baptist Health in Winston-Salem, North Carolina, followed suit in early 2014. And the momentum is building as other organizations adopt transparency strategies.

These bold organizations are not scrubbing the data they publish. They know that true transparency involves public disclosure of all patient experience data. Every qualitative rating—along with every positive, neutral, and negative patient comment (except those that would violate patient confidentiality)—is posted and attributed to the appropriate physician who cared for the patient.

Selecting a physician can be challenging, even for healthy patients seeking preventive care. It can be anxiety provoking for patients seeking care for an illness or injury. Having access to robust and reliable information about an organization's physicians empowers patients to make choices about their care.

Promoting patient autonomy allows the patient to be a full participant in guiding his or her care and reduces the avoidable suffering that could otherwise be caused from a lack of information.[16] It signals to the patient that the organization provides compassionate and empathic care even before he or she has a first care encounter.

A commitment to data transparency not only helps grow market share by attracting new patients but also acts as a powerful way of retaining current patients. A recent analysis found that the most important predictor of patient loyalty was patient confidence in care providers.[17] Data transparency builds credibility and cultivates public trust and confidence in organizations and their physicians.

When new and existing patients conduct an online search for a physician, the website with the most reviews will be listed first in the search results. Organizations that are innovating by capturing patient experience data using census-based surveying have a wealth of reliable, valid data at their disposal. The high volume trumps the amount of data that any opt-in consumer review website can provide. Healthcare organizations that consistently update their websites with the most current qualitative and quantitative physician data will drive online traffic directly to their own pages rather than independent sites that house a handful of responses many years out of date.

Before publishing online reviews, Utah's physician profile page views totaled 32,144. Three months after implementation, monthly page views increased nearly fourfold to 122,072. Piedmont observed similar results with a 200% to 300% increase in web traffic. Both organizations' find-a-doctor websites offer significantly more reviews than any third-party review site, and there has been a marked increase in their visibility in search results.[14]

The advantages of data transparency culminate in a formidable strategic and competitive advantage for organizations willing to lead this charge. Physicians want to practice good medicine and reduce suffering for their patients. Data transparency that is built on robust sample sizes drives improvement by motivating an epidemic of empathy among providers to deliver the best possible care.[18] They value reliable and valid data that show them how they are doing, where they need to improve, and which high-performing colleagues may have the best practices to share.

After Utah launched its online review website, physician performance on patient experience measures improved at an accelerated pace. The system's overall experience rating increased steadily from the bottom to the top quartile of Press Ganey's national database, and the percentage of top-performing physicians increased dramatically. Likewise, since going live with online physician reviews, Piedmont physicians have owned their data. They take advantage of patient experience coaches in their practices to discuss patient comments and to determine how they can improve.[14]

Everyone in healthcare recognizes the value of transparency. However, stakeholders get nervous about exposing their data. They are quick to cite the potential downsides—that patients will not be able to understand the limitations of the information or that risk adjustment will be inadequate to explain why their performance looks below average.

Pioneers in transparency are showing these fears to be unfounded. These organizations have taken the bold position that more patient experience data reveal the truth about the type of care being provided. Publishing patient data on the Internet is not mere marketing—it creates a powerful motivation for physicians to give every patient empathic care. Financial incentives to improve the patient experience in and of themselves could never have produced the kind of change being experienced at Utah, Piedmont, and Wake Forest.[19] What matters is physicians' awareness that every patient visit is a high-stakes encounter, an opportunity to reduce suffering and provide the best possible patient care.

CONCLUSION

Patient-reported data collection and analysis are rapidly evolving from a marketing function to a strategic focus. Organizations are seeking to maintain and increase their market share as well as improve care by enhancing their ability to meet their patients' needs, mitigate inherent suffering, and eliminate avoidable suffering.

Innovations in patient experience are making this type of true care transformation possible. To understand what drives patients' suffering, data that reflect how well patient needs are being met—including patient-reported outcomes for clinical subsets—have taken center stage. Data on amenities (e.g., food, parking) are increasingly peripheral.

Data are no longer collected solely by mailing paper surveys or calling patients by phone. Using electronic methods to capture data on unmet patient needs gives patients a louder voice than they have ever had in healthcare. And analyses of these data are no longer limited by small numbers of survey returns. The volume of data at organizations' disposal allows teams and individual clinicians to improve actual patient care for all patient populations.

The strategic imperative to create value in healthcare by measuring unmet patient needs and improving performance to better meet those needs has never been greater. The chaos that characterizes modern healthcare creates unnecessary patient suffering—but it can be overcome and remedied. The wheels are already in motion to do so. Pioneering organizations are differentiating themselves in the market by adopting patient experience innovations that help them reduce patient suffering, create value, and reengage the workforce in fulfilling the mission of healthcare.

REFERENCES

1. Lee TH, Mongan JJ. *Chaos and Organization in Health Care*. Cambridge, MA: MIT Press; 2009:x–xv.

2. Lee TH. Reduction of patient suffering as a strategic goal. *Med Practice Insider*. 2014. Retrieved from http://www.medicalpracticeinsider.com/blog/reduction-patient -suffering-strategic-goal.

3. Press Ganey. Reducing suffering: the path to patient-centered care. Retrieved from http://pressganey.com/resources/white-papers/reducing-suffering-the-path-to-patient -centered-care.

4. Lee TH. Why patient loyalty matters—and how to enhance it. *HFM Magazine*; 2014. Retrieved from https://www.hfma.org/Content.aspx?id=26243.

5. Cleveland Clinic. Empathy: the human connection to patient care. Retrieved from https://www.youtube.com/watch?v=cDDWvj_q-o8.

6. Lee TH. Patient experience data are outcomes. *J Clin Outcomes Manag*. 2014;21: 479–480.

7. Mylod DE, Lee TH. A framework for reducing suffering in health care. *Harvard Bus Rev*. 2013. Retrieved from https://hbr.org/2013/11/a-framework-for-reducing-suffering -in-health-care.

8. Lee TH. The word that shall not be spoken. *N Engl J Med*. 2013;369:1777–1779.

9. Press Ganey. Measuring patient needs to reduce suffering. Retrieved from http://pressganey.com/resources/white-papers/measuring-patient-needs-to-reduce -suffering.

10. Institute for Innovation. Redesigning Care to Fit the Needs of Specific Patient Groups: Patients Who Need Sleep More Than Nighttime Medical Interventions. Retrieved from http://www.theinstituteforinnovation.org/docs/default-source/innovation-stories /inspiring-innovation-stories_yale_quiet-at-night_final.pdf?sfvrsn=2.

11. Press Ganey. Targeted Performance Improvement. Retrieved from http:// pressganey.com/resources/white-papers/strategic-insights-targeted-performance -improvement.

12. Thackeray R, Crookston B, West J. Correlates of health-related social media use among adults. *J Med Internet Res*. 2013;15:e21.

13. Hanauer DA, Zheng K, Singer DC, Gebremariam A, Davis MM. Public awareness, perception, and use of online physician rating sites. *JAMA*. 2014;311:734–735.

14. Anderson E, Simester D. Reviews without a purchase: low ratings, loyal customers, and deception. *J Marketing Res*. 2014;51:249–269.

15. Press Ganey. Transparency Strategies: Online Physician Reviews for Improving Care and Reducing Suffering. Retrieved from http://pressganey.com/resources/white-papers/online-physician-reviews-for-improving-care-and-reducing.

16. Dempsey C, Wojciechowski S, McConville E, Drain M. Reducing patient suffering through compassionate connected care. *J Nurs Admin.* 2014;44:517–24.

17. Press Ganey. Protecting market share in the era of reform: understanding patient loyalty in the medical practice segment. Retrieved from http://pressganey.com/resources/white-papers/understanding-patient-loyalty-in-the-medical-practice-segment.

18. Lee TH. How to spread empathy in health care. *Harvard Bus Rev.* 2014, July 17. Retrieved from https://hbr.org/2014/07/how-to-spread-empathy-in-health-care.

19. Lee TH. Online reviews could help fix medicine. *Harvard Bus Rev.* 2014, June 3. Retrieved from https://hbr.org/2014/06/online-reviews-could-help-fix-medicine.

CHAPTER 21

Behavioral Economics and Stanford Health Care's C-I-CARE Patient Experience

Amir Dan Rubin

Abstract

Stanford Health Care, an academic health system affiliated with Stanford University and the Stanford School of Medicine, is known for excellence in patient care, education, and research. In recent years, Stanford Health Care has also become highly regarded for its outstanding patient experience. The achievement of high patient-satisfaction levels has largely been the result of Stanford Health Care's C-I-CARE philosophy and approaches, which lay out techniques and practices associated with effective, patient-centered communications. Although traditional management approaches for incentives and change management are incorporated in Stanford C-I-CARE, insights from behavioral economics have served as key differentiators in engendering broad team engagement and in supporting sustained habits and high performance levels.

Stanford Health Care is a $4–billion academic health system affiliated with Stanford University and the Stanford University School of Medicine. Located in the heart of Silicon Valley in Northern California, Stanford Health Care (just Stanford hereafter) is recognized for medical breakthroughs, including the first use of the linear accelerator, invention of the CyberKnife, the first heart–lung transplant in the world, and major innovations in stem cells, genomics, imaging, minimally invasive surgery, cancer, and the neurosciences. With seven

Nobel Prize winners currently on the faculty, Stanford has been the "go-to" place for cutting-edge research and for treating the most complex conditions. Even though Stanford's medical care has long been considered among the best in the world, the organization has not always been known for its high level of service. In late 2009, Stanford Hospital's "likelihood to recommend" national ranking according to Medicare, Hospital Consumer Assessment of Healthcare Providers and Systems, and Press Ganey surveys was in the 43rd percentile. By 2014, Stanford's rankings jumped to the 93rd percentile in the nation and number 1 in the entire San Francisco Bay Area (see Figures 21.1 and 21.2). This improvement in patient satisfaction has been largely the result of Stanford Health Care's implementation of its C-I-CARE patient experience program. The C-I-CARE approach lays out techniques and practices associated with effective, patient-centered communications. The program and its successful implementation heavily leverage insights from behavioral economics.

In his book *Thinking, Fast and Slow*, Nobel Laureate and behavioral economist Daniel Kahneman describes two models for how people make decisions.[1] In one model—"the slow model"—people are methodological and analytical in their decision making, as might be described by economic theory and probabilistic models. In the other model—"the fast model"—people make decisions by leveraging heuristics, rules of thumb, shortcuts, or biases to avoid the more effortful thinking required to deeply analyze decisions. Richard Thaler and

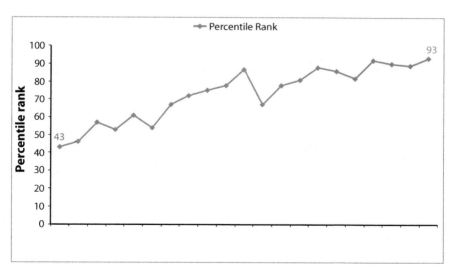

FIGURE 21.1 Stanford Hospital's rising inpatient-satisfaction scores.
Source: Press Ganey, All Hospitals in Database.

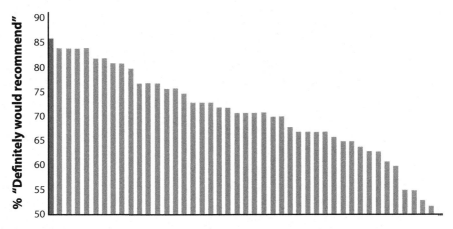

FIGURE 21.2 Stanford Hospital's number 1 ranking in patient satisfaction among all San Francisco Bay Area hospitals. Source: Medicare HCAHPS CY 2013, Bay Area Counties

Cass Sunstein in their book *Nudge: Improving Decisions about Health, Wealth, and Happiness* refer to this dichotomy in decision making as the difference between how theoretical "Homo economicus" or "econs" make decisions versus how "humans" actually make decisions.[2] Thaler and Sunstein describe how decisions made by "humans" can be affected by "nudges" or by the "choice architecture" around the decision. For the theoretical "econs," on the other hand, decisions are not affected by how a question is framed. In his book *Influence: The Psychology of Persuasion*, Robert Cialdini describes how people are influenced by several predictable approaches.[3] By leveraging approaches described by these researchers and many others in Stanford Health Care's implementation of C-I-CARE, organization-wide change has been accelerated and sustained at a broad scale.

In their classic management guidebook *The Leadership Challenge: How to Make Extraordinary Things Happen in Organizations*, Jim Kouzes and Barry Posner speak to the importance of organizations aligning on a shared vision.[4] Behavioral economists might describe the value of a shared vision as providing an anchor point for organizational team members from which adjustments can be made. Kahneman, Thaler, and Sunstein all conclude that it may be easier for people to make decisions by adjusting from an existing starting point, anchor, or default option rather than trying to make a decision without any prompting or launching point.[1,2] This approach to adjusting from an anchor supports what Kahneman calls *fast thinking* or what Stanford researcher B. J. Fogg calls a *tiny habit* change.[5] Such shifts may take less effort than a more fundamental consideration of an entirely new decision or direction. Accordingly, to help launch Stanford C-I-CARE, the organization developed a new vision statement: "Healing humanity through science and compassion, one patient at a time." This new vision anchored itself in Stanford's historical value of "science," yet made an adjacent connection to patient experience by noting that both science and compassion seek to affect humanity.

Lean or Toyota Production System approaches teach that engaging team members in incremental performance improvements, which are then built into standards and core processes, can lead to dramatic effects on performance.[6,7] Stanford Health Care's management system draws on insights from lean and is referred to as the *Stanford Operating System*. The Stanford Operating System involves three key managerial components: (1) how strategies are aligned and deployed, (2) how operations or value streams are improved, and (3) how performance is sustained though active daily management techniques. At the core of the system is the concept of engaging team members to develop best practices, also called *standard work* in lean parlance. At the core of Stanford C-I-CARE lie patient experiences with best practice standards. Although Stanford C-I-CARE is the descriptor for a broader set of approaches for improving the patient experience, at its basic level C-I-CARE includes a pneumonic and template to guide key components of great interactions (see Figure 21.3). The acronym or its components might be clever, but the concept of templates or scripting is well known. However, as referenced earlier, these core C-I-CARE templates leverage many insights from behavioral economics to help align team members and support sustained high performance levels.

At the inception of its patient experience efforts, Stanford Health Care took its core C-I-CARE template and asked all departments to describe best practice communication interactions in their respective areas—which were codified as C-I-CARE standard work. Moreover, patient experience scenarios were created and staff and physicians were asked how they would personally wish to be treated if they were receiving care at Stanford. This approach of making a scenario vivid and personal is a known decision-making bias in behavioral economics,[1] and it can be a more effective technique than asking staff to reflect in the abstract on areas needing improvement.

Moreover, Stanford Health Care regularly uses "design-thinking" techniques, including empathy mapping and ethnographic studies, to assess patient and family perspectives.[8] These approaches involve staff members regularly observing and engaging with patients and family members, which allows them to personally see the challenges patients face. These approaches, along c·i·care   c·i·care

c·i·care

CONNECT with people by calling them their proper name, or the name they prefer (Mr., Ms., Dr.)

INTRODUCE yourself and your role

COMMUNICATE what you are going to do, how long it will take, and how it will impact the patient

ASK permission before entering a room, examining a patient or undertaking an activity

RESPOND to patient's questions or requests promptly; anticipate patient needs

EXIT courteously with an explanation of what will come next

One Patient at a Time

FIGURE 21.3 Stanford Health Care's C-I-CARE template

with participation by patients and family members in every improvement project, leverage decision-making biases around the availability and vividness of information as people often assume that what they see in front of them is representative of the broader population set.[1] Moreover, the negative issues observed in patient interactions tend to be more vivid and memorable because people weigh such "numerator" instances often without regard to the "denominator" or the representativeness of their presence.[1] When pursuing a lean "zero-defect" philosophy for service, this focus on the instances of service deficiency has been quite helpful in engaging team members around C-I-CARE.

In their book *Switch: How to Change Things When Change Is Hard*,[9] Chip and Dan Heath describe how changes can be made easier for people if the "bright spots" or best practices are clearly highlighted and critical moves are clearly scripted out. C-I-CARE best practice templates indeed follow such an approach in laying out "standard work" for outstanding patient communications. Stanford Health Care takes these C-I-CARE best practice templates and folds them into job descriptions, interview questions, training videos, and performance reviews. Team members therefore have clearer road maps for following C-I-CARE, thus shrinking the perception of the magnitude of change.

To convert C-I-CARE from a best practice to a routine habit, Stanford Health Care has leveraged many other insights from behavioral economics and design thinking. Stanford behavior design faculty member B. J. Fogg describes that a behavior happens when motivation, ability, and a trigger come together.[5] In his book *The Power of Habit: Why We Do What We Do in Life and Business*, Charles Duhigg similarly describes how a habit loop consists of a cue, a routine, and a reward.[10]

C-I-CARE templates help improve ability and thus help develop habits by providing best practice routines. Increased ability to execute these routines is further supported through regular online training, in-person rounding and coaching, and daily huddles.

To help provide a cue or trigger in the habit cycle, signs of C-I-CARE can be literally found across the organization. Indeed, miniaturized C-I-CARE templates hang on the badges of every employee and physician across the health system. By making the idea of C-I-CARE ubiquitous—on badges, in newsletters, on posters, and in meetings—Stanford Health Care leverages the decision-making bias of the availability effect. In other words, decisions may be affected by what information is most available or that is seen most recently or frequently. C-I-CARE badges also take advantage of a "priming" effect, reminding people that C-I-CARE might be a good choice for conducting their next behavior.[1]

To reinforce behaviors and further support habit formation, Stanford C-I-CARE uses several reward mechanisms described by behavioral economics. Stanford Health Care leaders conduct regular coaching rounds to observe behaviors and ask questions about C-I-CARE practices. During such rounds, they often hand out C-I-CARE chocolates and share praises, and they often subsequently write thank you letters to staff regarding observed C-I-CARE excellence. In addition, patient comment cards are shared daily with staff and posted in break rooms. The chocolates, praises, and letters can serve as small rewards to reinforce C-I-CARE habit loops. Moreover, for busy and tired individuals, these rewards can help provide the slight energy boosts needed to support making a change toward C-I-CARE, addressing what psychologist Roy Baumeister calls "ego depletion" or the fatigue and energy expended in making decisions.[11] Moreover, such small rewards may also create a sense of reciprocity in team members, making people feel more obligated to follow C-I-CARE best practices given that they have received something of value.[3] In addition, to leverage the influencing power of vivid and memorable images and stories, patient testimonials are often shared during management meetings. These testimonials are then recorded on video and shared across the organization in regular huddle meetings.

Stanford Health Care also leverages environmental and physical design approaches to support making C-I-CARE the easiest choice for physicians and staff as described by Kerry Patterson, Joseph Grenny, David Maxfield, Ron McMilian, and Al Switzler in their book *Influencer: The Power to Change Anything*.[12] For example, new ambulatory clinics are being built across the Stanford Health Care system with shared common workspaces for physicians and staff, encircled by patient exam rooms (see Figure 21.4 on C-I-CARE centered design). This design supports physicians and staff remaining proximal to patient exam rooms and to each other, reducing time spent walking between distant physician offices, and therefore reducing patient wait times. In addition, Stanford leverages lean "5-S" approaches for placing the most frequently used supplies within an inpatient room to help keep staff closer to patients and increase

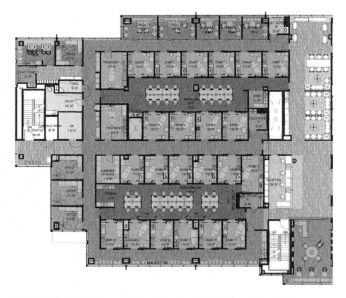

FIGURE 21.4 Stanford Health Care C-I-CARE centered design. The design uses patient rooms with doors on two sides: one external door for patients to enter from a circulating corridor, and one internal door for physicians and staff connecting the exam room to a shared internal workspace. Source: Stanford Health Care and Ratcliff Architects

the frequency of staff–patient contacts. Computers on wheels and bedside devices similarly create structural encouragement for caregiver–patient interaction, compared with traditional centralized nursing stations that create greater distances between caregivers and patients.

Stanford Health Care's C-I-CARE program also leverages traditional, "rational" reward mechanisms. Managers have annual financial incentive plans that include measures on C-I-CARE execution and patient-satisfaction scores. Stanford physicians also have annual financial incentives based on their individual satisfaction scores.

Yet insights from behavioral economics imply that some of the "irrational" incentives driving "humans" may be more powerful than the "rational" incentives driving "econs." In their groundbreaking paper on prospect theory, Daniel Kahneman and his Stanford colleague Amos Tversky describe that the prospect of a loss has more effect on decision making than the prospect of an equivalent gain.[13] One might therefore posit that "loss aversion" may have a stronger influencing factor on change than some equivalent traditional incentives that offer gains or rewards. To take advantage of such insights, Stanford Health Care regularly publishes C-I-CARE performance dashboards within the organization showing a manager's performance against every other manager on key C-I-CARE components, including satisfaction scores, C-I-CARE rounding, huddle execution, and staff recognition. Loss aversion may play a heavy motivating factor here in spurring improved performance because managers may not want to lose their existing standings or self-identities as good leaders by finding their performance at the bottom of any broadly shared list. Similarly for physicians, individual physician satisfaction scores are not only openly shared within departments but are also posted on the Stanford Health Care Internet site as part of a physician's biography for all the public to see. Loss aversion may play a strong factor here as well in driving C-I-CARE engagement because distinguished physicians with impeccable resumes and clinical track records likely do not want to lose their preeminent standings from lower patient-satisfaction scores. Indeed, Stanford physicians now rank among the very best in the entire nation in patient satisfaction. Accordingly, insights from prospect theory and its concept of "loss aversion" might imply that the desire to avoid the loss of group acceptance or reputational standing might be a more powerful influence factor than the pull of rewards and recognitions.

Stanford Health Care seeks to deliver "the absolute best patient experience anywhere, period" through its Stanford C-I-CARE approach. Yet patient experience is typically measured by retrospective patient-satisfaction surveys. Daniel Kahneman describes that the "remembering self" or the memory of any experience is often disproportionately weighted by the peak or nadir of an experience and the end of the experience. This insight further highlights the importance of every Stanford team member exceling in C-I-CARE because the lowest C-I-CARE performer may drive the patient's overall ranking of a care experience. It is also why the "E" in C-I-CARE refers to "Exit" because final communications may make for lasting memories. Although traditional management approaches for incentive and change management have been important to C-I-CARE, insights from behavioral economics have served as key differentiators in engendering broad team member engagement and in supporting sustained habits and high performance levels.

REFERENCES

1. Kahneman D. *Thinking, Fast and Slow.* New York, NY: Farrar, Straus & Giroux; 2011.

2. Thaler R, Sunstein C. *Nudge: Improving Decisions About Health, Wealth, and Happiness.* New Haven, CT: Yale University Press; 2008.

3. Cialdini R. *Influence: The Psychology of Persuasion.* Rev. ed. New York, NY: Harper Business; 2006.

4. Kouzes J, Posner B. *The Leadership Challenge: How to Make Extraordinary Things Happen in Organizations.* 5th ed. San Francisco, CA: Jossey-Bass; 2012.

5. Fogg BJ. BJ Fogg's Behavior Model. Stanford, CA; 2015. Accessed May 2015 at www.behaviormodel.org.

6. Liker J. *The Toyota Way: Fourteen Management Principles from the World's Greatest Manufacturer.* New York, NY: McGraw Hill Professional Publishing; 2003.

7. Ohno T. *Toyota Production System: Beyond Large-Scale Production.* New York, NY: Taylor & Francis; 1988.

8. Brown T. *Change by Design: How Design Thinking Transforms Organizations and Inspires Innovation.* New York, NY: Harper Collins; 2009.

9. Heath C, Heath D. *Switch: How to Change Things When Change Is Hard.* New York, NY: Broadway Books; 2010.

10. Duhigg C. *The Power of Habit: Why We Do What We Do in Life and Business.* New York, NY: Random House; 2012.

11. Baumeister R, Tierney J. *Willpower: Rediscovering the Greatest Human Strength.* New York, NY: Penguin Publishing Group; 2011.

12. Grenny J, Maxfield D, McMillan R, Switzler A, Patterson K. *Influencer: The Power to Change Anything.* New York, NY: McGraw Hill; 2007.

13. Kahneman D, Tversky A. Prospect theory: an analysis of decision under risk. *Econometrica.* 1979;47(2):263–291.

Impact of an Engaged Workforce on Patient Care

OUR CULTURE OF I CARE

Marc L. Boom

Abstract

Houston Methodist's culture is based on the simple values of integrity, compassion, accountability, respect, and excellence—which are all signified by the acronym I CARE. We all share these values, and our experience shows that our patients' experiences are positively affected by these values. Our workforce recounts stories to inspire and remind our employees that our patients are at the center of everything we do. We continue to focus on the future with a tireless emphasis on improving patient outcomes and sustaining a remarkable culture for our employees. Our values are the heart and lifeblood of Houston Methodist's mission and drive everything we do.

We love to tell stories at Houston Methodist. For the most part, these stories are not for our patients or for the public. We tell them to each other. The stories we share are about our employees and our patients, who are at the center of everything we do. That concept is not an abstraction or merely alluded to; it is the foundation of our culture.

Our hospital system has a rich history that parallels the progress of our home city. The Methodist Hospital had its beginnings in the catastrophic Spanish influenza epidemic of 1918–19, when local physician Dr Oscar Norsworthy offered his 30-bed hospital to the Texas Conference of the Methodist Episcopal Church. After struggling to stay open during the Great Depression, the hospital blossomed in the post–World War II years with the arrival of a young, ambitious surgeon: Dr Michael DeBakey.

DeBakey's breakthroughs and discoveries in the field of cardiovascular surgery earned him international acclaim, and his home hospital became a destination for hopeful patients from around the globe. For more than 50 years, DeBakey's work defined the hospital and deepened its reputation. Our staff and physicians looked up to the famed surgeon as a leader, and he once famously described The Methodist Hospital as "a hospital with a soul."

Today the hospital is called Houston Methodist Hospital, and it is the flagship of a system with seven community hospitals serving the country's fifth-largest metropolitan area and its population of 6.5 million. We are a major academic medical center with a research institute, a global healthcare component, and a comprehensive residency program. Our 19,000 employees and 4,000 physicians serve more than a million patients from 92 countries each year.

But no matter how large and diverse we may become, Houston Methodist's hospitals will always have that soul that DeBakey described. What sets Houston Methodist apart, we believe, is the daily emphasis on our I CARE values—integrity, compassion, accountability, respect, and excellence—among our workforce.

Our employees see their work at Houston Methodist as more than a job. Our workforce is here to save lives, comfort the suffering, and help heal the sick.

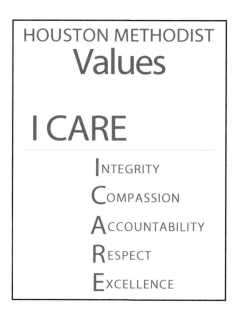

FIGURE 22.1 Houston Methodist Values defined

From the moment they are hired, Houston Methodist employees are encouraged to live our mission and I CARE values every day.

At Houston Methodist, we believe it is more important to demonstrate our values through action than to merely define them. Our stories come from our patients and our employees. In these stories, simple acts of kindness become testimonials to the power of compassion. We heard about Ashlee Sparks, a nurse at Houston Methodist West Hospital, who learned a patient in the emergency room was worried about her dog. The patient had locked the dog in a bathroom at home, thinking she would go home from the ER the same day. The patient had to be admitted to the hospital, so Ashlee went to the patient's home, fed the dog, and enlisted neighbors to care for the pet until the patient was able to return home.

We told the story of Carol Beachy, a physical and occupational therapy assistant at Houston Methodist San Jacinto Hospital, who made sure a patient received a walking aid he was promised. This patient was discharged home and expected to receive delivery of a walker. However, the walker was not ordered because of a miscommunication. Carol intervened by purchasing a walker with her own money, making sure the patient received it.

Then there was the story of Charlotte Kinnard, a social worker for case management at Houston Methodist Hospital who encountered a patient undocumented in the United States and not entitled to government assistance for his healthcare. The patient was homeless, without income, and severely disabled following a stroke. He had no family and only one friend with limited resources. Charlotte worked with a skilled nursing home and Casa Juan Diego, a local charity, to accept the patient for a small payment. The organization offered him a bed and care during his recovery; he was later provided a permanent home when he was no longer in need of skilled services.

Frequently these stories illustrate small deeds that make a big impact on patients. Angela Harless, a registered nurse at Houston Methodist West Hospital, learned that a patient's procedure was canceled. The patient had a two-hour drive to the hospital, and when Angela could not reach him by phone she waited in the hospital lobby until the patient and his wife arrived. Angela apologized and offered to buy them breakfast, which touched the patient and his family.

The subjects of these stories do not always receive awards. This was the case with a group of nurses at Houston Methodist Hospital who were moved by the plight of a pregnant woman with a brain tumor. The patient's baby had to be delivered prematurely so the mother could receive surgery, and nurse Michelle Schoen in labor and delivery changed her shift hours to help with the delivery. The baby was taken to nearby Texas Children's Hospital while the mom had surgery. As the new mother recovered, she longed to see her newborn daughter. So nurses in neurology intensive care made arrangements to take the patient in a wheelchair to visit her baby at the children's hospital. Each excursion required extensive planning because the patient had external monitors and an IV following her brain surgery. The daily trip to see her child was essential to the patient's healing and a powerful illustration of the compassion our nurses have for their patients.

Another story we love begins with a patient in the emergency room at Houston Methodist San Jacinto Hospital. While she was in severe pain, someone came in to her room, hugged her, and sat beside her. This person held the patient's hand and reassured her things would be all right. The visitor stayed until the patient felt better. After the emergency had passed, the patient went to find her benefactor; to her surprise, she saw Maria Lopez emptying a trash can and mopping the floor. The visitor the patient had assumed was a nurse was actually a housekeeper.

We communicate these stories and many others throughout the year so all employees can share in the ways coworkers exhibit our I CARE values. The stories are shared at award recognition events, all employee meetings, and gatherings for special events such as National Nurses' Week. We print these stories in newsletters that go out to employees from the administrators of all our hospitals, and we recognize the employees who are at the heart of these stories.

The I CARE values at Houston Methodist go back to 1998 when the organization began to redefine itself with a return to our faith-based roots. A committee appointed by our board of directors researched hospitals across the country and returned a recommendation that Houston Methodist better integrate spiritual values across its entire system.

Because our workforce is so racially, ethnically, and religiously diverse, we had to work hard to seek a common ground for everyone. We sought to identify a set of values that crossed all lines and would appeal to all our employees.

We created a special committee of employee representatives from all of our hospitals and from all disciplines and job categories. This group eventually created Houston Methodist's first vision and belief statement and rewrote our mission statement to reflect the reintroduction of spiritual values. This group worked with senior management to distill the process into a set of core values identified by the I CARE acronym: integrity, compassion, accountability, respect, and excellence.

But these were just words and abstract concepts to most of our employees. No one realized at the time that a catastrophic event would bring these values to life for everyone in our hospital system.

In June 2001, tropical storm Allison rolled out of the Gulf of Mexico into southeast Texas, meandering across the state and dropping nearly 40 inches of rain in just a few days. Houston received the worst of the resulting flooding: More than 2,700 homes were destroyed, suddenly making as many as 30,000 people homeless.

At Houston Methodist Hospital in the Texas Medical Center, Allison's impact was devastating. The hospital's two levels of basements flooded, destroying the backup generators needed to operate lifesaving machines during the storm. With all power out in one of the city's biggest hospitals, our employees had to rally in the middle of the night to care for patients in rough conditions.

Staff members manually operated equipment needed to keep some patients alive. In the stifling June heat, volunteers carried patients down flights of stairs one by one. Some staff members stayed at work for days, not knowing if their own homes were flooded in the storm.

Although the hospital never closed, it had to operate at limited capacity for 10 weeks. We managed to discharge nearly all of the patients who were there when the storm hit, so we spent much of that time getting back the services necessary to begin treating patients again. Floodwaters destroyed some of the hospital's facilities, and it would take at least two years to rebuild.

Allison could not wash away the hospital's spirit. As our workforce rallied to care for patients and for each other, we saw the I CARE values come to life. We all lived those values every day, and no one forgot them.

Even as we rebuilt our facilities, we also rebuilt our culture. We gradually worked the I CARE values into every aspect of our business, creating a program that reinforces these values to our employees.

The I CARE program for the workforce involves training, work group sessions, and annual recommitments made by all employees to adhere to these values. The I CARE theme is consistent in all internal communications, and employees are encouraged to exhibit these values and behaviors at all times. In fact, many departments at Houston Methodist share an I CARE affirmation each morning to remind and inspire employees to uphold these values.

When employees assess their own performance, the first thing they ask is, "Do I exhibit the I CARE values?" In their annual evaluations, all employees are measured on how well they live up to the I CARE values and are given a numerical score.

Each Houston Methodist hospital rewards employees for exhibiting I CARE behavior. Twice a year, employees who noticeably demonstrate these values are nominated by their peers and recognized as part of a program directly tied to the I CARE mission. Winners are honored at a special luncheon, their photographs are prominently displayed on posters and in employee newsletters, and each winner receives his or her choice of $1,000 or a full week of paid time off, as well as a gold ID badge for easy recognition of their special status among their peers. The winner's manager or supervisor and selected coworkers are also invited to the awards luncheon. Managers and supervisors are also eligible for an I CARE award, and selected winners receive $500 cash as well as money to spend on leadership-development opportunities.

During the celebration of our I CARE award winners we begin to tell our stories. These stories not only feature nurses who give patient care but also housekeepers, patient care assistants, painters, social workers, and anyone else who is a keeper of our values. In some cases, we secure the permission of patients and employees to share these stories with the outside world. Employees also take pride in sharing these stories as well; we all believe the focus on our I CARE values helps to make our hospital system a great place to work.

In 2015, Houston Methodist earned a spot on *Fortune* magazine's "100 Best Companies to Work For" list for the 10th consecutive year. Only a handful of U.S. hospitals consistently appear on this list. Since 1998, the list has been assembled by the Great Place to Work Institute, a research and training firm, through surveys of employees in U.S. companies that determine which employers provide the best workplace cultures.

The company's Trust Index Employee Survey solicits opinions and perceptions through a series of questions designed to gauge employees' levels of trust and satisfaction in their jobs. The accumulated data are then used to rate organizations that eventually appear on the "100 Best Companies to Work For" list.

Our surveyed employees consistently rank Houston Methodist high on key attributes such as pride (in 2015, 96% agreed with the statement "I am proud to work for Houston Methodist"), opportunities for advancement (92%), and a desirable workplace atmosphere (94%). Most of those surveyed described Houston Methodist as consistently friendly, and 8 of 10 respondents characterized their workplace as caring, fun, and cooperative and with the feeling of a family.

This annual survey is a useful yardstick in measuring our employees' attitudes toward the company and their workplace. Perhaps the most important way for employees to provide valuable opinions and criticism is through the annual employee survey, which has been conducted each fall since 2001. Morehead Associates Inc. (a division of Press Ganey, a company that measures and analyzes healthcare data) manages the annual survey and each year ranks its client hospitals according to their employee and workforce satisfaction. For 2014, Houston Methodist maintained its ranking in the 98th percentile among more than 350 healthcare organizations across the country.

Our scores are consistent on items that reflect Houston Methodist's focus on values. The item our employees rank as the company's greatest strength in comparison to other healthcare organizations is how it treats employees: "Houston Methodist treats employees with respect." Employees also express high satisfaction with job security and agree that Houston Methodist is a great place to work. They also give high marks to tools and resources available for them to do their jobs and to the organization's respect for diversity. In general, employees express confidence in our future success and the quality of our care and service.

The employee survey is our most effective communication tool to measure attitudes, level of engagement, commitment, and possible areas for improvement. Results from the survey are shared with managers and employees via departmental meetings. Managers are asked to review the results with their staff and create action plans to improve in those areas identified as most important by employees. These action plans ensure not only that are employees' voices heard but also that the feedback results in workplace enhancements. This openness and receptiveness to feedback empowers employees to initiate innovative processes to improve patient care and the work environment.

In addition, we believe completely in rewarding and recognizing our employees for their work. We issue a quarterly bonus to each employee; the amount depends on levels of patient-satisfaction survey results in each hospital. At a hospital reaching or surpassing its target patient-satisfaction level, an employee can receive as much as $300 for that quarter.

We know from practice that efforts to reinforce employee engagement and satisfaction directly affect the levels of patient satisfaction. Satisfied employees have a desirable effect on the quality of care; we have seen that notion reinforced at studies conducted at other hospitals.

"The Relationship Between Employee Satisfaction and Hospital Patient Experiences" in 2009 found that surveyed patients that were treated by hospital departments with more satisfied employees were more likely to recommend the hospital to others. Those patients also rated the quality of the care they received as higher.[1] John Griffith's study—also from 2009—of 34 community hospitals that won the Malcolm Baldrige National Quality Award for healthcare found that employee morale was the leading factor in patient satisfaction.[2] Both studies pointed out that employee satisfaction starts with hospital leadership.

Our own plan, which was presented to employees in 2014, is called "Vision for the Second Century." It proposes to advance several initiatives important to our system, including research, education, advancements in clinical care, and

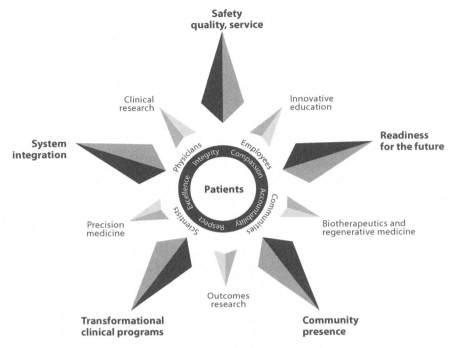

FIGURE 22.2 Vision for the Second Century star

continuous improvement in the quality of our care. Illustrated by a star (Figure 22.2), this vision places the patient at the center of everything we do, surrounded by our I CARE values of integrity, compassion, accountability, respect, and excellence. One point of the star dealing with long-term organizational goals is readiness for the future—specifically, how we continue to serve our patients in the new marketplace created by the Affordable Care Act (ACA).

When it was signed into law in 2010, the Affordable Care Act changed the way hospitals do business. The ACA moved hospitals away from a volume-based model to a quality-based model, applying a yardstick to meet measurable standards for quality and rewarding them according to how well they meet those standards. This is a good thing: When hospitals are forced to compete on quality, consumers win.

The hospitals that consistently find success in this new environment are those that deliver the outcomes and experiences patients want. Traditional clinical outcomes such as mortality are still vital to patients, but other measures such as the hospital experience are growing more important.[3]

As an academic hospital system, Houston Methodist seeks individuals who value patient care, teaching, and research. We need to know that our employees—even those who do not interact directly with patients—are dedicated to the cause of health and wellness. Potential hires are asked to agree to our I CARE values before applying for open positions. I have always believed that if you want to win the World Cup, you must first put together a World Cup team.

We seek people who are in tune with the concept of service to others, who are compassionate and respectful, and who understand that we seek to always deliver a great experience for our patients.

Creating this experience is an important part of our employee training. The patient experience at our hospitals—we call it the Houston Methodist Experience—is built on the foundation of our I CARE values. Everything our employees and physicians do for our patients should reflect these values.

All new employees are trained in the Houston Methodist Experience as part of their initial orientation. New hires fill out a survey asking about their preferences and likes: "What do you want to be called?" "What's your favorite type of snack?" Managers are then provided this information to make each employee's first day unique and enjoyable by ensuring they address the employee by the right name and make the employee's favorite snack available. This not only makes new employees feel welcome but also provides an example of the power of offering patients a personalized experience—an important part of the Houston Methodist Experience.

The Houston Methodist Experience has been in place since 2003, and the employee training module was introduced throughout the system to ensure that our patients and guests have a similar experience no matter which hospital they visit.

In the first few years of the Houston Methodist Experience, each employee was trained in the basic concepts for good service and a good experience. Now education is ongoing in the form of events and competitions that allow employees to place their own distinctive stamp on this form of service. For example, a photo and art contest encourages employees (including physicians) to create visuals that are displayed and judged in a competition. Following the competition, all artwork—not just that of the award winners—is put into permanent display around the hospital campus.

Employees are also encouraged to create a setting or environment that enhances the patient experience. For example, staff members are given the freedom to come up with names for their conference rooms or decorating and color schemes that they see as soothing to the patients. This is an important component of the culture at our hospitals; the Houston Methodist Experience is designed to give employees tools to demonstrate and express their values.

The Houston Methodist Experience measures its success each year with increases in patient-satisfaction figures and favorable responses from employees during an annual employee-satisfaction survey. The initiative is now deeply embedded in the culture of our hospitals. By providing a quality and spiritual environment, our employees know they make a difference.

Of course, the most important part of the Houston Methodist Experience training is enhancing the I CARE values for employees. We believe in conducting ourselves with the utmost integrity because we are honest and ethical in all we say and do. We apply compassion to our interaction with patients—embracing the whole person and responding to patients' emotional, ethical, and spiritual concerns as well as to their physical needs. We practice accountability and stand by our actions. Respect is how we show that we value every individual, and we treat everyone as a person of worth and dignity.

It is easy to promise excellence, but it takes work and dedication to deliver it time and time again. Our patients deserve nothing less than our best effort at all times. We constantly work to make our hospitals more hospitable, and the most important way we do this is by nurturing a culture of I CARE among our employees. This culture makes our work more meaningful and gratifying, and it keeps our patients at the center of everything we do.

REFERENCES

1. Peltier J, Dahl A, Mulhern F. The relationship between employee satisfaction and hospital patient experiences. Forum for People Performance Management and Measurement; 2009. Available at http://www.info-now.com/typo3conf/ext/p2wlib/pi1/press2web/html/userimg/FORUM/Hospital%20Study%20-Relationship%20Btwn%20Emp.%20Satisfaction%20and%20Pt.%20Experiences.pdf

2. Griffith J. Finding the frontier of hospital management. *J Healthcare Manag.* 2009; 54:1.

3. Competing on Patient-Driven Value—The New Health Care Marketplace. Press Ganey Special Report, 2015.

INDEX

AAMC (Association of American Medical Colleges), 83, 167

academic health centers, population health management in, 126

access to healthcare, 292–293; in fee-for-service model, 304; in Grand-Aide visits, 180; problems in, 167–169; in retail clinics, 197; in telemedicine, 164, 165–166, 169–171, 172, 174, 175; wait times in (*See* wait times for healthcare)

accountability: in culture of safety, 5, 53, 54f–56f; in Houston Methodist I CARE approach, 345–354; public reporting on healthcare quality improving, 87, 95, 98; in Robust Process Improvement, 14; type of work affecting, 53, 54f–56f

accountable care organizations (ACOs), 106, 113, 124, 283, 307–308

accreditation: ACGME standards in, 76–80; culture of safety standards in, 52, 53; of retail clinics, 209

Accreditation Council for Graduate Medical Education (ACGME), 76–80; Clinical Learning Environment Review (CLER), 79–80; competency standards of, 76–79; Next Accreditation System (NAS), 79

activity and motion monitoring, 67; with telemedicine, 164; with wireless body sensor network systems, 145, 146, 148

acute conditions: gap between recommended and actual care in, 227; mobile health technology in, 155–156; team-based care in, 129

acute coronary syndromes: clinical practice guidelines in, 221–222; precision medicine in, 241

adherence to clinical practice guidelines, 227–231, 229f, 230t

adherence to therapy: in Grand-Aide program, 178, 182, 183, 184, 185; in mobile health technology, 148, 156; in population health management, 117; in shared decision making, 270, 271

administration of medications: electronic system in, 64–65; errors in, 33, 61, 64–65; smart pump technology in, 65–66

administrative data in public reporting, 89–90

Advance Payment ACO model, 307

adverse events, 32; cost of, 61; in culture of safety, 7; definition of, 32, 61; identified in chart review, 34; incidence of, 33, 34, 61; in medication errors, 32–33, 62, 65, 66; recovery phase in, 50, 51; reporting of, 51, 56

Affordable Care Act (ACA), 281–289; on clinical practice guidelines, 219; and convenience care clinics, 213; and cost of healthcare, 106, 107, 169, 289–290; and

CPSIA information can be obtained
at www.ICGtesting.com
Printed in the USA
LVOW05*2227270616

494346LV00016B/89/P